GROUNDS
FOR
DREAMING

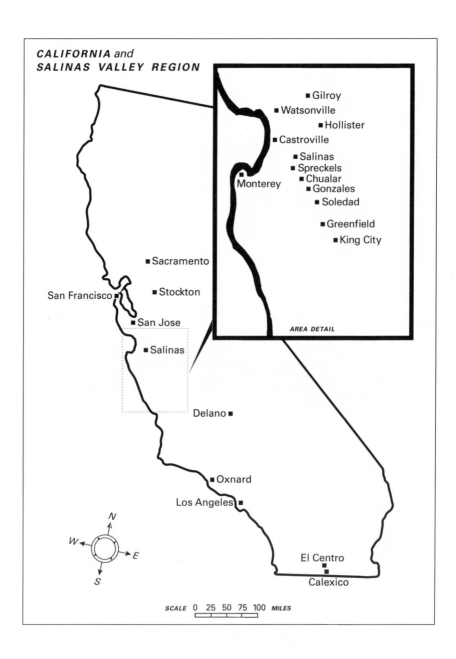

CALIFORNIA and SALINAS VALLEY REGION

AREA DETAIL

■ Gilroy
■ Watsonville
■ Hollister
■ Castroville
■ Salinas
■ Spreckels
■ Chualar
■ Gonzales
■ Soledad
■ Greenfield
■ King City
■ Monterey

■ Sacramento
■ Stockton
San Francisco ■
■ San Jose
■ Salinas
Delano ■
■ Oxnard
Los Angeles ■
El Centro ■
■ Calexico

N
W
E
S

SCALE 0 25 50 75 100 MILES

GROUNDS FOR DREAMING

MEXICAN AMERICANS,

MEXICAN IMMIGRANTS, AND THE

CALIFORNIA FARMWORKER MOVEMENT

LORI A. FLORES

Yale UNIVERSITY PRESS
New Haven and London

Frontispiece map by David Hackett.

Published with assistance from the Kingsley Trust Association Publication Fund established by the Scroll and Key Society of Yale College, and from the Mary Cady Tew Memorial Fund.

Yale University Press books may be purchased in quantity for educational, business, or promotional use. For information, please e-mail sales.press@yale.edu (U.S. office) or sales@yaleup.co.uk (U.K. office).

Set in Sabon type by Newgen North America.
Printed in the United States of America.

ISBN 978-0-300-19696-2 (cloth : alk. paper)
Library of Congress Control Number: 2015938235

A catalogue record for this book is available from the British Library.

This paper meets the requirements of ANSI/NISO Z39.48-1992 (Permanence of Paper).

10 9 8 7 6 5 4 3 2 1

To my father, Alfredo H. Flores (1934–2005)

Contents

Acknowledgments

At times when the words were not flowing, I often turned to drafting my acknowledgments. Doing so not only helped me visualize this book's completion but reminded me of all the gratitude I felt for the individuals and institutions that helped me along this journey. I received generous financial support for this project from the Stanford Center for Comparative Studies in Race and Ethnicity, the Stanford Humanities Center, the Haynes Foundation, the Southern California Historical Association, the Consortium for Faculty Diversity Postdoctoral Fellowship at Bowdoin College, a Faculty Development Research Award from Bowdoin College, the Faculty Diversity Program of the State University of New York, and the Sam Fishman Travel Grant from the Walter P. Reuther Library at Wayne State University.

The intellectual and moral support I have received during my graduate education and early career is immeasurable. Stephen Pitti, Albert Camarillo, and Estelle Freedman were wonderful advisors at Yale and Stanford who taught me, each in their own ways, how to be the type of historian I wanted to be. Their scholarly rigor, generous mentorship, and personal kindnesses have influenced the standards I hold for myself as an academic and as a human being. At Bowdoin College I had the pleasure of being around incredibly supportive colleagues including

Connie Chiang, Mariana Cruz, Kelly Fayard, Matt Klingle, Annelle Rivera-Beckstrom, Susan Tananbaum, and Allen Wells. At Stony Brook University (SUNY), I am lucky to have dynamic colleagues who nurture and challenge me. Particular thanks goes to Paul Gootenberg, Nancy Tomes, Gary Marker, Brooke Larson, Elizabeth Newman, Daniel Levy, Sara Lipton, Jared Farmer, Eric Beverley, Shobana Shankar, Eric Zolov, and Robert Chase for their advice, engagement with my work, and moral support. Serendipitously, my colleague April Masten's father wrote a song in 1966 about one of the climactic moments in this book, and I thank her for agreeing to let me reprint it in Chapter 5.

This book is better because of the numerous people who provided feedback on my work-in-progress at various conferences and workshops. To all my collaborators and audiences at the meetings of the Southwest Labor Studies Association; Pacific Coast Branch of the American Historical Association; American Studies Association; Western Association of Women's Historians; Ethnicity, Race, and Migration Program speaker series at Yale University; Stony Brook Latin American and Caribbean Studies New Faculty Colloquium; Stony Brook Initiative for Historical Social Sciences; Hunter College Labor and Working-Class History Seminar; the University of California–Berkeley Bancroft Seminar on Latino and Borderlands History; the "Boycotts: Past and Present" conference at the University of London; and the "Quarantine: History, Heritage, Place" conference at the University of Sydney—thank you for all of your comments, questions, and suggestions. José Alamillo, Estelle Freedman, Carol McKibben, David Montejano, and David Torres-Rouff read and commented thoroughly on the entire book manuscript, and I am beyond grateful for the time and energy they put into doing so. Magda Maczynska, Ana Minian, and Maria Montoya were fabulous writing buddies over the years; so many cafés, so many pastries. The conversations I have had with other colleague-friends—including but not limited to Mike Amezcua, Rick Baldoz, Cristina Beltrán, Nick Bravo, Gerry Cadava, Cecilia Cárdenas-Navia, Genevieve Carpio, Pedro Castillo, Ernesto Chávez, Miroslava Chávez-Garcia, Valerie Deacon, Alejandro Delgado, Rosalinda Garcia, Nanibaa' Garrison, Laura Gutíerrez, Jane Hong, Josh Howe, Mike Innis-Jiménez, Faith Kazmi, Kevin Kim, Shelley Lee, Beth Lew-Williams, Casey Lew-Williams, Mireya Loza, Rosina Lozano, Brian Luna-Lucero, Myra Luna-Lucero, Katherine Marino, Monica Martínez, Dodie McDow, Natalia Mehlman-Petrzela, Andrew

Needham, Gina Marie Pitti, Julie Prieto, Andrew Robichaud, Ana Rosas, Vicki Ruiz, Margaret Sena, Rachel St. John, Tim Tomlinson, Derek and Ariel Vanderpool, Tamara Venit-Shelton, Julie Weise, and Chris Wilkins—have buoyed me and made my work better. I always looked forward to my conversations about this book *en español con* Helena Celdrán en San Francisco y Joel Sanchez Bulnes en Oaxaca. I also thank my students, who have helped me think about how to make this work provocative and accessible, particularly Eduardo Castro, Emily Johneas, Kate Leifheit, and Molly Pallman.

My trips to various archives would have yielded less had it not been for the knowledgeable and supportive staff of the Stanford University Department of Special Collections; Beinecke Rare Book and Manuscript Library; Steinbeck Public Library; Southern California Library for Social Studies and Research; UCLA Charles E. Young Research Library; Huntington Library; National Archives branches in Washington, D.C., College Park, and San Bruno; University of California–Davis Department of Special Collections; Monterey County Historical Society; Monterey Public Library; Salinas City Hall; Salinas Courthouse; Walter P. Reuther Library; Monterey County Agricultural and Rural Life Museum; and Oaxaca City's Instituto del Atención al Migrante. At the end of long days in the archives, it was great to hang out with friends who hosted me in their homes. Thank you to Mariana and David Cass, Stephanie Eberle, Laura Harrison, Matt and Jessica Lewis, Carol and Scott McKibben, Ana and Abigail Rosas, Casandra Rosenberg and Jacek Mysior, Elizabeth Stanley, Joanna Sturiano, Julianna Prieto and the Vallor family for always giving me places to crash when I needed them. The other people who welcomed me into their homes and offices were those I interviewed for this project. I am grateful for, and humbled by, the generosity and vulnerability my interviewees demonstrated in sharing their memories, and all of them have enriched this work.

Speaking of enriching conversations, nothing balances me more than the ones I have with old friends. A special thank you goes to Ruth Yemane, Daniel Perez, David Stanley, Roxanne Flint Rosenberg, and Star Ramirez-Alvarez for always checking in and caring. I owe a tremendous debt to Mary Mendoza-Newman, Sylvia Marie Delgadillo, and Isabel Sanchez-Sachs for keeping me healthy over the years and advocating for my personal happiness. David Hackett created the maps and infographics for this book and I am so appreciative of his talent, humor, emergency microfilming skills, and steadfast support of this project. I feel very sentimental about publishing my first book with my alma mater, and I thank everybody at Yale University Press who saw its value and shepherded it through all stages of production. Special thanks goes to Laura Davulis, Eva Skewes, Philip King, Katie Golden, Mary Valencia, the readers who provided such constructive and incisive feedback, and my fantastic copyeditor Jessie Dolch.

My most profound gratitude goes to my family. My parents Mary Ann Flores and Richard H. Rocha and sisters Gina Marie Flores and Paige Rocha have been constant in their love and support. Gina in particular has spent many years being my "coach," brainstorming partner, proofreader, and best friend. She along with the rest of my family in Texas (too many people to name here, but you know who you are!) have always cheered me on in life. I love you all. I dedicate this book to my late father Alfredo H. Flores. His own story of growing up Mexican American, dropping out of eighth grade to save his family's small farm, returning to school two decades later, and earning a college degree to become a teacher continues to drive and inspire me. The following history of Mexican-origin people in agricultural California is in many ways the history of my own family, of others who toiled on the land, and of those who continue to do so today. To my dad, and to everybody else who has taught me the value of hard work, resilience, and respect for oneself and others, I hope this book is one measure of proof that I keep those lessons in my mind and heart.

Finally, to all the readers of this book, thank you. You are no longer the imaginary audience I have carried around in my head for years, but my real one, and your engagement with my work means so much. *Mil gracias.*

Abbreviations

AGIF	American G.I. Forum
AWOC	Agricultural Workers Organizing Committee
CRLA	California Rural Legal Assistance
CSO	Community Service Organization
GFLA	Growers Farm Labor Association
GSVA	Grower-Shipper Vegetable Association
INS	Immigration and Naturalization Service
LULAC	League of United Latin American Citizens
MAPA	Mexican American Political Association
MEChA	Movimiento Estudiantil Chicano de Aztlán (Chicano Student Movement of Aztlán)
NAWU	National Agricultural Workers Union
NFLU	National Farm Labor Union
NFWA	National Farm Workers Association
OEO	Office of Economic Opportunity
SNCC	Student Nonviolent Coordinating Committee
UFWOC	United Farm Workers Organizing Committee
UPWA	United Packinghouse Workers of America

GROUNDS FOR DREAMING

Introduction

BLOWING IN FROM the Pacific Ocean, a particular wind haunts a fifteen-mile stretch of California's Highway 101, a main artery of transportation from north to south. Here in the Salinas Valley, between the small agricultural towns of Chualar and Soledad, one can hear this shrieking wind and feel its force, strong enough to sway bodies and vehicles. During harvest season, lush green fields flank both sides of the highway. Stooped farmworkers, covered in hats and bandannas meant to protect them from the elements, dot the landscape. The vegetables they pick make their way into grocery stores, hotels, and restaurants in California and across the nation. At the end of each workday, workers are transported out of the fields in white labor contractor buses that almost seem to emanate their passengers' exhaustion.

On this busy strip of road, a freshly installed marker bearing the words "Bracero Memorial Highway" might make one wonder about the history of this place. Indeed, it was here that dozens of Mexican agricultural guestworkers (or braceros) perished in two major transportation accidents in the twentieth century. In June 1958, fourteen braceros burned to death when a lit cigarette sparked a sloshing can of gasoline in their labor bus, setting the back compartment ablaze. Unable to communicate with the driver, and trapped by chains tied on the outside of the bus's back doors, the workers could not escape. Five years later, in September 1963, a freight train collided with a shoddily constructed bracero bus at an unmarked railroad crossing in the town of Chualar. The crash killed thirty-one braceros and one other worker and injured numerous others.

These horrific accidents, particularly the latter, gripped the nation in their exposure of the substandard transportation conditions braceros endured in the United States. The multiple interests pulled in by the tragedies—Mexican American civil rights activists, California agribusiness, the Mexican consulate, the U.S. Federal Bureau of Investigation (FBI), and the U.S. Congress—belied the exploitation and invisibility braceros had suffered since arriving as a workforce reserve for the United States during World War II. The Salinas Valley, long praised as a center of national food production and called the "Salad Bowl of the World," was revealed to be a dark nexus of farmworker mistreatment. As activists used these bracero deaths to draw wider attention to the plight of the nation's agricultural workers, the Salinas Valley took center stage in debates over U.S. agribusiness, labor, and immigration policy during the 1960s.[1]

This book explores the Salinas Valley's past to show how this agricultural empire was continually a center, a microcosm, of significant transitions and moments in U.S. labor, immigration, and Latino history. Located in Monterey County on California's central coast, the valley encompasses several towns and 240,000 acres and is one of the most fertile farming regions on the planet. Temperate weather in all seasons, coupled with cool breezes and protective layers of fog from the Pacific Ocean, help vegetables such as lettuce, artichokes, celery, carrots, and broccoli flourish almost year-round. Because of this, many farmworkers nickname the region *la crema* (the cream) of the labor circuit and choose to make it their permanent home. In the early twentieth century, Salinas Valley growers began cultivating cash crops and taking advantage of railways that facilitated trade between the American West and East. As certain growers consolidated more land and power, the region transitioned from an agricultural society to an agribusiness society. What the writer and activist Carey McWilliams termed "factories in the field"—industrial systems of agricultural production that exploited successive waves of racialized working-class populations—came to characterize the California landscape. By the time the United States entered World War II, the diverse workers who had toiled in the state's fields included Native Americans, Asians, white migrants from the Dust Bowl, and Mexican-origin people. When the war began, Mexican braceros joined Mexican Americans to become the new agricultural proletariat of California and the Southwest. Today, the Salinas Valley's multibillion-dollar agricultural industry, and U.S. agriculture in general, continues to be highly dependent on Latino (mostly Mexican immigrant) labor.[2]

Popular knowledge of the Salinas Valley remains rooted in the work of the region's famed native son John Steinbeck, whose novels including *East of Eden* and *The Grapes of Wrath* are praised for their colorful depiction of California's agricultural workers and economy. The town of Salinas, where Steinbeck was born, makes much of its literary legacy, and thousands of tourists are drawn there each year. Yet the ways in which Salinas and California built their wealth on the backs of farmworkers during the twentieth century, particularly Latino ones, are often glossed over in tourist-driven historical narratives of places like "Steinbeck Country." A turbulent history of worker exploitation, racial segregation and discrimination, violence, and transnational suffering pervades this place and others like it. In chronicling the experiences of Mexican Americans and Mexican immigrants in the Salinas Valley, and their part in creating one of California's agricultural empires while being deprived of socioeconomic and political equality, *Grounds for Dreaming* presents a darker and more critical history of this region.

This book also contributes to the larger history of Mexican-origin people, both native and immigrant, in California. Agricultural California has been given less attention relative to urban California in histories of Mexican American life, labor, and civil rights politics in the post–World War II period. Although 60 percent of Mexican Americans lived in cities like El Paso, Chicago, and Los Angeles by the mid-twentieth century (Los Angeles claimed the largest Mexican-origin population outside of Mexico after 1930), the daily lives and political struggles of the others who lived in rural or agriculture-centered communities have been understudied. George Sánchez's landmark work on how people "became Mexican American" in Los Angeles before World War II left space open to tell the rest of the story, outside of an urban context. Over the past two decades, scholars have filled this historiographical gap. Studies of cotton pickers, cannery and packinghouse employees, and citrus workers have documented the politicization and activism of the Mexican-origin agricultural working class in southern California. Recent scholarship on the Napa and Silicon Valleys has produced more nuanced and multicultural histories of northern California, yet little ground has been broken on the history of central California.[3]

I argue that the history of the Salinas Valley is emblematic of how agriculture-centered environments and economies affected the politicization of U.S.-born and immigrant Mexicans in twentieth-century California. During the 1930s, agribusiness leaders there colluded with law enforcement to crush labor protests from "Okie" packinghouse workers and Filipino fieldworkers. This destruction of unions eliminated an important political avenue for Mexican Americans when they became the farmworker majority soon after. It was not until 1970 that the United Farm Workers Organizing Committee (UFWOC), led by Cesar Chavez, conducted one of the biggest agricultural strikes in U.S. history in the lettuce fields of the Salinas Valley. These two moments of militancy are well known in California and labor history, but what happened during the years between? How did Mexican Americans navigate their social place and political identity in an increasingly corporatized agricultural setting, particularly when the government-sponsored Bracero Program (1942–1964) brought a large influx of Mexican guestworkers into their midst? The years between World War II and the "Chicano" civil rights era of the late 1960s and 1970s were a crucial interstitial period during which Mexican Americans confronted restrictive racial, labor, and immigration policies; founded their own civil rights organizations; and developed complex relationships with Mexican nationals. In tracing these processes, this book provides important connective tissue between the histories of Mexican American activism in the World War II and Chicano Movement periods. Shifting the analytical focus from the cities to the fields, this book revises the cast of characters, turning points, and landmark moments in the postwar Mexican American labor and civil rights movements.

Specifically, the experiences of those living in agriculture-centered communities alter and augment the history of Mexican American politicization in three ways. First, Mexican Americans in agricultural settings had to contend with the effects of the Bracero Program in ways their urban counterparts did not. In the era of the New Deal and World War II, labor unions were often the singular avenue through which ethnic and racial minorities could articulate their civil rights demands.

When growers began replacing protesting U.S. workers with braceros, however, agricultural workers lost the ability to collectively bargain with their employers and from that point fell behind industrial workers in both earnings and working conditions. Through its importation of foreign nonunionized guest workers, the Bracero Program changed the labor landscape of the nation forever and placed urban and nonurban Mexican Americans on very different timelines of political activism and progress. Without unions that could successfully fight for their rights and upward mobility, Mexican Americans in agriculture-centered communities struggled longer to form other kinds of political organizations that could help them achieve their goals.

Second, Mexican Americans in agricultural regions experienced particularly complex relationships with Mexican immigrants that negatively affected the way both groups were treated by the wider public. David Gutiérrez has argued that "the more or less constant presence of large numbers of Mexican immigrants in Mexican American communities has forced Mexican Americans to come to daily decisions about who they are—politically, socially, and culturally," and other scholars have examined Mexican Americans' historically ambivalent attitudes toward Mexican immigrants. Some Mexican Americans have blamed Mexican nationals for stealing jobs, impeding union organization, and exacerbating the public perceptions of all Mexican-origin people as foreign, undesirable, and criminal.[4] When the Bracero Program produced a parallel stream of undocumented Mexican migration and the U.S. Immigration and Naturalization Service (INS) ramped up its border control efforts during the 1950s, three groups of co-ethnics—Mexican Americans, braceros, and undocumented migrants—negotiated tense relationships in work and public spaces. This book offers fine-grained analysis of these three groups' triangulated histories, showing how national labor programs and transnational migrations affected people's lives on the ground. Wary of braceros and undocumented migrants as labor competition, Mexican Americans grew more resentful when white Americans and immigration authorities targeted them as "foreign" too and challenged their identities and rights as U.S. citizens. Braceros found themselves in a liminal space as unprotected subjects of both their home and receiving countries and sought rights as guest-workers with little support from the Mexican Americans around them. Undocumented migrants, derogatorily termed "wetbacks," became the most vilified and vulnerable workforce of all.[5] They often led lives in the shadows until a traumatic event—apprehension by the INS, a work accident, or death—brought their journeys to light. Although the lives of Mexican Americans and Mexicans were intertwined by work, romance, family, and common forms of discrimination, the backdrop of the Bracero Program and anti-"wetback" sentiment prevented any ethnic solidarity or political mobilization among these three groups for several decades. This book suggests that Mexican American–Mexican tensions and relations were just as significant in shaping the contours of Latino political activism in postwar California as Mexican-white tensions and relations were. It rubs against the common story of Latino community formation and solidarity to explain why, in an agricultural economy and context, some Latino communities did *not* get formed or took a much longer time to evolve compared with urban centers.

Finally, deeper examination of agricultural communities changes the narrative of the Chicano Movement's evolution in California. The majority of scholarship on *el movimiento* has focused on Los Angeles as the state's center of Mexican American political activity and chronicled the high school walkouts, antiwar demonstrations, and cultural production that characterized the movement's origins and ethos. Historians usually insert farmworkers into this story in 1965, identifying Cesar Chavez's grape strike and boycott in Delano, California, as the moment that inspired urban Chicanos to begin supporting the farmworker cause. I contend that this moment actually occurred earlier in the Salinas Valley. By 1960 protests were mounting against the Bracero Program by organized labor, the Catholic Church, and Mexican American activists infuriated by the program's continual extension. In September 1963, the deaths of thirty-one braceros on the railroad tracks of Chualar caused the Bracero Program to come under intense national scrutiny. The variety of Mexican American leaders and organizations that responded to the accident, and their mutual protests against farmworker exploitation, arguably constituted the first significant moment of urban-rural unity within the nascent Chicano civil rights movement in California.[6]

This book traces not only how people "became Mexican American" and articulated that identity in agricultural settings, but how, over the years, these Mexican Americans then became Chicanos. For the bulk of the twentieth century, I argue, the things that played a significant role in this process of identity and community formation were Mexican Americans' relationships with Mexican nationals and the racial notions of Mexican-origin people that formed within the world of agriculture. This study concurs with others which argue that "race" is not a biological reality but a socially constructed concept that people have used to distance and differentiate themselves from one another. Racial categories—formed on the basis of things such as skin color, physical characteristics, geography, and language—are employed in creating hierarchies of power that affect people's mobility, choices, and lived experiences in very real ways. Chapter 1 explores race-making in California after the U.S.-Mexican War and Gold Rush and explains how conceptions of racial difference led to the ethnic succession of Asian and Mexican workers in the state's fields. In the Salinas Valley, racialized beliefs that these two populations were "naturally suited" for stoop labor led to other forms of discriminatory treatment, including harmful stereotyping of Mexican-origin people in the local media. Along with describing the racial landscape of the town of Salinas, this chapter discusses the strikes conducted there by "Okie" and Filipino agricultural workers during the 1930s that provoked a violent response by agribusiness and law enforcement. The deep antiunion hostility displayed in these moments of labor militancy prevented Mexican-origin workers from unionizing when they became the Salinas Valley's new agricultural proletariat during the 1940s.

By World War II the region had become a booming center of U.S. agriculture and representative of the diverse international and interstate migrant population that California welcomed on a larger scale. When the Bracero Program began as a "temporary" wartime manpower initiative in 1942, braceros began working under labor contracts in all regions of the United States. The face of the American farmworker became even more "brown," hardening existing socioeconomic and racial hierarchies in which Mexican-origin people remained at the bottom. Continually renewed between the U.S. and Mexican governments until 1964, the Bracero Program was one of the longest-running guestworker programs in U.S. history. There is currently much valuable scholarship on the program, ranging from diplomatic histories of its negotiations to studies of braceros' working experiences in the United States to gendered analysis of the survival strategies of bracero families left behind in Mexico.[7] This is the first book to examine how the Bracero Program, and braceros themselves, shaped California race relations and the contours of Mexican American civil rights activism. Chapter 2 focuses on the World War II years and shows how different permutations of conflict played out not only between Mexican Americans and a white mainstream that denied them equal treatment, but between Mexican Americans and braceros as they came into contact with each other in a militarized, masculinized agricultural context. Though Mexican Americans reacted against racial discrimination by writing letters of complaint to local authorities or wearing the controversial zoot suit, these forms of resistance did not have the same effect that they had in urban California, where Mexican American civil rights organizations began taking shape in the immediate postwar period. This chapter argues for the Bracero Program's centrality in understanding why the activism of Mexican Americans living in agricultural California appeared weaker, or progressed at a slower pace, than that of urban Mexican Americans.

The Mexican world of agricultural California became even more complex as growers imported greater numbers of braceros and a parallel stream of undocumented Mexican migrants sought work in *el norte* (the United States). Chapter 3 analyzes the effect of the late 1940s and early 1950s, or "wetback era," upon personal relationships in the Mexican American–bracero–"wetback" triad. Although some moments of intraethnic bonding occurred in the spheres of work, religion, and romance, several fields of division, including nativity, citizenship, class, language, and political ideology, kept these three communities apart. The Mexican American agricultural working class felt betrayed by the state, which had created a Bracero Program and immigration system that did not protect them as worker-citizens but instead served at the pleasure of agribusiness. Meanwhile, some Mexican American middle-class civil rights leaders voiced concerns that undocumented migrants threatened their economic stability and social respectability. Two particular flashpoints—the INS's "Operation Wetback" of 1954 and the peak of the Bracero Program in 1956—brought the intraethnic conflict between Mexican Americans, braceros, and undocumented migrants into greater relief. Not wanting to be racially associated with deportable "illegal aliens" or braceros (who, in the 1950s, were being constructed as all-male masses of sexual deviants), Mexican Americans in the Salinas Valley struggled with whether to defend their co-ethnics or rally against them. Simply put, many Mexican Americans living in agriculture-centered communities felt that fighting for their own rights was a daunting enough task. At best, they defended Mexican nationals indirectly by protesting their exploitation but avoided engaging in activism on their behalf. Interestingly, when personal connections were made across lines of citizenship, it was often Mexican American women who decided to socialize with Mexican nationals. This was noteworthy in a male-dominated agricultural environment and signaled women's importance in future moments of community-making.

Against a Cold War backdrop of labor and political repression, xenophobia, and heightened border surveillance, California's Mexican Americans tried to assert their Americanness and good citizenship by founding and joining organizations like the Community Service Organization (CSO). Extant literature has focused on this organization's founding in Los Angeles and the activism of its male and female members but has generally stayed confined to the urban realm.[8] Chapter 4 examines the formation and lifespan of a CSO chapter in Salinas that was founded in 1954 after a group of friends mobilized to fight for the fair trial of a Mexican American youth accused of murdering an Italian American peer. During the 1950s the CSO conducted successful voting and citizenship drives, fought cases of police harassment and housing discrimination, sponsored social events, and gained the respect of city officials who otherwise would have doubted the good citizenship of Mexican Americans. In addition to offering a detailed look at the workings of a CSO chapter outside of the organization's base in Los Angeles, this chapter complicates historical analysis of the organization by exploring how the Salinas Valley CSO both succeeded and failed. While it empowered its members—and Mexican American women in particular—as community organizers, the organization limited its own power and dissolved by the early 1960s because it failed to create interracial alliances, involve the larger Mexican-origin community in specific protests, maintain stable leadership, and risk its cultivated image of respectability. By examining the membership, goals, and trajectory of this CSO chapter, Chapter 4 shows how a prominent urban-origin Mexican American civil rights organization replicated and existed in an agricultural climate. It also discusses how the California CSO at large had to come to grips with the different goals of its urban and rural constituencies.

Chapter 5 situates the 1963 bracero deaths at Chualar as a pivotal moment in the history of the Bracero Program and California's Chicano Movement. After the accident, urban and agricultural Mexican American leaders came together to protest the Bracero Program's exploitation and safety hazards. Arguably, this was the first time that farmworkers' concerns claimed a place of priority on the agenda of California's nascent Chicano Movement. The Chualar incident produced enough protest from organized labor, church leaders, and civil rights advocates to accelerate Congress's decision to discontinue the Bracero Program in 1964. Scholars have periodized the program through its administrative phases—the early wartime years dominated by government control (1941–1947), a negotiation period with Mexico over program extension (1947–1951), and a more restrictive and exploitative phase dominated by grower control (1951–1964). In California, however, the Bracero Program lived a longer life until 1968 because the state and federal governments continued to bend to grower requests for Mexican guest labor. It was not until a group of Salinas farmworkers turned to the legal aid organization California Rural Legal Assistance (CRLA), and made history by filing and winning lawsuits against growers who sought to continue importing braceros and prevent their employees from joining Cesar Chavez's UFWOC, that the Bracero Program officially died. These legal actions and victories, I argue in Chapter 6, were evidence that a farmworker movement long suppressed had finally blossomed again in the Salinas Valley. "Chicano" rhetoric and protest began to emerge as well in the Mexican American political community and student population. Even before Chavez arrived to organize lettuce workers in 1970, Mexican Americans were directing their energies into increasingly coordinated, direct, and assertive forms of social and political action. Chavez did not bring the Chicano Movement to the Salinas Valley—there was a *movimiento* already waiting for him there.

Much has been written about Chavez, mostly in reaction to decades of literature and a recent biopic that praised his contributions to the farmworker rights movement and elevated him to heroic or saintly status as a Mexican American civil rights icon. More critical analysis of his union leadership style and personal flaws has enriched our view of this charismatic yet complicated man. While this study engages with that scholarship, it does not seek to make Chavez the main character of the Salinas Valley farmworker movement story. Rather, it pays greater attention to the less exalted farmworkers, volunteers, students, and supporters who helped Chavez become such a successful organizer. The 1970 lettuce strike in Salinas played an essential role in cultivating that success but has been overlooked compared with the Delano grape strike of the 1960s and the later United Farm Workers' strikes of the late 1970s and 1980s. The final chapter of *Grounds for Dreaming* provides necessary and deep analysis of the 1970 strike and parses the various groups of UFWOC supporters and detractors involved. The size of the strike, the racialized violence that erupted, the activism of women, and the unprecedented cooperation seen between Mexican Americans and Mexicans made it a remarkable moment in California labor and Chicano history.[9]

The agricultural hub of the Salinas Valley negotiated, and shaped, key moments and transitions in labor and immigration policy, race relations, and civil rights activism in the postwar American West. The story of how its Mexican American and Mexican residents confronted particular struggles and became political actors reveals how shifting our analytical lens to an agricultural context helps our narratives of the California Latino experience become more inclusive and multidimensional. It also illuminates how intertwined the histories of native-born and immigrant Mexicans have been and continue to be. Mexican American identities have been formed relationally to, or consciously against, those of Mexican nationals and vice versa. This continues to be relevant after 1970 and into the twenty-first century. Latinos in the United States have grown in number, become increasingly diverse along various lines, and spread throughout the country to settle in places unaccustomed to their presence. In many ways, this demographic seems to be continually new. Yet old debates around citizenship, rights, immigration policy, border control, guestworker programs, and farmworker justice continue to resurface, sometimes predictably but other times in disturbing ways. This book provides the backstory to these modern conversations, through the lives of people both long gone and still here.

1 The Racial and Labor Landscapes of the Salinas Valley Before World War II

NATIVE AMERICANS WERE the first inhabitants of the land that became the Salinas Valley. The Ohlone, Salinan, Costanoan, and Tehesselen tribes made their homes in the region for seven centuries before the Spanish, who colonized Mexico in 1521, established a presence in present-day California. The Spanish government built a presidio in Monterey (1769) and missions in Carmel (1770), Soledad (1791), and San Juan Bautista (1797). Spanish soldiers and missionaries recruited Indians to be vaqueros, laborers, or neophytes, and over time the Indian population decreased dramatically because of European diseases, poor living conditions, and cruel treatment. After Mexico gained independence from Spain in 1821 and the missions were secularized in 1828, the Mexican government parceled out mission property and other lands to Spanish-Mexican *Californios* and to foreigners if they agreed to adopt Mexican citizenship and Catholicism. Native Americans, though freed from the missions, often did not have the financial resources to buy property and thus remained in the laboring class for *Californio* landowners.[1]

Just two decades after California's transition from Spanish to Mexican rule, everything changed once more. After the formation of the Texas Republic in 1836 and the annexation of Texas in 1845, a boundary dispute over what actually marked Texas's southern border—the Nueces

River or Rio Grande—set in motion the U.S.-Mexican War of 1846 to
1848. The United States ultimately prevailed with its greater military
power and its Manifest Destiny–driven hunger for a large swath of the
Mexican empire. The resulting Treaty of Guadalupe Hidalgo carried
the following terms: the United States would pay $15 million for more
than half of Mexico, including California and most of the Southwest
(the Gadsden Purchase of 1854 acquired southern Arizona and southwestern New Mexico for an additional $10 million), and Mexican citi-
zens residing within the ceded territory had one year to decide whether
they wanted to keep their land and become U.S. citizens or leave their
homes and retain their Mexican citizenship. Only two thousand people
left for what was now Mexico, while one hundred thousand people became the United States' first Mexican Americans. They had not crossed
the border; the border had crossed them. This significant addition of
people, land, and natural resources to the American West was followed
by the Gold Rush of 1849, which brought one hundred thousand more
people from places as varied as New York, France, Mexico, Australia,
China, and Chile.

In this multicultural and economically competitive environment,
people of Latin American and Asian origin fared badly. Derogatorily
nicknamed "greasers" by whites and stereotyped as lazy, dirty, and culturally backward, Latin American prospectors were subjected to a state
antivagrancy act known as the "Greaser Act," which targeted those of
"Spanish or Indian blood . . . who [were] armed and not peaceable
and quiet persons," and a "Foreign Miners' Tax," which initially required them to pay a monthly tax of twenty dollars for access to the
gold mines. Many could not afford this tax and were thus deprived of
the opportunity for possible wealth. This racial exclusion transpired
despite the fact that it was Mexican miners who had introduced the
batea, a wooden bowl used in washing out gold, and the *arrastra,* a
piece of equipment used in placer mining operations. Asian miners
were subject to the tax as well, and, according to one writer, their payments from 1850 to 1870 amounted to half of California's total state
revenue. Those Chinese who could not afford to be prospectors became
"coolies" or contract laborers in mines, fields, or railroads.[2]

The exclusion of Latinos and Asians from the goldfields was compounded by widespread land dispossession that occurred after California's incorporation into the United States in 1850. Although the Treaty

of Guadalupe Hidalgo had guaranteed the rights of all new Mexican Americans to their property, in 1851 landowners with Spanish or Mexican titles were ordered to appear before the U.S. Land Commission and present documentary evidence of their landownership. For those who may not have had tangible proof on paper—perhaps land had been informally passed down through generations, or documents had been lost or destroyed during wartime—this was a difficult task. All lands for which claims were rejected were regarded as public domain and could be usurped. Mexican-origin landholders in the Salinas Valley and elsewhere in the Southwest were confused and outraged as they struggled to defend their land claims in English-language courts of law. Ultimately, the Land Commission and District Court of Appeals upheld three-fourths of land grant titles, but petitioners accumulated significant debt over litigation that lasted on average for seventeen years. Many ended up losing their land via costly court fees, tax delinquency, squatters, or lawyers who asked to be paid in property instead of cash. Meanwhile, the federal government sold huge tracts of land to railroad companies, including the Southern Pacific Railroad, and to state government speculators who purposefully devalued properties and then bought and subdivided them to sell at a profit.[3]

The post–Civil War migration of easterners to the West would only accelerate this process of land transferring out of the hands of Mexican Americans into those of Euro-Americans. This was how so many places in the U.S. Southwest, including the Salinas Valley's central town of Salinas (Spanish for "salt marsh"), came to be. Jacob P. Leese, who bought the vast Rancho Sausal from *Californio* Feliciano Soberanes for six hundred dollars in 1852, sold eighty acres to Deacon Elias Howe, who then erected a two-story inn called the Halfway House in 1856 to serve as a small way station between San Francisco and Los Angeles. Around this inn Howe built the beginnings of Salinas—a tavern, country store, and stagecoach station that became the site of political meetings and other public gatherings. In 1865 Howe sold his property to Italian-born tinsmith Albert Trescony, whose construction of a small hotel, blacksmith shop, and stable expanded Salinas further. Over time, grocery and clothing stores, hotels, banks, saloons, schools, and doctors' offices sprouted and attracted a diverse array of inhabitants.[4]

Salinas's first residents were mostly migrants from the eastern United States, Canada, England, Germany, Ireland, Denmark, Italy, Portugal, and Switzerland. A small *Californio* population persisted, along with a few Chinese immigrants. The first African American resident of Salinas was a slave from Mississippi brought to California and freed by his master, but not many followed. By the time of Salinas's first census in 1870, only two of the town's six hundred residents were classified as "colored." More settlers arrived when the Southern Pacific Railroad Company extended its line to Salinas and established a depot in 1872. Praised by the County Board of Supervisors as the "most important commercial city in the county" with its paved streets, electric lights, hotels and businesses, fraternal halls, and opera house, Salinas was officially incorporated into Monterey County in 1874 and replaced Monterey as the county seat. This was partly because many county residents believed the once-desirable coastal town of Monterey had become "a Mexican town that had not taken on the comforts and improvements modern civilization has found essential for health and convenience." Meanwhile, Salinas was a town of 1,865 people, with a steady influx of Euro-American immigrants, making it the more modern, prosperous, "white" town of the valley.[5]

The value placed on whiteness affected how different elements of the Spanish-speaking population were treated. Those of more "Spanish" or European heritage were considered "whiter" and more socially respectable. White men, particularly those who wanted to achieve higher status as landowners or politicians, learned Spanish and married into *Californio* families. The *Monterey Weekly Herald* affirmed that "no sensible man would ever think of depreciating an alliance with a Spanish family, new or old. In fact, it is an honor to all who are fortunate enough to win a fair bride connected with an 'old Spanish family.'" One Mr. Webb, described as being "affiliated with a Spanish family," was elected Monterey County Judge in 1875, no doubt helped along by extra votes gained from the Spanish-speaking community. Meanwhile, *Californianas* assented to marry white men out of love, a desire to protect their family's resources and possessions, or a wish to maintain their status in what they observed to be a rapidly changing society. According to Maria Raquel Casas, only a few hundred intermarriages between *Californianas* and Euro-Americans occurred between 1820 and 1880, but those that did had a profound effect on the marital partners and their communities. In Monterey County, for example, the 1825 marriage of failing English trader William E. P. Hartnell and

privileged Spanish-Mexican *Californiana* María Teresa de la Guerra y
Noriega secured his financial status and maintained her social status.
Hartnell eventually acquired a share of Rancho del Alisal from the Soberanes family, opened California's first organized school, and served
as a tax collector, mission overseer, and translator for the California
government. Thanks to his wife's family and connections, Hartnell rose
in prominence, and today Hartnell College in Salinas bears his name.
By contrast, Mexican-origin people of lower class or darker skin were
considered more "Indian," racially inferior, and undesirable for intermarriage or other forms of social accommodation. In fact, in 1855
the California state legislature passed a law prohibiting school boards
from using funds to educate nonwhite students. Mexican Indians and
Mexican mestizos with a weak claim to "European" or "white" identity
were thus deemed ineligible for a public education. The law changed in
1864 but still stipulated that nonwhite students be instructed in separate schools funded only by other nonwhites' property taxes.[6]

By the 1880s, whites had assumed more control over land, businesses, and positions in politics and law enforcement in California. As
Albert Camarillo explained in his pioneering study of Santa Barbara,
Mexican-origin people in the state experienced the two processes of
proletarianization and barrioization in the late nineteenth century. Rel-
egated to unskilled or semiskilled work in the new white capitalist labor market, many Mexicanos had to take on migratory and seasonal
labor to survive. This resulted in their becoming the new agricultural
working class in the U.S. Southwest by the end of the century. This
proletarianization was accompanied by racial segregation that pushed
Mexican-origin people into lower-class neighborhoods, or barrios, by
the late 1880s and 1890s. These two processes were not limited to California. By this time Mexican-origin people had become the new proletarians of the copper smelters and cattle ranches of Texas and mines of
New Mexico and Arizona, where workers labored under a race-based
dual-wage system. While white "American" miners in Arizona earned
between thirty and seventy dollars a month plus board, for example,
Mexicano workers received between twelve and thirty dollars a month
and a weekly ration of flour.[7]

While Mexican-origin people became the agricultural proletariat of
much of the U.S. Southwest by the 1920s, this process was delayed in
the Salinas Valley because of the large Asian immigrant labor force

that first served the region's agricultural economy. By the late nineteenth century the Salinas Valley was supplying grain for half of the bread eaten in the U.S. West, and the Spreckels sugar beet refinery was thriving. With the completion of the railroad system at the turn of the century and the commercial connection of the West and East Coasts strengthened by the use of refrigerated railcars, the Salinas Valley became a booming national center of food production. Each region of California had its cash crops; vegetables flourished in the Imperial and Central Valleys, citrus orchards covered the area surrounding Los Angeles, fruits and nuts made the Santa Clara Valley rich, and vineyards were the domain of northern California. Because of its year-round temperate climate, the Salinas Valley could produce crops as diverse as lettuce, potatoes, beans, carrots, celery, artichokes, and broccoli. Additionally, immigrants from Switzerland, Italy, the Azores, and Denmark had moved to the valley and established hundreds of successful dairies. Jack Ferrasci, whose family emigrated in the 1920s from the Italian canton of Ticino, Switzerland, remembered how he and other Swiss Italians were drawn to the valley by word of mouth, hearing that it had "the richest soil in the world." The Ferrasci family's farming enterprise went on to accumulate in excess of one thousand acres of land, and by 1930 there were 19,645 other Ticino natives in California.[8]

While Anglo Americans and European immigrants became the vast majority of growers and farmers in the Salinas Valley, Asian immigrants—first Chinese, then Japanese, then Filipino—made up the first agricultural working classes. Chinese laborers toiled in the region's grain fields after the completion of the transcontinental railroad in 1869, and the miles of irrigation ditches they dug boosted the value of the land from twenty-eight dollars an acre in 1875 to one hundred dollars an acre two years later. A Chinatown district quickly emerged northeast of Salinas's center to house and serve this laboring population. During the economic panic of 1873, however, many white Californians accused the Chinese of undercutting other workers and being a menace to the state. Groups such as the San Francisco–based Workingmen's Party endorsed anti-Chinese measures and immigration restrictions, and in 1882 the Chinese Exclusion Act barred all new Chinese immigration to the United States. Those already living in the country, and U.S. citizens of Chinese descent, were permitted to stay along with incoming merchants, students, and diplomats, but those in the latter three categories were deemed ineligible for U.S. citizenship. In Salinas, China-born merchants took refuge in Chinatown for their housing and business operations. They, along with the few dozen other Chinese residents, likely recognized the passing of the Chinese Exclusion Act as a pivotal moment in the history of the United States as a gatekeeping nation.[9]

As smaller numbers of Chinese entered California after 1882, Japanese laborers became the state's new agricultural workforce. From 1902 to 1907 approximately thirty-eight thousand Japanese plantation workers immigrated to the American West from Hawai'i, and thousands more came directly from Japan. By the early 1900s, however, the notion that the Japanese represented another "yellow peril" had seeped into political and public discourse. The Gentlemen's Agreement of 1907, an informal agreement between the United States and Japan, restricted further Japanese emigration. Some regions of California, including the Salinas and Santa Clara Valleys, continued to embrace Japanese farmworkers as disciplined and obedient labor. Yet as these workers became more successful at cultivating, leasing, and buying farmland, California growers perceived them as an economic threat. Agribusiness interests threw their support behind the Alien Land Acts passed by the California legislature in 1913 and 1920 that prohibited aliens ineligible for U.S. citizenship—specifically, Chinese and Japanese immigrants—from purchasing, owning, selling, or leasing property in the state. In essence, those who had cultivated the land with their labor found themselves without any rights to it. Japanese landholders responded by forming land companies or asking a U.S. citizen (sometimes a second-generation Japanese American, or nisei) to lease land for them, yet they could not escape the "unassimilable" identity imposed on them because of their national origin. Punjabi migrants from British colonial India, often referred to by the American misnomer "Hindus" regardless of their actual religion, worked on California farms and orchards during the early 1900s. Several marriages between Mexican-origin women and Punjabi men took place in the San Joaquin and Imperial Valleys, but the Immigration Act of 1917—which prohibited emigration from a designated "Asiatic Barred Zone" that included much of eastern Asia, south Asia, and the Pacific Islands—prevented this population from growing.[10]

Early-twentieth-century immigration legislation, including the Alien Land Acts, Asian restriction, and the Johnson-Reed Immigration Act of 1924 (which imposed yearly quotas on European migrants), did not affect Mexican migration. At this time the U.S.-Mexico border was marked by stone monuments, but these markers were separated by miles with no walls or fences between them. Congress had created a Bureau of Immigration in 1891, and a few years later its field organization, the U.S. Immigration Service, had established a Mounted Guard of seventy-five men to patrol the Mexican and Canadian borders for undocumented Chinese immigrants, but no personnel had been deployed to monitor the movements of Mexicans. As Cleofas Calleros, who immigrated from Mexico to the United States during the early 1900s, recalled, "All you had to do coming from Mexico, if you were a Mexican citizen, was to report at the immigration office on the American side ... give your name, the place of your birth, and where you were going to." At the turn of the century Mexico's economy was deteriorating, largely because of President Porfirio Diaz's policy of allowing foreign capitalists and companies to invest in or buy land. To that end he eliminated *ejidos* (communal land used and owned by peasants), which then displaced small farmers. These impoverished Mexicans went first to northern Mexico in search of work, but with the railroad's penetration into the borderlands, it was easy to hop a cheap train into the United States. Mexican migrants settled in Texas and throughout the Southwest and Midwest, venturing on their own or following the promises of an *enganchador,* a labor recruiter who lured workers to U.S. railroads, fields, mines, and factories with offers of free transportation and higher wages. These promises were often empty—migrants frequently found that their travel costs and lodging were deducted from their wages—and many became *enganchados,* or "hooked ones," trapped in a vicious cycle of debt and low-wage labor.[11]

The Mexican-origin population of the United States increased with the social and economic chaos of the Mexican Revolution. Between 1910 and 1920 more than one million Mexicans—one-tenth of Mexico's population—migrated to *el norte.* Mexican immigrant men took on work in the steel and meatpacking plants of Chicago, the auto factories of Detroit, the cotton fields of Texas, and the citrus and vegetable fields of California. Women did the same or became maids, laundresses, garment workers, or cannery workers. During World War I, at the request of agribusiness interests and industrialists, the U.S. government exempted the Mexican population from the 1917 Immigration Act's required literacy test, ten-dollar visa fee, and eight-dollar head tax from the years 1917 to 1921.[12] Though the government welcomed Mexicans as laborers, not all Americans welcomed them as neighbors. A "100 percent American" movement and Red Scare hysteria during the war, along with concerns over public health and disease, led to the stereotyping of Mexican-origin people as filthy, ignorant, or politically subversive. Meanwhile, American Federation of Labor (AFL) president Samuel Gompers and other labor union leaders tried to have Mexican immigration drastically reduced throughout the 1920s because of fears that Mexican workers were depressing wages and being used as strikebreakers. They pointed to the numbers as justification for their anxieties. By the 1920s more than one-third of all employed Mexicans worked in agriculture. In California, the Mexican-born population had risen to almost half a million by 1920, and Mexicans formed the largest single ethnic group among the state's farmworkers. Mexican migration peaked during the 1920s, with 459,287 Mexicans entering the United States between 1921 and 1930. By 1930, California claimed almost one-quarter of the Mexican population living in the United States.[13] Some labor unions went as far as to exclude Mexican workers from membership altogether and were only partially placated when the U.S. Border Patrol was created in 1924 to begin policing Mexicans' entry into the country.

It was only after Chinese, Japanese, and Indian laborers left the fields of the Salinas Valley that Mexicans became a noticeable workforce there. Those Mexicans who decided to migrate to the town of Salinas in the early twentieth century hailed from various Mexican states, including Jalisco, Sonora, Chihuahua, Michoacán, Guanajuato, Durango, and Zacatecas. Traveling by train or on foot, they crossed the border at points of entry in Laredo, Eagle Pass, and Del Rio, Texas; Naco and Nogales, Arizona; and Calexico, California (fig. 1.1). By 1920 Mexican migration had helped Salinas grow to 4,308 people, with 3,219 "native whites" (U.S.-born Europeans and Mexicans), 713 "foreign whites" (European and Mexican immigrants), 224 Japanese, 104 Chinese, 26 blacks, and 22 people of "miscellaneous" origin, who were most likely Filipino. Because the Philippines became a U.S. territory after the Spanish-American War in 1898, Filipinos were considered "noncitizen nationals" or "wards" of the United States and exempt from anti-Asian

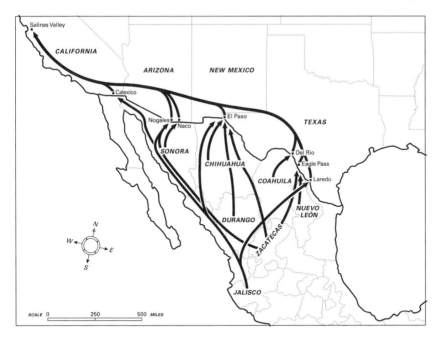

Fig. 1.1. Post–Mexican Revolution migration routes to U.S. ports of entry and the Salinas Valley. These routes are simplistic composites gleaned from naturalization records. Migrants did not always head directly toward the Salinas Valley from Mexico but followed family and work opportunities to different parts of the Southwest before eventually arriving in the region. (Map by David Hackett)

immigration laws. Yet they lived in what sociologist Rick Baldoz calls a "political twilight zone between citizenship and alienage," meaning they could move freely across and within the borders of the United States but were deemed ineligible for naturalized U.S. citizenship. Between 1907 and 1936, 150,000 Filipinos migrated to the United States to work in sugar plantations in Hawai'i, canneries in Alaska and Seattle, or agriculture in California. Because men were the more desired laborers, women's immigration was restricted and Filipinas made up less than one-quarter of newcomers. By 1930 approximately 45,000 Filipinos lived on the U.S. mainland, mostly in California.[14]

Working alongside each other in California fields by the 1930s, Mexicans and Filipinos experienced the same racialization that other workers before them had experienced. Many whites held preconceived notions about the "natural" ability of the two groups to perform stoop labor. "Due to their crouching and bending habits," claimed Dr. George Clements of the Los Angeles Chamber of Commerce, Mexicans and Filipinos were suited for fieldwork while whites were "physically unable to adapt" to such labor. A California Department of Industrial Relations report stated that Filipino workers were "more tractable and more willing to put up with longer hours, poorer board, and poorer lodging facilities . . . Where a white worker might feel restive and disgruntled because of bad conditions, the Filipino immigrant is satisfied to stay on the job without kicking." Meanwhile, Texas farmers claimed that "white people won't do the work and they won't live as the Mexicans do on beans and tortillas and in one-room shacks," and "whites cannot be as easily domineered, led, or directed as the Mexicans." To the west in the Imperial Valley of California, a vegetable growers' representative agreed: "We want the Mexicans because we can treat them as we cannot treat any other living man." A Professor R. L. Adams added these final words about the Mexican farmworker in 1930: "He will do tasks that white workers will not or cannot do. He will work under climatic and working conditions, such as excessive heat, dust, isolation, and temporary employment; conditions that are often too trying for white workers . . . He will work under direction, taking orders, and suggestions. He is not expensive labor." In arguing that Filipinos' and Mexicans' bodies were made for farm labor and that their minds did not object to "bad conditions," these agricultural industry professionals justified these workers' poor treatment and standard of living. Additionally, Filipinos and Mexicans suffered from labor segmentation by being restricted to field labor and barred from working in fruit and vegetable packing sheds alongside white women and men.[15]

Filipino men labored under other racialized assumptions when it came to their sexuality. Because of the restricted immigration of Filipinas, men essentially became members of a bachelor society. "We became an entire generation that was forced by society to find love and companionship in dancehalls," said Philip Vera Cruz, who migrated to the United States in 1926 and went on to become a well-known labor leader. In Salinas's Chinatown district Filipinos could patronize "girly houses" and dancehalls but quickly provoked the ire of local residents if they dared to cross the color line and openly date or marry white women. California's miscegenation law prohibiting marriages between whites and "Negroes, mulattoes, Mongolians, and Malays" meant that Filipinos were considered unacceptable sexual and romantic partners for Euro-American women. In early December 1929 in the Salinas Valley town of Watsonville, police arrested a Filipino man after seeing him with a white teenage girl. He was later released after the girl's mother affirmed they were engaged. The next month the Northern Monterey County Chamber of Commerce passed a resolution written by local judge D. W. Rohrback that condemned Filipinos as "a menace to white labor" and a "moral and sanitary threat" and demanded their expulsion from the county. When a taxi-dance hall, or private club, opened in Watsonville for Filipinos to dance with white women, gangs of young white men attacked Filipinos at the hall over a period of several days while a mob of four hundred whites ransacked the Northern Monterey Filipino Club and a crowd of white youths shot up a Filipino labor camp, killing worker Fermin Tobera. Rohrback blamed Filipinos for provoking this violence. "Damn the Filipino! He won't keep his place," he fumed. "The worst part of his being here is his mixing with young white girls . . . buying them silk underwear and . . . keeping them out till all hours of the night. And some of these girls are carrying a Filipino's baby around inside them." Rohrback actually presided over the original court trial of the eight men charged with the rioting, but fanatical public support of the vigilantes caused the case to be relocated to Salinas under Judge H. S. Jorgensen, who sentenced the men to two years in a state penitentiary for the murder of Tobera. Jorgensen, however, suspended the sentences, and the men never served any prison time. This violent episode in the Salinas Valley—and attacks against Filipinos elsewhere in California and other parts of the West Coast—traumatized the population.[16]

Like Filipinos, Mexican-origin people experienced discrimination because of their ethnic and national backgrounds. Despite residing in California long before it became part of the United States, Mexicanos were treated as foreign inferiors. Growers' propagation of the idea that Mexican laborers were "birds of passage" who would return to their home country during harvest breaks further encouraged local whites to treat all Mexican-origin people, U.S. citizens included, as temporary residents and social outsiders. In the Salinas Valley during the late nineteenth and early twentieth centuries, newspapers were the main outlet through which negative perceptions of Mexican-origin people as violent, drunk, stupid, dirty, and sexually deviant were circulated. Having already placed them low on the labor hierarchy, whites asserted Mexicanos' social undesirability and racial inferiority through words that would lead to, and seemingly justify, their ongoing mistreatment.

MEXICANNESS AND THE MEDIA

Mexican-origin people in the Salinas Valley became the targets of racially charged media coverage and criminalization almost immediately after whites began settling in the region. An early popular stereotype was that of the Mexican bandit, primarily because of notorious *Californios* Tiburcio Vásquez and Joaquín Murrieta who were allegedly driven to vigilantism against white settlers during the 1840s and 1850s. According to legend, Murrieta became vengeful when his claim to gold was stolen because of his racial background and white miners hanged his half-brother on a false charge of horse theft. Murrieta became a horse thief himself, raiding ranches and killing several men while redistributing stolen wealth to the poor. Often referred to as the "Robin Hood" of California, Murrieta was only twenty-two years old when he was reportedly killed. Born in Monterey in August 1835, Tiburcio Vásquez was labeled by media as a "wily little Mexican" who stabbed the constable of Monterey to death at the age of nineteen. Vásquez achieved folk-hero status by robbing the stagecoaches of white travelers near Salinas. After serving two terms in San Quentin and breaking out of prison four times, Vásquez was accused of robbery and murder at a California store, and an all-white jury convicted him of first-degree murder with a sentence of death. Calling Vásquez's name "a synonym for all that is wicked and infamous," the trial judge ordered him hanged in San Jose on March 19, 1875. Before his execution, Vásquez explained to a newspaper reporter that he had become a bandit after witnessing so many *Californios* being "unjustly and wrongfully deprived of the social rights that belonged to us."[17]

Vásquez's case was probably the most famous of its kind, but the hanging of Mexicans was not an uncommon practice. Lynching of all types of people by vigilante committees in the American West dated back to the Gold Rush, but Californians of Mexican descent were lynched at a rate disproportionate to their overall population. Historians William D. Carrigan and Clive Webb have made the compelling case that Mexican-origin people ran an equal if not greater risk of being lynched or victimized by vigilante violence in the turn-of-the-century U.S. Southwest as African Americans in the U.S. South. Some documented reasons for *Californio* lynchings included things such as murder, theft, rape or sexual assault, and miscegenation but also "being of Mexican descent," "cheating at cards," witchcraft, "courting a white woman," "refusing to play the fiddle," and "taking a white man to court." Out of the 143 lynchings of Mexican-origin people that occurred in California from 1848 to 1928, 19 of them occurred in Monterey County. The victims included father and son pair José and Juan Higuera, who allegedly murdered Anglo enforcement officers in 1854 and 1865, respectively, and others accused of murder or theft. In one May 1856 case, three "unknown Mexicans" were hanged "on rather slight proof" of a crime. In almost all the cases, the victims were taken from their jail cells and hanged or shot by a group of vigilantes.[18]

As the stock character of the Mexican bandit began to develop, so did other ideas about Mexican-origin people's alleged propensity toward violence, drunkenness, uncleanliness, and unlawful behavior. Nineteenth- and twentieth-century Salinas Valley newspapers' coverage of murders, fistfights, and petty theft involving Spanish-surnamed people—such as "Lizzie Escobar, a wayward 15-year-old" servant arrested for stealing items from her Anglo employer—led the reading public to make assumptions about Mexican-origin people as a whole. An 1875 *Monterey Weekly Herald* article, for example, called Mexican parents "entirely indifferent concerning education," and after the discovery of Theophile D. Baca, "a Mexican about 25 years of age" whose murdered body was thrown in a gulch, the *Salinas Weekly Index* reported that Baca was "a man of more than ordinary personal neatness and intelligence for one of his class." Even if the newspaper's use of the term "class" referred to Baca's lower socioeconomic status rather than his ethnic background, there was evidence that even the old *Californio* population fell victim to assumptions about their inherent criminality. One of the most discussed political scandals involved Salinas tax collector Manuel Castro, "a member of one of the oldest and well-known families in California," who was accused of embezzlement and arson. Authorities later found that Castro's deputy had gambled away the stolen money, but as a local historian later argued, "the scandal

contributed to the further decline of the role of the Spanish 'Los Californios' in the life of the county."[19]

In consistently using the simple referent "Mexican" regardless of the
subject's actual citizenship status, newspapers made a point of emphasizing these individuals' racial identity while never doing the same for
white subjects. With each headline such as "Mexican Worker Dies in
Fight," "Mexican Stabbed," or "Mexican Arrested on Drunk Driving
Charge," the public association between Mexicanness and criminality
solidified. Additional associations between Mexicanness and other negative traits ranging from stupidity to sexual deviance covered the pages
of papers. One article read, "Jose Urdes, an ignorant Mexican, will serve
120 days in the county jail for wife beating," and another mentioned
José Franco, a forty-eight-year-old "Mexican laborer" who had too
much to drink, fell into some mud, and had to be fished out by police
who then charged him with disturbing the peace. A rape case in which
seven Spanish-surnamed men were accused of assaulting a prominent
white Salinas woman garnered much media attention. Mexican-origin
women were hardly mentioned, but when they were—like Rose Pico
and Agnes López, who were charged with vagrancy and expelled from
Monterey County for two years—they were associated with unlawful
activity and sexual promiscuity. In rare instances when Mexican-origin
people appeared as victims in media reports, they were still implied to
have been at fault. During the 1930s and 1940s several Mexican laborers walking home from the fields were killed in hit-and-run accidents.
In all cases, white drivers' mental clarity was never questioned, and
none were given jail time, while Mexican workers' drunkenness or lack
of attention on dark roads was stated to be the cause of the accidents.
In cases where Mexican-origin people were the drivers, however, they
were consistently arrested and charged. Forty-year-old laborer Rafael
López was charged with a felony for his driving, and a *Salinas Daily
Post* article poked fun at one William Rojas, who would "have to do
without his tortillas and frijoles for six months" after pleading guilty
to a hit-and-run accident.[20]

Infrequent moments of positive media treatment occurred when the
"Mexican colonies" of Salinas Valley towns commemorated holidays
such as El Dieciseis de Septiembre, the day of Mexican independence
from Spain, with public celebrations. To keep their culture alive and
create a venue for financial and social support, Mexican-origin people

in the Southwest had founded mutual aid organizations (*mutualistas*) such as the Alianza Hispano-Americana (founded in Tucson in 1894) and El Primer Congreso Mexicanista (founded in Laredo in 1911) in their local communities. *Mutualistas,* in addition to Spanish-language political clubs and newspapers, sponsored Mexican holiday celebrations. Yet even when white residents recounted or mimicked these festivities, they erased their original "Mexican" character and origins. At a local "fiesta" held by white Salinas Valley residents in 1939, for example, Mexican food was served but media coverage focused on the "Spanish" entertainers, music, and dancing. This elevation of a Spanish culture and erasure of a Mexican one, Carey McWilliams first opined, created a "Spanish Fantasy Past" in which municipal authorities and boosters whitewashed California's indigenous and Mexican history for white consumption.[21] This fantasy-making had very real consequences. The stereotypes of the dirty Mexican bandit, drunkard, buffoon, prostitute, and rapist that were circulated by individuals and the media continued to follow Mexican-origin people, both U.S.-born and immigrant, well into the twentieth century. They also worked to justify the erection of racial boundaries between different groups of Salinas residents. Community leaders worked on building Salinas's reputation as the new successful "white" town of the valley and in the process pushed Mexican-origin people and other racial minorities to live on its outskirts, where they would be joined by new migrant populations arriving during the Great Depression.

Imagined racial differences between people heavily shaped the mapping of access to residential and commercial space. In Salinas, which had grown to ten thousand residents by the late 1920s, specific neighborhoods and their boundaries began to be clearly defined (fig. 1.2). Middle- and upper-class whites lived in central or north Salinas, along with a very small number of *Californios* who had retained a merchant or white-collar status. Chinese, Japanese, and a few Filipino residents lived in Chinatown, northeast of the town's center. A string of vegetable packing sheds lay along the railroad tracks that meandered through Salinas, for easy transportation of produce. Housed on the margins of Salinas, Filipino and Mexicano farmworkers lived in labor camps owned by contractors and often hitched rides from their bosses into Chinatown on the weekends to take advantage of the district's restaurants, pool halls, brothels, and Catholic churches.[22]

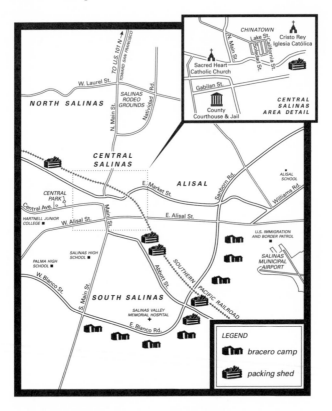

Fig. 1.2. Salinas, California, ca. 1940s. (Map by David Hackett)

Because immigration of Mexican women was not limited at this time like that of Filipinas, several Mexicano laborers opted not to live in labor camps but instead in family dwellings in an unincorporated neighborhood to the far east of Salinas. This area, originally part of the land granted to W. E. P. Hartnell from a *Californio* landholder, was called Alisal (Spanish for a grove of alder or sycamore trees) and was home to Mexicanos and a very small number of African American residents. When Joe Pradia arrived in Salinas from Texas in 1929, he discovered only fourteen fellow blacks. "I was used to seeing a lot of colored people," Pradia remembered. "Here [in Salinas] I'd see one one day, then it'd be two or three days till I'd see another." Later, Alisal (and California in general) became home to Tejanos (Texas Mexicans) seeking farmwork and "Okies" and "Arkies," mainly white migrants from

Oklahoma, Texas, Arkansas, and Missouri fleeing the drought- and Depression-ravaged Dust Bowl. During the 1930s four hundred thousand Dust Bowl migrants moved to locales in agricultural California, with many basing their resettlement on the fact that they had relatives already living in the state. Evidence of chain migration could be seen in the Salinas Valley town of Greenfield, for instance, which amassed two hundred residents from the same community in the Arkansas Ozarks. In Alisal, more than four thousand "Okies" and Tejanos purchased small parcels of land by 1935.[23]

Often called "Little Oklahomas" or "Okievilles" by Californians who resented their creation, Dust Bowl migrant subdivisions cropped up on the outskirts of other agricultural towns such as Bakersfield, Modesto, Fresno, Stockton, and Sacramento. As Alisal became a more migrant-heavy and working-class neighborhood—most inhabitants became farmworkers, dishwashers, waitresses, carpenters, or hotel employees—Salinas residents quickly labeled the area "Texhoma." They believed the neighborhood's mix of modest homes, simple tents, and hastily constructed shacks of old lumber, corrugated iron, and tar paper to be an eyesore, and Monterey County officials denounced Alisal as a shantytown of "makeshift adobes" overflowing with trash. The idea of a racially diverse working class living in a "grove of trees"—not in the cleared or settled part of town—positioned Mexicanos, African Americans, Tejanos, and "Okies" as spatial outsiders. They were fringe people living in a forestlike environment meant for nonhuman creatures. When county officials likened their dwellings to "makeshift adobes," they characterized Alisal residents as primitive and poor, creating a racialized sense of space while ignoring the fact that Alisal's unincorporated status was the cause of the neighborhood's lack of order and cleanliness. Meanwhile, local Salinas whites were characterizing their Dust Bowler counterparts as "dirty, shiftless, dishonest, bad, always fighting, lazy, immoral, [and] white trash." Even with their "white" racial identity, "Okies" suffered discrimination similar to that of Mexicanos and blacks because of their migrant and working-class status. "They [Salinas whites] resented us and it was very hard to get loans at banks," remembered Ruby Bond, cringing at the memory of being called an "Okie." Vernon Appling, who went to Salinas with his wife and child from Texas in the mid-1930s, recalled, "The people used to make snotty remarks all the time about Little Oklahoma, and joke about it." Salinas was not the only place in California that discriminated against "Okies"; a resident of the San Joaquin Valley at the time recalled that a sign directing "Okies and Negroes upstairs" was displayed prominently in the foyer of a local movie theater. Most "Okies" had assumed that their race and heritage would always guarantee them the "American" stamp of approval, and they were shocked to discover that this was not the case.[24]

A common working-class identity and "outsider" status bound together Alisal's diverse residents and forced them to coexist in ways that those living in incorporated Salinas did not experience. Mexican American resident Delfina Chaparro Sánchez, for instance, became a loved figure in Alisal soon after she moved there from the multiracial Los Angeles neighborhood of Boyle Heights. She established herself as a community matriarch, doling out marital advice and blessings and throwing holiday celebrations. "People came to her for cures, for counseling, for religious instruction, for chewing out, for a free meal, and a party," remembered her grandson Alex Zermeño. "Most of them were Mexicanos, [but] a lot of the whites came too. I mean, she fed anybody who came in that door . . . if somebody was sick, she was there with a pot of soup or beans." The act of sharing was frequent in Alisal because of the common struggle with poverty. Zermeño remembered that "Okies" with jobs in canneries and packing sheds often brought home crates of discarded food from work to share with neighbors in need. In some ways, similar economic struggles blunted the potential sharpness of racial difference. Alisal's population grew significantly over the course of twenty years, doubling from 2,355 to 5,501 between 1920 and 1930, and reaching 12,937 by 1940.[25] Even if its inhabitants were not officially considered residents of Salinas proper, Alisal certainly influenced the town's political and economic life. This was particularly noticeable during the mid-1930s when Filipino lettuce workers and "Okie" packing shed workers decided to strike for higher wages and better working conditions. The violent resistance they encountered from their grower-employers and local law enforcement only reaffirmed how powerful Salinas agribusiness had become in a short time.

LABOR STRUGGLES OF THE 1930s

Members of Salinas's grower class came from a variety of backgrounds. Some had migrated from Europe and immediately purchased land, while others came from humbler roots in the U.S. South and had worked their way up from trimming lettuce and loading produce trucks to positions as farm managers and owners. Three major growers who planted roots in Salinas in the 1920s and 1930s and continued to be powerful throughout the twentieth century were Bruce Church, T. R. "Russ" Merrill, and Eugene "Gene" Harden. A descendant of Irish immigrants who went to California by way of Canada and New York, Church was born in 1900 and graduated from the University of California with a degree in business economics. He worked for a produce shipper, eventually acquired thousands of acres in lettuce fields, and formed the Bruce Church Company in 1933. Merrill was born in Nebraska in 1898 and went to California in 1928 as a produce buyer for the large eastern grocery chain A&P. He moved to Salinas in the 1930s and entered the iceberg lettuce packing business. His company Merrill Farms then expanded to ship lettuce, celery, broccoli, and asparagus. Harden was born in Wyoming in 1892 and moved to California as a young man, founding a lettuce and melon farming operation in the Imperial Valley before relocating to Salinas in the 1920s and forming the E. E. Harden Packing Company. These three prominent growers, Salinas resident Joan Santoro remembered, "were the gods of the town . . . they had a certain brotherhood." This brotherhood was fostered by the men's families' personal closeness as well as economic competition. "You'd hear one refer to another as a 'son of a bitch' or that 'damn no good bastard,'" Santoro remarked, "but the next day they'd be eating and drinking together while sharing information of their profits, or how much of their produce had been shipped and sold."[26]

In 1930 Church, Merrill, and Harden—along with other prominent grower-shippers—joined the newly founded Grower-Shipper Vegetable Association (GSVA). Created as a voluntary trade organization aimed at promoting the interests of regional agribusiness, the GSVA sought to level the playing field for an unpredictable industry in which a drought or flood, crop disease, or economic depression could result in huge losses and bankruptcy. To that end the GSVA encouraged collective decision-making and discouraged members from individual actions such as lowering prices or signing a union contract that would raise workers' wages. Foreseeing a decade in which the Salinas Valley would boom in population and wealth because of its lettuce crop, the GSVA created an agricultural industry impervious to labor union penetration.

Meanwhile, California farmworkers had created their own associations. An early collaboration between hundreds of Japanese and Mexican American farmworkers in Oxnard resulted in the formation in 1903 of the Japanese Mexican Labor Association (JMLA), the first interethnic labor union in California. When the association applied for an AFL charter, however, the umbrella labor organization declared that a charter would be granted only if the Mexican members dismissed their Asian counterparts. "We will refuse any other kind of charter, except one which will wipe out race prejudices," the association responded. The JMLA went on to strike and succeeded at doubling wages for farmworkers in Ventura County. Then, between 1914 and 1917, the Industrial Workers of the World (IWW or "Wobblies") worked in tandem with the anarchist Partido Liberal Mexicano (Mexican Liberal Party, or PLM) in leading a series of worker walkouts in California fields, orchards, and vineyards at harvest time. These protests resulted in wage hikes and the state's construction of more farmworker camps.[27] Since the IWW-PLM collaboration did not yield a formal labor union, however, these one-time improvements had no lasting effect.

The lack of a central vehicle for farmworker protest in California was particularly alarming during the years of the Great Depression. Nationally, more than 1.5 million people left cities for farms in 1932, and the 1933 farm population of 32 million was the largest in history, with two workers competing for each available farm job. Daily wages for California field laborers dropped from an average of $2.55 in 1930 to an all-time low of $1.40 (between fifteen and sixteen cents an hour) in 1933. It was that year that a wave of thirty-seven labor strikes by various unions, including the International Longshore and Warehouse Union, the International Ladies' Garment Workers' Union, and the Cannery and Agricultural Workers Industrial Union (CAWIU), rocked California. The CAWIU led thousands of agricultural workers in a series of strikes and achieved victories at pear ranches in San Jose and beet fields in Oxnard, among other places. In the cotton fields of the San Joaquin Valley, twelve thousand Mexican, black, white, and Filipino workers defied growers and local police during their strike and won a major wage gain.[28] In response to the 1933 CAWIU strikes, many prominent California agriculturalists came together to form the Associated Farmers to combat unionization, targeting CAWIU members with violence, harassment, and legal prosecution.

In this militant atmosphere of 1933, the Salinas Valley experienced its own strike by Filipinos, who comprised 40 percent of the region's agricultural workforce. In August, seven hundred members of the Salinas chapter of the Filipino Labor Union (FLU), which had been founded in Stockton in 1930, walked out of the lettuce fields to protest their low wages. Their walkout failed, however, when growers simply replaced them with Mexicano, East Indian, and Asian strikebreakers. Another protest did not happen until the next year, when the AFL-affiliated Salinas Vegetable Packers Association (VPA)—a union made up of mostly white packing shed workers that excluded Filipinos, Mexicans, and other racial minorities from membership—agreed to strike with the FLU to persuade growers to come to the bargaining table. On August 27, 1934, this coalition of white and Filipino workers began its strike. Growers, merchants, and local law enforcement immediately responded with intimidation and physical violence. Police and local vigilantes beat strikers, and ranchers shot two Filipino picketers. Meanwhile, tensions emerged between the FLU and VPA because the latter felt the former was making unreasonable wage demands, and the FLU wanted more recognition as an independent union. On September 3 VPA members returned to work without the consent of the FLU, leaving Filipino lettuce workers to continue striking alone.[29]

Residents of Salinas displayed immense hostility toward these Filipino laborers. A local physician publicly declared that Filipinos were "more disturbing and more dangerous than any other Asiatic group," while growers circulated stories about radical socialists and communists infiltrating FLU ranks. On September 21 an armed mob of thirty Salinas farmers and business leaders fired one hundred rounds of ammunition into FLU cofounder Rufo Canete's labor camp. After forcing five hundred Filipino workers out at gunpoint, the mob burned the camp to the ground, killing one Filipina. Farmworker George Montero claimed that conspirators set off a false fire alarm in Chinatown to occupy Salinas's two fire trucks so that none was available to save the camp. Fearing for the remaining protestors' lives, Canete declared the strike over on September 24. In the first settlement between California growers and organized ethnic workers, the FLU settled with the GSVA for more reasonable work hours, a wage increase from ten to forty cents an hour, and the recognition of the FLU as a legitimate union.[30]

The violence of the 1934 strike was only exceeded by another strike two years later and a different group of agricultural workers. In August 1936 negotiations broke down between the GSVA and the Fruit and Vegetable Workers Union No. 18211, made up of white (mostly "Okie") lettuce packing shed workers and truck drivers. On September 8 more than three thousand workers—along with five hundred sympathetic FLU members—declared a strike. The protest quickly escalated into "a local civil war" as riots erupted on the streets among employers, strikers, and local residents. The GSVA hired Army Reserve officer Colonel Henry Sanborn to organize raids against strikers, giving him the top floor of a Main Street hotel for his strategic headquarters. When strikers gathered to tear loose crates of lettuce from produce trucks and spill them onto the street, law enforcement officers including 150 highway patrolmen sent in by California governor Frank Merriam attacked picketers with clubs and tear gas. Salinas sheriff Carl H. Abbott deputized at least one thousand of the town's men to form a "citizen's army," encouraging them to use any weapons they had—rifles, baseball bats, billy clubs, and ax handles fashioned by Salinas High School students. Growers' alliances with local and state officials and law enforcement, as well as several newspaper photographers' images of Salinas workers left beaten and bloody, captured national media attention. In an October 1936 article for *The Nation*, Edward Robbin observed: "What may be found today in Salinas, California, is perhaps the first open alliance in America of industry and government to crush civil rights. This is the definition of fascism." A National Labor Relations Board report on the strike denounced the "inexcusable police brutality, in many instances bordering on sadism" that occurred. The violence that characterized the Salinas strike, as well as others in Lodi, Brawley, Orange County, and Santa Paula during the 1930s and early 1940s, provoked John Steinbeck to brand California agribusiness as heartless: "No one complains at the necessity of feeding a horse while he is not working. But we complain about feeding the men and women who work our lands. Is it possible that this state is so stupid, so vicious, and so greedy that it cannot clothe and feed the men and women who help to make it the richest area in the world? Must the hunger become anger and anger fury before anything will be done?" After the Monterey County Board of Supervisors passed an emergency antipicketing ordinance, the strike ended on November 3, 1936. Although the Fruit and

Vegetable Workers settled with growers for an eight-hour workday and overtime pay, the harsh resistance of the grower establishment was enough to crush agricultural unions in the Salinas Valley for the next three decades. In other parts of the country during the 1930s, union membership continued to shape the identities of working-class people, but in the Salinas Valley the idea of an agricultural labor union was literally beaten out of those who wanted to believe in it.[31]

The 1936 strike was one of the most violent in California labor history and highlighted the power structures in place that kept Salinas Valley farm laborers from successful large-scale organizing. Meanwhile, on a national level, farmworkers were being excluded from protective New Deal legislation such as the Social Security Act and the 1935 National Labor Relations Act (NLRA, or Wagner Act), which gave industrial workers collective bargaining rights. Many spoke out in response. Carey McWilliams, California's commissioner of immigration and housing, published *Factories in the Field* (1939), which called for farmworkers to be covered by the NLRA and to be granted the same rights as factory workers. That same year John Steinbeck published *The Grapes of Wrath,* which painted a vivid picture of the sufferings of "Okies" in California. Finally, hundreds of witnesses testified before the U.S. Senate Labor Committee, chaired by Senator Robert M. La Follette Jr., about the widespread legal repression of California farmworkers.[32]

The Depression era also brought about a disturbing transition in the treatment of Mexican-origin people by state and local governments. During the 1920s, in the spirit of social progressivism, reformers had led Americanization programs (sponsored by churches, public health agencies, and employers) to teach Mexican-origin people "proper" hygiene, parenting, nutrition, language, and religion. Mexican men and women responded in a variety of ways, from acceptance to selective program participation to taking refuge in their culturally familiar barrios.[33] Americanization programs operated on the belief that Mexicans were assimilable and could eventually "belong" in the United States as long as they were socially controlled and given an Anglo-centric education. Yet when the stock market plummeted and the unemployment rate rose, xenophobia reemerged in the form of a "Mexican problem" in the public imagination. In March 1930 the *Saturday Evening Post* editorialized: "The dilution of the people and the institutions of this country has already gone too far . . . We may be obliged to absorb great numbers of Porto [sic] Ricans, Hawaiians, and Filipinos . . . we are under no obligation to continue to make this country an asylum for the Mexican peon, and we should not do so." The *New York Times* agreed: "It is folly to pretend that the more recently arrived Mexicans, who are largely of Indian blood, can be absorbed and incorporated into the American race." In 1930 more than 1.4 million Mexican-origin people lived in the United States, representing a 75 percent growth in the country's Spanish-speaking population since the 1920 census. This population explosion, coupled with financial hard times, caused many Americans to believe that Mexicans were a demographic and economic burden. Several white factory workers wrote letters of complaint to officials in Washington, D.C. One laid-off steelworker from Gary, Indiana, wrote to the Bureau of Immigration: "Most of these Mexicans are not citizens . . . They are about the lowest class of people that have entered this country. Because they will work cheaper than Americans will . . . [t]he American has to walk the streets and a Mexican has the work. That's not justice." Another unemployed steelworker from Mansfield, Ohio, wrote that "the place to start [is] by deporting thousands of these foreigners." The AFL also called for Mexicans' removal with the catchphrase "Employ no Mexican while a white man is unemployed." Meanwhile, the U.S. Census Bureau—for the first and only time—added a new racial category of "Mexican" in 1930, positioning this population as officially nonwhite while once-ostracized eastern and southern European immigrants became absorbed into white America.[34]

The assimilation programs of the 1920s were quickly replaced by voluntary deportation and forced repatriation drives during the 1930s financed by both the U.S. and Mexican governments. Mexican consuls distributed flyers reading "México llama a sus hijos" ("Mexico calls out to her children") to encourage movement back to the homeland, while the U.S. Bureaus of Immigration and Naturalization merged to become the INS and began restricting legal Mexican migration into the country. Admittance numbers dropped sharply from 38,980 in 1929 to 11,915 in 1930, and then to 2,627 in 1931 and stayed below 2,000 for several years after. Voluntary and forced deportation and repatriation drives took place in major cities like Los Angeles, Chicago, and Detroit, and immigration officers conducted raids in public plazas. In total, more than half a million people were transported to Mexico by train from 1931 to 1937. An estimated 60 percent of the deportees and *repatriados* were actually U.S. citizens by birth but had either been rounded up in public raids or were forced to leave along with their immigrant family members. They found themselves in the Mexican interior, with no memory of or emotional connection to the country that deportation advocates thought they should "go back to." Meanwhile, medical officials in various parts of California regulated bodies in their own way by forcibly sterilizing and deporting "feeble-minded" Mexican men and women whom they deemed unfit to reproduce. By 1933, one-third of the Mexican population in Los Angeles—the city with the largest such population—had vanished. The reaction to Chinese-origin people during the late nineteenth century had been repackaged and reenacted against Mexican-origin people in the twentieth, making them the new population whose labor was no longer needed during a time of national economic hardship.[35] The flow of Filipino migration was halted as well. The 1934 Tydings-McDuffie Independence Act transformed Filipinos' status from "U.S. national" to "alien" and limited their entrance to fifty migrants per year, and the Filipino Repatriation Act passed the next year offered Filipinos free transportation back to the Philippines if they agreed to forfeit the right to reenter the United States. These immigration policies had a great effect upon the demographics and agricultural labor system of California. With the Filipino population prevented from growing over time, it became more common to see Mexican faces in the fields than Asian ones.[36]

After the deportation and repatriation drives of the 1930s, the more than two million Mexican Americans who remained in the United States were left disillusioned and angry at the ways in which their federal and state governments had deemed them undesirable. By 1940 the Mexican-origin population had transitioned from being heavily immigrant to heavily American. In California almost two-thirds (220,120) of the total Mexican-origin population (354,432) were U.S. citizens and less than half claimed two foreign-born parents. Although Mexican Americans did not suffer from de jure segregation like African Americans, they still experienced discrimination and de facto segregation in their workplaces, neighborhoods, and public spaces such as schools, swimming pools, restaurants, and movie theaters. In response, as historian George Sánchez describes, many Mexican Americans began to engage in a "politics of opposition" dedicated to making their legal rights as U.S. citizens manifest in social reality. Some joined labor unions affiliated with the Congress of Industrial Organizations (CIO), while others became members of civil rights organizations such as the League of United Latin American Citizens (LULAC, founded in Texas in 1929) and the Congress of Spanish-Speaking Peoples (El Congreso, founded in Los Angeles in 1939).[37]

Mexican Americans in the Salinas Valley, however, were severely limited in their opportunities to participate in these organizations because of both geography (major branches and chapters of these organizations remained in cities) and politics. By 1940 the Salinas Valley had become known worldwide for its tremendous lettuce and vegetable production, and its labor hierarchies had shifted in significant ways. Local residents' antipathy toward "Okies" had been tempered over time by Dust Bowlers' white privilege and upward social mobility. Although they were initially treated as outsiders, "Okies" were not "alien" and "foreign" like Mexican- and Asian-origin people. Thus, during the 1930s and 1940s, many were able to move from field labor into work as packing shed employees, truckers, and foremen.[38] Those Filipinos who remained in Salinas vied for nonfieldwork in the agricultural sector and transitioned into irrigator, labor contractor, and labor camp operator and cook positions. This left Mexicanos at the bottom, trapped in low-paying field labor positions. Having observed the systemic collusion between agribusiness, law enforcement, and citizen vigilantes that crushed farmworker unionization attempts in Salinas, Mexican Americans knew they would have to articulate and fight for their rights in other ways. This would become even more challenging as the United States entered World War II and instituted a guestworker program that imported hundreds of thousands of Mexican braceros to work in U.S. fields and on U.S. railroads. In being simultaneously conflated with and placed in opposition to this new population of Mexican workers, Mexican Americans in agricultural settings would face even larger roadblocks to achieving integration and equality.

2 Racial Meeting Grounds and Battlegrounds During Wartime, 1941–1947

ON THE AFTERNOON of December 7, 1941, Filipino farmworker George Montero entered his bunkroom at a Salinas labor camp and turned on the radio. He was looking forward to the next day, when he and his fiancée Harley planned to drive to Vancouver, Canada, to marry. As George packed for the trip, his excitement suddenly turned to shock. Over the radio came an announcement that the Imperial Japanese Navy had launched an attack on the U.S. fleet at Pearl Harbor, Hawai'i, a few hours before. The United States was entering the Second World War. Though horrified by the news of the bombing—and knowing his father would be drawn into the war in the Philippines—George was still determined to marry. The trip was not one of leisure but of necessity, for his fiancée was white, and the couple could not legally wed in California. In 1941, Washington and New Mexico were the only states that permitted intermarriage between "Caucasians" and Filipinos; California did not legalize such unions until 1948. George had chosen Canada because, as he had learned since migrating to the United States in 1930, "that's where Filipinos [went]." The couple married on December 9 and returned to Salinas, which was already planning to send many of its own off to war.[1]

George and Harley's story illustrates two realities that people of color, including Latinos, had to navigate during wartime. First, their marital union exemplified the racial mixing that characterized the era, as Americans of every background came into closer contact with each other in the armed forces or on factory lines, dance floors, and the streets. Though Salinas was still a small town of 24,523 people (including the 12,937 residents of Alisal), it claimed an impressive diversity of residents who ranged from long-settled Anglo, Mexican, and Asian Americans to recently arrived "Okies" and "Arkies," African Americans, Europeans, and Tejanos.[2] Second, George's desire to marry Harley, even in the instability of a recently declared war, showed how much he wanted his relationship to be respectable and legitimized. In a climate of heightened attention to one's Americanness, patriotism, and belonging, Latinos and other people of color in the United States pushed back against racial discrimination in efforts to gain legitimization and respectability in the public sphere.

This chapter examines how Latinos negotiated their relationships with other racial groups—and with each other—during the war years, and how an agriculture-centered context simultaneously produced racial meeting grounds and battlegrounds. The two federal decisions to intern Japanese-origin people in the United States and to institute the Bracero Program—in which Mexican braceros (literally, "arm-men") would fill the wartime labor shortage by working in U.S. fields and on U.S. railroads—changed the nation forever. These two initiatives, one of Japanese expulsion and the other of Mexican importation, altered landscapes of labor and power and affected race relations as several states suddenly became more "brown" with an influx of braceros. It was not only whites who reacted strongly to the braceros' presence, but Mexican Americans as well. Intraethnic conflict manifested in encounters between four groups of Mexican-origin men—military servicemen, braceros, U.S.-born farmworkers, and "zoot suiters." Though all had the common aspiration to be visible and respected, each group expressed its own brand of masculinity, which created tension in the larger Latino community. It was this intraethnic tension, and the changes the Bracero Program wrought, that arguably slowed the evolution of a postwar Latino civil rights movement in the Salinas Valley, making it and other agricultural regions quite politically different from their urban counterparts.

EXPULSION AND IMPORTATION

Along with the military draft, Japanese internment created the wartime labor shortage that justified in many political and agribusiness leaders' minds the need for a Bracero Program. After the bombing of Pearl Harbor, the U.S. government assumed that all people of Japanese origin might harbor loyalty to Japan. In February 1942, President Franklin Delano Roosevelt signed Executive Order 9066 ordering all people of Japanese descent to be evacuated from the West Coast and placed in internment camps. Out of a total Japanese-origin population of 127,000, 110,000 were forcibly relocated; 62 percent of them were U.S. citizens. People of Italian background were also asked to leave the West Coast but were not forcibly relocated, and several actually moved to Salinas to help build an internment assembly center there. The Salinas Rodeo Grounds served as one of seventeen assembly centers throughout the U.S. West designed to hold those heading to internment camps. Local teacher Leon Amyx wondered "what the hell in the world those people must have felt when they were taken out of their homes and they were really [U.S.] citizens . . . it wasn't fair, it certainly wasn't fair." Sympathizers like Amyx were few, however, as Salinas became the town with the strongest anti-Japanese sentiment in the valley. This was largely due to the 194th Tank Battalion, heavily populated with Salinas men, being captured four months after Pearl Harbor, with fewer than half of the men surviving the Bataan Death March. When the Salinas Chamber of Commerce distributed a survey about Japanese internment to residents after the capture of the battalion, only *one* of 769 respondents approved of allowing "loyal" Japanese people back into Pacific Coast states during the war. Many respondents made additional comments on their surveys. "I was looking at the High School graduation class pictures in a studio window the other evening, and it certainly was a pleasure to see no Japanese faces amongst our children," local Plumbers and Steamfitters Union secretary Louis R. Jenkins wrote. "We hope that we never see another live Jap on the Pacific Coast," added farmer William Casey. "We don't want any of them back at all," agreed farmer Tony Garcia and his wife. "There are no loyal Japanese," asserted banker Oliver Bardin, while hotel owner W. L. Young proclaimed, "the only loyal Jap perhaps is a *dead one*." The survey eventually made its way into state media. "The People of Salinas, Who Know

Japs, Oppose Their Release," blared a headline in the *San Francisco Call Bulletin.* "The sentiment of California, we believe, is reflected in a recent poll of the city of Salinas," the *Los Angeles Deal News* affirmed, while the *Sun-Herald* of Colusa remarked, "Until some means can be found to segregate the Japanese into 'safe' and 'unsafe' brackets, the entire Pacific Coast will vote with Salinas."[3]

Shortly after internment began, in the summer of 1942, the U.S. and Mexican governments negotiated an emergency farm labor program that would import Mexican men to work on U.S. farms and railroads. The Bracero Program was not the first time the United States had formally requested guest labor from Mexico. During World War I, approximately seventy-three thousand Mexican men entered the country to work in the mining, construction, agriculture, and railroad industries. Despite claims that the program was a temporary war measure, it lasted from 1917 until 1922 and was characterized by tremendous abuses of Mexican workers by employers who did not honor contract terms. Interrupted briefly by the repatriation and deportation drives of the Great Depression, the United States' desire for low-wage Mexican labor returned with the beginning of World War II. As during World War I, the Bracero Program was conceived as a temporary wartime program, but instead it lasted for more than twenty years and distributed between 4.6 and 5.2 million labor contracts. On average, two hundred thousand Mexican men entered the United States per year, and though they worked in almost all parts of the country, the majority went to California, Texas, and other southwestern states. Puerto Rican laborers were recruited during wartime as well to work on the East Coast, and some worked on farms, but they were smaller in number than the African Americans who tended to hold these agricultural positions. The U.S. government promised braceros decent housing and food, transportation to and from work sites, the local "prevailing wage" for their labor, and steady work for at least 75 percent of their contract period. These terms, however, were upheld minimally or not at all during the life of the program, with enforcement mechanisms proving weak or nonexistent. This has led many to argue, including Truman Moore in his book about migratory farm labor, that braceros' poor living and working conditions made them the rented slaves of the twentieth century.[4]

Though the Mexican government had strong reservations about resurrecting a guestworker program, it had reasons for doing so. The nation remained in the grips of an economic crisis, and the program seemed to offer a "safety valve" for struggling Mexicans who could gain exposure to U.S. culture and agricultural methods, send remittances to their loved ones, and help modernize Mexico upon their return. The Mexican media emphasized braceros' importance as "soldiers of the plough" producing food for the Allies, with newspapers like *Excélsior* running headlines such as "Only Mexicans Can Save California Harvests." Mexican program officials used similar rhetoric, encouraging each man to regard himself as a soldier and fighter for democracy. Braceros embraced this military discourse in describing their function. "We weren't workers; we were practically soldiers, because we were replacing the soldiers," Juan Bravo Saldaña said, couching his labor in the language of duty and responsibility. Ignacio Gómez agreed: "We came to the United States to fight, to fight hunger . . . We did not fight with weapons, but with our arms, to feed the people."[5]

Upon receiving an order for braceros from a prospective employer—funneled through that employer's respective State Department of Employment and the U.S. Employment Service in the Department of Labor—Mexico's Bureau of Migrant Labor in the Ministry of Foreign Affairs assigned bracero recruitment quotas to particular states. Jalisco, Michoacán, Sonora, Veracruz, and Zacatecas were the first to recruit and screen workers for contracting at designated "migratory stations." Thousands of Mexican men—some from as far south as Oaxaca—swarmed these states' government offices, while throngs of others converged upon border cities like Calexico, California, where an "avalanche" of braceros created such chaos that U.S. and Mexican police turned a hose on the crowd of men. Prospective braceros (*aspirantes*) occupied a multitude of regional, cultural, and ethnic identities. Some were highly educated and cosmopolitan but unemployed, whereas others were struggling *campesinos* (farmworkers) from small rural villages. Some had been deported from the United States during the Great Depression and were trying to find a way back home. Others hailed from indigenous communities in Mexico and had difficulty communicating in both English and Spanish. What held these men together was their common desire to earn higher wages in *el norte,* and many were the sons or grandsons of migrants who had done the same in earlier eras (fig. 2.1). Ninety percent of *aspirantes* were between the ages of twenty-one and forty-five, two-thirds were married, and at least

Fig. 2.1. Father and son Jesus Gutierrez (above) and Jose Merejo Loredo (right), who migrated at different times from San Luis Potosí, Mexico, to work as braceros in the United States. (Courtesy of Sonia Chapa)

half were fathers. Their relatives often expressed fear or reluctance at sending their loved ones north. Pedro de Real Pérez remembered that his family in Zacatecas was "afraid that something would seduce me in the United States" but eventually accepted his departure because of their poverty. As Espiririón Salazar ruminated: "When you are young and the need is such, borders are the last things you worry about. We needed work and the Americans needed our labor."[6]

Since a limited number of bracero contracts were available, competition for them was intense and costly. One had to pay an initial 250 pesos, roughly equivalent to four months' earnings for a rural Mexican family, merely to be considered for the program. The next step was traveling to one of a few migratory stations scattered throughout Mexico. Some men spent their life savings or took out loans to be able to make the journey. Once at a migratory station, *aspirantes* had to wait for their state and name to be called over the station's loudspeakers. Men waited for weeks or even months outside stations, and Mexican women eventually began selling food, clothing, blankets, and sex in those areas. As their money for food and shelter ran low, men resorted to sleeping on the street and digging through trash for food. One bracero remembered witnessing others eating banana and watermelon peels, and even pieces of newspaper, to keep from starving. Some men paid *coyotes* (human smugglers) to arrange their border crossing without a contract or gave *mordidas* (bribes) of up to one thousand pesos to migratory station employees to be given a contract faster, but several were swindled and left with nothing. One man, speaking for himself and five of his friends who were rejected from the Bracero Program, communicated their disappointment to an interviewer: "All of us are ruined, since all of us went deeply into debt in order to come here for a contract. I sold my *milpa* (small farm) in Aguascalientes to raise money for the trip. My wife and six children are waiting at home, waiting for me to send them money from the United States. Now there will be no money, and there is nothing for me to go back to. I guess my children will have to beg in the streets. I wish I were dead."[7]

If an *aspirante* did hear his name called, he entered a line in which his body was inspected and farming knowledge tested to ensure his fitness for agricultural labor. A grower-employer's representative would frequently use cordial gestures, such as shaking a man's hand or patting him on the shoulder or back, to gauge his strength and physique.

Oaxaca-born Heriberto Cortes remembered officials checking whether his hands were calloused to prove he possessed adequate experience. These tactile and visual modes of inspection echoed past practices in the American slave market. As scholar Henry Anderson observed when he visited a bracero reception center in Calexico, California, a guide made pronouncements on the fitness of each *aspirante* he passed, reminding Anderson of "the slave markets as I imagined they existed a hundred years ago in Baltimore, or Charleston, or New Orleans." Men quickly became aware of this particular valuation of the body and tried to accommodate employers' desire for strong and docile labor. Some rubbed rocks in their hands to create blisters, while others altered their posture and behavior. "We learned how to stand, you couldn't stand up too much, stand too erect. [That person] was considered too independent, too rebellious," one bracero said. Another affirmed that employers "want[ed] us to be dumb and dirty," so he and others acted the part of obedient and ignorant workers. Indeed, one representative of a major bracero-employing association in California was recorded making these statements while picking his braceros at El Centro:

> You see this fellow here? He's the ideal bracero. He's the right size. He's built right. He's a farmworker, you can tell he hasn't any big ideas. He's got the right attitude. He's humble, not fresh or cocky. He's an Indian type, probably from Jalisco or Guanajuato.
>
> This one is a type I don't care for. He's no peon. He's too well dressed. Looks too intelligent. Almost white . . . They end up telling off the foreman and then there's trouble. Let them stay in Mexico.[8]

Chosen braceros were then evaluated by a psychologist, photographed and fingerprinted, registered by U.S. INS officers, and given a physical exam by Mexican and U.S. Public Health Service officers that included examinations of the lungs, eyes, kidneys, heart, and limbs; tests for tuberculosis and venereal diseases; and vaccinations. The last stage was delousing, during which every man was required to undress and be sprayed from head to toe with DDT, a chemical still commonly used at the time for mass cleansing. This process of disinfection was particularly humiliating and remembered vividly by ex-braceros. "They fumigated us as if we were a herd of cattle, goats, hogs, dogs, and it was the worst experience I ever had," Ignacio Gómez said. Isidoro Ramírez agreed: "there was no privacy . . . many older men were almost close to crying to do that." Liborio Pérez added that braceros' brown bodies "would be left white" from the DDT spraying. Cleansing braceros until they were literally white, border health officers shared southwestern public health officials' preoccupation with ridding Mexicans of dirt and disease. The final step in the contracting process was signing a two-page contract that bound a man to work in the United States for between three and nine months but did not specify an employer or details about wages and work sites. Loaded onto chartered buses or trains, contracted braceros were transported to one of five U.S. reception centers—El Centro, California; Nogales, Arizona; or Hidalgo, Eagle Pass, or El Paso, Texas—to receive their assignments. During these journeys, food and space were scarce. Juan Bravo Saldaña remembered receiving only one piece of white bread and coffee "so bad it tasted like drain water" during his train ride, which lasted several hours. Men assigned to work in California passed through El Centro, where they were processed by U.S. Department of Labor representatives and disinfected yet again. At this point, relatives and friends were often separated if they could not persuade one employer to take them together. While Isidoro Ramírez's brother was sent to work in Salinas, for example, Isidoro was sent to Los Angeles County. "It wasn't important who was separated . . . one was a slave," Ramírez lamented.[9]

An inaugural shipment of five hundred California braceros arrived in Stockton on September 29, 1942. The next month, the Salinas Valley's first shipment of 380 braceros arrived by train, waving American flags and shouting, "Long Live America and Mexico!" After being greeted by U.S. Employment Service and Farm Security Administration representatives, grower representatives, and members of the local community, the braceros (who ranged in age from eighteen to sixty years of age) posed for photos in front of flying U.S. and Mexican flags and sang the Mexican national anthem while raising their hands into the wartime "V" sign for victory. Officials gave welcome speeches and briefed the men on their work assignments over a meal of chili beans, stew, tomatoes, pudding, and coffee served by twenty "local Mexican women" before leading the workers to trucks waiting to take them to their labor camps. The braceros contracted to work in the lettuce, strawberry, carrot, and artichoke fields of the Salinas Valley made up one-fourth of the 4,189 braceros employed in the United States in 1942. If one looked in other parts of California, one could find braceros knocking walnuts and almonds in Sutter County, training hops in Sacramento County, picking apples in Sonoma County, gathering olives in Tulare

County, harvesting citrus in Los Angeles County, and working in date groves in Riverside County. A small number of Jamaican farmworkers worked alongside braceros during the war years, but they tended to be employed in northern and southern California rather than the central part of the state.[10]

As the supervisor of the Salinas Valley's Bracero Program operations, New Mexico transplant Benigno "Ben" López had to ensure that braceros received adequate housing, food, transportation, and employment for at least 75 percent of their contract period at the "prevailing wage" rate. He was also responsible for making sure that braceros did not displace domestic (U.S. resident) workers or adversely affect the latter's wages. Yet López and other program supervisors around the country were working within a largely unregulated infrastructure. The U.S. federal and state governments did not employ enough people to monitor working conditions in states where braceros were being used. As a result, grower-employers colluded to establish record-low "prevailing" wages in their own regions. The Pacific Northwest offered braceros the highest average wage at $1.25 per hour, while California paid $1.00 per hour. Braceros in the South earned far less, as low as forty cents an hour in Texas and thirty cents an hour in Arkansas.[11] If domestic farmworkers refused to work at these "prevailing" rates, growers could claim a labor shortage and thus request more braceros, leading to a vicious cycle of wage depression and domestic worker displacement.

Braceros' substandard wages were matched only by their living quarters. Growers often housed braceros on the outskirts of towns in camps mostly maintained by Filipino or Mexican American operators. Styled after military barracks, bracero camps were often constructed from old barns, tool sheds, vegetable packing sheds, or chicken coops. Bunkrooms held rows of beds sometimes made of only slats of wood and sacks of straw, and camps lacked enough showers, heating, lighting, and ventilation for the hundreds of men who inhabited them. Without easy transportation to nearby towns or daily interaction with other residents, braceros became the nation's most immobile, invisible, and vulnerable labor force. Meanwhile, the media lauded braceros as "Good Neighbor Mexicans" and allies in the war effort but emphasized their temporary stay. A Salinas Valley newspaper assured its readers that "they will remain in this country until no further need of their assistance is required. They will then return to their homes in Mexico."[12] Braceros were deemed necessary from an economic standpoint, but they were an ephemeral workforce not to be woven into the national social fabric.

BRACEROS' DAILY LIVES

The long and difficult workdays braceros endured in the Salinas Valley reflected the ways in which agriculture had shifted to agribusiness. Working from early morning to evening, braceros and domestic farmworkers earned one dollar an hour for ten to fourteen hours of labor with the two-foot short-handled hoe, commonly known as *el cortito* (the short one). Growers claimed *el cortito* was preferable to a long-handled hoe because of its greater efficiency at thinning and weeding. Farmworkers, however, believed it was a tool of control that forced them to work in an uncomfortable stooped position that made it easier for supervisors to see who was working and who was attempting to stretch and rest (fig. 2.2). Over prolonged periods of time, using *el cortito* caused a degeneration of the spine, leading to permanent disabilities. Even if one did not work with this tool regularly, discomfort and pain still characterized the work. Picking strawberries, for example, required one to crouch between the plants, rapidly select the best berries without bruising them, fill up a cart, and race the cart down the row to a berry checker. This routine only got tougher for domestics when employers began employing more braceros. One Salinas Valley strawberry worker complained: "I remember they would give us a 10-minute break every two and a half hours. They don't do that anymore. They don't have to. The braceros never ask for a break." An irrigator from Sacramento concurred: "Braceros don't walk, they run. I went to the boss, and I said it just didn't make sense to push a man that way. He said for me to get out. Since they got the braceros, they have figured out all kinds of ways of getting more work out of you for less money." The greater speed with which domestics, who were mostly Mexican American, had to work to keep up with braceros and keep their jobs led others to continue to believe in the "natural" ability of Mexicans to perform stoop labor. "Americans won't do [stoop labor]," one white Salinas woman affirmed. "In the first place, our backs are too long . . . the Indian Mexican has a short back, it's easier for him to stoop over to get to the ground. Doesn't hurt him as much." In discussing the arrival of a new group of braceros, a *Salinas Californian* article stated, "Stocky Mexican peons—389 of them—arrived in Salinas last night . . .

Fig. 2.2. Salinas Valley braceros work in a lettuce field with *el cortito, 1956.*
Photographer Leonard Nadel received funding from the Fund for the Republic to
document the bracero experience. (Courtesy of Leonard Nadel Bracero Photographs, Archives Center, National Museum of American History, Smithsonian
Institution)

[they] are of the short, husky type found to be best for field work."[13]
This association between Mexicanness and physical suitability for farm
labor sustained a deterministic notion of which racial groups naturally
"belonged" in the fields.

The only respite field laborers received during the day was lunch-
time, when cooks laid out buckets of rice, beans, and meat for workers
to eat either standing or sitting in the dirt beside the fields. Some braceros, like Aquilino Zarazua, however, remembered working twelve-
hour days and receiving nothing to eat until they returned to their labor camp for dinner, which often consisted of soup or bits of meat
alongside beans, tortillas, canned fruit, coffee, and soda. In her memoir
Farmworker's Daughter, Rose Castillo Guilbault described braceros
as she remembered them during her youth in the Salinas Valley, re-
creating the atmosphere of loneliness and isolation that pervaded their
labor camps:

> The men who arrived alone from Mexico led mostly ascetic lives . . . To
> them the United States meant work and, therefore, their lives revolved
> around it. They woke with the chill of dawn and returned in the cool
> of dusk to their bare, crowded, cell-like rooms. I'd see these men piling
> out of trucks and trudging up the long dusty trail at the edge of the field
> that led to their housing. "Pobrecitos. Poor men," my mother would

say. They resembled battered birds—straw hats covering hair matted gray from layers of dust, and ragged, thin shirttails over mud-splattered khaki pants.

After dinner, leisure options within bracero camps were limited. Living far from a major city or the U.S.-Mexico border, Salinas Valley braceros did not have the same ease of travel or social opportunities that their compatriots in the Imperial Valley, for example, enjoyed. Many men placed radios in their bunkrooms and either listened to a local English-language radio station that played a few hours of Spanish-language programming each night or tried to catch the faint signal of a Los Angeles– or Texas-based Spanish-language station. While listening, braceros smoked, played cards, or wrote letters to their loved ones in Mexico, enclosing cash or promising to send Western Union money orders. Sleep followed shortly after, as the men had to rise before dawn for another long workday. "It was a very, very limited life deprived of many things because we did not have the means of leaving those places [camps] . . . We had no choice but to stay there . . . we were pure work people," Pedro de Real Pérez said (fig. 2.3).[14]

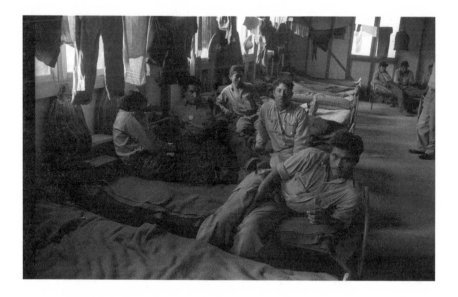

Fig. 2.3. The homosocial world of the bracero camp, 1956. (Courtesy of Leonard Nadel Bracero Photographs, Archives Center, National Museum of American History, Smithsonian Institution)

As one observer commented about the Bracero Program, "For the growers the program was a dream: a seemingly endless army of cheap, unorganized workers brought to their doorstep by the government." With a vast reservoir of foreign labor to draw from, profit-driven employers myopically ignored how their harsh work demands were destroying bracero bodies. Subjected to *el cortito,* low-quality food, not enough water, and poorly maintained segregated housing, braceros frequently suffered from respiratory illnesses, chronic back pain and permanent spinal injuries, hunger, dehydration, and the emotional effects of isolation. Though they were feeding the nation through their labor, they were not being nourished themselves. Ben López, who lived with his family at Camp McCallum (a thirty-two-acre bracero camp seven miles outside Salinas), regularly brought in nurses to treat ailing braceros. He was the exception, however, as most bracero supervisors offered little if any medical attention to braceros unless they had broken a bone or appeared in near-death condition. When José Barajas-Chávez cut his hand, for instance, he recalled that his foreman "told me that I was going to have to eat the lettuce that I had bled on . . . No one asked if I was all right. No one cared." Frequently known just by their work numbers instead of their names, braceros felt neglected and dehumanized. Audómaro Zepeda worked in multiple California locations but affirmed of Salinas in particular that "they treated people very badly. They treated one like a slave until one cried." Isidoro Ramírez agreed: "The life of a bracero [was] one . . . [of] a slave. The conditions that they placed on us, one could not say anything . . . [it was] the worst experience that I have had in my life." In other parts of California, braceros were being used in dangerous and unauthorized ways. Federal correspondence revealed that the U.S. Forest Service hired braceros to fight forest fires, a violation of the bracero agreement that prompted a shocked Mexican Embassy to protest to the U.S. Department of Labor. Compounding the abuse of braceros' bodies was their further exploitation by those closest to them in their labor camps. Some Mexican American and Filipino American labor contractors and camp managers made illegal deductions of three to five dollars per month from braceros' paychecks for their use of blankets and mattresses, and at times they added fake names to work lists so that when an entire crew got paid, they pocketed the *muertos'* (dead men's) wages and left each bracero with fewer earnings. Salinas Valley carrot workers had to pay

Fig. 2.4. A peddler impresses braceros with various goods at a Salinas Valley labor camp, 1956. (Courtesy of Leonard Nadel Bracero Photographs, Archives Center, National Museum of American History, Smithsonian Institution)

several dollars per week out of their own pockets for "twistems," the wires used for bunching carrots, until an investigation in the 1950s discontinued the practice. Then, at the end of every harvest season, peddlers visited labor camps and bombarded braceros with overpriced goods such as blankets, toothpaste, radios, and watches (fig. 2.4). Ray Villanueva, who grew up among braceros in a Salinas labor camp operated by his Filipino labor contractor father and his Mexican American farmworker mother, lamented that braceros bought these consumer goods at inflated prices in order to avoid the racial discrimination they faced in stores downtown.[15]

From its early years, the Bracero Program was harmful and even fatal to its recruited workers. From the program's beginning in August 1942 to March 1946, 344 bracero deaths were reported nationwide (fig. 2.5). In examining the reasons for fatalities, one could argue that death by "natural causes" likely included respiratory illnesses caught from cold mornings in the fields or cold nights in drafty bunkhouses, heat stroke, or other internal damage from continuous stoop labor without adequate rest, water, or sanitary facilities. Being "struck by

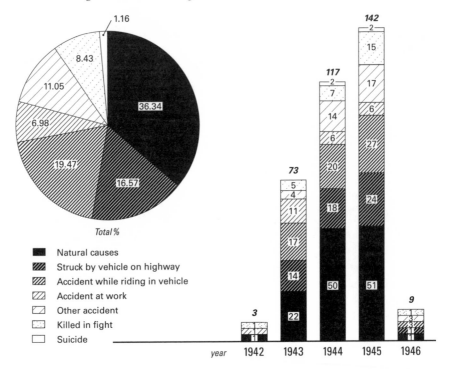

Fig. 2.5. Bracero deaths nationwide from August 1942 to March 1946. (Infographic by David Hackett. Source: U.S. Department of Agriculture, Special Report on Foreign and Domestic Agricultural Workers, Table XI: Causes of Deaths of Mexican National Farm Workers from the Beginning of the Program to March 1, 1946, Folder 5, Box 9, Roth Papers, 1936–1977, University of California at Davis Special Collections)

vehicle on highway" was the result of bracero camps being marginally located and braceros not having access to transportation other than walking along dark highways at night and on weekends. An "accident while riding in vehicle" resulted from the cramping of dozens of braceros into poorly constructed work vehicles unregulated by safety standards. "Accident at work" plagued braceros working on railroads as well as in the fields. Smashed fingers, broken limbs, and fractured skulls could be the harrowing result of swinging and laying rail ties. "Killed in fight" and "suicide" comprised two other disturbing categories, and the death toll rose with each passing year. The low number for 1946 is not because of any improvements in braceros' conditions, but because data stopped being collected in March of that year.

Threatened with contract termination and deportation if they complained about work conditions or inhumane treatment, braceros could not unionize or bargain for better wages and living conditions. In the words of one scholar, the Bracero Program constituted "a recipe for docility and exploitation" that allowed the U.S. economy to flourish on the backs of cheap Mexican labor. Meanwhile, the Mexican government did not provide much support to braceros once they arrived in the United States. Though studies of braceros in the Pacific Northwest and South have shown that braceros exerted power at times by organizing strikes or requesting Mexican consular intervention in recovering wages and punishing employers for labor violations, Salinas Valley braceros went largely ignored by the Mexican Consulate. Ex-bracero Ismael Nicolás Osorio, who worked in Arizona, Texas, Colorado, Washington, and California, remembered that the Mexican consul in San Francisco rarely visited Salinas, and when a bracero did muster the courage to complain about conditions, the consul responded, "If you don't like it, go back to Mexico."[16] Not treated as full citizens by either the United States or Mexico, braceros lived and worked in a liminal space, neglected by both their home and receiving countries.

In spite of the dangers and dehumanization evident in the Bracero Program early on, Mexican men kept signing up for recruitment out of economic need. Remembering the financial aspirations of the Salinas Valley braceros he supervised, Ben López remarked, "Ninety percent of them had a goal that they wanted to achieve." In addition to sending remittances, many men often took seed, sewing machines, irrigation and farming equipment, barber tools, shoes, cloth, and silk stockings back with them to Mexico to use or sell. Two bracero brothers shipped hogs from Salinas to Mexico, starting a pig farm that eventually sold meat to local markets and hotels in Guadalajara. Another man shipped thirty-five bicycles home to open a rental business in Mexico City's Chapultepec Park, while several others purchased taxicabs in Mexico every time they returned from their multiple bracero contracts and eventually opened their own taxi businesses. Letters written to braceros from their relatives in Mexico shed additional light on what must have been consuming braceros' minds and driving their work. Salvador Perez Rico's mother reported that earth was falling on his land, likely because of the eruption of the Paricutín volcano in Michoacán in 1943. Jesus Caldera's family wrote to him that his beans in Zacatecas had frozen during the winter and his corn did not thrive, throwing the whole family into hunger and poverty. Teresa Garcia wrote to her husband that she was able to use the 165 pesos he sent to support her mother, pay the rent, and buy shoes for their two children. Conversely, Francisca Negrete asked her husband Juan, "Why haven't you answered me so as not to worry me?" and requested a picture. Other letters reveal the financial and emotional neglect that bracero relatives in Mexico suffered. "Well, Papa, tell me what is the reason for not having written us," Jose Estrada's child wrote to him. "Tell me if you do not have the will to write me . . . [so] that I may get to work . . . to support us because it seems that you have forgotten that you have a daughter."[17]

Indeed, some braceros had difficulty bridging the gap between the money the Bracero Program promised them and the money they actually made for their families after taking into account low wages, paycheck deductions, and the temptations of consumer goods. As a child growing up in Mexico, Sonia Chapa remembered her bracero father Jose Merejo Loredo (see fig. 2.1) returning home "dressing differently" in new shirts and slacks, boots, a watch, and a hat from the United States.[18] Clothing, accessories, and other things that signified "America" were very appealing to braceros as symbols of social belonging in their receiving communities and as symbols of upward mobility and success in their sending communities. A photograph of Plutarco Chavez-Ruiz, standing in front of a field in Salinas, keenly evokes the consumption habits of certain braceros (fig. 2.6). He wears an outfit of leather dress shoes, khaki pants, a leather belt, collared shirt, and a black leather jacket, all items presumably bought in Salinas shops. The shine of his jacket and slicked hair contrasts with the blue sky and green lettuce rows in which he probably worked every day in much shabbier clothes. The caption written on the back of the photograph, "Recuedo [sic] de Salinas [Memory of Salinas], 1959," begs several questions. Did Plutarco send this picture home to his family during his stay in Salinas to reassure them that he was doing well, or was the recuerdo for him to keep as a memory of all he had done, bought, seen, and endured as a farmworker in the United States? Did he buy the camera that produced this picture, or did he ask a camera-owning bracero to take a photograph for him? Was this photo taken on a weekend or right before his contract ended and he returned to Mexico? Whatever the answers, this photograph shows what success meant to braceros—to be able to endure the hard work of the fields, earn enough money to send to their

Fig. 2.6. Plutarco Chavez-Ruiz, a bracero, poses in a Salinas field. (Photograph originally in color; courtesy of the Bracero History Archive and the National Museum of American History)

families and purchase the occasional luxury, and stand proudly at the end of a workweek or contract term.

WARTIME RACE RELATIONS AND RACIAL BORDERS

During the first years of World War II, Monterey County's bracero population remained fairly steady at between two thousand and twenty-five hundred, or 15 percent of the county's farm labor force. At the end of braceros' contract terms grower-employers either requested that their contracts be renewed or ordered new groups of braceros once old groups left, distributing them among the county's seventy labor camps. Largely out of the sight and minds of white locals during their six-day workweek, braceros used Saturday nights and Sundays to go into town, pooling money for taxis or hitching rides from friends or foremen. Many chose Salinas as their leisure destination. The Mexican restaurants there provided a familiar taste of home; Main Street shops offered "cowboy-style" boots and clothing, radios, suitcases, and Singer sewing machines; and the Crystal Theatre showed Spanish-language films starring Mexican actors like Pedro Armendariz, Dolores Del Rio, Cantinflas, and Pedro Infante. By 1945, the Crystal played Spanish-language films two days a week to accommodate Salinas's bracero population. The nearby Fox and El Rey theaters followed suit and began playing Spanish-language movies as well.[19]

During their weekend excursions, braceros surely noticed that they were the newest members being folded into a diverse mix of Californians. Tejanos and Dust Bowlers continued to arrive, and according to alien registration figures, more than five hundred thousand immigrants from around the globe resided in the state. Meanwhile, the war had drawn many people to work on military bases and in defense industries, and Mexican nationals who had completed U.S. military service were naturalizing as citizens and establishing roots. In this way, braceros found themselves not only at the crossroads of the world, but at the crossroads of what Américo Paredes deemed *Mexico de afuera* (greater Mexico), where U.S.-born and immigrant Mexicans blended and created an in-between culture. Between 1940 and 1950, California's population increased by 55.3 percent, four times that of the rest of the country. Though most migrants settled in defense industry cities such as Los Angeles, San Francisco, Oakland, and Richmond, Monterey County experienced the fifth largest population gain.[20]

In the town of Salinas, some residents made efforts to establish positive relationships with each other across lines of race, class, and citizenship. In the thirteen-hundred-person neighborhood of Alisal, Mexicanos and "Okies" bonded over their common working-class identity. "I remember eating biscuits and gravy from an 'Okie' family, and they would come over to our house and eat tortillas and frijoles," remembered Ray Villanueva. Because of continuing flows of migration from Mexico and south Texas, Mexicanos remained cognizant of their diversity along lines of nativity, region, immigrant status, and citizenship. When braceros began arriving, some Mexican Americans showed interest in socializing with them. In November 1943 a group of Salinas Mexican Americans and braceros made a joint contribution of more than three hundred dollars to a local war fund for Mexicanos serving in the U.S. military. In addition, when *mutualistas* hosted dances or celebrated Mexican holidays, they invited braceros and migrant workers to attend. Some white residents befriended braceros as well. Gary

Hollis, a teenager working at a Salinas ballpark in the early days of the Bracero Program, noticed three braceros lingering outside the park and admitted them for free. Learning that all three were silversmiths from northern Mexico who spoke little English, Hollis lent them some schoolbooks and offered to teach them the language. The friendship among the four lasted until the braceros' contracts expired. Before leaving Salinas, the braceros left the books and a gift of silver cufflinks on Hollis's doorstep.[21]

More often than not, however, bracero-local relationships existed within limits in 1940s Salinas. Bracero Ignacio Gómez, for example, noticed that his former supervisor, a white man, would regularly invite Gómez to his home for meals but never suggested public outings. This was likely due to the looks and words that a person of Mexican descent could receive at this time in public. Though Bracero Program terms had stipulated a strong antidiscrimination policy, braceros and U.S.-born Mexicans were routinely refused service at restaurants, bars, and other business establishments. Controversy erupted in Texas when braceros, Mexican American soldiers, and Mexican diplomats all complained of rampant discrimination during wartime. As a result, the Mexican government blacklisted Texas from the Bracero Program in July 1943. Headlines such as "No More Mexican Workers Will Go to Texas in Humiliation" and "Mexican Workers Will Not Go to Texas Because of Racial Discrimination Which Exists There" covered the pages of Mexican newspapers. Under pressure from agribusiness, Texas officials established the Good Neighbor Commission, and Governor Coke Stevenson passed the 1943 Caucasian Race Resolution, which stated that Mexican Americans were "Caucasian" under the Treaty of Guadalupe Hidalgo and thus merited equal treatment in public places. This equal treatment, however, never materialized in social reality. Mexico maintained its Texas bracero blacklist for the entirety of the war, and California became the state with the largest bracero population.[22]

Though other states did not get blacklisted, this did not mean that race relations there were not fraught with division and segregation. During the 1940s, bathrooms and restaurants featured "No Mexicans Allowed" signs, movie theaters restricted Mexican and African Americans to balcony seats, and public swimming pools allowed Mexican and African Americans to swim only on pool-draining days so that whites would not have to swim in the supposedly "contaminated" water. In schools, Spanish-surnamed children were customarily placed in remedial classes or separate buildings because school boards generalized that they required separate instruction in language and hygiene. And in residential neighborhoods, home renters or buyers of color were prohibited from living in certain areas by racially restrictive covenants. Covenants had existed since the 1890s and often manifested in property deeds brandishing clauses such as "no part of the premises . . . shall be permitted to be occupied or used by any Mexican, Asiatic, Negro, Filipino, or person born in the Turkish Empire . . . except those persons [who] may be employed as household servants or farm employees." By 1940, 80 percent of realtors were using covenants, and they only increased as westward migrations of communities of color changed national demographics. From 1940 to 1950 the nonwhite population of the United States increased by 15 percent, from almost 13.5 million to almost 15.5 million people.[23] Out of 110 *Salinas Californian* real estate advertisements that explicitly used the terms "restricted" or "nonrestricted" between October 1943 and January 1969, 38 listed nonrestricted properties while 72, almost twice as many, advertised restricted ones. One ad took a different angle on the era's Good Neighbor Policy by asking: "Do you want Good Neighbors? You will find some of the best people living here . . . As this subdivision is restricted you will always be protected." Advertisements for restricted neighborhoods clearly marked racial boundaries, as did those for nonrestricted properties. The phrases "no race restrictions to Filipinos, Chinese or Mexicans" or "suitable for any nationality" might have relieved homebuyers and renters of color scouring the newspaper, but they performed the same work of letting racial minorities know where they belonged and where they did not.[24]

Those who tried to defy the rules of this housing battleground discovered how strongly many people felt about keeping whites and nonwhites apart. When Filipino farmworker George Montero and his white wife Harley wanted to buy a home in Alisal, for instance, two white female residents attempted to halt the bank's processing of the Monteros' home loan and circulated a petition calling for the family's exclusion. It took a meeting with a visiting Filipino consul for George to secure his loan and affirm his identity as a respectable and deserving homeowner. By and large, real estate agents refused to sell homes to buyers of color or showed them properties only at night. When Ignatius

Cooper and his wife, both black, attempted to move into a neighborhood where prominent growers Bruce Church and Gene Harden lived, neighbors signed a petition for their dismissal. In fact, realtors urged many blacks to buy shacks in Alisal or move twenty miles away to the coastal town of Seaside.[25] Despite the 1948 *Shelley v. Kraemer* U.S. Supreme Court ruling that racial covenants could not be legally enforced, they continued to be a Salinas custom until 1969.

Kept at a physical distance from spaces of whiteness, people of color had to create their own spaces for socializing and engaging in leisure activities. In Salinas, this space was Chinatown. Historical studies of other Chinatowns, including those in Los Angeles, New York, San Francisco, and Vancouver, have shown how such districts initially fostered community between Asian residents and then became more commercial, interracial zones as tourists, business owners, and consumers moved through them. By the 1940s Salinas's Chinatown was no different. A Filipino Presbyterian church, Buddhist temple, and Church of Confucius stood alongside Chinese restaurants, an African American–owned pool hall, and Mexican American–owned eateries and dance-halls like the Mexico City Café and Mariano's Nightclub. The Lotus Inn, a two-story building that held a cocktail lounge, restaurant, banquet room, and boarding house, was owned by Chinese business partners Wallace Ahtye and Bow Chin but operated by Mexican Americans Hank Mar and Gonzales Gutíerrez (fig. 2.7). The back rooms of the Hop Hing Lung general store and the Paradise Cocktail Lounge offered illegal gambling to locals, braceros, and the diverse servicemen of the nearby Fort Ord military installation. Salinas resident Wellington Lee recalled his childhood memories of Chinatown's multicultural atmosphere: "I fell asleep and awoke to the mixture of soul music and Mexican love songs blaring from poolhalls and cafes. I saw the winos, transients, field laborers, and Fort Ord soldiers weave their way down the main thoroughfare, Soledad Street, on a Saturday night or a Sunday morn."[26]

What made Chinatown even more alluring was its reputation as a sexual as well as racial meeting ground. Intermarriages were relatively few in Salinas during this time, with some unions occurring between Mexican men and Italian women and Mexican women and Filipino men (in part because of the three groups' shared Catholic identity, Mexicans' and Filipinos' common use of Spanish, and the skewed

Fig. 2.7. Signs adorning the old Lotus Inn as of 2011 serve as a historical re-minder of the mixed Asian-Latino commerce that characterized Chinatown in Salinas. (Photo by David Hackett, 2011)

gender ratio that resulted in a male-heavy Filipino immigrant flow). Yet in Chinatown, interracial sexual encounters happened frequently in dancehalls, nightclubs, and brothels and on the streets where white, black, and Mexicana prostitutes stood waiting for clients. Prostitutes of various racial and ethnic backgrounds serviced bracero camps as well and were allowed in by camp operators. Those who chose to spend their leisure time in Chinatown transformed it from a segregated neigh-borhood created out of racial and labor hierarchies of the nineteenth century to a wartime zone of interethnic freedom and experimentation. They deterritorialized it as exclusively Chinese and refashioned it as an inclusive multicultural space of vice and excitement. "Chinatown" had become a misnomer and continued to be used only out of tradition. With disapproving eyes, some residents and city authorities labeled Chinatown as a dirty, diseased, and immoral district and its patrons as dirty, diseased, and immoral people. The multicultural nature of the space and the willingness of its patrons to cross racial borders made it seem particularly deviant.[27]

At the same time that it served as a meeting ground for its diverse patrons, Chinatown became a battleground when violence broke out between four groups of men—braceros, Fort Ord servicemen, Salinas Mexican Americans, and Tejano migrant farmworkers. In the case of servicemen and braceros, both came to Chinatown dressed in a manner that asserted their own brand of masculinity. Servicemen wore their uniforms as literal and figurative evidence that they were well suited for first-class citizenship and respect. Meanwhile, fueled by the same masculine ideals of servitude and protection, braceros wore "American" boots, dress shirts, jeans, and hats to communicate their ability to financially provide for themselves and their families. At crowded taxi stands, fights erupted when servicemen disregarded lines and piled into cabs, stealing them from waiting braceros. These confrontations became so frequent that in June 1945, attorney George Pollock (who, coincidentally, was the one respondent sympathetic to the Japanese in the Salinas Chamber of Commerce internment survey) asked the Salinas City Council for police protection at the downtown cab stand, where three taxi companies operated on weekend nights.[28] While racial tension may have been a primary factor in these incidents, newspaper accounts of intraethnic violence between braceros and Mexican American servicemen suggest that other factors, such as class and social status, were at play. In 1943 two "Mexican" soldiers from Fort Ord were arrested for stabbing bracero José Lopes, and later a "tall Mexican" from a Salinas labor camp stabbed two Mexican American soldiers.[29] Although these occurrences and others may have emerged out of personal animosities, it is possible that braceros and servicemen—the first considered unarmed "soldiers of the plough" and the second, armed soldiers of the nation—recognized and reacted to their different roles in wartime America. Both groups of men could claim important roles in the war effort, but braceros occupied a far less prestigious position as manual laborers. One could speculate that Mexican American servicemen's remarks about braceros' work and noncitizen status, and braceros' resentment of Mexican American soldiers' assumed superiority, likely led to outbursts of aggression on both sides.

Meanwhile, other tensions developed as a steady influx of braceros and Tejano migrant farmworkers into California seemed to threaten local Mexican Americans' jobs in agriculture. As has been documented for the citrus and packinghouse industries of southern California, local Mexican Americans came to resent braceros as competitors in labor and romantic relations with Mexican American women. Similar conflicts in Salinas resulted in a high rate of intraethnic crime, including two 1943 incidents when braceros fatally stabbed local Mexican Americans. The only thing that exceeded violence between braceros and Mexican Americans was violence between braceros themselves, who sometimes brought familial disputes and hometown grudges with them from Mexico. In one of many cases throughout the 1940s, two bracero cousins fatally stabbed bracero Eduardo Díaz because he had not been sending remittances to his wife in Mexico (the sister of one of the attackers) and had "mistreated" the same attacker's fifteen-year-old sister.[30] With men at the center and women sometimes the subjects of dispute, these confrontations reveal how Salinas's male-centered agricultural economy—and proximity to a military installation—produced specific home front conflicts during wartime. Not only did Mexican-origin people have to battle the prejudices of whites, but they had to confront the same among each other.

MEXICAN AMERICAN AND BRACERO RESISTANCE DURING THE 1940s: WEARING, WRITING, AND SKIPPING

Despite the fact that five hundred thousand Latinos (four hundred thousand Mexicans and Mexican Americans, sixty-five thousand Puerto Ricans, and thirty-five thousand Central and South Americans) served in the U.S. Army during World War II—and came back with more Congressional Medals of Honor, Purple Hearts, and other military honors than any other ethnic group—this population continued to be treated as second-class citizens in wartime America. In addition to discrimination in housing, education, employment, and political representation, Latinos experienced excessive patrolling and brutality at the hands of police. In the Southwest, this was in large part due to the persisting stereotype of the Mexican juvenile delinquent and gang member. The infamous 1942 Los Angeles Sleepy Lagoon case, in which twenty-two youths (all Mexican American but one) were charged with the murder of José Diaz at a house party, linked Mexicanness and violent crime in the public imagination.[31] Then, the "Zoot Suit Riots" rocked the same city in June 1943. A weeklong episode of violence between Mexican American youth and white servicemen, the riots centered on the controversial zoot suit, an outfit consisting of a long and broad-shouldered

Fig. 2.8. A U.S. serviceman examines zoot suiters' attire at the Uline Arena in Washington, D.C., June 1942. (Photo by John Ferrell. Farm Security Administration/Office of War Information Photograph Collection, Library of Congress Prints and Photographs Division, Washington, D.C.)

"finger-tip" coat and billowing pants that tapered at the ankle. The zoot suit was popular not only with Mexican Americans, but with African Americans in Harlem and Detroit, Jews in Brooklyn, Italians in Boston, and Asian Americans and whites in California (fig. 2.8). Some Mexican American male zoot suiters, also called "pachucos" (a term associated with gang activity that the Los Angeles media pounced upon), added a long watch chain and hat, combed their long hair into a pompadour or ducktail, and spoke in *caló,* a mix of Spanish and English. Women zooters, referred to as "pachucas," "zooter girls," "black widows," "zooterinas," or "slick chicks," often wore a long, broad-shouldered coat, a knee-length pleated skirt, dark lipstick, and bouffant hairstyles. Some women chose to wear the masculine version of the zoot suit, pushing gendered fashion boundaries even further. Whichever form of the suit they chose, pachucas were considered "little tornadoes of sexual stimuli, swishing and flouncing down the streets" and threatening contemporary standards of femininity, decorum, and female sexuality.[32]

The majority of zoot suiters were second-generation Americans whose Mexican parents had immigrated to the United States during the early twentieth century. By World War II, 77 percent of the estimated 3.5 million Spanish-speaking people in the country were native-born citizens, but foreign-born Mexicans still claimed a significant presence. According to historian David Gutíerrez, of the 354,432 people of Mexican extraction living in California in 1940, 85 percent had at least one parent born in Mexico.[33] This blending of first- and second-generation identities and experiences led to differing views on acculturation, citizenship, and rebellion in Mexican American families. While Mexican immigrants still may have felt somewhat like outsiders in the United States, young Mexican Americans coming of age during the 1940s embraced "American" life and customs and saw possibilities for constructing new identities. Many may have simply viewed the suit as "cool," but as historian Robin D. G. Kelley has argued, "while the zoot suit was not meant as a direct political statement, the social context in which it was created and worn rendered it so." Likewise, Mexican writer Octavio Paz observed of the pachuco: "He knows that it is dangerous to stand out and that his behavior irritates society, but nevertheless he seeks and attracts persecution and scandal. It is the only way he can establish a more vital relationship with the society he is antagonizing. As a victim, he can occupy a place in the world that previously had ignored him; as a delinquent, he can become one of its wicked heroes." The zoot suit provoked critiques from both the white mainstream and more culturally traditional Mexicans. The War Production Board had eliminated extra material and features in suits in early 1942 as part of its cloth rationing measures, and thus many regarded the conspicuous consumption of the suit as a disrespectful and "un-American" act.[34]

Though Mexican American youths were not the only ones wearing the zoot suit, they became targets of violence as the media linked the suit to the idea of the pachuco gangster and sexual deviant. On June 2, 1943, the day before the riots, Los Angeles newspapers reported that a pachuco gang had kidnapped and raped two young married white women in a "zoot suit orgy," provoking one angry white sailor to declare, "We're going to do what the police haven't been able to . . . We're going to make the streets of Los Angeles safe for sailors' girls, and for the general public." Echoing the vigilante violence that followed the myth of the black rapist in the nineteenth-century South, groups of white servicemen and civilians made it their mission to start searching streets, bars, movie theaters, dancehalls, restaurants, and even private homes to beat and strip zooters. "Street cars were halted while Mexicans, and some Filipinos and negroes, were jerked out of their seats, pushed into the streets, and beaten with sadistic frenzy," reported Carey McWilliams. In many cases police stood idly by, waiting until afterwards to arrest the victims for "disturbing the peace" while taking only a handful of servicemen into custody. Mexican Americans not wearing zoot suits were attacked as well, revealing the racism that lay at the core of the riots. In harming and humiliating Mexican American bodies, white servicemen could reassert their power as Americans and as men. The riots ended on June 10, 1943, when the U.S. War Department declared parts of Los Angeles "out of bounds" to military personnel.[35]

Three hundred miles north of Los Angeles, Salinas residents were paying close attention to the riots. In November 1942 the *Californian*'s editor assured anxious readers that the town "never saw a zoot suit [and] we never hope to see one." Almost immediately after this proclamation, however, young Mexican American men and women began wearing zoot suits on the streets of Salinas. In fact, the zoot suit fad had migrated from cities such as Los Angeles and San Francisco to other agricultural hubs including Stockton, Fresno, Gilroy, Delano, and Oxnard. Zooters were arrested in droves, not only for criminal activity but sometimes for merely looking the part. In one case, a Salinas judge convicted four zoot suiters with "duckbill" haircuts of disturbing the peace and ordered them to return the next week with haircuts and clothing taking them "out of the zoot suit class" and "from the ridiculous to the conventional." In another case, nineteen-year-olds Sally and Estelle Reyes were charged with vagrancy and jailed for dressing in the "zoot suit fashion." Despite repeated warnings from the judge to keep quiet, the two women laughed and disrupted the courtroom until the judge ordered them back to the jail for the afternoon. The Reyeses continued to be disruptive when they reappeared. After sentencing Estelle to thirty days in jail and Sally to a one-hundred-dollar fine and fifty days in jail, the judge ordered the two women to "abandon the type of dress they were wearing for something more conventional." By flouting gender norms and literally laughing in the face of authority, the Reyes women demonstrated their "unwillingness to stay in [their] traditionally assigned place."[36] Young Mexican American zooters defied racial hierarchies that had made them invisible by making themselves very visible, unsettling white residents and local authorities. This white discomfort manifested in traditional legal punishment and in unmaking the zooter look itself. By dictating how zooters should change their hair and dress, judges sought to regulate Mexican American bodies and exercise control over their stylistic expression.

Salinas underwent its own zoot suit "riots" soon after those in Los Angeles had ended. In early July 1943 nine zooters who were all farmworkers and "American citizens of Mexican parentage" appeared in court for their involvement in a fight that broke up a city-sponsored dance. The nine, who were "dressed in the regalia which has offended Salinas boys and provoked several near riots," according to news reports, insisted they had been attacked solely because of their attire. City Manager V. J. Barlogio hypothesized that the zoot suit was not so much the cause of trouble as the youths' "attitude toward girls which is resented by other young men." Two days later this "attitude" was reinforced by a Mrs. Hughes, who reported being grabbed and "accosted by insulting zoot suiters" as she waited for a cab. As in Los Angeles, Mexican American men's perceived sexual transgressions against white women—from flirting to actual physical contact—infuriated white men in Salinas.[37] Exhibiting a boldness far from the stereotype of the passive *campesino*, the zoot suiter was a threat to racial, class, and sexual order. White youths began gathering in downtown Salinas in the evenings and lingering outside of movie theaters and other business establishments to "clean up on zoot suiters." In early July 1943 Salinas police arrested two groups of white youths for fighting with zooters downtown. A few evenings later, a fight between "nine Mexican boys in zoot regalia and seven other youths" at a local dancehall resulted in police taking all sixteen boys into custody. Other incidents included the beating of "Mexican" Rudolph Lares by a group of youths who had planned to "cut the hair of the first zoot suiter they saw."[38] Salinas newspapers continued to omit the names of whites involved in criminal activity, identifying them by the race-neutral term "youths," while always identifying people of Mexican descent as such and providing their names. In this case, however, the identification of Lares as "Mexican" raises important questions: Was he a bracero rather than Mexican

American, and if so, was he even wearing a zoot suit? Or was the group of "underage youth" merely looking to cut the hair of any "Mexican" who had the longer hair associated with the "pachuco" style? If the figure of the "zoot suiter" had indeed become conflated with the figure of the "Mexican" in the minds of white youth, no type of "Mexican" in Salinas was safe from criminalization and possible attack.

What makes the history of zoot suiting in Salinas different from conventional historical narratives of the trend is the position that zoot suiters occupied in this agricultural community's social hierarchy. Unlike in Los Angeles, where zooters suffered brutal attacks by white locals and servicemen, in Salinas zooters were often the perpetrators of violence against their Mexican American and bracero co-ethnics. On several occasions, Mexican American servicemen on furlough from Fort Ord reported being harassed, beaten, and robbed by zooters. Whether zoot suiters attacked them because of negative associations with the Los Angeles riots, or because the two groups exchanged taunts and insults about each other's masculinity and dress, is unknown. Zooters also victimized local Mexican Americans and braceros. In July 1943 three zoot suiters were placed in custody for an attempted robbery of M. J. Hernandez and José Navarre at a local bar. Later, three braceros reported being threatened and robbed by eight club-wielding zoot suiters.[39] Possible explanations for this pattern could lie in zoot suiters' view of braceros as men of lower social status. They were foreigners, temporary workers, and men of lesser economic means. The zoot suit, in its style and in the attitude of the wearer, pushed back against the stereotype of the poor, stooped-over Mexican farmworker—in other words, what the bracero embodied. In Los Angeles, the zoot suiter seemed to be at the bottom of the totem pole, but in Salinas and other communities where the Bracero Program functioned, braceros occupied that lowly and vulnerable position. The history of zooter-bracero conflict places a crucial twist on what we know about zoot suiting in Latino life.

When zoot suiters continued to be arrested for altercations into the spring of 1944, Salinas police chief George C. Wight accused Los Angeles of producing the violent youths. "Such crimes are not prevalent among the native born boys of Mexican families [in Salinas]," he affirmed. Some of the Mexican families to whom Wight referred likely agreed, as the zoot suit craze had also created a generational battleground between older Mexicanos and younger Mexican Americans.

While the first group attempted to construct a "respectable" image by hosting benefit dances and Mexican holiday celebrations, the latter disrupted these events on multiple occasions. In April 1944 a group of zoot suiters disturbed a Red Cross benefit "fiesta" dance sponsored by the Comité Cívico Mexicano. Resisting arrest, the group of zooters and some bystanders started a "riot" by assaulting white police officers with beer bottles. Disparaging the actions of the zooters, Comité chairman N. H. Alvarez distanced himself and other members from this younger "rowdy element." Having been historically criminalized by Salinas media, Mexican Americans who wished to eradicate this stereotype through their respectable public actions became angered with zooters who reenergized links between Mexicans and violence. Over the next few months multiple zoot suit "gangs" created disturbances at "wholesome" Mexicano community dances. Zoot suit–related violence persisted in Salinas until the end of 1946, far longer than it did in Los Angeles.[40]

Historian Edward Escobar has argued that police repression during the zoot suit era ultimately gave rise to a new ethnic consciousness and political solidarity among Los Angeles Mexican Americans. In Salinas and other communities where the Mexican American population was still small, however, there was no critical mass to redirect attention from the zoot suit "problem" to civil rights activism. A few individuals attempted to protest racial discrimination by writing letters to local newspapers. In a letter to the *Californian* Manuel C. Jiménez linked Mexicanos' second-class status in California with "Hitlerism" abroad by sharing his experience entering a bar with a bracero friend. The bartender denied service to the two men and shouted at them, "We don't serve Mexicans and don't ask why." A week later, a letter signed "A soldier's mother" echoed Jiménez's previous statements: "Such discrimination is all right in a nazi country but not in a country of democratic ideals as America. I have a friend whose son was working in a shed here in Salinas. Having a light complexion he was not noticed among the other nationalities. One day he started talking about the Mexicans and mentioned that he was Mexican himself . . . The next day he was fired." The author continued by describing an incident in which a group of Salinas girls, asked to identify their racial backgrounds at a dancehall, were not admitted when they replied "Mexican." The anonymous mother concluded by reminding *Californian* readers that Mexicanos' valiant efforts in World War II merited their equal treatment: "Our ancestors were here long before any European set foot on American soil. Our husbands, sons and other relatives are fighting and dying on the battlefields for a better way of life and an equal chance to live decently." Other letter writers, such as Clarence C. Castro, complained about municipal neglect of Salinas's Mexican neighborhoods, asserting the need for a city water supply, sewer and sanitation facilities, and streetlights in these areas.[41] Though they did not have the political organization to say so as a group, individual Mexican Americans took it upon themselves to let Salinas authorities know, through the written word, that racial discrimination was not going unnoticed.

Meanwhile, braceros were using various strategies to contest their unsatisfying working conditions. Some persuaded program supervisor Ben López to let them choose their own work crews made up of friends and acquaintances with whom they wanted to share a labor camp. On less frequent occasions, braceros asked for work transfers if they felt their employers had pushed them to work too many hours during their first few days on the job. Others voiced complaints about their living conditions to the Mexican Consulate. One group of California braceros, for example, packaged and mailed a sample of the unappetizing meals they were being served to the nearest consul, along with an invitation to visit their labor camp. Across the nation in Baltimore, nineteen bracero railroad workers went to Washington, D.C., and complained to the Pan-American Union that they were not receiving medical attention, adequate food, or a chance at enjoyable social lives. A particularly powerful form of bracero resistance was leaving the program altogether and "skipping out" on one's work contract. The phenomenon of "skipping" emerged not long after the Bracero Program began in 1942. Braceros skipped for various reasons, including dissatisfaction, homesickness, an offer of higher wages by another employer, or the desire to craft an entirely different existence in *el norte*. Isidoro Ramírez, for example, skipped out on his contract picking tomatoes in Stockton and escaped to San Francisco to work as a garbage man; other unhappy braceros in his crew followed. By 1947 a total of 18,294 braceros had gone missing across the nation, becoming part of a historical legacy of runaway workers. Though the Farm Security Administration asserted that less than 1.5 percent of braceros in the United States failed to complete their contracts, the number of "skips" in Salinas consistently stayed between 10 and 15 percent during the life of the Bracero Program. According to a March 1946 federal report, for instance, out of 160 braceros missing from California, the highest number were from Salinas (28), with Fresno (16) and South Pasadena (14) following behind. The high percentage of bracero skips in Salinas was in part due to the town's position as a major Bracero Program hub but surely also reflected the particularly poor working and living conditions that braceros suffered there.[42]

As a racially diverse place in 1940s California, Salinas was both a meeting ground and a battleground. Some people developed relationships across lines of race and citizenship that ranged from the friendly to the sexual, while others clashed over issues of race, class, social status, and generation. The scholarship on Mexican Americans, race, and World War II has largely focused on the relations between Mexicans and whites. Yet when one looks inside the "Mexican" world, one gleans a complicated and fragmented societal portrait. Intraethnic conflicts between Mexicanos themselves, whether physical or ideological, transpired because three important things were at stake: visibility, respectability, and upward mobility. Servicemen wanted to be treated like first-class citizens for their sacrifices; local farmworkers wanted to protect their jobs, romantic prospects, and family lives; zooters wanted to be noticed as an important constituency in the world of cultural consumption; and braceros wanted to be recognized and rewarded as guest laborers filling a wartime void. The ways in which these four groups converged and clashed with each other illuminate the twists that agriculture-centered communities place on the history of Mexican Americans and the World War II home front.

Historians have agreed that the war marked a turning point for Mexican Americans because of the socioeconomic and political changes it wrought. Those who served in the military experienced racial integration in the trenches and a feeling of civic inclusion through their patriotic acts. On the home front, those who entered the defense industry and other workplaces received a taste of slightly better wages and—especially for women—more social independence. Yet when veterans of color returned home from fighting fascism and genocide to find the same segregation and racial discrimination they thought they had left behind, it was clear that they remained second-class citizens in the United States. As a result, these veterans and other activists founded civil rights organizations in the immediate postwar period. In 1947 the CSO was founded in Los Angeles, first to support Mexican American politician Edward Roybal and later to tackle issues such as voter registration, housing discrimination, worker unionization, and educational segregation. The next year, veteran and physician Hector P. Garcia founded the American G.I. Forum (AGIF) in Corpus Christi, Texas, which emphasized Americanism, conducted its meetings in English, and urged its members to better their education and participate in civic life. The organization gained national attention when it protested the refusal of a funeral home in Three Rivers, Texas, to bury decorated Mexican American veteran Felix Longoria in a "white" cemetery. After securing the assistance of Texas senator Lyndon B. Johnson, the forum arranged for Longoria's burial at Arlington National Cemetery with full military honors. The AGIF soon broadened its concerns to voting and educational segregation, supplementing the civil rights work of LULAC in Texas. On a national level, many workers of color took advantage of their membership in CIO-affiliated labor unions to fight for their labor rights and equality.

In the Salinas Valley, however, the postwar era played out very differently from this larger national context. Though labor unions were invaluable vehicles for Mexican American political empowerment, they could not emerge in an environment where the Bracero Program constantly threatened to replace class-conscious or "rebellious" Mexican American workers with cheaper, nonunionized workers from across the border. During the program's first year, the United States imported slightly more than 4,000 braceros to work on U.S. farms and railroads. By the end of 1943 the number had jumped to 56,114, rising again in 1944 to 63,432. Between 1942 and 1947, the United States imported between 200,000 and 300,000 braceros. California received half of this number over these five years (with a whopping 90 percent of braceros in 1945), making it the nation's biggest bracero-employing state.[43] The Bracero Program's popularity led Congress to approve a renewed agreement with Mexico in 1947 in which grower associations, rather than the federal government, would pay the costs of contracting and caring for braceros. Mexican American workers realized that their labor competition was here to stay, and the fear of losing their jobs only further hindered the development of any coherent agricultural labor movement. In communities where it operated, the Bracero

Program became a wedge that blocked certain avenues of dissent for Mexican Americans in agricultural communities, placing them on a separate—and arguably slower—political trajectory than their urban counterparts.

Although they tried to contest their invisibility and subjugation through wearing distinctive fashion, writing letters of protest, emphasizing their respectability, or running away, Salinas Valley Mexicanos found that their actions had only a minimal effect on their white-controlled, agribusiness-dominated surroundings. As one resident observed, "Salinas, whose wealth depended on brown labor, remained a white town."[44] Things would become even more complicated as the growth of the Bracero Program created a parallel stream of undocumented Mexican migrants seeking work in *el norte*. The U.S. government began targeting these "wetbacks" as the new national invaders of the late 1940s and 1950s. In addition to braceros, Mexican Americans now had to confront another population of co-ethnics that threatened their economic livelihood and civil rights struggles. In a national climate in which "Mexican" identity implied undesirability and illegality, the challenges of being Mexican American in an agriculture-centered community only came into sharper focus.

3 Bound in Tension
Mexican Americans, Braceros, and Undocumented Migrants, 1947–1960

ONE MORNING IN April 1953, Salinas Border Patrol inspectors James Maloney and George Ward noticed "a group of men appearing to be Mexicans, working in a field." The two drove their truck, which already held some apprehended "wetbacks," into the field to conduct a raid. From his father's small strawberry farm next door, Mexican American Tomás Diaz reportedly shouted to the workers—whom he did not know—"Run for your life! That's the Immigration!" As the group of men scattered, Maloney and Ward struggled to catch as many as they could. Diaz ran into the field shouting, "You guys should not treat those wetbacks like dogs." He ran to Maloney, who was shoving the migrant Leopoldo Rodríguez-López into the truck. "You have no right to handle that Mexican that way! They have their rights," Diaz yelled. Calling Diaz a "son of a bitch," Maloney pushed and kicked him out of the way, and in the chaos six undocumented workers escaped. "Obviously Mr. Diaz put on his demonstration near the government vehicle for the sole purpose of detaining the Patrol Officers as long as possible in order that the aliens would have a better chance of escaping," Salinas immigration inspector Bruce Long remarked in an official statement. "Why did you yell at the Mexicans to run?" an examining officer asked Diaz during his interrogation. "No reason at all," Diaz calmly replied. The INS, part of the U.S. Department of Justice, ultimately determined that there was insufficient evidence to prosecute

75

Diaz. As for Rodríguez-López, who had crossed into the United States four times since 1928 (twice with documents, twice without), officials granted him voluntary departure back to Mexico.[1]

Diaz's behavior during the raid implied a sense of solidarity with Mexican nationals against *la migra,* or the INS, which had moved into the Department of Justice in 1940 and become a stronger presence in the U.S. Southwest. After the end of World War II, the railroad Bracero Program ended, but agribusiness clamored for more guest labor. Out of concern over racial discrimination and braceros' working conditions, however, Mexico delayed program extension negotiations from 1947 until 1951. During this period a variety of administrative agreements between U.S. grower-employers and the Mexican government allowed guestworkers into the country, but many Mexicans crossed into the country *sin papeles* (without papers), and this undocumented immigration continued even after an official Migrant Labor Agreement (also known as Public Law 78) was formalized in July 1951.[2] In the eyes of the INS, "Mexican" had become synonymous with "illegal," and Diaz attempted to challenge this automatic conflation. Moreover, in affirming to INS officers that "wetbacks" had rights, he communicated a simultaneous awareness that he had his own rights as a Mexican American. Being the son of a strawberry farm owner, however, Diaz was not the average agricultural working-class Mexican American competing with braceros and "wetbacks" for work in the fields. He thus held much less of a stake in making sure that any "wets" were caught and deported.

At this time many Mexican Americans felt differently from Diaz and believed a "wetback problem" was threatening their labor and civil rights agendas. Indeed, the landmark publication *What Price Wetbacks?* expressed this view in 1953. Coauthored by the AGIF, a Mexican American–founded veterans' and civil rights organization, and the Texas State Federation of Labor, an organization of AFL union locals, the study sought to "awaken the people of America to the danger of this wetback invasion." The Bracero Program and the parallel stream of undocumented immigration it had created, the study argued, were depressing wages and conditions for U.S. workers. The publication continued:

> *These are the wetbacks*—hundreds of thousands of them pushing across the Rio Grande day after day, pushing their blood brothers, American

citizens of Mexican descent, out of jobs . . . pushing wages down, down, down. *These are the wetbacks*—sad eyed and sick, desperate beings unaware that their illegal entry and existence bring with them to the areas they infest soaring statistics on syphilis, tuberculosis, infantile diarrhea and other diseases, along with a host of crime and other socio-economic problems.

At the same time that the authors recognized the economic desperation of undocumented Mexicans, they attacked them for being a criminal and diseased infestation harmful to the socioeconomic futures of Mexican Americans. Ed Idar Jr., the executive secretary of the AGIF and a member of the report's investigating team, was a prominent figure in the Texas Mexican American civil rights movement. The son of newspaperman and LULAC founder Eduardo Idar, Ed had served in the military during World War II and been active in the AGIF since 1950. Believing that "wetbacks" were both a labor and national security problem, Idar Jr. argued that a permeable border left the United States open to infiltration by "Communists and subversives of all types." In addition to distributing fifteen thousand copies of *What Price Wetbacks?* to members of Congress, state and national government agencies, and the media, the AGIF testified at various state and federal hearings that a continuous infusion of undocumented Mexican immigrants "materially retarded [Mexican Americans'] assimilation." Other Mexican Americans expanded this critique to braceros. LULAC of Texas declared that both braceros and "wetbacks" were robbing Mexican American farmworkers of a living wage; economist and labor activist Ernesto Galarza argued that the Bracero Program was corrupt and poorly regulated; and an anonymous Mexican American leader in Los Angeles was quoted as saying: "The braceros . . . hang onto the tail of our shirts. We can't brush them off, because that wouldn't be humane. But their weight is dragging us down."[3]

These juxtaposed accounts of sympathetic actions and antagonistic words toward Mexican nationals demonstrate that depending on their class, immigration status, or political ideology, Mexican Americans responded to Mexicans in varied ways during the "wetback era" of the late 1940s and early 1950s. Existing scholarship has explored Mexican Americans' ambivalent attitudes about Mexican immigration and immigrants in the twentieth century.[4] While some Mexican Americans sympathized with, cultivated transborder ties with, and included Mexican nationals in their own struggles for civil rights, others blamed Mexican nationals for stealing jobs, lowering wages, undermining the U.S. labor movement, and causing discrimination to fall upon both groups. This chapter examines Salinas Valley Mexican Americans' and Mexicans' experiences on the ground during the late 1940s and 1950s that kept them from forming a larger transnational Mexican-origin community. The INS raids that swept agricultural California beginning in 1947 turned the nation's attention to the "wetback problem" and framed undocumented Mexican migrants as inherently criminal, diseased, and threatening to U.S. citizens. This chapter uses the deportation files of the Salinas INS branch office to delve into the migration stories and eventual apprehensions of undocumented Mexicans, giving humanity to these migrants in the process. A large number of undocumented Mexican migrants eluded the grasp of the INS and found employment in California agriculture by agreeing to work for even lower wages and fewer protections than braceros. As a result, Mexican Americans of the agricultural working class came to resent both braceros and "wetbacks" for taking jobs and depressing wages in the fields.

Though the lives of these three populations intersected at times to create moments of intraethnic bonding—for instance, Mexican Americans and braceros worked together to build their own Catholic church in Salinas when they were ostracized by white churchgoers, and some Mexican American women engaged in romantic relationships with Mexican immigrant men—these moments were relatively rare compared with moments of intraethnic tension. Two particular flashpoints in the 1950s, the INS "Operation Wetback" of 1954 and the peak of the Bracero Program in 1956, fragmented the agricultural Mexican-origin population in significant ways. Driven by Cold War fears of border infiltration by communists, alien subversives, and diseased immigrants, the INS carried out a quasimilitary operation that deported approximately 1.3 million undocumented Mexicans from the Southwest from 1954 to 1957. Presuming that anyone who looked "Mexican" could be a suspected "illegal," immigration authorities targeted Mexican Americans as well and treated them as undesirable foreigners in their own home country. Meanwhile, the U.S. government's strategy of using massive deportation numbers to shore up the Bracero Program as a legal, regulated solution to the illegal immigration crisis produced higher numbers of bracero importations. Grower-employers imported almost half a million braceros in 1956—the program's peak year. When growers in Salinas proposed building labor camps in residential areas to accommodate this larger bracero population, protests erupted from white residents who viewed braceros as social problems and sexual threats. Mexican Americans, well aware of their racial conflation with braceros, struggled with whether to defend their co-ethnics or join in protests against their presence. In agriculture-centered places, Mexican Americans kept braceros and "wetbacks" at greater social distance during the late 1940s and 1950s and did not make great efforts to advocate on their behalf. To them, it was daunting enough to protect their rights as U.S. citizens during a time of xenophobia, state repression of labor militancy, and heightened surveillance of borders and individuals.[5]

THE "WETBACK PROBLEM"

After 1943 the center of operations for the U.S. Border Patrol shifted from the country's northern border with Canada to the southern border with Mexico. A few years later, the U.S. government and media began obsessively focusing on the country's "wetback problem" as reports estimated that tens of thousands of undocumented Mexicans were working in the United States. In 1947 Border Patrol officers conducted a sweep of northern and central California, apprehending 335 aliens in "Operation Sacramento" in March, 325 in "Operation Fresno" in April, 322 in "Operation Salinas" in May, and 159 in "Operation Stockton" in June. Recognizing that the Salinas Valley was a prime "wetback" destination, officials returned there in December 1947 and apprehended 659 undocumented Mexicans in fields, labor camps, bus depots, and street corners and deported them. Another 462 were apprehended in May 1948, and then in the spring of 1950 a special crew of twelve U.S. immigration officers apprehended 3,000 more. The fact that immigration raids took place with such frequency in the Salinas Valley even before the beginning of Operation Wetback in 1954 proved that immigration authorities had already singled out the region as one saturated with a "wet" workforce.[6]

The majority of those apprehended had been employed at the time of their capture, proving that Salinas Valley growers and labor contractors were more than complicit in the region's "wetback" problem. Agricultural employers all across the country were using undocumented workers, offering them no labor protections and even lower wages than domestic farmworkers and braceros. Some undocumented workers were making as little as twenty to thirty cents an hour for a twelve-hour workday, or nothing at all if unscrupulous employers claimed that the harvest did not bring a profit or called the INS to raid their farm on payday. By 1951 an estimated one million "wetbacks" had entered the United States. That year the President's Commission on Migratory Labor recommended sanctions against and fines for employers who knowingly hired undocumented workers, but the agribusiness lobby in Congress succeeded in adding the "Texas Proviso" to the Immigration and Nationality (McCarran-Walter) Act of 1952, which stated that employing an undocumented worker was not considered "harboring" and thus not punishable by fines or jail time. Believing they were justified in hiring undocumented workers, agricultural employers in the Southwest railed against the INS. In Texas's Rio Grande Valley, locals posted anti–Border Patrol signs in store windows and accused the INS of violating their right to use Mexican labor. In the Salinas Valley, a prominent group of growers arranged a personal meeting with immigration officials and asserted their right to use mixed bracero and "wetback" crews, given the delay in Bracero Program negotiations. They justified their use of undocumented labor in other ways. "The average American type can't take stoop labor," Salinas Chamber of Commerce director and GSVA member S. V. Christierson said. "The ones we do get . . . work a half day and quit." Blaming the deficiencies of citizen workers rather than low wages for the region's labor shortage, Christierson continued: "We don't know who's legal and who isn't . . . we don't have Gestapo methods and we don't ask for passports, identification and work cards. But an illegal Mexican looks just like an American citizen of Mexican descent and we hire him in good faith."[7]

While Christierson attempted to imply a kind of egalitarianism in growers' lack of distinction between Mexican American citizens and non-citizen Mexicans, the former faced the consequences of such conflation. The physical and racial similarities that Christierson noted between the two groups were also noted by INS officials who often mistook Mexican Americans for "wetbacks." Salinas resident Salvador Menares Mendoza, for example, was charged with resisting arrest when he was accused of being an "illegal." Mendoza was later found to be a U.S. citizen and was released. Another man, Jose Martinez-Aguirre, was taken in by INS officials but later proved to be from the

United States. Across the Southwest INS agents used a broad brush in searching for "illegal aliens," often stopping "Mexican-looking" U.S. citizens on the street and deporting U.S.-born children along with their undocumented parents. The location of the Salinas INS branch office in Alisal, near the homes of several Mexican Americans, undoubtedly disturbed and intimidated residents and led to "wetback" accusations. As the California State Advisory Committee of the U.S. Commission on Civil Rights later reported, these government-sponsored raids "made every brown American suspect." While urban Mexican Americans were railing against "stop and frisk" practices by law enforcement officers, rural Mexican Americans were resenting being asked to show their papers. Reminded of Depression-era deportations and zoot suit–related police brutality, Mexican Americans in the Southwest were angered at being branded "alien citizens" in their own home country and begrudged undocumented Mexican migrants for marking them by association as undesirable foreigners.[8]

By September 1952 federal agents reported that of the 530,000 "wetbacks" apprehended in the United States, more than half (275,000) had been caught in California. As domestic agricultural workers complained of depressed wages and unemployment, and as anti-foreigner and pro–border enforcement sentiment increased during the McCarthy era, the U.S. government institutionalized a formal roundup of undocumented Mexicans beginning on June 13, 1954, termed Operation Wetback. Led by Lieutenant General Joseph M. Swing, 750 Border Patrol investigators and officers raided public spaces, workplaces, and private homes and expelled undocumented migrants from the U.S. Southwest by bus, train, plane, and boat. Close to 1,500 people were arrested every day, and by the end of the year the U.S. Border Patrol had arrested slightly more than 1 million people around the nation, with 638,033 of them apprehended in California.[9]

Deportation files reveal much about the undocumented Mexican migrants, mostly male, who decided to cross the border during the time of Operation Wetback. While some ventured into *el norte* on foot, others stowed away in vehicles or hopped onto freight trains, hiding in refrigerated railcars or squeezing their bodies between railcar frames. One group of thirty-eight "wetbacks" traveled so far on the Alaska Railroad that they were arrested at the end of the line closest to the Arctic Circle. The thousands of undocumented Mexicans who went to the Salinas Valley were drawn to its flourishing agricultural industry and the possibility of blending in with its heavily Mexican-origin labor force. According to migrant smuggling case files, white and Mexican American smugglers drove undocumented migrants from Tijuana and Mexicali to Salinas for $80 to $125 apiece. Because of a lack of communication between INS district and subdistrict offices near different ports of entry, migrants who were apprehended found that they could reenter the United States several times. Fortino Avalos-Presiado, for example, evaded inspection at the border and found employment as a farmworker in the Salinas Valley before being apprehended and granted voluntary departure to Mexico. He reentered the United States and was granted voluntary departure three more times from different locations in California (including Salinas) because his apprehending agents did not have access to a centralized record about him. If a migrant was deported, an action more severe than voluntary departure, this often did not deter repeat migration. José Solano-Ruíz was granted voluntary departure three times and deported twice before being deported from Salinas. José Hernandez-Brambila testified that he had "entered the United States unlawfully on more occasions than he can remember," been granted voluntary departure numerous times, and been deported twice before being apprehended by the Salinas INS. Border corruption made some migrants' crossing even easier. After a stint in the United States as a dishwasher, one migrant returned to Mexico and encountered border officials in Mexicali who offered to let him cross the border again for a bribe of forty dollars. Meanwhile, the INS was "drying out wetbacks," or permitting those apprehended in the fields to become regularized as braceros on the spot.[10] The rate of undocumented immigration kept increasing as word spread that one did not have to wait for weeks at a migratory station to get a bracero contract but merely had to cross the border and get caught working in agriculture.

Although men were apprehended more often than women—between 1950 and 1960 only five women (four Mexican, one Chinese) appeared in Salinas INS deportation files—the stories of undocumented women migrants are equally striking. Carolina Venegas-Sinchon, who claimed a Mexican mother named Manuela Soto and an Indian father named Inder Singh-Shine, was arrested by the Salinas INS in 1954 under the name Caroline Shine-Soto (fig. 3.1, left). At her deportation hearing, she explained to Special Inquiry Officer P. R. McLaughlin that she had lived in Holtville, California, until she was two years old, after which she lived with her mother in Jalisco, Mexico, where she eventually married a man named Javier Venegas and followed him to the United States. A disbelieving McLaughlin confronted Venegas-Sinchon with evidence that a woman had since appeared at the Calexico immigration office asserting that *she* was the real Caroline Singh Shine of Holtville. After a two-day hearing, a frustrated McLaughlin and Venegas-Sinchon held a tense exchange:

> MCLAUGHLIN: Mrs. Venegas, what I am trying to convey to you is that . . . you are an imposter.
>
> VENEGAS-SINCHON: Evidentally [*sic*] there are two of us . . . I realize that it is a serious thing and that I am likely to lose because this other person seems to have all the proof; but I have always carried that name and when I came my mother gave me those papers . . . if I had known that it was a lie . . . I would not have come [to the United States] in the first place.
>
> . . . .
>
> MCLAUGHLIN: Mrs. Venegas, if you are not Caroline Shine, who are you?
>
> VENEGAS-SINCHON: I don't know who they want me to be.

McLaughlin tried various strategies to prove Venegas-Sinchon's guilt, even going so far as to state that she "show[ed] no indications of having an East Indian national as a father insofar as [her] racial characteristics." A month after her hearing, which proved so confusing it was continued indefinitely, Venegas-Sinchon returned to Mexico on her own out of either fear or frustration that she would not be able to live an easy life in the United States.[11]

Whether or not Venegas-Sinchon had told the truth about her name, her complaints about the unequal and confusing access to documents of citizenship was correct. Identities had become commodities that were being bought, sold, created, duplicated, and stolen on a regular basis. Venegas-Sinchon's husband Javier Venegas proved so through his own immigration history. With two other wives besides Carolina living in Arizona and Mexico, Venegas had crossed the border several times under various aliases. He met another woman, Maria Socorro Chávez, in Mexicali in May 1954 and offered her transportation to the United States and a kitchen job in his Salinas Valley restaurant (fig. 3.1, right). Upon her arrival, Venegas then suggested Chávez make extra money

Fig. 3.1. Deported migrants
Carolina Venegas-Sinchon
(above) and Maria Socorro
Chávez (right). (Salinas INS Sub-
Office Files, National Archives
and Records Administration, San
Bruno, California)

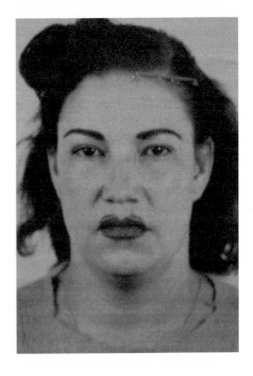

as a prostitute. A few weeks later, Chávez was solicited by an under-cover police officer at Venegas's restaurant and arrested for vagrancy. Although Chávez identified Venegas as her transporter, the INS was unable to prosecute him for lack of evidence. Chávez's migration story and deportation epitomized the difficulties some Mexican women confronted in journeying to the United States. If they wanted to avoid the vulnerability of migrating *sola,* they often chose to travel with a man who was a relative, friend, *coyote,* or romantic partner, and often these relationships posed their own gendered problems. Chávez became vulnerable as Venegas's employee and then more so once he "suggested" she sell her sexuality to improve her economic condition in the United States. Finally, she became vulnerable to *la migra* through her position as an exposed service worker in a restaurant, while Venegas succeeded at disappearing, perhaps taking refuge at the home of one of his multiple wives.[12]

Deportation file photographs are fascinating sources that not only tell us more about what was important to the INS in terms of record keeping, but provide a sense of undocumented migrants' diversity and humanity. Taken mug shot–style against a plain white background, these photographs attempted to capture every detail about an apprehended migrant's features from the chest up. Information about hair and eye color, complexion, height and weight, and distinguishing scars or marks on the body were also entered in the files. As two migrants who challenged *la migra* with their numerous recrossings, José Solano-Ruíz and José Hernandez-Brambila did not express the fear of a first-time apprehension in their Salinas INS deportation photographs (fig. 3.2). While Ruíz seems almost defiant with his slightly lifted chin and blank stare, Brambila appears resigned to the reality that he will have to cross the border once more. As both men are not wearing work shirts with signs of wear or dirt, it is likely that they were apprehended on the street, in a public establishment, or at their homes. The staples that bound the men's pictures to their deportation papers are visible in the photographs, bordering Ruíz's profile and driven through Brambila's head, a virtual puncturing of his attempt at clandestine crossing.

The stories and photographs of youths who migrated to the Salinas Valley are particularly poignant. Antonio Vásquez, an eighteen-year-old from Jalisco, had to abandon his dream of becoming a doctor because of his poverty. He crossed the border on foot at Calexico and lived in

Fig. 3.2. Deported migrants José Solano-
Ruíz (above) and José Hernandez-
Brambila (right). (Salinas INS Sub-Office
Files, National Archives and Records
Administration, San Bruno, California)

Salinas for one year before being deported, after which he returned
immediately to Salinas and was apprehended a second time. Raul
Savedra-Leiva, a sixteen-year-old from Sonora, returned to Salinas
eight days after being apprehended, while Ernesto Angulo-López, an
eighteen-year-old from Sinaloa, reentered the United States by freight
train five days after. Seventeen-year-old Pedro Martínez-Velasquez re-

entered the United States on the very same day of his apprehension. Guadalupe Naranjo-Bravo from Michoacán crossed into the country three times before the age of seventeen, and Enrique Reyes-Padilla, an eighteen-year-old from Mexicali, was deported from Salinas after his sixth trip to the United States. The faces of Savedra-Leiva, Angulo-López, and Reyes-Padilla might well have been found among those in a high school yearbook but instead appeared in mug shots taken by the Salinas INS office (fig. 3.3), reminding viewers that many young Mexicans did not experience a childhood but were instead forced into the undocumented migrant stream and criminalized at an early age.[13]

Some migrants were apprehended in Salinas after only days or weeks in the United States, but others succeeded in staying for several months or years undetected. Migrants' most common strategy was to obtain false documents. After crawling through a fence at Nogales, Arizona, in June 1952, Gustavo Ramírez-García sought out a local priest, who sold him a baptismal certificate in the name of Francisco Ramírez-Escarzaga. Ramírez-García was able to obtain a social security card and driver's license and register for military service under his assumed name. After presenting these documents to immigration officials in Porterville, Delano, Visalia, Sacramento, and Watsonville in California, he was finally arrested and deported from Salinas in October 1954. Gilberto Román-Méndez impersonated one Antonio Morales-Herrera from Los Angeles. José Gonzáles-Cisneros pretended to be Antonio Aguirre-Mata from Chicago. Trinidad Hernandez-Soto presented the birth certificate of a Jesus Rodríguez-González born in Nebraska upon his apprehension. José Rueda-Medina identified as Raoul Patrick Barajas-Velasquez from San Francisco. Maria Estela Jimenez Arce, who was trying to join her mother, grandmother, and sister in the United States, used the birth certificate of a Margarita Terrango that she obtained from a friend in Mexico. All six were deported.[14]

In other cases, false documents were not enough to keep a migrant safe from suspicion. Sacramento Ferrel-Rodríguez, age twenty-four, stole the identity of his U.S.-born cousin Uvense, acquiring a copy of his birth certificate and registering with the U.S. military under the same name. Ferrel-Rodríguez then married U.S. citizen and Salinas Valley resident Gerada Contreras, with whom he had a daughter. In his frequent trips back to Mexico to visit his mother, he continued to claim his cousin's identity, fooling immigration officers in Delano, San Diego,

Fig. 3.3. Deported youths Raul Savedra-Leiva (above), Ernesto Angulo-López (right), and Enrique Reyes-Padilla (facing page). (Salinas INS Sub-Office Files, National Archives and Records Administration, San Bruno, California)

and Soledad for two years before Salinas INS officers received anonymous information that Ferrel-Rodríguez was not a U.S. citizen. After a short period of interrogation, he admitted the truth. "I knew it was against the law to say that I was a citizen of the United States and use my cousin's name and birth certificate," he told Salinas INS officers,

Fig. 3.3. (*continued*)

"[but] I thought that no one would discover me and that I could have a good life."[15] The anonymous informant—perhaps his employer, someone with a grudge, or the real Uvense himself—singlehandedly destroyed Ferrel-Rodríguez's artifice of U.S. citizenship. When he said "I thought that no one would discover me," he implied that he made great effort to "belong" in the United States. Performing the role of a U.S. citizen required various props. One could carry documents such as a birth certificate or driver's license to assert an "American" identity, but one could also carry other markers of belonging, such as the ability to speak English or evidence of "American" material consumption. Braceros, and likely undocumented migrants as well, placed high importance on how they dressed and bought cowboy boots, hats, radios, and other commodities that helped them fit in with locals.

No doubt some Mexican Americans, frustrated with being racially conflated with "wetbacks," alerted the INS of undocumented migrants' presence in order to assert their own identity as law-abiding U.S. citizens. In other cases, it was Mexican families themselves who notified the INS of their relatives' presence in the United States. Ignacio Farias Mora's parents, for example, informed Salinas INS officers by mail that their son was living in Salinas illegally and asked for him to be sent back to Guadalajara. In revealing interviews he conducted with 493 "wetbacks" during their deportation processing, University of Notre Dame professor Julian Samora found that at least 17 percent of his sample was reported to immigration officials by a Mexican American, Mexican national, friend, or relative. Despite communication networks that allowed them to know which migration routes worked best or how to acquire false documents, some undocumented migrants found that the social networks they created with Mexican Americans in *el norte,* or preserved with their families in Mexico, could at times work against them.[16]

In addition to undocumented migrants, INS officers had to patrol the high number of bracero "skips" who chose to leave their employers and become "wetbacks" themselves. Braceros and undocumented immigrants were often envious of each other's positions and believed the grass was greener on the other side. Undocumented immigrants who did not have the patience for or faith in the bracero contracting system crossed the border in hopes of blending in with braceros in the fields or being regularized by the INS as a bracero with a work contract. Meanwhile, a bracero tied to an exploitative employer envied the freedom of movement a "wetback" had in leaving an undesirable work situation and seeking better wages and conditions elsewhere. An INS report covering the brief period of January 30 to February 25, 1952, showed that 485 of 1,115 apprehended undocumented Mexicans were "abscondees from agricultural contracts." In 1953 a total of 7,547 California braceros skipped, with 916 of them fleeing from the Salinas Valley Growers Farm Labor Association (GFLA), which employed 5,659 braceros at the time. This percentage of skips (16 percent) was the highest found in any growers association in the nation, even though the Imperial Valley employed twice as many braceros at this time.[17]

As skips began drawing more media attention on both sides of the border, the INS knew it had to persuade the American public that it was performing its job correctly. If braceros continued to act out their dissatisfaction and choose illegality as the preferable identity, it not only would be embarrassing to the country but would threaten the continuation of the Bracero Program. Future program renewals depended on the U.S. government proving, to its citizens and to Mexico, that the

Table 3.1. Braceros contracted and undocumented
migrants apprehended, 1951–1964

Year	Braceros contracted	Undocumented migrants apprehended
1951	190,745	500,628
1952	197,100	543,538
1953	201,380	875,318
1954	309,033	1,075,168
1955	398,650	242,698
1956	445,197	72,442
1957	436,049	44,451
1958	432,857	37,242
1959	437,643	30,196
1960	315,846	29,651
1961	291,420	29,877
1962	194,978	30,272
1963	186,865	39,124
1964	177,736	43,844

Bracero Program was a regulated and effective solution to the illegal immigration problem. Operation Wetback was designed to both create and allay fears about permeable borders, and with each published roster of INS deportations the Bracero Program gained traction as the preferred method for employers to hire Mexican labor legally. When the U.S. government secured a renewal of Public Law 78 in 1955, the INS began publicly declaring that it had eliminated the "wetback" problem and scaled down its efforts (table 3.1). By 1957, Operation Wetback had fizzled.

MEXICAN AMERICAN–MEXICAN RELATIONSHIPS
IN THE TIME OF OPERATION WETBACK

Though many Mexican Americans toiled alongside braceros and undocumented migrants in the fields, others kept a social distance from Mexican nationals for fear of harsher discrimination than they already experienced. Racially restrictive covenants still kept Mexican Americans from living in certain neighborhoods, positions in local government or law enforcement remained closed to them, and children experienced segregation and racism in their schools. Even the son of Ben López, who claimed the closest relationship a Mexican American could with the white grower elite of Salinas when he accepted the position of GFLA director in 1947, remembered his high school teachers and counselors dismissing his dreams of becoming a lawyer or teacher and telling him instead that he would make a better plumber. Darker skin color only amplified some Mexican Americans' mistreatment. One group of young women complained that those who looked the "most white" obtained secretarial and clerical jobs while darker-skinned "Mexican-looking" ones were hired only by fruit and vegetable packing sheds. A Mexican American storeowner recounted the poor service he received at a Salinas bank simply because of his physical appearance: "It was late and I had been working in my old clothes taking stock inventory. I didn't have time to go home so I had to drive over in my old truck. When I got to the bank, I couldn't get anybody to wait on me—even though I had an appointment. It was the clothes. They thought I was just another Mexican."[18] Resentful of being viewed as "just another Mexican," this man and others sought rights and respectability as Mexican *Americans* that clashed with the social reality of being treated as simply *Mexicans*.

In the agricultural world, Mexican Americans' resentment of Mexican nationals (or at least their desire to distinguish themselves from them) manifested in working relationships in the fields. Although field manager and irrigator positions remained largely in the hands of whites and Filipinos, some Mexican Americans had worked their way into foreman, driver, labor contractor, and camp operator positions by the 1950s because their bilingualism made them useful intermediaries between workers and management. In these supervisory roles, Mexican Americans claimed a higher status, salary, and degree of authority over braceros (fig. 3.4). Some Mexican Americans used this power to form positive relationships with their bracero crews while others did the opposite. Rodolfo Jacobo Páramo remembered: "Some of the foremen would yell at us to bend back down if we stopped to stretch our backs . . . They said that they wanted to see us bend like staples." Oaxacan-born bracero Ismael Nicolás Osorio, who worked in Arizona, Texas, Colorado, and Washington before going to the Salinas Valley, remembered that some Mexican American foremen refused to

Fig. 3.4. A bracero picks lettuce while a Mexican American foreman watches him in a Salinas Valley field, 1956. (Courtesy of Leonard Nadel Bracero Photographs, Archives Center, National Museum of American History, Smithsonian Institution)

communicate with braceros in their shared language of Spanish. He admitted to once breaking down in tears because of the foremen's harsh commands and propensity to "treat us like animals."[19] Language, rather than serving as something that bonded people together, was sometimes used to divide people in the agricultural labor system.

To Mexican Americans who remained in the agricultural working class, braceros seemed a threat to their economic survival. Grower-employers had taken advantage of the INS's I-100 program, which allowed braceros to be recontracted for work without having to return to Mexican recruitment centers, as well as the "Specials" program, which had begun in the summer of 1954. "Specials" were supposed to be well-performing workers possessing specialized experience for a specific job, but employers often applied the label "special" to any bracero they wished to retain. In the Salinas Valley, many domestic farmworkers found themselves being fired and replaced with bracero crews. Women were particularly vulnerable to displacement because employers believed braceros to be physically stronger. "When I worked out in the fields," Annie Saldívar remembered, "I only got to work maybe about a month out of the year because . . . whenever the Mexicans would come from Mexico, they would lay us off." Even if a farmworker was willing to migrate and "follow the fruit" around the country for different harvest seasons, he or she found only a fraction of the employment that a bracero did. Furthermore, the average hourly wage of farmwork in the United States in 1954 was only 37 percent of that of industrial work. Many frustrated farmworkers began making the move from field to factory, including some Mexican Americans in Salinas who took jobs at new plants of the Firestone, Nestlé, and Smuckers companies.[20]

Packing shed workers, who included Mexican Americans but also "Okies" and people of Italian descent, were another group disgruntled by the Bracero Program. By the 1950s the Salinas Valley was the world's largest producer of table vegetables and supplied almost half of the U.S. head lettuce crop. To accelerate produce shipments, growers turned to the new technology pioneered by Bruce Church and Lester "Bud" Antle called vacuum cooling. Instead of being packed in cardboard boxes to be placed in crates with ice, freshly cut heads of lettuce would be packed and then placed in a vacuum cooler that would cool the leaves quickly, eliminate air, and prevent rot. It did not take long for growers to realize that they could make braceros pick lettuce and then pack it directly after in the fields. Whereas shed employees had earned between $1.32 and $1.67 an hour for trimming, weighing, wrapping, and grading produce, braceros were being paid less than 88 cents an hour to do all of this as well as picking the produce. By the summer of 1954, displaced shed workers made up 65 percent of the three thousand unemployed people in Salinas, and many of these workers traveled to Sacramento with CIO Local 78 of the United Packinghouse Workers of America (UPWA) to protest. Elsewhere in California, unemployed farmworkers were complaining about other grower-employer practices. After being told to apply for farmwork at their local Farm Placement Office, domestics were often given referral slips that misdirected them to work assignments or sent them to fields where bracero crews had already completed the work. "American citizens cannot get work . . . The wetbacks and [braceros] have the whole Imperial Valley," two southern California workers testified at a hearing of the President's Commission on Migratory Labor in 1952. "Men who fought in the South Pacific and Europe in World War II are turned away from the fields and packing sheds because growers, shippers and Mexican contractors prefer crews of illegals and Nationals [braceros]," added the National Farm Labor Union (NFLU).[21] Feeling betrayed by a federal government that continually extended the Bracero Program, U.S. farmworkers of every ethnic background expressed their hostility to bracero and undocumented Mexican labor.

In the midst of these tensions, there were occasional but significant moments when the Salinas Valley's Mexican American and Mexican communities came together. The construction of Salinas's first "Mexican" Catholic church, Cristo Rey (Christ the King), was one of these moments. In the early 1950s almost half of the population of incorporated Salinas (fourteen thousand) identified as Catholic. Sacred Heart Catholic Church was the most popular of the three Catholic churches in town and claimed a diverse congregation of whites, Mexican Americans, braceros, and Filipinos worshipping under Irish priest Patrick O'Connor. With its multicultural congregation Sacred Heart seemed to be a place of welcoming, but racial barriers and discrimination persisted within its walls. Mexican Americans and braceros customarily sat in the rear pews or stood against the back wall during mass and endured constant "suggestions" from white clergy and congregants that they might be happier in their "own" church. Sacred Heart churchgoer and GFLA director Ben López took individual action by allowing traveling missionaries and priests to minister to braceros in their camps and mobilizing a group of Mexican Americans to help build a bracero chapel at Camp McCallum to hold Spanish-language masses. Yet Mexican Americans and braceros wanted their own church in town, a place of faith where they would not be excluded on the basis of their national origin. Aided by a land grant from a donor, Mexican Americans and braceros began pooling resources to construct Cristo Rey. Braceros made particularly large financial donations and shipped in materials from Mexico, including stained glass windows and a statue of the female patron saint the Virgin of Guadalupe. "Their money made that church," Salinas resident Catalina Alvarez remarked. Cristo Rey opened its doors in December 1951, and Peruvian priest Humberto Hermosa led one weekday and three Sunday Spanish-language masses every week attended by hundreds of braceros, Tejano migrant workers, and local Mexican Americans (fig. 3.5). A group of Mexicana women cooked breakfast after each mass so that congregants could mingle.[22] Cristo Rey continued to be a religious and social hub for the Spanish-speaking community throughout the twentieth century and stood as

Fig. 3.5. Father Humberto Hermosa with a group of braceros in front of Cristo Rey Church in Salinas, California, November 1952. (Photo by Bayard Rucker. California Department of Employment Records, University of California at Davis Special Collections)

Fig. 3.6. Bracero Ismael Nicolás Osorio and his wife Lucina, who wed at Cristo
Rey Church soon after its founding. The two were both born in Jalisco, Mexico,
but met in the United States. (Courtesy of Lucina Ruiz de Nicolás)

a significant act of unity between Mexican Americans and Mexican
nationals (fig. 3.6).

Outside of the sphere of Catholicism and Cristo Rey, a transnational
mentality influenced the individual actions of Mexican American Salinas Valley residents who reached out to Mexican nationals during

the 1950s. Jose Enrique Friedrich was born in Mexico City in 1903 and moved to California as a young man to join his brother who was already living there. Though Jose had earned a law degree in Mexico, his undocumented status meant he had to take on jobs such as washing dishes at a Los Angeles drive-in and selling products door-to-door along the California coast. After meeting the woman who would become his wife, he moved to the Salinas Valley and became a bracero camp contractor. In the process of housing and feeding braceros, Jose developed a sense of kinship with these men who were, like him, Mexican and in search of a respectable living in the United States. "He knew why they were there," Jose's son Robert mused. "They needed the money for their families . . . yet they were not respected; they were looked down upon." It was true that braceros were sending much of their money home—in 1952 the Mexican newspapers *Excélsior* and *Las Ultimas Noticias* reported that bracero remittances totaled $30 million and constituted Mexico's third largest source of income after mining and tourism—but Jose knew that braceros wished to participate in local consumer culture. As he had acquaintances in Los Angeles who distributed Mexican films, Jose pursued the idea of building a Spanish-language movie theater for braceros in Salinas. He began with pop-up theaters at ranches, a local Buddhist temple hall, and a gymnasium, where he showed 16-millimeter films and charged nickels and dimes for admission. When he finally built the Plaza Theater on Pajaro Street in the early 1950s, it became a "little gold mine" popular with Mexicans and Mexican Americans alike and held showings from morning until night (fig. 3.7). Through his theater, Jose not only made braceros feel welcome in Salinas but gave safe haven to undocumented immigrants at certain times. During INS street raids Jose would inform his patrons, "If you're here illegally, don't leave." He would then close up the theater for the night, say a passing goodbye to lingering INS officers, and return in an hour to help those hiding inside escape through a back door. "He would help the guys stay one step ahead," Robert remarked. "A whole lot had to do with how he was treated when he first came to this country, where all of a sudden his education didn't mean squat . . . I know those things had to have really cut him and had a great deal to do with how he felt about immigration issues." In addition to his work in the theater, Jose helped at least fifty Mexican men bring their families legally into the United States through his knowledge of the law.[23]

Fig. 3.7. Braceros line up in front of the Plaza Theater, 1956. (Courtesy of Leonard Nadel Bracero Photographs, Archives Center, National Museum of American History, Smithsonian Institution)

The entity of the family was another way in which the lives of Mexican Americans and Mexicans were intertwined. Circuits of migration and social interaction produced romantic relationships and families between the two groups, and parentage and marriage bound citizens to noncitizens. The theme of romantic connection between Mexican men and U.S.-born women was particularly prevalent at this time, with songs like "El Bracero y La Pachuca" describing romances between braceros and Mexican American women, while films such as *Pito Pérez se va de Bracero* (Pito Pérez Becomes a Bracero, 1947), *Espalda Mojada* (Wetback, 1952), and *El Fronterizo* (The Border Man, 1952) all featured migrant protagonists tempted by U.S.-born women whom they met in dancehalls, bars, and brothels. Eulalio Gonzáles's *corrido* "Natalio Reyes Colás" ("Nat King Cole") used wry humor to describe how a bracero named Natalio quickly Americanized his name and himself after meeting a Mexican American woman.[24]

Though Salinas's position as a Bracero Program hub made the town a male-dominated space, it was often Mexican American women who experienced the closest connections with braceros and undocumented

Mexican men. Some Mexican American women grew up being prohibited from dating Mexican men by their parents, who might have held prejudices against noncitizens or believed that these men were financially unstable womanizers who saw marriage as a way to remain in the United States. Mexican American women discussed the matter with each other as they socialized or worked alongside each other in fields, restaurants, or packing sheds. Rose Castillo Guilbault remembered her mother being told by a family friend upon their arrival in the Salinas Valley: "You must marry an American. It's your best chance for a good life . . . all the Mexican men here are braceros. There's no future for someone like you with one." Oftentimes against the advice of friends or family, Mexican American women engaged in friendships, sexual relations, or romantic partnerships with braceros as well as undocumented men. During Operation Wetback, however, a relationship with an undocumented immigrant could have serious consequences upon one's heart and family, as deportation files show. When he was deported from Salinas in 1954 for reentering the United States after his bracero contract expired, Guadalupe González-Chávez left behind a local woman with whom he had been living. A Salinas woman bore three of Roberto Mendoza-Martínez's children before losing him to deportation. Rafael Ramírez-Trujillo had to leave his pregnant U.S.-born wife in Salinas after being apprehended by immigration authorities.[25]

The life story of one Salinas woman, Catalina Alvarez, showcases the multiple relationships that Mexican American women cultivated with braceros and undocumented Mexican migrants.[26] Born in Texas, Alvarez moved to Salinas with her husband and five children in 1955 in search of better work opportunities. She eventually found work in a Salinas strawberry field earning 95 cents an hour alongside three hundred braceros, a few other Mexican American women, a Filipino couple, and some Tejano migrant families. When Alvarez's boss discovered she was bilingual, he promoted her to translator and berry inspector with a salary of $1.50 an hour. In this supervisorial position, Alvarez confronted traditional gender roles and men who tried to resist her authority in the fields. Some braceros audibly complained that she was too strict, while male cooks and contractors became angry with her if she asserted that braceros' food was not satisfactory. "I had some scary moments . . . I thought [one man] was going to hit me because I was being *metiche* [meddling]," she recalled. Alvarez was not safe from conflict at home either as her husband grew increasingly jealous of how much time she spent with braceros. Like some other Mexican American men, he viewed braceros as thieves of local jobs and local women. The couple eventually separated, and Catalina accepted some braceros' offers to visit them and their families in Mexico after the harvest season. She delighted in witnessing the success of braceros who had opened grocery stores, Laundromats, and taxi services in Mexico with their program earnings. Conversely, Alvarez saw the poverty that pushed others to fight for bracero contracts again and again. "It was heartbreaking for me to see why they would come," she said, recalling a visit to a bracero, his wife, and six children in Morelia, Michoacán, during which the family gave her their single bed while they all slept on the floor. Although she was the daughter of two Mexican immigrants, Alvarez realized what privileges her U.S. citizenship gave her only after she saw the Bracero Program from the other side of the border.

Back in the United States, Alvarez confronted the traumatic consequences of the program's lack of regulation and attention to braceros' well-being. For instance, she had to rush a bracero to the hospital for a ruptured appendix when their employer refused to call for a doctor, and in June 1958 she was called to the town of Soledad to identify the remains of fourteen braceros from her crew after their labor bus caught fire from a cigarette and chains tied on the outside of the bus's back doors prevented the men from escaping. Eventually, through her job, Alvarez became romantically involved with a bracero whom she identified only as 208 (his work number). "We didn't have anything in common, I was the boss and he was the worker," she said, but 208 was determined to impress Alvarez by rushing to pick berries and frequently visiting her checking table. After overhearing another worker invite Alvarez to a dance in Watsonville, 208 borrowed pants and shoes from other braceros and arranged a ride to the dance to surprise her there. A romantic relationship lasted between the two for thirty years, and Alvarez accompanied 208 back to Mexico after every harvest season to help him cultivate land he purchased with his program earnings. After 208 suddenly abandoned Alvarez, she became romantically involved with a Mexican immigrant working in Salinas, helping him raise the two children he had brought to the United States. Reflecting on her personal bonds with braceros and Mexican immigrants, Alvarez considered herself exceptional in an environment hostile to Mexican men. "[The 1950s were] a time where these men [braceros] stayed by themselves," she said. "They were kept out of town . . . Very few people were like me [and] knew they were human." During a time when cross-national relationships were fraught with divisions and risks, Alvarez and other Mexican American women became border-crossers who gained intimate knowledge of Mexican men, including and beyond the romantic.

WANTED AS LABOR BUT NOT AS NEIGHBORS: BRACEROS AS A PATHOGENIC PROLETARIAT

After Operation Wetback, another important flashpoint that heightened tensions between Mexican Americans and Mexicans was the peak of the Bracero Program in 1956, when U.S. employers imported the largest annual number of braceros (445,197) to date. Whereas braceros comprised only 16 percent of all farmworkers in the United States in 1950, they made up 52 percent by 1956. Meanwhile, in Monterey County, braceros went from being 4 percent of all seasonal farm labor in 1950 to 63 percent by 1956. On other side of the border, people were noticing the Bracero Program's large drain on the Mexican citizenry. Articles from Oaxaca's daily newspaper *El Imparcial* in 1956, for example, bemoaned the "exodus" of thousands of *aspirantes* searching for the "vellocino de oro" (golden fleece) in the United States. In reality, braceros were finding nothing golden in *el norte*. Under Public Law 78 the ordering and distribution of braceros now fell under the Farm Placement Service, a grower-controlled agency, rather than the U.S. Farm Security Administration. Grower-employers were now responsible for paying for braceros' transportation, food, and lodging instead of the U.S. government. With this administrative shift, abuses against braceros increased significantly. In Texas, a labor contractor (and local judge) was caught serving braceros meat that had been imported into the United States as dog food. In Arkansas, a bracero complained to the Mexican newspaper *La Voz de Mexico* about his and other braceros' "miserable salaries" and the "pigpens" in which they were forced to sleep. Thousands of braceros continued to skip out on their contracts, and in California, the Salinas Valley GFLA continued to have the highest percentage of skips in the entire state.[27]

Braceros pushed back against their mistreatment by filing thousands of formal complaints with Bureau of Employment Security compliance representatives, bracero reception center officials, Mexican consuls, U.S. labor union representatives, and the INS during the 1950s. These complaints concerned a range of violations, including low wages and illegal paycheck deductions, substandard food and housing, abuse by foremen, and employers' use of undocumented labor. The resulting investigations revealed that employers nationwide had underpaid or wrongfully deducted hundreds of thousands of dollars from braceros and that a disturbingly high number of bracero transportation vehicles violated safety standards. On average, half of the complaints braceros made were substantiated by investigators and remedied. In the Salinas Valley, bracero Vicente Perez-Munoz succeeded in having his physically abusive foreman removed from his position while another group of braceros received an apology from their foreman after reporting that he called them *cabrones* (bastards) when they complained about the unsatisfactory meals in their labor camp. In addition to filing complaints, some braceros sought membership in U.S. labor unions such as the NFLU or the National Agricultural Workers Union (NAWU) to strike with domestics for better working conditions. Because Public Law 78 prohibited braceros from unionizing, however, employers could deem such strikes invalid. Some braceros found that even an interest in unionization automatically placed a target on their backs. Salinas Valley bracero Francisco Hernandez Cano had his contract terminated for wearing a union button, but after his compatriots paid for a bus ticket to Washington, D.C., Cano made a last-ditch effort to complain about their working conditions to a Mexican ambassador and a U.S. Department of Labor representative. The Bureau of Employment Security opened an investigation, but it is not clear whether any improvements were demanded of the braceros' employers. Cano returned to Mexico and later reentered the United States as a bracero but used a different name to disguise his "agitator" past, again demonstrating how a culture of surveillance and hostility to labor activism during the 1950s constrained the lives of farmworkers.[28]

For all the dangers and violations they encountered as guestworkers in the United States, braceros were constructed as the dangerous ones—racially and sexually—as their numbers peaked in 1956. Braceros knew they had been contracted for their bodies but quickly found that locals wanted their bodies to stay in the fields and not to come in contact with them. The idea that Mexican migrants were a pathogenic proletariat bringing dirt and disease across the border had existed for some time, but during the 1950s braceros came to embody the threat of sexual deviance and sexually transmitted disease. In the Salinas Valley, locals and the media characterized bracero camps as unhygienic, disordered all-male spaces lacking the structure of the idealized 1950s nuclear family. What they failed to acknowledge was agribusiness's role in requesting single men instead of families and creating such crowded and unsanitary living quarters. Newspapers jumped to publish stories about bracero camps as dens of criminal activity ranging from marijuana dealing to violent altercations, and spatial associations between braceros and the "red-light" district of Chinatown led to assumptions about braceros' promiscuity and lack of morals. The Catholic Church joined in the conversation, arguing that the Bracero Program tore Mexican families apart and exploited men so much that they lost spiritual fortitude in the face of temptations such as gambling, alcohol, and women.[29]

This notion that braceros were inherently prone to making poor moral and sexual decisions led to the beginning of venereal disease testing in 1953 at bracero reception centers along the border by the Communicable Disease Center (later the Centers for Disease Control and Prevention). Initially, this testing proved a lengthy process. By the time results were wired back from laboratories, braceros were already at work in the fields and had to be tracked down for penicillin treatment. When a rapid blood plasma test that could deliver results on-site was instituted in 1957, braceros began receiving penicillin treatment at reception centers at a cost of sixty cents per worker billed to grower-employers. Across all five centers, between 6 and 7 percent of braceros received this treatment, but at California's El Centro center, nearly 10 percent of entering braceros tested positive for venereal disease. This heightened association between Mexicanness, maleness, and sexual contagion only created more anxiety in those who already saw the Mexican migrant body as problematic in the 1950s. In Monterey County, officials blamed the high venereal disease rate on the eighteen thousand braceros who had worked in the county's lettuce and strawberry fields the previous year, and UPWA representative Bud Simonson wrote in a letter to Senator Hubert Humphrey that braceros were "largely responsible for corrupting the morals and health of the girls" of the Salinas Valley.[30] Pathologizing braceros as sexual predators and their bodies as vectors of disease, media and residents linked Mexicanness, masculinity, and danger.

Constructed as a gendered "social problem," braceros seemed all the more threatening when U.S. grower-employers imported close to half a million of them in 1956. Out of the 187,861 contracted to work in California, the town of Salinas absorbed 11,294 (a significant addition to the town's 21,133 residents) and scrambled to find a housing solution. When growers proposed building bracero camps in residential areas, protests erupted from homeowners who argued that the camps would be "eyesores," lower property values, and corrupt community morals. Resident Sally Gutíerrez remembered that "the locals, and Mexican [American]s too, objected to having the braceros close to where families lived because they were all single men. They didn't want them close to the children and things like that." Numerous people attended City Planning Commission meetings to oppose bracero camp construction. Citing braceros' drinking and carousing, one housewife asked, "Will we have to lock our homes?" while another complained about "not being able to walk on the streets without being embarrassed by single men." The commission ultimately approved only two forms of bracero housing—a group of tents and a fenced-in camp—but rejected all other proposed camps and declared them a "moral hazard to children" and "too close for comfort." With this, braceros were characterized as not only hypersexual but pedophiliac and criminal. Labor camp operators continued to propose new bracero facilities, but residents kept protesting, as well as some local clergy members. Expressing "great concern" about the high concentration of foreign workers and labor camps, the Salinas Ministerial Association wrote in a letter, "We believe this constitutes a threat in a number of ways . . . [to] women and children . . . if these men spent leisure time walking about our areas." The letter continued that since bracero camps would only increase "racial tension and other destructive forces," all future camps should be located "in an uninhabited area of this county." Braceros were dangerous and needed to be confined to the margins, the association argued, but not completely eliminated for labor reasons.[31]

As they witnessed the virulent opposition to integrating braceros into community life, Mexican Americans in Salinas were painfully aware of how their racial status subjected them to similar scrutiny and discrimination. Some Mexican Americans made efforts to defend braceros' characters and in the process defend themselves as people of Mexican descent. When labor camp contractor Valentina Reyes proposed the construction of a six-hundred-bracero facility inside Salinas city limits, for example, dozens of Mexican Americans signed a petition circulated by Rev. Humberto Hermosa of Cristo Rey Church in support of the camp. The very fact that braceros had helped build Cristo Rey with their hard-earned money, the petition attempted to remind the city, stood as proof of the men's religiosity and respectability. The City Council ultimately rejected Reyes's permit, but Mexican Americans continued to be vocal at subsequent hearings. When the City Council approved the expansion of two labor camps in south Salinas in February 1957, local residents sent 113 letters in protest and appeared in person to complain. Owners of an apartment complex argued that their tenants in the army and navy could no longer leave their wives at home alone, and one man added that police would not be able to control the "biological urges of men." Louis John Valenzuela, a self-professed representative of "the Mexican people of Salinas," then asked white protestors why they would object to his walking in front of their houses. County Commissioner Chet Ramsey quickly responded that the issue "was not a racial one," and others replied that it was "the concentration of single or married men away from their families" that was problematic.[32] Using gender instead of race to justify their opposition, the protestors probably did not persuade Valenzuela and others who were well aware that it was *Mexican* men, not all men, who had been historically characterized as hypersexual deviants.

Meanwhile, there were Mexican Americans joining the anti-bracero camp faction. Some did so out of fear that their image as respectable citizens would be destroyed by whites racially associating them with braceros. Others, including members of the Salinas chapter of the CSO (founded in 1954), opposed bracero camps because of the corruption behind their construction. The organization discovered that Monterey County Housing Authority director Eleanor Walters had embezzled money and evicted numerous Mexican American residents from low-income housing in order to sell the property to bracero contractors and camp operators. The CSO gathered enough evidence against Walters to have her imprisoned in 1957. While the Salinas CSO's actions targeted those depriving Mexican Americans of housing and not braceros themselves, its members showed no desire to include braceros in their social or political world. This was also evident in the national CSO leadership. In a 1958 letter to California Republican senator Thomas Kuchel, CSO officer Tony Rios expressed the organization's opposition to the

Bracero Program because "our members have seen the deterioration of the economic, social, and *moral* life of communities where the Bracero Program is in effect."[33] During the 1950s many Mexican Americans felt that their rights of citizenship and respectability were tenuous, and for this reason they kept braceros on the other side of the figurative border between citizens and noncitizens that had hardened in Cold War America.

A strengthened Bracero Program working in tandem with heightened border surveillance and national "wetback" paranoia pulled Mexican Americans, braceros, and undocumented migrants apart, holding them in a triangulated tension that left them all socially, economically, and politically vulnerable. In agricultural communities where the Bracero Program and undocumented immigration placed a tremendous weight on the workings of local economics and politics, Mexican Americans and Mexicans experienced complex and strained relationships on the ground. To Mexican Americans, the "wetback problem" and renewal of the Bracero Program felt like a binational betrayal that depressed wages in agriculture and perpetuated the association between Mexicanness and marginality. Braceros felt betrayed by the lack of provisions in Public Law 78 for their sustenance and safety and did not feel welcome in communities that characterized them as sexually dangerous and undesirable neighbors. Undocumented immigrants gained little sympathy from both Mexican Americans and braceros as the workers at the bottom of the agricultural labor hierarchy. This is not to say that meaningful relationships were never formed; this certainly happened at particular moments and on individual levels. But in an agricultural hub like the Salinas Valley, Mexican Americans viewed a continuous infusion of Mexican newcomers as a complication to their civil rights struggles. Defending themselves *and* their migrant counterparts seemed a daunting, perhaps even self-destructive, task in a Cold War climate that emphasized "Americanness" and good citizenship. During the 1950s and 1960s Mexican Americans would gravitate to civic action groups to present their proof of both of these things. The Los Angeles–based CSO, which had become the most prominent Mexican American civil rights organization in California by midcentury, seemed a promising avenue for the political empowerment and social acceptance that so many people desperately wanted.

4 The Community Service Organization, 1953–1963

THE COMMUNITY SERVICE Organization, the first Mexican American civil rights organization in the Salinas Valley, was founded after two rival groups of students at King City High School—one Mexicano and one white—decided to battle each other on a summer night in 1953. Bad blood had existed between the groups for some time, manifested in dirty looks and insults exchanged in school hallways. Though racial segregation was commonplace in primary schools, high schools were racially integrated and for many students the first place where they regularly encountered others of different backgrounds. Alex Zermeño, who attended primary school with Mexicano and "Okie" students of his socioeconomic class, remembered that when he arrived at Salinas High School in 1953 there was noticeable class and racial tension. "I got a bit of wetback jokes and stuff like that," he said. Peter Crawford, who attended King City High School during the mid-1950s, agreed that "there was still a latent kind of tension" between the Anglo and Mexican American student bodies.[1]

On the night of August 27 the rival groups rendezvoused at Pine Canyon near King City. Some of the youths' parents and friends knew about the planned fight but did nothing to stop it. When the group of sixteen Mexicano boys arrived at the canyon, they were surprised to find eight parked cars and thirty white youths, including many members of the school's football team and their female companions, waiting for them. Realizing they were outnumbered, the boys fled back to their three cars and drove away, only to be chased by the others. One of the lead cars crashed into a small bridge, prompting the occupants of every car to climb out with weapons such as baseball bats, bicycle and harvesting machine chains, shovel handles, pieces of pipe, and knives. With only car headlights punctuating the darkness, the youths could not clearly see who they were attacking, or who was attacking them. Struck in the head with a bicycle chain, nineteen-year-old farmworker Santiago "Jimmy" Ortiz reacted by slashing a knife in the direction of his assumed attacker. A few moments later, the fight ended when someone noticed the body of seventeen-year-old football player Max Montalbetti lying in a pool of blood with a stab wound to the heart. He was rushed to a hospital and pronounced dead on arrival. That night the Salinas sheriff and district attorney interviewed thirty-five of the youths and held fourteen in jail for further questioning. Authorities interrogated Ortiz alone for twenty hours until he admitted he had used a knife during the fight. Claiming self-defense, Ortiz could not confirm whether Montalbetti was the person he blindly attacked. Ortiz was the only one charged with Montalbetti's murder. The others were charged with rioting by the Juvenile Department of the Superior Court in Salinas, with a court hearing scheduled to determine punishment. All parents of those involved received citations for failing to prevent the incident.[2]

In the Salinas Valley media, the fight and Montalbetti's death immediately became events marked by race. "Involved in the initial fight were a Mexican descent boy of King City and a Greenfield youth," the *Salinas Californian* stated, racially tagging Ortiz while giving Montalbetti a normative "youth" identity for being a white boy of Swiss Italian descent. Other newspapers followed suit by labeling the two rivals as a group of "Mexican boys" versus an "American" or "high school" group, attributing U.S. citizenship and student status to the white youths while stripping their Mexican American counterparts of both. Also highlighted was the class contrast between Ortiz, a "ranch hand" and "laborer" who was presumably no longer a student, and Montalbetti, a rising football star. Newspapers' racialized language and sensationalistic portrayal of the fight as a "gang war" and "riot" greatly affected public perceptions of the event. The day after news of Montalbetti's death emerged, a "prominent" white woman in the Salinas Valley town of San Lucas walked into a local business exclaiming that all the "dirty Mexicans should be kicked out to where they belong." A letter to the editor of the *Soledad Bee* responded to the anti-Mexican vitriol of this woman and others who were "using this tragedy to vent their race hatred on the Mexican people," affirming that "these hate breeders should look around and see how many of our boys have gone to war . . . both gangs were equally to blame." Others blasted media giants like the *San Francisco Chronicle* for making the "Mexican" identity of some of the youths so salient in their coverage. "Some of the other boys who participated in the fight . . . are obviously of foreign extraction also. However, no mention of their ancestry is made," a Cupertino couple wrote to the newspaper. Another person added, "Many people of Mexican origin who have proven themselves good citizens, and who are fully respected, are constantly being offended by such articles that create a discriminative attitude." These two letters prompted the *Chronicle*'s editor to acknowledge that the article's emphasis on some of the participants' Mexicanness was "perhaps erroneous."[3]

Amidst this polarizing media coverage, a group of Mexican Americans in Salinas came together over the King City incident. A close-knit circle of friends and relatives—husband and wife pairs Abelicio (Abe) and Anna Chávez, Albert and Cecilia Sánchez, Dean and Jennie Diaz, Manuel and Sophie Cásarez, and Gregorio and Consuelo Zermeño and their son Alex—collectively discussed the media's portrayal of the brawl. They also learned that Salinas authorities had prohibited Ortiz's parents from speaking to or visiting their son in jail and that the family lacked sufficient funds for a defense attorney. The group began soliciting donations for Ortiz's legal defense from the local Mexicano community. At Ortiz's preliminary hearing the Monterey County Grand Jury declined to indict him for murder, concluding that he had acted in self-defense and that the incident was largely due to poor parenting by the guardians of the youths involved.[4] Ortiz's exoneration was a tremendous victory for the Mexican American community.

The hearing for the other forty-five youths, however, proved more complicated and took place over three nights beginning September 2 in the Monterey County Board of Supervisors' chambers. The hearing was not open to the public, but the number of defendants, parents, and law enforcement officials present made it the largest juvenile court gathering in local history. On October 8 Judge Henry Jorgensen finally determined that "racial antagonism or race prejudice was the cause of the riot," adding that local "schools, homes and churches . . . failed to properly educate and train these youths to be good Americans." In a voice "occasionally choked with emotion" Jorgensen delivered sentences. One youth (not identified by nationality) was ordered deported while another received a ten-day sentence in the county jail. Nine received probation, and sixteen were dismissed. Jorgensen left those present in his courtroom with a final assertion that "one thing that will destroy America is racial intolerance." Clearly affected by this episode of violence between young people, Jorgensen made a rare statement about race relations in the Salinas Valley. The region had become increasingly diverse during and after World War II, but some residents had become more intolerant of this diversity.[5] Jorgensen's ruling also reflected a certain ethos of the early 1950s. Concerns about proving oneself to be a "good American" and good citizen went hand in hand with being aware of what one should not do or be—in other words, what could "destroy America." In a Cold War climate of heightened border surveillance, McCarthyism, and purging of left-wing "radical" labor or political activity, following the rules and demonstrating one's loyalty to home became essential.

It was in this context that Mexican Americans looked to civic-minded civil rights organizations to prove their good citizenship while making claims that they deserved equal treatment. Organizations such as the AGIF, founded in Texas in 1948, and the CSO, founded by Saul Alinsky–trained community organizer and West Coast director of the Industrial Areas Foundation Fred Ross in 1947, offered the opportunity to do both. By making activities like registering voters and "Americanizing" immigrants key parts of their agendas, the AGIF and CSO sought to show local and state authorities that they sought to do only good for their communities. It was this patriotic "American" image that allowed these organizations to survive during a time when efforts to create civil rights change were being severely limited.

By the early 1950s two organizations existed for Mexican-origin people in the Salinas Valley, but both focused on cultural preservation rather than civil rights. The Comité Cívico Mexicano hosted Mexican holiday celebrations, dances, beauty pageants, and blood drives. The Comisión Honorífica Mexicana, a Mexican Consulate–sponsored organization that emerged in the Southwest during the 1920s, encouraged loyalty to the "homeland" in similar celebrations and events. After the King City incident, those people who had fought for Ortiz's fair trial desired to effect greater change. Aware of the CSO, the group contacted Ross and asked for his help. Ross, CSO organizer Gene Lowry, and a young Cesar Chavez (who would officially be hired as a CSO organizer the next year) arrived in Salinas on December 10, 1953 to establish a chapter in Monterey County. Over the next ten years the chapter proceeded to register hundreds of voters, helped numerous Mexican immigrants obtain their U.S. citizenship, battled discrimination and police harassment cases, and opposed growers' attempts to convert low-income housing to bracero camps. As the first Mexican American civil rights organization in the Salinas Valley, the CSO provided an institutional locus of empowerment where there had been none.[6] The organization quickly branded itself as "respectable" and curried favor with local leaders who otherwise would have doubted the "Americanness" of Mexicano residents. Furthermore, it was the first organization that gave Mexican-origin women the opportunity to become more visible community organizers. Unlike its contemporaries LULAC and the AGIF, the CSO did not limit women's leadership and participation to auxiliaries. Women organized fund-raisers, registered voters, and served as witnesses in naturalization proceedings while keeping full-time jobs or caring for their families. Largely because the CSO was a family-centered organization and heavily populated by couples and relatives, women had the opportunity to build the organization from within and serve as its public representatives.

For all its success, however, the CSO limited its power in the Salinas Valley by failing to do four things: build a stable membership, involve the larger Mexicano community in its activism, create interracial alliances, and risk its "respectable" image. During the late 1950s the chapter split into two—one made up of residents from the town of Soledad who sought to confront local authorities directly about racial discrimination, and another made up of Salinas residents reluctant to do the same. Preferring to maneuver within established power structures rather than challenge them, Salinas CSOers eventually chose to concentrate on forming social rather than political community among Mexican Americans. These differences in political style and goals resulted in the demise of both chapters by the early 1960s. Respectability served as the draw, but also the downfall, of this important civil rights organization in the Salinas Valley.

Existing scholarly studies of the CSO have detailed its founding in southern California, its role in Edward Roybal's 1949 election to the Los Angeles City Council, and its function as a training ground for future leaders, including United Farm Workers union cofounders Cesar Chavez and Dolores Huerta. Stephen Pitti's examination of the San Jose CSO provides a rare look at the organization outside of southern California, but on the whole, existing literature provides little information about CSO chapters in rural or agriculture-centered communities, even though 70 percent of the CSO's membership was made up of agricultural workers in the mid-1950s.[7] This chapter examines how this organization of urban origin operated in the agriculture-centered environment of the Salinas Valley and ends with addressing how, on a wider state level, the CSO of California struggled to represent both its urban and rural constituencies. As debates over the Bracero Program and domestic farmworkers' suffering raged during the early 1960s, the question of whether California's Mexican American civil rights movement should stay in the cities or move into the fields became one the CSO could no longer ignore.

THE CSO'S BEGINNINGS

In establishing the Monterey County CSO, Fred Ross had to rely on techniques that helped him build the first CSO chapter in Los Angeles. Before moving there, Ross had served as a Farm Security Administration director of a migrant labor camp in Arvin, California; resettled Japanese American internees through the War Relocation Authority; and worked in Chicago with Saul Alinsky, whose Industrial Areas Foundation had become known for the "Back-of-the-Yards Neighborhood Council," a citizens' group dedicated to neighborhood improvement. Ross returned to California as West Coast director of the foundation in 1946 and met a group of Mexican Americans who were supporting one of their own in the 1947 Los Angeles City Council election. Thirty-five-year-old Edward Roybal ran for the Ninth District—a multiethnic district composed of Mexicanos, Asians, blacks, Jews, and other European immigrants—but lost because of low voter turnout. Ross, who had organized civic action organizations called Unity Leagues in the

Pomona Valley, sought to create a similar organization for the East Los Angeles neighborhood of Boyle Heights that would mobilize residents to become voters and citizens. In "house meetings" where neighbors gathered at each other's homes to hear about the CSO's purpose, Ross recruited five thousand new members in three months. Through door-to-door registration campaigns CSO volunteers registered fifteen thousand new voters, and when Roybal ran a second time for City Council in 1949, he won and became the first Mexican American councilman in Los Angeles since 1886.[8]

Though its initial purpose was voter registration and mobilization, the CSO crafted its mission statement and principles to encompass broader goals. In a pamphlet distributed to potential members, the CSO proclaimed itself "a self-help civic action agency" that sought to "promote inter-community harmony" and "protect, remedy and prevent violations of human and civil rights." During the early 1950s, the organization addressed problems plaguing Los Angeles that included school segregation, housing and employment discrimination, municipal neglect of barrios, and police brutality. A disturbing incident on Christmas Eve of 1951, in which a group of Los Angeles police officers arrested and then severely beat seven men at the Lincoln Heights jail, prompted the CSO to aid the victims. In the end, five officers were imprisoned for the "Bloody Christmas" beatings, and seventeen others were dismissed or suspended. The CSO confronted police brutality again in 1952 when its chairman (and United Steelworkers union leader) Anthony Rios was arrested, stripped, and beaten along with Alfred Ulloa in the Lincoln Heights jail when the two tried to stop plainclothes officers from beating a man outside of a bar. The CSO assisted Rios and Ulloa in their trials, after which both men were acquitted. The CSO's involvement in these and other police brutality cases led *The Nation* to proclaim in March 1953 that the organization had brought about "the political awakening of the Spanish-speaking minority" in Los Angeles and was sure to do so in other parts of California. With memories of the Bloody Christmas and Rios-Ulloa trials fresh in his mind, Fred Ross saw the opportunity to mobilize Salinas Valley Mexican Americans around their own episode of violence in King City. Salinas seemed the natural choice for Monterey County CSO headquarters since it had just surpassed Monterey as the largest city in the county with a population of eighteen thousand and another seventeen thousand people living in the unincorporated Alisal district.[9]

The founding members of the Los Angeles CSO tended to be U.S.-born and from white-collar or union backgrounds, but the first members of the Monterey County CSO represented a wider variety of class positions, immigration experiences, and backgrounds closer to the world of agriculture. Anna and Abe Chávez were both born and attended college in New Mexico, where they married. After Abe's Korean War stint in the Air Force, the couple moved to Salinas, where Abe's aunt already lived. Abe became a counselor at Soledad Prison while Anna became a teacher at Fremont Elementary School in Alisal. The Chávezes soon realized that their college education and middle-class jobs set them apart from a large segment of the Mexican-origin population. "When we came to Salinas, and we saw what the [Mexicano] farmworkers were going through . . . we couldn't believe it," Anna remarked. Because Abe "saw helping this population as his mission," the couple gravitated toward helping farmworker Jimmy Ortiz.[10] By this time, the Chávezes were friends with several other couples, including Dean and Jennie Diaz and Albert and Cecilia Sánchez. The Diazes owned and operated a shoe store and repair shop in Salinas that was particularly popular with braceros. Albert was an upholsterer and the son of well-known Alisal resident Delfina Sánchez. Cecilia had toiled with her family in the fields of Colton and Castroville during the 1930s and the shipyards of the San Francisco Bay Area during World War II. In the late 1940s the family returned to the Salinas area, and fourteen-year-old Cecilia found a job in a lettuce packing shed. After meeting Fred Ross, Albert and Cecilia volunteered their large home in Alisal for the first CSO house meetings. This prompted more of the Sánchez family to become members. Albert's sister Consuelo, a U.S.-born cannery worker, and her husband Gregorio Zermeño, a Mexican immigrant employed as a labor camp operator, were also homeowners in Alisal and were considered "upper-class" residents of the neighborhood. Consuelo and Gregorio's sixteen-year-old son Alex became the chapter's youngest member. Speaking of the emergence of his own and others' political awareness, Alex affirmed: "it all started when the veterans came back from World War II. They had a totally different image of themselves. And that's where I remember the rub happening in Salinas, is when these vets started saying 'No, we ain't putting up with that no more.'"[11] The CSO provided a long-awaited institution through which Mexican Americans in Salinas and elsewhere could fight racial discrimination and other injustices.

Some Monterey County CSO members lived and worked closer to the world of agriculture. Charles Villegas, a clerk at a grocery store where most county welfare food orders were processed, noticed that many elderly or disabled farmworker customers had little to no knowledge of welfare laws and raised that concern at CSO meetings. Jose Friedrich had daily interactions with braceros who lived in his labor camp and later patronized his movie theater. Manuel and Sophie Cásarez worked in the transportation and packing segments of the agricultural industry. A Tejano, Manuel worked as a truck driver for the Southern Pacific Railroad, and Sophie, who emigrated from Mexico with her family at age two, worked as a packing shed employee. By the 1950s Mexicanas had taken the majority of jobs in sheds cleaning, sorting, and packing produce on conveyor belt lines, replacing white women who had moved up to supervisor or "floor lady" positions in sheds or to jobs in local banks or hospitals.[12] Two CSO members, Ben López (Abe Chávez's brother-in-law) and Sally Gutiérrez, were important intermediary figures between farmworkers and grower-employers. Through his position as Salinas GFLA director, López had a foot in two worlds—that of the braceros he contracted and supervised, and that of the growers to whom he supplied this bracero labor. Gutierrez immigrated to the United States with her Mexican parents when she was an infant and became a U.S. citizen. After getting married, she took a job in a cannery. Later, while her husband served in World War II, Gutíerrez worked in Gilroy's War Food Office where she managed braceros' payroll records as well as their complaints about labor camp food. She then served as a traffic clerk for the Salinas Municipal Court, where her Spanish-language skills earned her attention from local law enforcement officials. As a result she became the first certified interpreter in Salinas, specializing in mediating bracero-employer matters and translating in court trials. Even before she joined the CSO, Gutiérrez showed an interest in politics, as evidenced by her membership in the League of Women Voters.[13] Taken together, the founding members of the Salinas CSO were diverse in their birthplaces, occupations, and social positions in the wider community.

THE CSO AS AMERICANIZING AGENT

Excited about their newly founded chapter, Monterey County CSO members made the short drive to Asilomar, a coastal town twenty-five miles away, to attend the annual CSO convention in March 1954. In his keynote speech to the gathering, Edward Roybal spoke of Mexican Americans' history and present situation: "We have been socially and politically ostracized. We have been deprived of our civil liberties and we have turned the other cheek. Our children have been segregated . . . This is the convention in which we are now going to fight back . . . [T]hose who fought in the battlefields of the European and Korean conflicts are back, ready to assume their responsibilities in the community and do their civic part . . . We are no longer Mexican hyphen Americans . . . we are Americans." Inspired by Roybal's words and the convention, the Monterey County CSO membership returned to Salinas ready to show that people of Mexican descent were just as "American" as any other group and deserved to be treated as full citizens. One of the first things the chapter did was visit the manager of the *Salinas Californian* to complain about its continual use of the referent "Mexican" in its crime headlines, including those about the King City fight. "They would never mention it if the person arrested was Italian or Irish," Sally Gutíerrez recalled. "The newspaper agreed with us and they stopped doing it." The chapter then began work to increase the number of citizen-voters in the local Mexicano community. With passage of the McCarran-Walter Immigration and Nationality Act in 1952, anyone over the age of fifty-two who had lived in the United States for at least twenty-two years could take the U.S. citizenship exam in their native language. To that end the chapter established two "Americanization" centers, one located at Cristo Rey Church in Salinas and the other at a Mexican American–owned grocery store in the town of Gonzales, where CSO members could explain necessary documents and procedures to Mexican immigrants interested in naturalizing. Some members even volunteered to teach free Spanish-language citizenship classes at night to prepare applicants for their examinations.[14] "Americanization" was a loaded term in a Cold War climate and shrewdly communicated to the public that the CSO posed no threat as a "Mexican" organization but rather encouraged the adoption of an "American" identity.

In part due to CSO's citizenship drives, 46,080 Mexican nationals were sworn in at citizenship ceremonies alongside other immigrants from 1950 to 1959. The naturalization records of the sixty-two Mexican residents of Salinas (thirty-seven men, twenty-five women) who acquired their citizenship between 1953 and 1961 provide more information about those who likely benefited from their local CSO's citizenship drives and classes. A large number of people over the age of fifty-two took advantage of the McCarran-Walter Act's Spanish-language concessions, but more than half of Salinas's Mexican naturalizees were younger than fifty, indicating that young and old alike wanted to reap the benefits of citizenship. The CSO would later begin offering free basic English courses to meet the needs of these younger immigrants. Applicants for naturalization ranged from Mario Luis Marquez, age nineteen, to Raul Francisco Fernandez, who took his oath of citizenship at the age of seventy-three. A few men did not live in the United States long before naturalizing, as they had recently completed their service in the Korean War, but the majority (two-thirds) of this group of naturalizees had migrated to the United States before 1940 and lived in the country for several years, if not several decades, before deciding to become citizens.[15]

The ages at which many of these naturalizees migrated, coupled with the length of time they had lived in the United States before they naturalized, suggest that they decided to become citizens because they felt somewhat "American" already. More than one-fourth had immigrated before the age of ten, walking across the border as small children or being carried as infants by their parents. With very little memory of or attachment to their home country, immigrants like Manuela Cota Bautista, who entered through Nogales, Arizona, at the age of two, and Cecilio Ramírez Torrez, who crossed into El Paso by train at age eight, had probably long viewed themselves as Mexican Americans. Proper citizenship documents only affirmed and protected this identity during a time of INS racial profiling and deportation roundups. In fact, figures show that the number of naturalizations spiked in 1955, soon after Operation Wetback. Some naturalizees went even further in "becoming American" by Anglicizing their names. Sixty-year-old warehouseman Celso José Carrasco officially changed his first name to Charles, and Korean War veteran Rodolfo Aguirre Pérez changed his to Rudy. For others, the decision to become a citizen was made in connection to marriage and one's partner. More than one-third of the sixty-two naturalizees were married to a U.S. citizen. All of these cross-nativity unions were between Mexican immigrants and Mexican Americans with the exception of one Mexican man who married a white woman and two Mexican women who married Philippine-born men. Some pairs of spouses who were both Mexican immigrants took citizenship classes or oaths together. Clotilde Estrada from Jalisco and Federico Rocha Acosta from Michoacán, for example, married in San Francisco on Valentine's Day of 1943, later became vegetable workers in Salinas, and took their citizenship oaths on the same day in January 1954.[16]

It was common for neighbors, friends, employers, or CSO members to serve as witnesses for those filing naturalization papers. Sally Gutiérrez and Consuelo Zermeño were present for multiple applicants' naturalization. Adela Acevedo became a citizen and then served as a witness for Bruno Espino. CSO founding member Sophie Cásarez became a citizen in 1954 and then served as witness for Marguerite Villegas, who joined the Salinas CSO with her California-born husband Arnulfo and later went on to be elected a vice president for the national CSO. Texas-born Josefa Gonzales, who had lost her U.S. citizenship upon marrying Mexican immigrant Jesus Enriquez in 1913, naturalized in Salinas in February 1957, with Jesus following suit in April 1959. The couple, who became CSO members, then served as witnesses for Mexican immigrant Teresa López Gilpas, who took her oath in July 1959. For naturalizees and those who knew them, taking the oath of citizenship was cause for celebration. Robert Friedrich remembered his father, Plaza Theater owner and CSO member Jose Friedrich, enjoying a champagne celebration at his home with friends, where "everyone was joking about him being an American" after naturalizing at the age of fifty-two in June 1956, twenty-six years after he first entered the United States.[17]

In addition to showing the networks created between CSO members and Mexican immigrants, naturalization records yield additional information about Salinas's Mexican-origin community during the 1950s. The addresses and occupations of applicants, for instance, confirm that the majority of Mexican immigrants lived in the Alisal district and held working-class jobs in agriculture, construction, or auto repair. A large number of women were categorized as "housewives," which likely obscured many women's positions in the informal economy as seamstresses, caretakers, and food sellers, among other things. Meanwhile, by viewing the occupations of witnesses, one learns that there was a Mexican American baker, tailor, carpenter, gas attendant, barber, minister, restaurant manager, and two grocers in the town.[18]

Along with citizenship drives, the Salinas CSO conducted voter registration drives to increase the Mexican American community's political power. Radio and telephone campaigns, leaflets, and door-to-door visits all formed the "Get Out the Vote" effort. After identifying eligible voters, CSO volunteers either personally escorted them to the courthouse clerk's office to complete their registration or directed them to the homes of CSO members Dean Diaz and Albert Sánchez, who had become Salinas's first Mexican American, Spanish-speaking deputy registrars. One Mexican American taxi driver even took it upon himself to drive through Salinas and Soledad and give people free rides to registration sites. By March 1954 CSO members had registered more than five hundred Spanish-surnamed people in Monterey County, nearly doubling the population's voting strength. The chapter had 179 dues-paying members, at least 200 attending citizenship and language classes, and inspired a group of Mexican Americans in the nearby town of Hollister to form their own CSO chapter in 1955.[19]

During the mid-1950s the Salinas CSO took on important discrimination and harassment cases. It filed a complaint against a school superintendent for discrimination against Spanish-speaking students that resulted in the official's termination and promises from the school board that the students would receive greater attention. In October 1955 CSO member Dean Diaz filed and won a damage suit against police officers who broke into his home without identification and assaulted him, and in May 1956 the organization sent a letter of protest to the Salinas sheriff when a deputy sheriff "interrogated a local Spanish-speaking girl and in the process exceeded his authority and what is considered reasonable good taste." After conducting his own investigation, the sheriff agreed and praised the CSO for bringing the matter to his attention. "Since that date there has been noticeable improvement in the attitude of the sheriff's deputies toward Spanish-speaking people," a chapter report read. The CSO began turning heads as representatives of Salinas city government took notice of the organization's sway over the growing Mexican American electorate. "City Hall and everybody started paying a little more attention, school boards, you know," Alex Zermeño said, remembering that the once-difficult process of requesting a stop sign for a Mexican American neighborhood became vastly easier.[20]

The CSO's engagement with the larger community only increased its appeal. The chapter sponsored youth sports teams, collected survey information from Mexican American residents for the Monterey County Tuberculosis and Health Association, and hosted free film screenings. Its reputation as a respectable, civic-minded, and "American" organization was solidified when Democratic state senator Fred Farr—who began attending the chapter's meetings to court Mexican American members' votes—set forth a Senate resolution in June 1957 praising the organization. Pointing out its dedication to nonpartisan voter registration and aiding people in acquiring their U.S. citizenship, Farr declared that the Monterey County CSO's mission "to better integrate the Spanish-speaking people of California into community life" had demonstrated its "devotion to our basic American principles."[21] The chapter had succeeded in showing influential people that it knew what good citizenship meant. Citizenship was bequeathed on a piece of paper, but it was practiced and validated in other spheres, including military service, schools, the workplace, and local politics. In downplaying the ethnic identity of its members while emphasizing its desire to secure "American" rights and privileges for those it served, the CSO showed a willingness to work within existing political systems. In turn, the organization earned approval from authorities who may not have otherwise considered it respectable during an anticommunist and anti-Mexican Cold War era.

WOMEN OF THE CSO

In the process of empowering its members to exercise their political rights and articulate their grievances, the CSO gave Mexican American women the opportunity to become community organizers. As various scholars have noted, historicizing ethnic women's activism requires closer attention to nontraditional forms of political action or protest. This expanded notion of activism becomes particularly important for the 1950s, a decade marked by Red-baiting, the retreat of organized labor, and the postwar resurgence of traditional gender norms in the workplace and the home. In contrast to the "June Cleaver" stereotype of the 1950s woman who returned to the private sphere after having stepped out of it during World War II, many working-class women and women of color continued working outside the home because of economic necessity and participated in community organizations like the CSO. Unlike LULAC or the AGIF, which limited women's membership and participation to auxiliaries, the CSO considered women equal members and allowed them to take leadership roles within the organization. During the early 1950s, men tended to hold president and vice president positions in the national and local CSOs while women served as secretaries or treasurers. In March 1956, there were only two female chapter presidents out of twenty-five chapters in California and Arizona. By the early 1960s, however, Monterey County's own Marguerite Villegas had risen to national CSO vice president, and other women had become CSO chapter presidents.[22]

Formal titles did not reflect the varied contributions and leadership that numerous women exhibited in their local chapters. Because the CSO welcomed families, mothers often brought their children to meetings to interact with playmates and absorb the organization's culture. Danny Robles, who attended CSO meetings as a child, remembered that the women of his family used to point out desirable role models or warn him about who did not get along. "They were giving you the whole rundown on everybody that was there . . . and so you learned a lot of people skills," he remarked. The Monterey County chapter was not alone in the practice of children being at meetings. A northern California CSO area conference in 1955 doubled as a "family affair" that included swimming, hiking, and dancing for members' children, and an amusing tidbit from a Stockton CSO report revealed that "some of the children no longer play cowboys and Indians but play little CSO."[23]

Some members like Alex Zermeño affirmed that there were "very clear male and female roles" in the Monterey County CSO because men tended to speak the most at meetings while only some women, such as Sophie Cásarez and Jennie Diaz, voiced their concerns. Yet women's actions affirm that their roles went beyond wifely support and caretaking. Cecilia Sánchez and Anna Chávez, for example, registered voters, educated their neighbors about their entitlement to Social Security benefits, prepared food for the chapter's monthly fund-raiser dances, taught citizenship classes, and served as witnesses in naturalization proceedings. Genevieve Ramirez served on the CSO's statewide committee on old age assistance (or *pensiones*) that fought for legislation to eliminate the citizenship requirement for state aid to the elderly and disabled. Ramirez collected hundreds of signatures from Salinas Valley residents for pension legislation and coordinated four delegation trips to Sacramento to fight for the bill, which Governor Edmund "Pat" Brown finally signed into law on July 14, 1961. Statewide, five women—Sarah Lopez (Madera), Amalia Corona (Oakland), Mary Ayala (Riverside), Rosemarie Ornelas (Sacramento), and Rita Medina

(Santa Clara County)—were chapter presidents out of a total of thirty-seven chapters, while Dolores Huerta of Stockton headed multiple national CSO committees, demonstrating that women formed the organization's backbone at every level.[24]

One reason why female CSOers were able to do as much as they did was because the organization's membership was heavily made up of couples and families. A Monterey County CSO roster from the late 1950s shows that at least sixteen pairs of spouses or groups of relatives made up the membership. Husbands and wives could be activists at the same time that they socialized with friends, and parents did not have to negotiate issues of child care since all were welcome at meetings. The chapter had begun as a group of relatives and friends, and it continued to make its members feel part of a familiar community. This worked to the CSO's advantage when an incident in late 1956 targeted some of its female members. The chapter had rented a church hall in Soledad for a fund-raiser dance, and three women were preparing food in the church kitchen. After one woman accidentally dropped a pan of water, the church priest stumbled into the kitchen, drunk and looking "like a wild man," and called them "goddamn Mexicans," "dirty women," and "a bunch of hoodlums." When the women later requested an apology, the priest refused and proceeded to make anti-Mexican remarks during his masses. After their attempts to communicate with the bishop in Fresno failed, the CSO made its disapproval known in a more creative way. During one Sunday mass, they instructed every Mexicano parishioner to drop a metal washer into the donation plate instead of money. Everyone followed the order because they were related to, friendly with, or protective of the women involved in the incident. By the next Sunday, the Irish priest had been replaced with one who delivered masses in Spanish. "We knew the only thing that would change [the church] was money," Anna Chávez remarked. "There's so much creativeness when a community wants to do something."[25] In great part fostered by women, the CSO's use of unconventional resistance could at times successfully replace more traditional forms of protest.

THE LATE 1950s AND THE BRACERO QUESTION

During its first years, the Monterey County CSO waged battles on behalf of the town's Mexican American residents while making efforts to include longtime Mexican immigrant residents in the body politic through naturalization and pension legislation. The chapter had not made any efforts to reach out to the local bracero population, or address these men's presence, but this changed in 1956 when the United States imported a record number of braceros and Salinas growers requested more Mexican men to work in their fields.

While CSO members as individuals surely had differing views about braceros depending on their level of interaction with them, the chapter voiced its opposition to growers' proposals to convert low-income resident housing into bracero housing. As early as 1954, the CSO fought against the idea of residents and braceros living in close proximity. They helped move thirty-two farmworker families out of Camp McCallum into standard public housing because 350 "single male farm workers" were living in the same quarters and creating a "social problem." The chapter then investigated Monterey County Housing Authority director Eleanor Walters, who was known for giving low-income housing residents invalid rent receipts written on scraps of paper or cereal boxes and later evicting them, claiming she had never received their rent. Her plans were to then sell the vacant property to growers and bracero housing contractors. The CSO collected enough testimonies of Walters's wrongdoing to persuade the district attorney to begin its own investigation, and Walters was eventually found guilty and imprisoned in 1957.[26]

Although Walters's jailing was a notable victory for the chapter, Fred Ross feared a loss of momentum after the incident and pressed chapter president Abe Chávez to keep members campaigning against braceros in public housing. Yet because the CSO had not included the actual Mexican American families who lost their housing in the fight against Walters, the campaign against additional bracero camps fell flat after Walters's imprisonment. By the end of 1960, Monterey County claimed 247 labor camps. Ross had long been anxious about the Salinas CSO because of its pattern of mobilizing around isolated incidents but failing to connect them in a more sustained fight against discrimination. The chapter had "missed the ball" on the bracero and housing issues, Ross wrote in his work diary, and the group's meetings had not attracted a consistent core membership. In part, this was because the chapter alternated its biweekly meetings between Salinas and Soledad. Though the chapter's total membership stood at 150 people, only 20 attended each meeting on average because most members chose to attend the meetings closest to their homes. The chapter was accomplishing important victories—registering more than fifteen hundred voters in three years, consistently drawing students to citizenship and English classes, and persuading California politicians to fight for *pensiones*—but there was no critical mass to take action on civil rights issues at the local level.[27]

The content of the Monterey County CSO's meetings also worried Ross. Many times, meetings turned into discussions of race and Mexican American identity provoked by Abe Chávez. "Abe used it [the meeting] as a counseling session, as a therapy session," Alex Zermeño remembered, chuckling. "He would throw out a question [like] 'What do you think when someone calls you a greaseball Mexican?' . . . and regardless of what response we gave him, he would always say, 'Why do you think that?' 'Well that's interesting, why?' Always 'why' . . . He made you dig." Chávez's direct questions and confrontational style drove some members away, which led Ross to worry about the chapter's sustainability. In August 1956 he wrote in his diary: "I told [Abe] he better get on the ball and go out after a larger 'nucleus' . . . his 'group dynamics' ideas clutter up his work at times. I think he believes my organizing approach is too 'aggressive.'"[28] By not directing more energy to recruiting new members or establishing a larger core of regular attendees, Chávez unwittingly diminished the power of the chapter.

Another crack in the Salinas CSO's foundation was its members' refusal to create interracial coalitions. The Los Angeles CSO had been a multiethnic chapter from its beginnings as it developed political support for Edward Roybal. Whites, blacks, and Asians were members alongside Mexicans, and the chapter created relationships with the National Association for the Advancement of Colored People and the Japanese American Citizens League as well as with organized labor groups such as the United Steelworkers of America, the United Automobile Workers, the International Ladies' Garment Workers' Union, and the Jewish Labor Committee. With these diverse supporters, Roybal was able to be elected in a district in which fewer than one-fifth of voters were of Mexican origin. Closer to Monterey County, the San José CSO made news when it helped two black men sue the Mexican American owners of a tavern and dancehall who refused them service. The chapter used the incident to demonstrate its dedication to civil rights for all. Members of the Salinas CSO, on the other hand, were reluctant to reach across racial lines. At a May 1957 meeting Abe Chávez raised the issue, commenting, "it appeared to me that they didn't want any Anglos in CSO. It was obvious that they were unwilling to face direct examination of their attitudes." He went on to tell Ross in a letter that when he suggested that the chapter accept an Anglo Protestant minister's offer to provide church space for CSO rummage sales, members shot back that the minister had not assisted them in their fight against the Soledad priest the year before. "This group expects and unconsciously demands the other racial members to move more than half way," Chávez wrote, speaking of the Soledad-based members in particular. He then revealed that the discussion resulted in nobody attending the next meeting and concluded, "It is possible that I touched a more sensitive area than I thought."[29]

In his letter Chávez alluded to a fundamental difference between the Salinas and Soledad CSO members that led to the chapter's fracture. By the late 1950s Salinas claimed a population of 22,500, and nearly 40,000 if one included the Alisal district. Soledad was a smaller community of 3,200 people ten miles away, and its Mexicano *colonia* (neighborhood) looked like, in Ross's words, "a big mud puddle" with its unpaved roads and no stoplights and signs. Poorer and hungrier for change, Soledad CSOers such as Aurelio Ramirez and Frank Ledesma wanted to directly tackle school desegregation and municipal improvements. Meanwhile, Salinas residents contended with racial discrimination that, according to Alex Zermeño, was "very subtle . . . [and] very economic." Choosing not to confront local authorities but instead use them to achieve their goals, Zermeño remarked, Salinas CSOers knew "how to play the game" and were more comfortable maneuvering within local power structures. This difference in political technique caused some Salinas members to ponder breaking away from Soledad members in February 1957. At the time Jennie Diaz scolded them "for even considering such a move when the Soledad people needed so much help," yet a year later, Salinas members had done just that. The chapter split into two in 1958—a Northern Monterey County chapter headquartered in Salinas and a Southern Monterey chapter based in Soledad. In his work diary, Ross wrote about the aftermath and his disappointment: "Since the split the Salinas leaders, who have always been at a higher economic & educational level than those of Soledad—have leaned more and more toward the 'cream puff' operation, social affairs, fund-raisers, etc. . . . While they were joined with the Soledad group they had to fight these [racial] issues—which made some of them pretty uncomfortable. This more than anything else, probably explains the genesis of the 'split.'"[30] The difference in how Soledad and Salinas CSOers wanted to function as leaders in their communities—the former as activists and protestors, the latter as respectable ethnic representatives—affected each chapter's accomplishments. In 1960 the Salinas CSO was still teaching a citizenship class, registering voters, fighting for the *pensiones* bill, and being vigilant against racial discrimination in local schools, but membership had decreased to 119 people. The chapter was devoting most of its energy to social events that helped to create a sense of ethnic community for Mexicanos, but not a political one. Meanwhile, the Soledad CSO had come into its own and recruited 160 members, registered 150 voters, conducted two basic English classes, filed lawsuits against the local chief of police and the City of Soledad for illegal search practices, made requests for improvements in the Mexican *colonia,* and assisted in welfare and naturalization cases. As CSO member and organizer Cesar Chavez once said of respectability's potential to smother activism: "If a minority group does 'nice' things, like taking a petition to the Mayor, or having tea parties with the PTA, it's going to become respectable. And once you become a respectable group, you're not going to fight anymore." Once they had the attention of local authorities, Salinas CSOers wanted to keep it and found it too risky to be "radical." Meanwhile, their poorer farmworker counterparts in Soledad were less afraid to directly confront authority since they felt they had nothing more to lose. Without any new emerging leaders, a stable core membership, and the organizational momentum to keep battling local racism and discrimination, the Salinas CSO dissolved in 1961, with the 1962 national CSO report showing no membership dues or attendance for either the Salinas or Soledad chapters. CSO directories listed Joe Piñedo and Alfredo Dominguez as Salinas and Soledad presidents for 1963, and Piñedo and Frank Ledesma as presidents for 1964, but these posts were most likely nominal since both chapters appeared to be defunct.[31]

The CSO's decline in these two Salinas Valley towns is important to include in the history of the CSO in California, particularly because the literature has largely focused on the organization's victories. In many ways, the story of the Salinas and Soledad chapters is a story of missed opportunities and lost momentum. The Salinas chapter's fight for respectability and rights became blurred, particularly because attaining the first felt like a breakthrough in and of itself. The Soledad chapter, on the other hand, did not have the critical mass to sustain its goal of making deeper, structural changes in its community. Despite its dissolution, however, the Monterey County CSO served as an important training ground for its founding members and those of the next generation who enjoyed more upward socioeconomic mobility. Frank Ledesma was elected mayor of Soledad and served for six years before serving on the Soledad school board for twelve. Abe and Anna Chávez's daughter became a surgeon, and Dean and Jennie Diaz's son a successful business owner. Alex Zermeño became the first Mexican American student body president of Hartnell College and received a degree in public administration from Harvard University before working as a probation officer in Alameda and San Quentin, an antipoverty activist in the Mission District of San Francisco, and deputy director of the National Council of La Raza. His brothers Ernie, Greg, and Andy—also CSO alumni— became a school principal in the Salinas Valley, the director of the California Youth Authority, and an artist who designed logos and cartoons for Cesar Chavez's United Farm Workers union, respectively.[32]

Just as it shaped its members' lives on a local level, the CSO dramatically changed the profile of California's Mexican-origin population. Before the organization was founded, less than 10 percent of Spanish-surnamed people in the state were registered to vote, and the great majority of members of the parent generation were not U.S. citizens. From 1947 to 1960, close to forty CSO chapters assisted forty thousand Mexicans in obtaining their U.S. citizenship, registered almost a quarter of a million voters, and helped elect or appoint more than one hundred Spanish-surnamed leaders to public office. By the end of the 1950s, 85 percent of the more than 3.4 million Spanish-surnamed people in the Southwest and 80 percent of California's more than 1.4 million Spanish-surnamed residents were U.S. citizens either by birth or through naturalization. By serving citizens and making new citizens, the CSO contributed to 1960 being a peak year in the number of people who culturally and legally identified as Mexican and American at once.[33]

THE URBAN-RURAL DIVIDE

While the Monterey County CSO chapter had to confront the reality of its two different constituencies, the national CSO (which claimed ten thousand members and more than forty chapters in California and Arizona by the end of the 1950s) had to do the same with its urban and rural members. Headquartered in Los Angeles, the CSO continued to privilege an urban agenda. As early as the mid-1950s, however, some CSO leaders tried to speak out for rural Mexican Americans and farmworkers in particular. In March 1955 former farmworker, realtor, and CSO national vice president Albert Pinon (a member of the San Jose chapter) testified before the Senate Subcommittee on Migratory Labor and expressed the CSO's concern for agricultural workers who, according to his testimony, made up 70 percent of the organization's membership. When bracero importations peaked the next year, Mexican American farmworkers suffering from wages of less than one dollar an hour and a lack of collective bargaining rights turned to the CSO for help. As CSO leader Cesar Chavez remembered of the farmworkers with whom he met in Oxnard: "Every meeting they hit me with the bracero problem but I would dodge it. I just didn't fathom how big that problem was, I would say, 'Well, you know, we really can't do anything about that' . . . finally I decided this was the issue I had to tackle."[34]

Born and raised near Yuma, Arizona, Chavez began work on the California migrant farm labor circuit at the age of twelve when his family was dispossessed of their homestead because of unpaid property taxes. As a young man, he participated in the zoot suit trend, joined the navy during World War II, and resisted discrimination when he encountered it. In one incident, he and his wife, Helen, were asked to move from their seats in the "Anglo" section of a movie theater in Delano. Chavez refused and was charged with violating the theater's seating policy. When Fred Ross began organizing the CSO in San Jose he met the Chavezes, who helped him build a CSO chapter there before moving to southern California to accept a bigger leadership role. Cesar's initial efforts to organize farmworkers began in 1956 when he received a grant from the UPWA to study the effects of the Bracero Program in

Oxnard. The Ventura Farm Labor Association was using braceros and trying to circumvent placing domestics in the fields by rejecting their job referral cards or assigning them to distant work sites that meant prohibitive costs in gas or other transportation. Through confronting the association, Chavez succeeded in getting domestics hired and raising the prevailing farm labor wage from sixty-five to ninety cents an hour.[35]

These were notable successes, but isolated ones. Overwhelmingly, agricultural workers' unions were being busted by the Bracero Program. Between 1954 and 1959 NAWU members were replaced by braceros when they attempted to strike in carrot fields in Monterey County, asparagus and tomato fields in San Joaquin County, peach orchards in Sutter County, and cantaloupe fields in Fresno County, as well as other crop areas. During the same period the Salinas Valley's UPWA Local 78 conducted multiple strikes only to have them all broken. Twelve thousand California growers continued to employ braceros, making the state second only to Texas in number of bracero importations. In Monterey County, braceros working with lettuce, strawberries, apricots, tomatoes, celery, carrots, and other vegetables made up a whopping 72 percent of all seasonal farm laborers in 1959. Growers continued to justify their high bracero usage by using the old technique of castigating domestic farmworkers for a supposedly poor work ethic. A Salinas Vegetable Growers Association report, for instance, claimed that of 843 domestics sent to its members from the Department of Employment, 431 either quit or were fired for such reasons as "failure to report for work," "talked to girls on ranch too much," "got drunk," and "can't take it."[36]

Bracero Program opponents kept pointing to evidence that the program was a stain upon the American conscience. The Agricultural Workers Organizing Committee (AWOC) stated in 1959, "Public Law 78 warps the lives of everyone it touches; it throws a shadow across our collective conscience; it cripples our country's moral stature before the world." The CBS documentary *Harvest of Shame,* which aired the day after Thanksgiving of 1960, graphically depicted the poverty and despair of millions of U.S. migrant farmworkers. AFL-CIO president George Meany complained of "going to international conventions and being needled by labor people from smaller, poorer countries, who could point out that at least they had organized farm workers, while the American labor movement hadn't." According to government reports, the more than two million U.S. citizens performing farm work averaged only 128 days of work and an income of $961 per year, far below the living wage. Almost four hundred thousand children between the ages of ten and thirteen were legally employed on farms by 1960, and many more were illegally employed. Farmworkers were still excluded from the protections of most workmen's compensation and unemployment insurance programs, collective bargaining rights, and a federal minimum wage. In California, while the average factory worker's earnings had risen 63 percent, from $1.60 an hour in 1950 to $2.60 in 1960, the average farmworker's earnings had only risen 41 percent, from $0.85 an hour to $1.20 (fig. 4.1). Criticizing agri-business's transition from family farming to "ruthless coldblooded big business exploitation of people and the land," AWOC organizer Louis

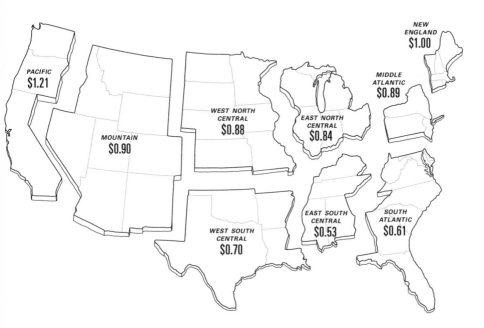

Fig. 4.1. Average hourly earnings of U.S. farmworkers by region, 1961. (Info-graphic by David Hackett. Source: Department of Labor, Bureau of Employment Security, "Hired Farm Workers in the United States," June 1961, Folder 11, Box 3, Farm Worker Organizing Collection, Southern California Library for Social Studies and Research, Los Angeles)

Krainock presented by contrast how many privileges the agricultural industry enjoyed: "Agribusiness is free to recruit and use semi-slave labor, free to maintain and use wage-breakers and strike-breakers, free to operate without minimum wages, maximum hours, unemployment insurance, or any of the social, ethical and financial controls society imposes on the rest of the industrial community."[37]

In January 1961 AWOC joined with the UPWA in a strike against Imperial Valley lettuce ranches that employed nearly two thousand braceros. The two unions demanded collective bargaining rights for twenty-five hundred striking domestics, a thirty-five-cent raise to a minimum hourly wage of $1.25, and the termination of the Bracero Program. They also persuaded the U.S. Department of Labor to investigate thirteen Imperial Valley lettuce growers—including Salinas-based companies Arena Imperial, Garin and Company, D'Arrigo, and the Salinas Valley Vegetable Exchange—that were suspected of contracting braceros before recruiting domestic workers. These growers were found guilty and lost their bracero privileges in late February (after the Mexican government demanded such a punishment), but the strike ended the next month with no improvements to domestic farmworkers' conditions.[38] Salinas Valley lettuce giant Bud Antle, who owned several ranches in the Imperial Valley, evaded his colleagues' penalty by surreptitiously signing a four-year contract with Local 890 of the Western Conference of Teamsters to prevent the AWOC-UPWA strike from affecting his operations. The Teamsters union had a national membership of nearly 1.5 million and covered various types of workers, including field, cannery, clerical, transportation, and warehouse workers. The contract gave fifteen hundred domestics a $1.25 hourly wage and overtime pay but stipulated that Antle could fire any worker without explanation and that the Teamsters would assist him in importing braceros if necessary. Antle's contract infuriated not only the UPWA and AWOC, but the Salinas Valley GSVA, which expelled Antle for acting against the status quo of nonunionization. AWOC and the UPWA led another strike at the Salinas Strawberries Company in April 1961, but when the U.S. Department of Labor did not order braceros' removal from the ranches, the protest collapsed after ten days. The Salinas Valley continued to stand alongside the Imperial and San Joaquin Valleys as the three biggest bracero-employing, antifarmworker union regions in California.[39]

Recognizing the severity of the Bracero Program's economic toll upon its farmworker membership, the California CSO attempted to integrate this constituency more fully in its statewide goals. Although only 15 percent of Spanish-surnamed people in California lived in rural areas by this time, Spanish-surnamed men made up 42 percent of all men working as farmworkers or foremen in the state, and Spanish-surnamed women made up 30 percent of all female farmworkers. In 1961 the CSO declared its intent to fight for a minimum wage for farmworkers and the elimination of the Bracero Program alongside its other goals of protecting low-income homeowners' rights, extending old-age pensions, and expanding the California Fair Employment Practices Commission to serve all minorities.[40] As impressive as this proclamation sounded, the actual level of support the CSO gave farmworkers was minimal. "A lot of [CSO members] were farmworkers themselves . . . [but] we had too many lawyers and doctors and schoolteachers at the top," Fred Ross admitted. Alex Zermeño and other Monterey County CSO members remembered observing this divide between urban and rural CSO chapters. "When we got together on state conventions and stuff like that . . . L.A. tried to dominate . . . there was always that dichotomy of small town and big town," Zermeño said. Cesar Chavez, who became the CSO's executive director in 1959, believed the organization was growing increasingly disconnected from its verbal commitment to the agricultural working class. At the seventh annual CSO convention in March 1960 in Fresno, Chavez made a poignant plea for the organization to pay more attention to the plight of farmworkers: "We aren't doing anything for the field worker . . . Some of this group here today feel there's no problem. They too, were agricultural workers once." Chavez envisioned leading a farmworker union, on his own terms, as one of his CSO responsibilities. In 1962, he stood again before the CSO convention at Calexico to propose this independent farmworkers' union and put it to a vote. When the convention voted against his motion, an angry Chavez announced his resignation. He went with his family and fellow CSO leader Dolores Huerta to Delano, where the two founded the National Farm Workers Association (NFWA), which would later merge with AWOC to form the United Farm Workers Organizing Committee (UFWOC).[41]

The Bracero Program remained the biggest obstacle to any future farmworker unionization. After it had first passed in 1951, Public Law

78 had been renewed every two years. In 1961 when Congress approved another extension until December 31, 1963, President John F. Kennedy signed the bill but expressed his anxiety that the program did not include adequate protections for domestics. In February 1963, California growers persuaded Representative Alan G. Pattee (R-Salinas) and Senator Robert J. Lagomarsino (R-Ventura) to introduce resolutions extending the Bracero Program once more. In late May 1963, the House voted for a final extension to December 1964.[42] Agribusiness had won out again, and Bracero Program opponents, including Mexican American activists, labor unions, religious groups, and civil rights and antipoverty activists, steeled themselves for a fight. The contract labor system that fed off unemployment and poverty in Mexico only to create unemployment and poverty in the United States, they believed, needed to be killed. What neither the pro– nor anti–Bracero Program factions could predict was a horrific event in Salinas in the fall of 1963 that would kill thirty-one braceros, place the Bracero Program under greater scrutiny, and create a window of opportunity for urban and agricultural Mexican American activists to collaborate on a political agenda encompassing both of their worlds.

5 A Town Full of Dead Mexicans

The Salinas Valley Bracero Tragedy of 1963

They are viewed as commodities, as objects, as chattels . . . the average bracero-holder probably has less respect for his chattels than the average slave-holder had for his a hundred years ago . . . You rent a bracero for six weeks or six months, and if he gets damaged, you don't care. You'll never see him again. You get next year's model—a newer, younger, healthier one.

    —Henry Anderson, Advisory Board of Citizens for Farm Labor, 1963

Oh, you wave to your sweet Chiquita as you cross the Rio Grande,
You are bound for Salinas town, you're gonna work for a gringo man.
And soon you're cutting lettuce, and sweatin' for your pay;
You grab a hoe and you bend down low when you hear the boss man say:
I wanna see hindends and elbows as you go on down that row.
Field hand, you don't stand 'til you're back in Mexico.
    . . .
You ride to the field one morning in the rear of a crowded truck.
It overturns and then it burns, in the flaming wreck you're stuck.
You think about Chiquita and then they drag you out.
"This man is dead," the Padre said, but the boss man he just shout:
I wanna see hindends and elbows as you go on down that row.
Field hand, you don't stand 'til you're back in Mexico.
    —Ric Masten, "Hindends and Elbows," 1966

IN THE EARLY morning of September 17, 1963, the bracero crew that lived at the Earl Meyers Company labor camp in Salinas boarded a bus to begin their work in two local vegetable fields. After a ten-hour workday harvesting celery and other crops, the men reboarded the bus near the town of Chualar, twelve miles south of Salinas, to return to camp. This "bus," a flatbed produce truck with an affixed canopy and four long wooden benches inside—two on the sides, two in the middle—was one of many converted vehicles growers used to transport braceros throughout California (fig. 5.1). The fifty-six men crammed into the back of the truck, some sitting on the floor beside long harvesting knives or atop large food containers. A chain tied on the outside of the bus's back doors kept the workers locked in the compartment, and the crew could not communicate with their driver and foreman, thirty-four-year-old Francisco "Pancho" Espinosa, or thirty-two-year-old co-foreman Arturo Galindo, who sat next to Espinosa in the passenger seat checking timesheets.

Around 4:25 p.m. Espinosa approached an unmarked railroad crossing eight miles south of Salinas. To the east and west, miles of vegetable fields flanked the stretch of track. Not seeing or hearing a train,

Fig. 5.1. Braceros enter a converted truck-bus in the Salinas Valley, 1956. (Courtesy of Leonard Nadel Bracero Photographs, Archives Center, National Museum of American History, Smithsonian Institution)

Espinosa inched the bus's front wheels over the tracks. He suddenly heard a whistle but still did not see anything. Espinosa gunned the motor to get across, but it was too late. A seventy-one-car Southern Pacific Railroad freight train traveling at sixty-five miles per hour smashed into the right side of the bus with a force so great it sheared the vehicle in half. The passenger compartment detached, sending bodies, pieces of wood, and work tools flying. Before the engineer could bring the sugar beet–carrying train to a stop, almost all of the workers lay scattered around the track, some thrown three hundred feet beyond the point of impact. Twenty-three died instantly. Tony Vásquez, a Mexican American foreman whose crew was thinning broccoli in a nearby field, witnessed the collision in horror and called authorities before rushing to the scene. "Bodies just flew all over the place," the twenty-nine-year-old Vásquez said. A truckload of soldiers from Fort Ord saw the wreckage from the highway and stopped to offer aid. Meanwhile, other drivers slowed their cars to observe the accident, delaying ambulances trying to reach the workers.[1]

Paramedics and Monterey County coroner Christopher Hill Jr. came upon a gruesome scene. "One body was hooked under the engine," Hill observed. "Shoes, hats and cutting knives were all around. Everywhere you could hear the injured moaning." Isidro Hernandez Tovar, a nineteen-year-old from Zapotlanejo, Jalisco, who was sitting near the front of the bus, remembered waking up after the crash: "I saw ambulances and many people. The bodies were already covered with an orange tarp. I was looking for my friend, Sixto Robles Urzua, also from Zapotlanejo, but I didn't see him. I walked to the bodies, uncovered the tarps, saw two or three bodies, but I didn't recognize any of them. They were completely disfigured. I kept walking and when I couldn't walk anymore, I sat by the edge of the field." Court interpreter Sally Gutíerrez, who was at home when she heard ambulances speeding across Salinas, was summoned to Chualar to help authorities interview the surviving Spanish-speaking braceros. It was the biggest accident Gutíerrez had seen since fourteen Salinas braceros had died in a bus fire in Soledad in 1958. As daylight faded, fifteen ambulances—and several local residents with vehicles—removed the dead and transported the injured to multiple Salinas hospitals, where three men died on arrival and two more died in surgery, bringing the death toll to twenty-eight. Salinas ambulance driver Gary Hollis recounted the stories his co-workers told him about the tragedy. "They said that when they brought one ambulance back to the garage from transporting the victims, they opened the back doors and the blood flowed out like water," he recalled.[2]

The dead braceros, who hailed from the Mexican states of Jalisco, Guanajuato, Sonora, Zacatecas, Puebla, and Michoacán, ranged in age from nineteen to fifty-nine. José Gómez Martínez died on his twenty-seventh birthday. Out of three pairs of brothers in the bus, Federico and Salvador Olmedo Gallegos perished, and José Meza Huerta and Salvador Orozco Contreras lost their brothers Roberto and Luis. Only one person was unharmed in the collision—driver Francisco "Pancho" Espinosa. In shock, he emerged from the bus with only minor cuts and bruises. After being questioned by the California Highway Patrol and the district attorney, Espinosa was arrested and placed in the Salinas jail on charges of felony manslaughter. He, along with the Bracero Program at large, would become the central figures of blame in what the National Safety Council deemed the biggest fatal vehicle accident in U.S. history.[3]

The Chualar accident has been recognized by some scholars as an important event within the history of the Bracero Program, yet analysis of the event has been limited to details of the accident and the program's lack of enforcement mechanisms for ensuring braceros' safety.[4] This chapter provides new critical examination of this tragedy, the communities involved in and affected by it, and the role it played in the death of the Bracero Program and the evolution of California's Chicano Movement. Producing the largest number of bracero fatalities to date, the Chualar accident reminded the nation of these guest-workers' vulnerability and exposed the Salinas Valley—long praised as the "Salad Bowl of the World"—as a dark nexus of farmworker mistreatment. Desperate to maintain their access to bracero labor, Salinas growers and officials attempted to control public opinion about the accident by handling the bracero victims' funeral, impeding federal investigations, and silencing the crash survivors. Yet they would not be able to escape critiques from union leaders, religious representatives, and Mexican American political activists who argued that Chualar was only symptomatic of the larger transnational tragedy that was the Bracero Program, which simultaneously exploited Mexican laborers and displaced U.S. workers in need of agricultural jobs. The tragedy at Chualar helped to amplify and galvanize these groups' opposition, proving a critical accelerant to Congress's decision to terminate the program the next year in 1964.

The accident also served as a pivotal point in California's embryonic Chicano civil rights movement. Before 1963, urban and agricultural Mexican American activists and organizations in the state had not collaborated on issues of concern in significant ways. The various injustices of the Chualar incident, however, pushed them to act together in protest of the Bracero Program's exploitation of Mexican-origin workers and its lack of safety standards enforcement. Recognizing that they could elevate their national profiles and lift some barriers to Mexican American upward mobility by eliminating braceros from the U.S. labor landscape, Mexican American activist groups in California spoke out together against the Bracero Program in a way they had not before 1963. Arguably, this collaboration constituted the first moment in which the concerns of Mexican American farmworkers were enfolded into California's emerging Chicano Movement agenda, even before famed farmworker union leader Cesar Chavez took the national stage with a grape workers' strike in Delano in 1965.

WORLDS COLLIDE: REACTIONS TO CHUALAR

By the morning of September 18, headlines about the crash covered the front pages of U.S. newspapers, including the *New York Times, Washington Post, Chicago Tribune, San Francisco Chronicle,* and *Los Angeles Times.* Mexican newspapers, including *Novedades, Excélsior, El Día,* and *El Imparcial,* also reported on the accident, but details about who had lived and died remained sketchy for horrified bracero relatives. "We held prayers and vigils for the dead and injured braceros," Inez Sosa said of her Mexican community. "We didn't have any news about the dead . . . people were anguished." Juanita Delgado, who was living in Jalisco, Mexico, at the time of the accident, lost her father Jose Mendoza Delgado. "I was only 9 years old, but that day changed our lives," she said. "My mother was left with six children, including the youngest that was only 6 months old. It was devastating. At the moment he died, my father had been doing something for his family. He was working [in California] to send us money for food because there were no jobs or money for food back in Mexico. He died sacrificing for us, as did all the men who died that day."[5]

Before he could read his own newspaper in San Jose, California, scholar and labor activist Ernesto Galarza was awakened at his home by a telephone call from the Salinas Central Labor Council. "Turn on your radio," the caller said. "There's been a farm labor bus collision at Chualar. Better come and look. This town is full of dead Mexicans." A Mexican immigrant with degrees from Occidental College and Stanford University and a Ph.D. in economics from Columbia University, Galarza was the former director of research and education for the NFLU. At that time, he had hoped that the NFLU would become a transnational representative of domestic farmworkers and braceros. An NFLU branch called SANTA (Sindicato Nacional de Trabajadores Agrícolas) had partnered with the Alianza de Braceros Nacionales de México en los Estados Unidos (Alliance of Mexican Braceros in the United States) to allow braceros to become NFLU members. Several Alianza members secured bracero contracts and went to the United States, and those who received work assignments in the Salinas Valley attended NFLU meetings and helped Galarza recruit new members. During the 1950s, however, the failure of NFLU strikes and guest-workers' ambiguous place in U.S. labor organizations plagued Alianza unionists. Their presence in the United States eventually faded, and Galarza—who had published multiple exposés of the Bracero Program, including *Strangers in Our Fields* (1956), *Merchants of Labor* (1964), and *Spiders in the House and Workers in the Field* (1970)—became less optimistic about transnational labor organization and focused instead on ending the Bracero Program altogether.[6]

As he came upon the Chualar railroad crossing, Galarza observed glass shards, broken planks, and blood-smeared farm implements strewn across the area. Black utility poles looming above the track formed somber crosses, while in the fields that flanked the intersection, braceros working with lettuce, beets, and carrots dotted the landscape. Along with Galarza, numerous public agencies had turned their attention to the site. The California Highway Patrol; the Monterey County Sheriff, District Attorney, and Coroner's offices; the California Department of Industrial Relations; the State Compensation Insurance Fund; the Public Utilities Commission; the Interstate Commerce Commission; the U.S. Department of Labor; and the Mexican Consulate had all sent representatives to carry out their own investigations. The presence of so many agencies pointed to how profoundly embedded the Bracero

Program was in California's and the nation's economies. The program had been renewed multiple times by the U.S. and Mexican governments, and braceros had become institutions of the U.S. labor market and agricultural landscape. Of the 186,865 braceros who worked alongside almost 3.6 million U.S. citizens on American farms in 1963, California claimed 65,000, while Texas, Michigan, Arizona, and Colorado followed close behind. Almost one in three California braceros—including everyone involved in the Chualar accident—was contracted by the Salinas Valley GFLA. The GFLA was one of the most persistent grower associations in persuading state and federal representatives to renew the Bracero Program time and time again, arguing that braceros were indispensable amidst a shortage of U.S. workers willing to perform stoop labor. Grower-employers' unwillingness to admit that higher wages might rectify this domestic "shortage" had led AWOC director Al Green to tell the *Lodi News-Sentinel* a mere three weeks before the Chualar incident: "California agriculture is sick. Here you have a 3.5 billion dollar a year industry—with corporation farms making enormous profits—built upon the labor of peasant workers imported from a foreign country and American workers who are kept at a level of bare subsistence."[7]

By this time three more crash victims had died, increasing the death toll to thirty-one. Fearing the accident would persuade Mexico to end the Bracero Program, California governor Pat Brown rushed a telegram to Mexico's president, Adolfo López Mateos, reassuring him, "we will make every effort to determine the cause of this tragedy and take every step to prevent such accidents in the future." Meanwhile, California growers argued that the accident could have happened anywhere, had nothing to do with the program, and that the bus involved had been in good mechanical condition. Salinas newspapers took the growers' side, maintaining that the tragedy of the bracero deaths was only being compounded by the condemnation of the program by "emotional, uninformed" opponents such as Mexican American Democratic representative Henry B. González. A Texas state senator from San Antonio who had been elected to Congress in 1961, González reminded his fellow politicians that 316 Mexican nationals had been killed in U.S. labor accidents during the previous five years and requested that they not extend the Bracero Program again. In response, an editorial in the *Salinas Californian* claimed that González had "stooped to a new low" and "mixed politics with tragedy" by calling braceros "slave labor." The paper urged its readers: "we must not let our shock and heartsick feelings spread and endanger a worthwhile farm labor program that has solved the age-old problem of how to get our produce to market in the most feasible way." Similarly, prominent Salinas grower William Garin criticized González in a letter to anti–Bracero Program Catholic priest James L. Vizzard: "It would seem that if this terrible tragedy of this bus train collision had happened anywhere else in the country and with no [Mexican] nationals involved someone like your Mexican friend in Congress from Texas would figure out a way to slant the story and make capital against the continuation of the national program. It is sad that these things ever happen and this one came at a most unfortunate time."[8] Dismissively referring to González as Vizzard's "Mexican friend," Garin made clear that he and other growers did not believe that the Chualar accident proved the Bracero Program to be dangerous, but only that it came at a "most unfortunate time" for agribusiness.

Indeed, heated debates in the nation's capital hinted that agribusiness was losing some of its sway. Some, like Representative Ezekiel Gathings of Arkansas, argued that braceros were treated well in the United States and speculated that ending the Bracero Program would result in rotting harvests and soaring crop prices. Others, such as Congressmen Jeffery Cohelan and B. F. Sisk of California, opposed the continuation of the program. Opposition forces won their first battle in late May 1963, when the House of Representatives voted 174 to 158 to terminate the program on December 31, 1964. In August the Senate agreed to grant the same one-year extension. Growers believed that they could still use agribusiness's lobbying power to push for an additional extension, or "phasing out," of the program into 1965 before the full Congress voted on the matter in December.[9] The Chualar crash and the dead Mexican bodies it produced, however, violently collided with their ambitions.

Meanwhile, the Catholic Church, organized labor, and Mexican American civil rights organizations, including the CSO, the AGIF, and LULAC, viewed the Chualar incident as the ultimate manifestation of the program's dangerous exploitation. Paid an average of one dollar an hour in California (and even less in other states), braceros endured long days of backbreaking labor and inadequate housing, food, rest, and medical services. As a result, they frequently suffered from respiratory illnesses, permanent spinal injuries, malnourishment, and intense isolation. The Chualar incident added the element of sudden death to what program opponents already saw as the slow death of braceros in the program. Meanwhile, U.S. agricultural workers suffered from substandard wages or unemployment because employers wanted cheaper, nonunionized bracero labor. It was not that domestic workers were unwilling to perform stoop labor, Bracero Program opponents argued, but that they were not being adequately recruited and paid to do so.

Moreover, Bracero Program opponents emphasized, the Chualar accident was not without precedent. Since the mid-1940s California farmers had crowded braceros into poorly constructed vehicles with untrained drivers to transport them from field to field. In 1953 fourteen braceros from Salinas and Brawley were killed in two separate crashes when their labor buses collided with trains. In 1955 eight braceros died and six were injured in a bus-train crash three miles north of Chualar. And in May and June of 1958, two of the most horrific bracero accidents occurred when a bracero ordered to drive a tractor in an Imperial Valley field (an activity prohibited by Public Law 78) was decapitated by a low-flying crop-dusting plane, and fourteen braceros burned to death in Soledad when two cans of gasoline in their labor bus caught fire from a cigarette. Chains tied on the outside of the bus prevented the workers from escaping, as in the Chualar case. Braceros dying from entrapment brought to mind past labor tragedies, such as the Triangle Shirtwaist Factory fire of 1911, in which 146 New York City garment workers—mostly Jewish and Italian immigrant women— died because their managers regularly locked the doors to factory exits. That incident led to legislation requiring improved safety standards for the industrial sector, but not the agricultural. In California from 1952 to 1962, 125 farmworkers were killed and 2,754 injured in transportation accidents, figures highly disproportionate to the state's general accident rate. More than a thousand child farmworkers were seriously injured in farm accidents from 1950 to 1957, and over the course of the decade three thousand farmworkers experienced chemical poisoning from pesticide exposure. Finally, the California press printed a striking series of articles about braceros who had died "mystery deaths" in their sleep after having violent nightmares. Dr. Irma West of the California Department of Public Health observed that workers in the Philippines and Hawai'i had died in similar fashion in what some were calling voodoo-induced "dream deaths." After investigating, West concluded that two of the California braceros had died from organic phosphate insecticide poisoning, and one had starved himself to death to save his wages, but the rest of the deaths remained unexplained.[10]

Farmworker tragedies were not limited to California. In May 1955 fifty-four men, women, and children being transported from Texas to Wyoming were injured when their overloaded truck flipped twice near Agate, Colorado. Eleven-month-old Daniel Luco died in the crash, suffering a crushed chest, skull fracture, and collapsed lung. The same year as the Chualar crash, a bus transporting forty-two migrant workers through the heart of Florida's citrus belt collided with a truck and plunged into a canal. Twenty-seven workers drowned, including twelve children. Disturbingly, as of 1963 the U.S. government still classified farmworkers as "types of loads" for vehicles along with metal, wood, and hay. "Farm laborers should be promoted in the law from the category of things to that of persons," an appalled Galarza declared. After an accident in Del Rio, Texas, where seven braceros were killed and sixty injured when the driver of the cattle truck in which they were being transported dozed off and crashed, a *Corpus Christi Caller* editorial emphasized racial minorities' lack of personhood in U.S. working spaces: "North Americans, so the propaganda line will go, speak freely of 'human values' and the 'decency of man' and the 'importance of the individual.' In practice, of course, they herd minority groups, such as Mexicans, into cattle trucks . . . North Americans never consider them as anything but human cattle anyway."[11]

The day after Thanksgiving in 1960, millions of Americans had tuned into the CBS documentary *Harvest of Shame*, presented by journalist Edward R. Murrow, which graphically depicted the poverty and despair of U.S. migrant farmworkers across the country. Along with showcasing the dirty beds, unsanitary toilets, and lack of running water in many migratory labor camps, the special featured interviews with workers struggling to find steady employment in the midst of the Bracero Program. The viewing public reacted by swamping the network and Congress with "outraged and conscience-stricken" mail.[12] In a letter to the film's producer David Lowe, AWOC organizer Louis Krainock wrote, "Had this program been shown Thanksgiving Day, I'm confident a lot of dinners would have savored of ashes and bitterness." The fact that both U.S. and Mexican farmworkers were continuing to suffer, and even die, from inadequate working conditions seemed all the more horrific amidst the civil rights ethos of the 1960s and U.S. politicians' efforts to craft a national image of freedom and equality. "We call ourselves the leaders of the free world, and yet we have tolerated a system of imported peonage within our borders for these many years," declared Henry Anderson, who had served as AWOC's research director, written extensively on bracero health and working conditions, and founded the Citizens for Farm Labor organization in the San Francisco Bay Area. In one of his radio broadcasts over station KPFA in Berkeley, California, Anderson mused: "Do you believe, as I believe, that freedom ought to mean choice between viable alternatives? Braceros have no choices. They must work for whomever they are told, doing whatever they are told, wherever they are told, for as long as they are told, under whatever conditions they are told." For Anderson and many others, the Salinas bracero deaths served as the last straw. It was the accident with the most bracero fatalities to date, and the most recent racialized labor injustice that could not go ignored. If the United States really was a beacon of freedom and equality in a Cold War world, it could not allow the mistreatment of its Mexican guestworkers to continue.[13]

Mexican American activists and civil rights organizations were particularly outspoken opponents to the Bracero Program, out of both humanitarianism and self-interest. Mexican Americans still endured racialization and discrimination as "Mexicans" in their daily lives. Braceros threatened not only the livelihoods of many Mexican Americans (as more lost their agriculture jobs to braceros and undocumented Mexican labor) but their social citizenship and acceptance in the United States. After the Chualar crash the Mexican American Political Association (MAPA)—a bipartisan organization founded in Fresno in 1960 to help more Mexican Americans become elected to political positions—presented a formal resolution against the Bracero Program to President Kennedy that directly addressed this intraethnic conflict. "PL 78 allows the agricultural industry of California to take advantage of our brethren from Mexico, the braceros . . . [T]hey have been used to create an artificial pool of cheap labor which entirely displaces many local seasonal farm workers, most of whom are Mexican American," the resolution read. Mexican Americans had formed "Viva Kennedy" clubs and given Kennedy 85 percent of their votes in 1960; in their eyes, it was now time for their leader to return the favor.[14]

Communication and collaboration among various Mexican American civil rights organizations increased significantly after Chualar. Chapters of the CSO, MAPA, and the AGIF began formulating joint resolutions against the Bracero Program and calling on Kennedy and Congress to end the program once and for all.[15] The AGIF had already spoken out in Texas against bracero and undocumented Mexican labor in *What Price Wetbacks?* (1954), but this was the first time in California that multiple Mexican American civil rights organizations collaborated in protest of an agricultural labor issue. If they could eliminate braceros from the U.S. labor landscape, Mexican American activists believed, they would be performing a transnational service—preventing more deaths of exploited Mexican citizens while ensuring future work and unionization opportunities for Mexican Americans.

Meanwhile, some program critics made a striking link between Chualar and a concurrent tragedy in the U.S. South to further articulate the injustice of unnecessary death during the civil rights era. In a September 27 article titled "Two Kinds of Blame in Birmingham and Salinas," the *East Bay Labor Journal* memorialized the Salinas braceros together with the "four little girls in Sunday school dresses" murdered in a September 15 bombing at an African American church in Birmingham, Alabama. Likewise, the Santa Clara County AFL-CIO's *Union Gazette* published an article titled "There Is Blood on Your Salad!" in which author Jeff Boehm linked "in memoriam" the deaths of the young African American girls and braceros. "We must stop ignoring the fact that these workers are treated worse than animals," Boehm wrote. "We must end forever the slave labor which stains our food with human blood!" Catholic priest James Vizzard drew the attention of U.S. Catholics by writing: "Just as the killing of the four Negro children at Birmingham has revulsed [*sic*] the Nation, and may well be the turning point in the civil rights battle, so it can be hoped that . . . [these] bracero deaths will not be in vain. The Mexican farm labor program should be ended now." As historian Gina Marie Pitti has argued, Vizzard and others used the Chualar tragedy as evidence of how "Mexican laborers suffered indignities and physical peril as frequently as African Americans encountered violence and racism in the South."[16]

By linking two separate tragedies suffered by racial minorities in the United States, these opponents of the Bracero Program drew the West and South together at a charged moment during the 1960s in hopes of gaining sympathizers across the country.

Rhetoric surrounding death, the racialized body, and personhood continued as autopsy reports provided further grisly details about the Chualar bracero victims. Twenty had suffered extensive trauma to the head, chest, abdomen, and extremities. One body had been transected by the wheels of the train, another was decapitated, and many bodies had been dragged along with the debris of the bus. Only twelve of the dead had been positively identified, not just because of the bodies' condition, but because supervisors often knew braceros only by their work numbers instead of their names. This custom of anonymity forced coroner Christopher Hill Jr. to ask some surviving braceros, including twenty-six-year-old Manuel Silva, to help him identify the dead. Silva had escaped the Chualar accident altogether by choosing to stay behind in the celery field stacking cartons. When he accompanied Hill to the mortuaries holding his dead co-workers, he had the heartbreaking task of identifying his roommate and best friend Juan Razo-Segoviano. Like Silva, Razo-Segoviano had been a citizen of a rancho near Guadalajara in the Mexican state of Jalisco. He left behind a widow and six children. The mystery of the other victims' identities eventually led Hill to seek help from the FBI, which sent a team to Salinas with fingerprints that had been taken from the braceros when they had entered the United States.[17]

When an FBI disaster squad arrived on September 21, investigators learned more about the doomed crew that complicated the story of the Chualar accident. Fifty-three braceros contracted by the Salinas GFLA had indeed been riding in the bus, but so had two domestics and one undocumented Mexican. The domestics, two white men from Chicago and Redwood City, could not be found after their release from Salinas hospitals. Twenty-two-year-old Antonio Gómez Zamora, who died in the crash, had worked as a bracero in Salinas in 1959 but returned to his hometown of Mexicali after his contract expired. He reentered the United States without papers in 1963. Zamora's undocumented status made the crew a "mixed" one, revealing that grower-employer David E. Meyers not only transported his employees poorly, but violated Public

Law 78 by employing an "illegal" Mexican.[18] This fact, along with others, would be covered up quickly as the GFLA began planning a public funeral for the thirty-one fallen braceros.

THE BATTLE OVER THE BODIES

Funeral arrangements soon turned into a public relations fiasco as Salinas authorities and the Mexican Consulate clashed over who would handle and memorialize the bracero bodies. Salinas Valley newspapers such as the *Watsonville Pajaronian* and *Salinas Californian* reported that a "battle over the bodies" and "macabre funeral hassle" had developed. Mexican consul Francisco Jaime Rivera requested that Fresno's Sánchez-Hall Mortuary, "the only completely Mexican mortuary in northern California," handle the funeral. GFLA director Ben López pressured Rivera to let Salinas host the memorial mass, fearing that not doing so would give the city "a bad image." The Mexican government's Department of Exterior Relations, through Rivera, finally relented.[19] In demanding control over their bodies and memory, Salinas representatives claimed the braceros as their own in a way they never had when the men were alive. Nameless before their deaths, the bracero victims became mourned members of the Salinas community in a public display designed to position California agribusiness as sorry about, but not directly accountable for, this loss of Mexican lives.

On the evening of September 25, 1963, six thousand braceros clad in jeans and work shirts disembarked from dusty vehicles and somberly walked toward the entrance of Salinas's Palma High School gymnasium, where the funeral was held (fig. 5.2). Some had known the victims personally, whereas others came to pay their respects or absorb a terrifying reminder of their own vulnerability. "I remember going and praying for them," said Aquilino Zarazua, who worked in the Carmel Valley and did not know the victims. The men filed silently by an American flag fluttering at half-mast at the gym's entrance. Inside the building, a Mexican flag and a pennant of the Virgin of Guadalupe stood at the head of thirty-one simple gray caskets arranged in the shape of a cross. Mourners filled the gym's bleachers to capacity, forcing three thousand people to stand outside the building. Salinas Valley clergy, growers, and representatives from the Mexican, U.S., and California governments stood together near the caskets. The nine thousand attendees belied the isolation and invisibility that braceros had endured

Fig. 5.2. Coffins of the Chualar bracero victims form a cross at the public funeral in the gymnasium at Palma High School. (Photo by the *Salinas Californian*, 26 September 1963)

in the Salinas Valley since 1942. Father Humberto Hermosa of Cristo Rey Catholic Church delivered the mass and a sermon in Spanish, and the choir of Sacred Heart Catholic Church—the same Salinas church that had excluded braceros and Mexican Americans from its congregation in the early 1950s—provided the music at the ninety-minute ceremony. The public memorial service was, in many ways, local growers' attempt to deflect attention from their longtime neglect of Mexican employees' safety. Braceros lacked a personhood while working in the United States that, in the case of Chualar, was acquired only through death. Through this public spectacle, Salinas agribusiness demonstrated that it could memorialize the dead while still exploiting the living.[20]

The GFLA had failed to ensure safe transportation to these braceros while they were alive, yet it readily paid for the transportation of almost half of the braceros' dead bodies across the border to their grieving families in Mexico. The thirty-one deceased men had left thirty-seven dependents under the age of sixteen. Seventeen had designated a wife as the beneficiary of their GFLA-financed State Compensation

Fund insurance policies, and twelve had designated a mother. Childless widows of deceased braceros were promised $18,100 paid over five years, while widows with one or more children would receive $20,500. These payments did not come quickly, prompting some braceros' widows and mothers to contact the Mexican Consul and even Ernesto Galarza for help. Margarita Vasquez, the mother of Trinidad Vasquez, wrote the following to Galarza:

> In the middle of November last year, I received a check of $56.14 that was my son Trinidad's salary at the time his death occurred. After this, I did not receive anything more and they have listened to me two times at Hermosillo and I have had to make the trips with much sacrifice, because I do not have help. My only boys are still very young and all of my family was being sustained by the work of Trinidad.
>
> I understand that the U.S. government has to give me an indemnity for the death of my son and I would like to have the money sent to me directly to this address, because I cannot make any more trips and I am in need, I have nothing to eat and I am sick.

A year after the accident, a group of bracero widows traveled to Salinas to speak directly with the Mexican Consul about their insurance policy compensation. According to Sally Gutíerrez, who served as the women's translator, the widows coordinated the meeting themselves out of frustration that they were not receiving their payments in a timely fashion. Resisting the culture of impunity that pervaded California agribusiness, these women confronted those financially responsible for robbing them of their loved ones and an important source of family income.[21]

The posthumous personhood bestowed upon the Chualar victims at their funeral did not, however, extend to the accident's thirty-second and lone undocumented victim. Antonio Gómez Zamora was buried separately in a Salinas cemetery; it is not known who paid for his burial or whether his family in Mexico ever tried to claim his body. Zamora's exclusion from the braceros' memorial mass was most likely very intentional by the GFLA. With its formal recruitment and contracting procedures, the Bracero Program had long been touted as the solution to unregulated Mexican immigration to the United States. Yet Zamora's death illuminated the reality that neither the Bracero Program nor immigration initiatives such as Operation Wetback had solved the problem of undocumented migration. Mexicans *sin papeles* continued to cross into the United States out of economic desperation or impatience with the long bracero contracting process.[22] Meanwhile, dissatisfied braceros were skipping out on their contracts to work elsewhere for better wages as "wetbacks." The program had failed to deliver on its promise of immigration control, and with the Chualar accident revealing even more of the program's flaws, Salinas grower interests rushed to clean up the mess. With the amount of local power they held, agricultural interests attempted to impede Ernesto Galarza's investigation of the Chualar victims' deaths while hiding the surviving braceros from public attention.

THE LIBERATED AND IMPRISONED: ESPINOSA'S TRIAL AND THE MISSING WITNESSES

After the bracero funeral multiple agencies continued to investigate the Chualar accident. The U.S. Department of Labor and California assemblyman Edward M. Gaffney (D-San Francisco), the chair of the assembly Interim Subcommittee on Industrial Relations, conducted hearings in Salinas to determine whether farm labor transportation safety standards had been violated. The Mexican Consulate monitored the compensation rights of the bracero victims and their dependents. Meanwhile, the chairman of the U.S. House of Representatives Committee on Education and Labor, Adam Clayton Powell, appointed Ernesto Galarza to conduct a formal investigation.[23]

Galarza immediately encountered accusations of being a biased investigator for his well-known opposition to the Bracero Program and previous involvement in labor organizations such as the Pan-American Union, the NFLU, and AWOC. The California Farm Bureau Federation argued that picking Galarza for the job was like "asking the fox to investigate a raid on a henhouse." Representative Charles Gubser (R-Gilroy), a former beet grower, spent an hour in front of the House demanding Galarza be removed from the investigation because he was neither objective nor qualified. In Salinas, Galarza ran into further obstacles. The firm that had converted the Chualar bus from a flatbed truck denied him access to their blueprints, and GFLA executive vice president Jack Bias and director Ben López declined to furnish the labor contracts of the workers involved in the accident, most likely to conceal the fact that many of the contracts had expired by the time of the crash. Indeed, eight men's records showed that their labor contracts had expired—Raul Pureco Servin, for example, was supposed to have returned to Mexico a full three months before the accident. This placed the GFLA in violation of Public Law 78 and, if discovered to be a more widespread problem, would prohibit all of its 239 user-members from requesting any more braceros.[24]

Meanwhile, bus driver Francisco "Pancho" Espinosa's manslaughter trial had begun. A Mexican immigrant who entered the United States at Hidalgo, Texas, in 1954, Espinosa made his way to Oxnard, California, where he climbed the agricultural labor ladder from field hand to foreman before moving to Salinas. He became one of the approximately nine hundred workers in Monterey County who had a green card, which bestowed a resident status that lifted Espinosa above the mostly bracero work crews he supervised in the fields and drove to and from work assignments; however, he likely did not earn much more money than them. According to California State Department of Employment data, "green-carders" were paid according to prevailing wage rates just like braceros and domestics.[25]

At his preliminary hearing on September 26—coincidentally (or not) the day after the braceros' public funeral—the Monterey County Grand Jury recommended leniency, and District Attorney Bertram Young reduced Espinosa's charges to thirty-two counts of misdemeanor manslaughter. Attorney Robert Ames, the first Native American graduate of Stanford Law School and an eight-year resident of Salinas, was appointed to defend Espinosa. After meeting his client, Ames gleaned the impression that "Pancho was a very, very sympathetic and expressive kind of person. You could tell from his body language, from his facial expression, what was going on inside of him . . . You could almost see the accident happening, and you could see the impact and the remorse and guilt . . . [of] a moral individual. He seemed to me to be a very simple, a very honest, a very responsible man . . . he was a kind of fellow that you would want to have as a friend." Aware of circulating rumors that the dead braceros' relatives in Mexico were plotting to kill Espinosa, Ames believed his client's best strategy was to remain in jail to avoid harm. Moreover, this jail time could count as time already served if Espinosa were convicted. Ames refused offers from Espinosa's friends, employer David E. Meyers, and other sympathetic Salinas residents to post his $5,500 bail. Galarza, already suspicious of Ames being a partner in the same law firm as pro–Bracero Program congressman Burt Talcott, grew more dubious when Ames refused him an interview with his client.[26] In Galarza's eyes, Ames was encouraging Espinosa to perform penance that could downplay his role as the Chualar villain. In turn, the accident could become just that, an accident, rather than the result of shoddy bracero transportation and Espinosa's reckless driving.

Espinosa's trial began in Salinas Municipal Court on December 9, with the prosecution's opening argument that Espinosa should have seen and heard the train. Prosecutors called only eight witnesses, including Espinosa's co-foreman Arturo Galindo and interpreter Sally Gutíerrez, but none of the crash survivors testified. Ames then defended Espinosa by arguing that strong Pacific Ocean winds had prevented him from hearing the train, that utility poles and Galindo in the passenger seat had prevented him from seeing the train, and that Espinosa had been diagnosed with poor peripheral vision, perhaps caused by his preexisting diabetes. The failings of Espinosa's body had caused him to fail to protect the bodies of others. During his four-day trial Espinosa remained largely silent, flanked by Gutíerrez and his nine-months-pregnant wife, Guadalupe. When Espinosa finally took the stand, Galarza observed: "there was only one moment of sharp alertness, of visible emotion, and that was when he told of his reactions during the seconds following the crash. He described himself, and reenacted with motions and gestures, sitting in the cab, his hands gripping the broken steering wheel, his face jerking right and left as the freight cars flashed past him, hardly six feet away. Espinoza [*sic*] indicated the extent of his panic and shock when he testified that he could not tell from which direction the cars were coming." Presented as a family man in a profound state of shock, Espinosa emanated a sense of confusion and remorse that clearly affected jury members, who, after less than two hours of deliberation, acquitted him of all charges. Espinosa, his wife, and their newborn child left Salinas soon after. The next year, rumors swirled that Espinosa had been killed in Mexico by relatives of the dead braceros, but these were later discounted. After that, nothing further was published about him.[27]

Galarza found Espinosa's acquittal disturbing for the jury's inattention to Espinosa's negligence and, on a larger scale, agribusiness's inattention to bracero safety. In his report on the trial, Galarza wrote, "there was no disposition in the community to make a scapegoat of the driver, and this good will was to some degree undoubtedly encouraged by the fact that none of the victims had been local residents."[28] Galarza's question of whether the Salinas jury would have reached a different decision had the dead workers been U.S. citizens instead of Mexican ones was valid. Locals did not treat braceros as community members, but rather as temporary inhabitants and social outsiders. The deaths at Chualar had been deemed an unfortunate accident that, to Salinas Valley agribusiness and Espinosa's jury, was best to forgive and forget. Although making Espinosa a scapegoat was an option, prosecutors pursued no additional testimonies or tactics to make him so, and growers did not encourage it, perhaps seeking to prevent any further investigation into their hiring and labor practices.

Determined to make safety violations a centerpiece of his investigation, Galarza sought out the forgotten bracero survivors. He eventually discovered that growers had sequestered twenty-two of them at the Stewart-Hill labor camp, an "almost deserted" and "terribly bleak and depressing" place in Salinas, after their release from various hospitals. Arguably, these survivors' testimonies would have bolstered the prosecutors' case against Espinosa and held tremendous weight in the jury's decision, yet they were never called to the stand or even allowed inside the courtroom. In illuminating interviews with eight of the survivors—Paz Encinas Acosta, Salvador Orozco, José Luis Valenzuela, Raul Puerco Servín, Luis Villalobos Martin, Dario Fuentes Ramirez, Asunción Trejo López, and Leopoldo Ochoa—Galarza acquired a very different picture of Espinosa. Calling him a "rough" and intimidating foreman who was "quick tempered" and "unresponsive to worker complaints" about wages and contracts, the braceros said that Espinosa often failed to stop at railroad crossings and "only got mad and paid no attention" when braceros complained about his reckless driving. In speaking of the Chualar incident specifically, the interviewees affirmed that Espinosa had "hardly stopped" before driving across the railroad tracks. Fearing the loss of their employment if they complained, surviving braceros did not file any grievances with their employer or the Mexican Consulate about their mistreatment and endangerment. Prohibited from returning to work in Salinas or returning home to Mexico, the Chualar survivors remained in limbo with no visits from the Mexican Consulate, whose representatives were instead publicly defending the Bracero Program against the protests of Mexican American civil rights groups. The U.S.

and Mexican governments were equally invested in keeping negative publicity about the program at bay—the former to maintain the flow of labor, the latter to maintain the flow of remittances.[29]

The surviving braceros of Chualar, along with braceros around the United States, occupied a liminal space in which they could not fully claim the rights of citizenship in either their home or host country. In his personal notes Galarza lamented, "The survivors of the crash have been forgotten. There was an impressive public relations mass for the dead but the living who are hurt or maimed are isolated, disperse[d] and bewildered."[30] Though they stood as important figures of witness to the accident and the dangers of the Bracero Program, the survivors were intentionally muted and hidden from public view by the GFLA, the very agency entrusted with ensuring their well-being. Those braceros who spoke with Galarza regained their voices and visibility, and their testimonies became part of Galarza's House Committee on Education and Labor report and subsequent 1977 book *Tragedy at Chualar*. But aside from one article published in the *Salinas Californian,* local residents were never made aware of the survivors' seclusion, and Espinosa's jurors never heard these men's recollections of the crash. It was clear that in Salinas, it was easier to care for and mourn dead Mexicans than it was to confront the traumas and exploitation of those still alive.

THE BRACERO PROGRAM ON TRIAL

What Salinas agribusiness was unable to silence was the growing vocal opposition to the Bracero Program. Union leaders sought to eliminate a labor force that undercut and displaced U.S. farmworkers. Religious organizations, including the National Council of Churches, the National Catholic Rural Life Conference, the Bishops' Committee for the Spanish Speaking, and the National Catholic Welfare Conference, argued that growers' greed went against the divine moral order and that the program hurt braceros spiritually by separating them from their families in Mexico. Father Anthony Soto affirmed, "[we] are not against him [the bracero] as a foreigner, but against his exploitation as a foreigner." Meanwhile, Mexican American activists began to forge stronger connections with each other in the wake of Chualar. Until this point, tension had characterized relations between different groups.

In answer to Notre Dame sociologist Julian Samora's 1962 national questionnaire concerning discrimination against the Spanish-speaking, more than one CSO member-respondent claimed that a lack of unity among Mexican American organizations was a noticeable problem: "Many of our leaders are jealous of each other and distrust of each other is always existent . . . we have tried to join some of these leaders before . . . [but there are] too many chiefs and no one willing to be an Indian." In 1963, however, the CSO, MAPA, and the AGIF all began expressing greater anti–Bracero Program sentiment and agreed to share the cost of publishing Galarza's report on the Chualar tragedy to reach a wider audience beyond a few government committees.[31]

The crash had reenergized conversations about labor, immigration, and the status of Mexican-origin people in the United States. Mexican American civil rights leaders of all stripes jumped on the anti–Bracero Program bandwagon, recognizing that it would draw more attention to their existence and elevate their organizations' national profile. In December 1964 representatives of LULAC, the AGIF, CSO, MAPA, the Latin American Civic Association (LACA), and the Council for Mexican-American Affairs (CMAA) convened in Sacramento to discuss issues that included agricultural labor policy, employment, education, poverty, and political appointments. Later, representatives of these groups, including Eduardo Quevedo, Bert Corona, and Herman Gallegos, appeared before a San Francisco hearing of the U.S. Department of Labor to specifically address the suffering of domestic farmworkers caused by the Bracero Program. Then, in 1965, leaders including Galarza, Quevedo, national LULAC vice president Jess Vela, and AGIF state chairman Charles Samarron met with Governor Pat Brown to discuss topics pertinent to California's Mexican American population. By 1965 a Mexican-American Unity Council had been formed to establish better communication and collaboration among these organizations. Chaired by attorney Manuel Ruiz, the Unity Council claimed as members MAPA president Bert Corona, CSO leaders James Delgadillo and Albert Pinon, Eduardo Quevedo, and Ernesto Galarza, among others. Later, at a MAPA convention, Corona reiterated the need for Mexican American activists to work together. "We must reject every effort to divide us and to weaken us. We must seek every way possible to cooperate with CSO, GI Forum, LULAC . . . [and the] UFWOC," he said in his welcoming speech to the convention. Indeed, one reason that Mexican

American political groups could not afford to act separately was that farmworker issues had become hot topics in national discourse, and these groups stood to benefit from this attention. In a way, the death of a group of braceros had helped birth a new phase of collaboration between California's Mexican American leaders. Thus, even before Cesar Chavez and Dolores Huerta gained fame as the leaders of the California farmworker movement through the UFWOC grape strike in Delano in 1965, the Chualar tragedy of 1963 galvanized the Mexican American activist community and enfolded farmworker concerns into the agenda of the nascent California Chicano Movement.[32]

Despite agribusiness's efforts to persuade Congress to extend the Bracero Program into 1965, the full congressional vote on December 4, 1963, maintained the program's scheduled end of December 31, 1964, twenty-two years after its beginning as a "temporary" guestworker program. During a time when the United States was preoccupied with its global image and addressing concerns about migrant labor, unemployment, and race relations in the form of War on Poverty initiatives and legislation such as the Civil Rights Act, the continuation of the Bracero Program became harder to justify. The Salinas Valley bracero deaths, along with the labor-, human-, and civil rights–centered rhetoric and protest that they evoked from multiple communities, undoubtedly influenced Congress's decision. As Henry Anderson had predicted in a radio broadcast the day after the accident, "The death of the thirty-one martyrs of the Salinas Valley may also prove to have been the death of the bracero system."[33]

On paper, the Bracero Program was dead, yet to noticeably "hysterical" California growers, it remained the ideal labor system that needed to be resurrected. Even some Mexican government officials lamented the program's end, as it would stop the outflow of surplus unemployed citizens and the inflow of remittances. "You're taking away our safety valve," one high-ranking official told the U.S. ambassador in confidence. Statistics from 1964 illuminate how dependent California still was on Mexican labor by the end of the program. Braceros constituted 75 percent of the state's lemon pickers; half of the southern coast's grape workers; more than 40 percent of the Palo Verde, Imperial, and San Joaquin Valleys' melon pickers; and 91 percent of the Coachella Valley's date palm workers. Some harvest associations experimented with importing other laborers—Tejanos; Native Americans from Arizona,

New Mexico, and South Dakota; African Americans from Louisiana and Mississippi; and Anglo day-haul workers from Los Angeles—but none of these domestic workforces met their expectations. As geographer Don Mitchell has argued, these domestic experiments failed not just because of "the rotten wages and conditions, but the very fact that it was now nearly impossible to provide the labor force the landscape required *unless* it closely resembled labor made available by the bracero program."[34]

Desperate for Mexican workers, California agribusiness tried to find loopholes. Some converted their favorite braceros into green-carders by sponsoring their applications. Others turned to Public Law 414, or the McCarran-Walter Act, under which U.S. Secretary of Labor Willard Wirtz could certify the importation of foreign workers if an insufficient number of U.S. citizens were unavailable at fair rates of pay and adequate working conditions. In a letter to President Lyndon B. Johnson, AFL-CIO president Walter Reuther condemned this strategy. "Such an approach would simply substitute one method of employing Mexican farm labor for another," he complained. In a joint statement, leaders of the AGIF, the CSO, MAPA, the CMAA, LACA, and LULAC denounced the "subservience" of government agencies to agribusiness, calling any further importations of braceros wholly "inconsistent with the crusade against poverty." While they waited for more braceros, California growers used Public Law 414 to hire approximately 1,200 Japanese, 120 Filipino, and 400 Basque workers to labor in their fields in 1964. Meanwhile, East Coast employers hired a total of 1,441 Canadian, Filipino, Japanese, and British West Indian workers, as well as 4,014 Puerto Ricans.[35] Appalled, labor unionists and activists argued that plenty of farmworkers could be found on the U.S. mainland, but inadequate working conditions and wages were keeping them away.

Determined to find out what exact grievances were causing a domestic labor shortage, Wirtz announced a seven-hundred-mile, three-day inspection tour to visit California farms and talk with workers, growers, union leaders, and government officials. One of his first stops was Salinas. At dawn on March 25, 1965, Wirtz and four of his aides (who included James Vizzard) made surprise visits to the labor camps of the Bruce Church Company, the C. W. Englund Company, and the S&W Company. According to Wirtz, the Church camp was "excellent. The facilities were spic-and-span and the breakfast was solid." Englund's camp, however, left Wirtz disgusted. "It makes me ashamed that anything of this kind exists in this country . . . The place is filthy," he told news reporters later. "It was a wonder anyone could look at the food, much less eat it." Englund, which operated fifty-six camps in California and Arizona serving up to ten thousand workers, was the biggest farm labor housing and feeding contractor in the United States. Wirtz said he would not discuss the S&W camp, a smaller grower-operated facility, because "it was so much worse than even Englund's facilities," but he concluded by blasting many California labor camps as "filthy, shameful blots on America." Wirtz also talked with Salinas Mexican American workers like eighteen-year-old Sal Castañeda, who had worked in the fields for two years to support his five brothers and sisters, and Bertha Rodriguez, who told Wirtz that three of her friends asked for jobs thinning lettuce but were rejected by labor contractors. These conversations and additional inspections persuaded Wirtz, a former labor law professor, that California could not justify leaving four hundred thousand people unemployed while importing one hundred thousand Mexican nationals. Wirtz declared to the media, and to California growers, that the bracero era was over.[36]

Some California growers responded to Wirtz's proclamation by sending very explicit messages that they would not tolerate his bracero ban. Orange County strawberry grower Jack Tabata, for example, plowed under twelve acres of his own crop to protest his not getting any braceros and then sent Wirtz a tray of bruised and unripe strawberries to demonstrate the incompetence of domestic workers (Wirtz allegedly ate the berries in response). Salinas grower William Garin began investing heavily in western Mexico where wages for cantaloupe harvesting averaged fifteen pesos a day (a little more than a dollar) while planning significant disinvestment in California land. To attract more domestics to agriculture, Wirtz increased the minimum wage for farmwork in California from $1.00 to $1.25 an hour, stipulating another increase to $1.40 by April 1, 1965. In Texas, where growers were paying braceros sixty to seventy cents an hour, the minimum hourly wage was set to $1.15.[37]

Yet by the beginning of May 1965, it was obvious that Salinas Valley growers had put great pressure on state and federal agencies to relieve their alleged domestic labor shortage. On May 4 the U.S. State Department and Mexican government agreed to import fifteen hundred

Mexican workers into Salinas along with one hundred Japanese and Filipino workers. Salinas farmers responded by audaciously requesting another twenty-five hundred braceros while the Salinas City Council ordered a telegram be sent to Wirtz and President Johnson urging the immediate return of braceros "to preserve the economic stability of the Salinas Valley." In late May 1965, Wirtz acquiesced and authorized another one thousand Mexicans for the Salinas area. Of the 3,500 foreign workers authorized for use in California during the first half of 1965, Salinas growers acquired 2,250 of them. That summer the U.S. government continued receiving letters pleading for the return of the Bracero Program from the Southern Monterey County Chamber of Commerce and Agriculture, Salinas Strawberries owner Thomas McNamara, and H. Stephen Chase, the president of Wells Fargo Bank, which had long handled the transfer of bracero pay deductions to Mexico. Meanwhile, in Sacramento, a group of California fruit and vegetable growers—including Jack Bias and William Garin of Salinas, Imperial Valley Farmers Association president Herbert A. Lee, and Western Growers Association executive vice president Frank W. Castiglione—visited Governor Brown in person and threatened to cut their plantings by 40 percent unless they received supplemental foreign labor. In an effort to prove that growers did not need guestworkers, the Mexican American Unity Council carried out its own domestic recruitment program along the central coast and recruited 1,849 farmworkers, but California Department of Employment director Albert B. Tieburg considered the effort a failure because it did not surpass previous domestic recruitment numbers by growers or the Farm Placement Service.[38]

Determined to put a stop to growers' requests, Wirtz developed a plan to recruit high school athletes from across the nation—or "A-TEAMS" (Athletes in Temporary Employment as Agricultural Manpower)—to work in California's fields. "Farm Work Builds Men!" was the program's official slogan. By the beginning of August 1965, 2,735 boys had begun work, but growers called A-Teams a "farce" and questioned their necessity if Wirtz claimed there were sufficient domestics available. When A-Teams arrived in the Salinas Valley in the summer of 1965, they failed almost immediately. Of the 718 boys initially employed, 268 quit within a month. Promised $1.40 an hour, A-Teamers were dumbfounded upon discovering that this rate applied only to their initial sixty-four-hour training period. After that they were to work on a piece-rate basis of one dollar a crate, a system that the youths claimed would not allow them to make a $1.40 hourly wage. The A-Teams also criticized their housing facilities and meals. In a C. W. Englund labor camp, several boys threw their plates on the floor and walked out of the mess hall in protest. Of the 876 A-Team members sent to the Salinas area, 52 percent left prematurely. In all other areas of California combined, only 16 percent did the same. This disparate rate suggests that, more than other places, the Salinas Valley had historically abused its workers without much surveillance or punishment. Representative Teno Roncalio (D-Wyoming) said of his state's A-Teams assigned to Salinas, "They were fed food that was unfit for human consumption . . . [and] lived in beds filthy with bedbugs." In denouncing these conditions as unacceptable for U.S. workers, Roncalio failed to acknowledge that braceros had endured these exact conditions since 1942. It had taken young citizen athletes complaining of similar sufferings to alert him and others to the mistreatment of farmworkers. Growers were eventually placated in September 1965 when the U.S. government imported 8,400 Mexican and Puerto Rican farm hands to the Salinas and San Joaquin Valleys, and then another 8,647 Mexicans to help harvest the state's tomato crop in 1966. It was clear that Wirtz and the U.S. government were losing the battle against ending the Bracero Program in practice as well as on paper. The official death of the Bracero Program was proving to be slow and painful, especially for those Mexican American farm-workers who still found themselves underpaid or unemployed.[39]

With the collision of a train and a bus came a collision of various communities—pro– and anti–Bracero Program, local and federal, Mexican and Mexican American—that proved an important moment in 1960s labor, social, and political history. As a site of tragedy, the Salinas Valley was thrust into the national spotlight and became a center of debate over the future of the most controversial guestworker program in the United States. As they lived, braceros stood as some of the least powerful workers in the country. Their dead bodies, on the other hand, held a catalytic power that accelerated not only the end of the Bracero Program, but the evolution of a Chicano civil rights movement in California that enveloped the goals of Mexican Americans in the barrios and the fields. As they realized they would be the ones to inherit the bracero legacy of exploitation, alterity, and invisibility, Mexican American farmworkers knew they had to act more boldly during the second half of the 1960s. In the Salinas Valley this boldness would manifest in public protests, landmark lawsuits against California agribusiness, and secretly joining Cesar Chavez's burgeoning farmworker union.

6 The Farmworker Movement in the Post-Bracero Era

THE CONTINUED IMPORTATION of braceros in what was supposed to be a post-bracero era was a painful thorn in the side of almost four million U.S. domestic farmworkers. Often forced onto the road and into an itinerant life, they suffered from a lack of a living wage and ineligibility for health insurance, welfare, voting rights, and other resources that required an extended period of residency in one place. Even if they did find employment, they endured long days of backbreaking fieldwork with unrealistic piece rates, inadequate rest periods, and exposure to pesticides. Their average life expectancy was only forty-nine years. Many female farmworkers experienced sexual harassment on the job, and U.S. Secretary of Health, Education, and Welfare Anthony J. Celebrezze called migrant children "the most educationally deprived group of children in our Nation" due to their families' peripatetic lifestyle. The disparity between farmworkers' and growers' wealth was shocking. Nationally, farmworkers' average annual income dropped from $1,125 in 1960 to $1,054 in 1961. Even in agriculturally rich areas like Monterey County, domestic laborers averaged only 129 days of employment and $1,247 in yearly earnings. Meanwhile, Monterey County agribusiness reaped $175 million in gross farm income in 1966, ranking eighth among agricultural counties in California and eleventh in the nation. Employers were doing little to create affordable family housing for migrant farmworker families (which averaged 6.5 people) and were using the excuse of a "domestic labor shortage" to hire Mexican nationals. In border regions like the Imperial Valley, growers hired Mexican commuter workers early in the morning before area employment offices opened to U.S. residents.[1] Although the Hart-Cellar Act in 1965 had imposed new quotas on Western hemispheric immigration, limiting entry to 120,000 people annually, these caps did not stop the flow of Mexican migrants into the country. In fact, the 20,000-person quota for Mexico fell drastically short of reality and historical immigration patterns and in effect created *more* undocumented immigrants whom U.S. employers were still willing to hire.

Though domestic farmworkers came from every racial background, the vast majority in the 1960s were Mexican American. By 1965 an estimated 5.5 million Spanish-speaking people lived in the United States, with between 4.5 and 4.8 million identifying as being of Mexican-origin. This population, in addition to comprising a vulnerable agricultural labor force, continued to suffer from discrimination in housing and employment, police brutality, being drafted to and killed in disproportionate numbers in Vietnam, and completing a lower median level of education than both whites and blacks. Many things had not changed, but one thing that had was the number of Mexican-origin people who were U.S. citizens rather than foreign-born. With a larger native-born population, the call for Mexican Americans' equal treatment and citizenship during a civil rights era grew louder. It was in this climate that the Chicano Movement, or *el movimiento*, emerged. This movement was an expression of Mexican American ethnic nationalism and civil rights protest that flourished during the 1960s. The term "Chicano" was believed to be derived from "Xicano," an abbreviated form of "Mexicano," and the ideology of "Chicanismo" involved a crucial distinction between a "Mexican American" and "Chicano" identity, with the latter encompassing greater ethnic pride and more militant politics. Instead of shying away from their Mexican heritage, Chicanos embraced their cultural roots and proclaimed a loyalty to "Aztlán," the original homeland that was now the U.S. Southwest. "A new Mexican-American militancy is emerging. Brown has become aggressively beautiful," an article in *Newsweek* remarked. Not all Mexican-origin people chose to identify as "Chicano" or "brown," preferring to stick with older assimilation-based ideologies instead. "I resent the term 'brown power,'" AGIF founder Dr. Hector P. Garcia said. "That sounds as if we were a different race. We're not. We're white. We should be Americans. But we should eat enchiladas and be proud of our names." Those who did want to be called Chicanos, however, believed it was time for more radical, confrontational political action against a white establishment.[2]

The CSO, LULAC, MAPA, and the AGIF still remained prominent Mexican American civil rights organizations, but new Chicano leaders came onto the scene in the mid- and late 1960s. In New Mexico, Pentecostal believer Reies López Tijerina founded the Alliance of Free Peoples (La Alianza) and led a land grant movement to reclaim land taken from Mexico by the Treaty of Guadalupe Hidalgo. His militant actions against law enforcement and the U.S. Forest Service landed him in federal prison at the end of the decade and made him a living legend. In Denver, Colorado, former sugar beet worker Rodolfo "Corky" Gonzalez founded the youth organization Crusade for Justice in 1966, held two Chicano Youth Conferences in 1969 and 1970, and wrote the iconic poem "Yo Soy Joaquin," which still stands as one of the most popular pieces of Chicano literature. In Texas, José Angel Gutiérrez founded the political party La Raza Unida (The United People), and in 1970 its Mexican American candidates swept a previously Anglo-dominated city council and school board in the town of Crystal City. Young people also become active *movimiento* participants. In March 1968, fifteen thousand high school students in East Los Angeles staged school walkouts (or "blowouts") to demand more culturally inclusive curriculum and more Mexican American teachers. Other students replicated these walkouts across the country. College students founded groups such as the United Mexican American Students, the Mexican American Youth Association, and the Mexican American Youth Organization, which were consolidated into Movimiento Estudiantil Chicano de Aztlán (MEChA) in April 1969. The Brown Berets, a youth group founded in California and modeled after the Black Panthers, demonstrated against educational inequality, police brutality, and the Vietnam War.

The individual who most successfully straddled the two worlds of the Chicano Movement and the U.S. political mainstream was Cesar Chavez. While beginning to organize Mexican American farmworkers in Delano, California, under the National Farm Workers Association,

Chavez and Dolores Huerta were approached by Filipino activist Larry Itliong, the leader of AWOC, to join his organization in a grape workers' strike in the Delano vineyards. By August 1966 the two unions had merged into the UFWOC. Because farmworkers in the American West did not yet have the same visibility as African American civil rights protestors in the American South, the UFWOC used multiple organizing tactics, including pilgrimages, fasts, and consumer boycotts, to capture national attention. Galvanizing union supporters in both the cities and the fields with his humble yet charismatic persona, Chavez rose to become an internationally known labor and civil rights leader.

Chavez was a successful organizer, however, only because of his union's co-leaders and the many farmworkers who welcomed him into their minds and hearts. In fact, it was in the Salinas Valley—a region where farmworker activism had been crushed for decades—that ordinary people laid extraordinary groundwork in the late 1960s that allowed Chavez to unionize thousands of people throughout California. They did this in three ways. First, many took initiative by financially supporting or joining the UFWOC during its early years. Though Chavez remained focused on the grape strike in Delano, his cousin Manuel moved to Salinas to lead a community action program funded by the federal government's Office of Economic Opportunity (OEO). Created by the Economic Opportunity Act of 1964 under President Johnson's War on Poverty, the OEO sponsored a number of vocational, literacy, volunteer service, and community programs dedicated to helping America's poor. Many farmworkers gravitated to Manuel Chavez and his program, knowing that both could serve as links to the UFWOC. Groups of farmworkers became union members and even arranged meetings with Cesar himself to request that he organize the Salinas Valley next. Second, farmworkers took advantage of another OEO-funded organization, California Rural Legal Assistance (CRLA), and filed two landmark lawsuits against California agribusiness in 1967 that protected farmworkers' right to unionize and stopped further importations of braceros into the state. These lawsuits would remove huge obstacles to agricultural unionization in general and the UFWOC's progress in particular. Finally, the region's Mexican Americans and Mexicans began creating greater political community. After twenty-five years of competing for agricultural jobs and other resources, U.S.-born, ex-bracero, and immigrant Mexicans came to realize that it was only by acting together that they could effect change in their laboring lives. This new collaborative spirit, coupled with an emerging Chicano Movement in the Mexican American middle class and student communities, benefited Chavez when he arrived in Salinas to organize lettuce workers in the summer of 1970. Chavez did not suddenly bring a farmworker movement to the valley—a vibrant movement had already blossomed and was waiting for him there.

THE RISE OF CHAVEZ AND THE UFWOC

Cesar Chavez, the man from Yuma, Arizona, who claimed humble migrant worker roots, captivated America by imbuing his farmworker cause with racial, religious, and civil rights overtones. He was a devoted Catholic who likened his philosophy of nonviolence to leaders like Martin Luther King Jr. and Mahatma Gandhi, and he used drastic techniques to highlight the deprivation and perseverance of poor laborers. He publicly fasted on numerous occasions, once for twenty-five consecutive days during which he accepted only water and prayers. In March 1966 he organized thousands of farmworkers to march three hundred miles with him from Delano to Sacramento to ask for California governor Pat Brown's support of the UFWOC. The marchers ranged in age from seventeen to sixty-three, and one-quarter were women. This pilgrimage, or *peregrinación,* complete with the union's graphically striking red and black Aztec eagle flag and iconography of the Virgin of Guadalupe, fascinated people living in communities along the route. Thousands lined up to watch, offer marchers food and drink, or even join the march themselves. By the time the march ended on Easter Sunday on the steps of the capitol building, it had grown to ten thousand people. Chavez then publicly announced that Brown had decided to vacation in Palm Springs instead of meeting the marchers, turning the *peregrinación* into a protest—and media gold (Brown had offered to return to Sacramento at the last minute, but Chavez rebuffed him). News photos and video of the limping and bleeding Chavez, along with the crowd roaring "Viva Cesar!" and "Viva Huelga!" (Long live Cesar! Long live the strike!) showed Americans everywhere that a farmworker movement was taking shape. The following Labor Day, Chavez joined another three-hundred-mile march of Texas UFWOC members at the end of their journey from Rio Grande City to Austin. Like their

counterparts in California, these Texan farmworkers were asking growers to pay higher wages and sign union contracts. They were also battling
the collusion between agribusiness and law enforcement, as the Texas
Rangers frequently partnered with local police to harass and disperse
union picketers. "There's a lot to the saying that all Texas Rangers have
Mexican blood. They have it on their boots," one witness told the U.S.
Commission on Civil Rights about the Rangers' legacy of violence.[3]

To initiate a national consumer boycott of grapes, the UFWOC capi-
talized on media attention and a civil rights era in which the practice of
the boycott had taken on new significance. Because farmworkers had
been excluded from the National Labor Relations Act since the New
Deal, the secondary boycott remained a viable tool for them to pair
with a strike. By picketing outside of grocery stores that sold nonunion
grapes, the UFWOC persuaded consumers to see that no matter how far
away they lived from California—Chicago, Detroit, New York, Philadelphia, Toronto—they could help Delano workers by choosing not
to shop in certain markets. This tactic worked particularly well with
housewives and other women who were often in charge of their house-
holds' food purchases. The UFWOC's clever strategy of crossing racial
lines and including consumers in a moral economy gained the support of people who otherwise might not have cared about the struggles
of Mexican American farmworkers. By connecting the commodity of
grapes to the crime of farmworker exploitation, the UFWOC banked
on the power of the purse to create social change. It became "cool"
for farmworkers and nonfarmworkers alike to wave the UFWOC flag,
shout "Huelga!," or wear a "Don't Buy Grapes" pin. When President
Richard Nixon tried to help growers circumvent the boycott by ship-
ping their fruit to U.S. armed forces in Vietnam and to Europe, Chicano
sailors threw boxes of grapes into the Gulf of Tonkin and activists
across the Atlantic made sure that hundreds of thousands of pounds
of grapes rotted on the docks of London and Hamburg. A blockade
on nonunion grapes extended to multiple ports in Scandinavia. This
cooperation around the globe took an economic toll on growers, and
Schenley Industries—a major liquor distributor that owned a grape
vineyard—became the first to sign with the UFWOC. California farmworkers erupted with excitement upon hearing the news via Spanish-
language radio, newspapers, or word of mouth from other *campesinos*
on the migrant labor circuit.[4]

UFWOC leaders made sure to let Salinas Valley workers know that a labor revolution was coming their way. "We made damn sure they knew about [Delano]," said UFWOC organizer Marshall Ganz. A rabbi's son born in Bakersfield, California, Ganz had dropped out of Harvard to volunteer in the African American civil rights movement. He participated in Freedom Summer, a 1964 Mississippi workshop run by a coalition of northern black youths and southern black activists to train students in the fight to enfranchise African Americans. During a trip home Ganz met Chavez, who asked him to join the union cause. With additional encouragement from Student Nonviolent Coordinating Committee (SNCC) activist Stokely Carmichael, Ganz joined the UFWOC as an SNCC liaison and soon became one of the union's top organizers.[5] Observing that Mexicano farmworkers in the Southwest suffered from injustices similar to those African Americans suffered, Ganz recognized that the U.S. civil rights movement was not isolated to the black-and-white South but encompassed other people if one looked west.

Even while he was focused on Delano, Chavez knew that the Salinas Valley was a critical site for farmworker organizing if the UFWOC was to succeed in California. To that end, he appointed his cousin Manuel to begin developing a stronghold there for the union. Because of the incorporation of Alisal in August 1963, Salinas had grown to a city of nearly sixty thousand, with Mexican-origin people numbering approximately sixteen thousand, or 27 percent. Manuel, who had been in and out of jail for grand theft and selling drugs, was already known in the union for his tough personality and cunning. "If Cesar was both the serpent and the dove, Manuel was all serpent," opined journalist Frank Bardacke, while others in the union characterized him as a "charming scoundrel" and the "evil twin in a Shakespearean drama." In February 1966 Manuel moved to Salinas to begin the most serious effort to organize farmworkers since the Filipino and "Okie" workers' strikes of the 1930s. He did not start with a full-blown unionization campaign, however, but with a community action program called the Committee for Salinas Valley Self-Help Farm Workers. Sponsored by the California Center for Community Development and funded by the OEO, the committee served as an agency to which farmworkers could go with grievances such as poor living conditions, the continued hiring of Mexican nationals over domestics, and unscrupulous labor contractors who, in the words of one farmworker, continued to transport them in vehicles like those used "when the braceros were killed a few years ago in Chualar."[6]

From February to June 1966 Manuel borrowed a successful CSO strategy and held more than fifty house meetings, speaking with more than five thousand Salinas Valley farmworkers about the benefits of mass mobilization. Although the committee was not formally acting under the UFWOC, it quickly became a proto-union. In early February 1966, three hundred unemployed male farmworkers protested in the streets against Monterey County's Department of Public Assistance. After being laid off by growers because of bad weather, the men had approached the department for indigent aid but were offered only county roadwork jobs to be paid in credits at a soup kitchen. Insulted by the low compensation, the three hundred men marched in tattered clothing through the streets of Salinas, carrying signs reading "Welfare Slavery Has Got to Go," "Give Us Real Jobs," "We Want to Live Like Equal Citizens," and "Let Us into the Great Society." County officials responded by offering the men three days of food for one day of work, but still no money. It had become painfully clear, not just to these protestors but to other Salinas Valley farmworkers, that a union was necessary to force county officials and grower-employers to take their labor rights seriously. Manuel's organizing stint in Salinas was only temporary (he relocated to the Calexico-Mexicali border to recruit new union members), but he had effectively created an important funnel organization for UFWOC membership.[7]

Meanwhile, the UFWOC's newspaper and mouthpiece *El Malcriado* ("The Ill-Bred One," or "Problem Child") was attacking the federal government and Governor Brown for bending to growers' demands for braceros after the congressional termination of the program. In one case in the spring of 1966, the UFWOC informed the Salinas Strawberries Company—the largest strawberry grower in the nation—that hundreds of workers in San Jose were available if the company would sign a union contract. Instead of negotiating, Salinas Strawberries recruited migrant families from Texas and charged them exorbitant rent to live in company-owned trailers, knowing the rates would scare away the recruits. Salinas Strawberries then telephoned Governor Brown and asked for one thousand braceros. "Congress abolished the bracero program two years ago, but these growers seem to be outside of the reach

BRACEROS FOR SALINAS

Fig. 6.1. A cartoon in *El Malcriado*, May 19, 1966, depicts a labor contractor leading chained braceros to Salinas. (Cartoon by Andy Zermeño)

of the law," *El Malcriado* declared and accused agribusiness and the federal government of being the real smugglers, or *coyotes,* depriving citizen-farmworkers of a decent livelihood. "When Governor Brown says he wants to help farm workers, and then smuggles in braceros, EL MALCRIADO says that he is a liar, a traitor to the Mexican-Americans who voted for him and a fool who will believe any lies the growers tell him. The farmworkers will not forget that," the article read (fig. 6.1).[8]

By March 1967 *El Malcriado* was being distributed in the Salinas Valley by residents like former Monterey County CSO leader Abe Chávez, Sally Gutíerrez, and teenage farmworker Teresa Serrano, who were all selling subscriptions. Farmworkers began writing to the paper to describe their poor working conditions and ask for information about how to join the UFWOC.[9] For a region in which growers and law enforcement had suppressed any farmworker unionization attempts since the 1930s, this was the beginning of a transformational period. As growers began discovering that their employees were secretly joining the UFWOC, however, they retaliated by threatening, evicting, and firing them. Just as they did with Filipino and "Okie" workers in the 1930s, Salinas Valley growers made it clear to Mexican laborers that they were not going to tolerate a union in the fields. What was different this time was that farmworkers had a new legal resource with which to fight back. Turning to California Rural Legal Assistance (CRLA), a newly founded legal aid organization for the agricultural poor, Salinas farmworkers filed lawsuits against California agribusiness during the late 1960s with effects far greater than they or others could have predicted.

CRLA AND THE SALINAS NINE

On July 31, 1967, an African American farmworker entered the downtown Salinas office of CRLA and asked for attorney Robert Gnaizda. The man, a carrot harvester for the Martin Produce Company, had just been fired by his employer, John W. Martin Jr., for being a suspected UFWOC member. As he asked Gnaizda for his help in suing Martin for unlawful termination, the man revealed that Martin's eight other carrot harvesters (another African American and seven Mexican Americans) had secretly joined the UFWOC as well and risked losing their jobs if they were discovered.[10] As he listened, Gnaizda doubted that one farmworker's firing would yield a strong legal case against Martin. Though he was aware of the antiunionism that pervaded Salinas agribusiness, the lawyer regretfully informed his prospective client that all nine men would have to be fired in order to win a case against Martin and the all-powerful GFLA. Not wanting to risk his co-workers' jobs, the farmworker left Gnaizda's office, believing nothing more could come of his grievance.

Brooklyn born and Yale educated, Robert Gnaizda was new to town, having been recently recruited to head the Salinas CRLA office by his friend Jim Lorenz, a Harvard graduate and lawyer who founded CRLA in 1966. CRLA received more than a million dollars in funding from the OEO under the War on Poverty and established offices in El Centro, Delano, Madera, Modesto, Marysville, Santa Rosa, Santa Maria,

Sacramento, Gilroy, and Salinas. Gnaizda agreed to head the Salinas branch under the condition that his colleague Marty Glick—a lawyer from Ohio who was working for the Civil Rights Division of the U.S. Department of Justice—be hired as well. Gnaizda and Glick, along with attorney Dennis Powell, opened the office in late 1966 and quickly realized how imbalanced the community's power dynamics were. "Salinas was run by agribusiness," Gnaizda recalled. "Farmworkers were irrelevant . . . there were no Latinos in any positions with any power at all." For this reason the CRLA office was moved to a central location on Main Street, rather than being in the "Mexican" neighborhoods of West Market Street or Alisal, to make the organization more visible to both Mexican-origin clients and white city leaders. Gnaizda acted further to make a strong impression. In the spring of 1967 he wrote a scathing letter to the editor of the *Salinas Californian* criticizing the "prevalent discourtesy and rudeness" of the INS in Monterey County and in particular its practice of addressing Mexican-origin people (both U.S.-born and immigrant) as "Pancho" when interrogating them.[11]

Gnaizda and Glick also hired a diverse branch staff to broaden the office's reach and appeal. Two bilingual Mexican American secretaries, Amelia Harris and Josephine Roar, joined four community workers, two of whom were former farmworkers and one who was a young Mexican immigrant who already had a reputation for political organizing. A resident of a dilapidated labor camp in Soledad, Hector De La Rosa had mobilized other camp families to protest their living conditions before the Soledad City Council. After months of fighting to put the matter to a vote, the citizens of Soledad voted 257 to 256 to raze the camp and give the families rights to build sixty new homes on the property with federal funds. A few months after this close victory, CRLA recruited De La Rosa to be a community worker and he began interviewing farmworkers in the fields, meeting with them at their homes in the evenings, and representing workers at legal hearings regarding unemployment, disability, and welfare issues.[12] By serving the agricultural poor and placing Mexican Americans in positions of leadership and visibility, CRLA served as an important Chicano Movement–era advocate for farmworkers. Unlike other civil rights organizations like the CSO or MAPA, CRLA made rural Mexican Americans its most important clients. Furthermore, the fact that most CRLA community workers had been farmworkers themselves lent an even greater sense of comfort and accessibility to Mexicano field hands who otherwise might have hesitated to ask for the organization's assistance.

As much as CRLA provided for its Salinas farmworker clients, it was the latter who directed the organization to particular cases of significance. In June 1967 ten Mexican American male strawberry workers approached CRLA to file a complaint against the Salinas Strawberries Company for attempting to evict them and their families from the company-owned La Posada trailer camp. Believing they had been fired because of their suspected UFWOC membership, the men argued that their trailers' lights, heat, and electricity had been shut off in an effort at further intimidation. Salinas Strawberries denied both charges, but when Glick came upon company records of the terminated employees on which was written "fired for union activities," the company's lies were exposed. In *Jaramillo v. Salinas Strawberries*, Judge Gordon Campbell ruled in favor of the workers and ordered Salinas Strawberries to reinstate all utility services, pay back wages, and rehire the workers with guaranteed future protection of their jobs.[13]

News about the case's outcome spread, and other Salinas farmworkers literally followed suit, using CRLA to file complaints against other grower-employers. Much-publicized cases filed in 1967 and 1968 concerned the lack of sanitation and health standard enforcement in California agriculture. At least three men—Rodolfo Lara, Magdaleno Botello, and Mauricio "Marty" Muñoz—were denied unemployment insurance benefits when they individually refused to accept farm labor jobs from the Department of Employment because of the employers' "filthy and grossly inadequate sanitary facilities." CRLA investigations found that of all Monterey County agricultural employers, most did not provide separate drinking cups for water for their work crews (separate cups were required by law to prevent the spread of diseases such as hepatitis, amoebic dysentery, typhoid, and tuberculosis between the workers and then to food consumers). Twenty-five percent did not provide toilets in the fields, and only a few provided hand-washing facilities. In Sutter, Yuba, Butte, and Colusa Counties, a CRLA farmworker survey found that of 173 employers concerned, more than 90 percent did not provide clean water, clean toilets, or hand-washing facilities to their employees. In June 1968 Lara was vindicated when the California Unemployment Insurance Appeals Board ruled in his favor. Muñoz, a

Korean War veteran who had refused to work for Salinas Strawberries after losing his job in the insurance industry, received a similar judgment the next year.[14]

One of the Salinas CRLA's most significant cases was its 1967 lawsuit against the Martin Produce Company, the same company that had fired the carrot harvester for being a suspected UFWOC member. After firing that employee, John W. Martin and GFLA executive vice president E. James Houseberg proceeded to intimidate the remaining eight workers. Manuel Ortiz, one of the "older field men" who had worked for Martin for eight years, was the first to be interrogated. Fearful of losing his job, Ortiz denied his and the others' UFWOC membership. In front of Ortiz, Houseberg advised Martin to fire all eight men and replace them with a new crew. Houseberg then ordered Ortiz "to go back to the fields and warn the boys that if they joined a union they would be fired." Martin would later go into the fields himself to discourage his "boys" from joining the UFWOC. Not wanting to risk the loss of their jobs, the eight men admitted nothing. Through the CRLA grapevine, Cesar Chavez heard about these intimidation tactics and decided to provoke Martin into action. On August 8, without the workers' or Gnaizda's knowledge, Chavez sent a telegram to Martin informing him that his remaining eight carrot harvesters were indeed UFWOC members. The next day, on August 9, Martin fired the entire carrot-harvesting crew. The fact that he did so after receiving Chavez's telegram meant that the nine men, including the original complainant—Fred Wetherton, John Watson, Jesus Robles, José Pérez, Manuel Ortiz, Domingo Longoria, Anthony Cervantes, Antonio Castañeda, and Ignacio Burgos—now had a case. CRLA filed a half-million-dollar lawsuit on their behalf against Martin, Houseberg, the GFLA, and the GSVA (the GFLA's parent association) for coercion, intimidation, and violation of the California Labor Code. Though they had not planned to be swept up into a larger movement that included Chavez and his union, the "Salinas Nine" would become key players in laying the groundwork for the UFWOC's future success in the Salinas Valley and throughout California.[15]

From the beginning, the men made sure that their CRLA lawyers knew their priorities. "What they wanted us to accomplish for them was to get back to work," Glick said. "They wanted their jobs." Although proud to be UFWOC members, the nine men considered economic security to be their primary goal. CRLA staff felt the same way, as the organization's OEO funding was contingent on its representation of individuals only and no labor unions or political groups. This point provoked some tension between CRLA and Chavez, who wanted the organization to act as an overt UFWOC advocate. A February 1967 letter from Jim Lorenz to Chavez addressed the issue: "I have the feeling that there have been a number of problems which are likely to persist between you and ourselves, unless we bring them out on the table . . . we are not representing you in negotiations with growers, and we are not bringing lawsuits on the Union's behalf. That's correct and it must continue that way, much as I personally sympathize with what you are doing. That was part of our original understanding with OEO, an understanding which you were willing to go along with." Chavez's files indicate that he did not directly reply to Lorenz's letter, only sending a formal notice that Dolores Huerta would be representing him at a CRLA board meeting in San Francisco a few days later. A few months later, Chavez demonstrated that he still desired some influence in, and benefit from, the Salinas workers' lawsuit. From union headquarters he urged the plaintiffs to bring more public attention to the case and to the UFWOC by picketing in front of the offices of Martin and the growers' associations. Mustering up the courage to disagree with their union leader, the nine men telephoned Chavez from Gnaizda's office to assert that their best strategy was to frame their firings as a violation of workers' freedom of association, an "all-American" right, rather than the right to join the UFWOC in particular.[16] In this act of resistance against Chavez, the Salinas Nine communicated their desire that the lawsuit result in the best conditions for themselves at that time, rather than for the larger farmworker movement.

At the preliminary injunction hearing on October 27, Judge Gordon Campbell affirmed there was a case to be tried, to the dismay of the GFLA and GSVA representatives who expected a quick dismissal. Gnaizda targeted Martin first, persuading him to break away from the associations and settle to avoid a prolonged lawsuit. In a letter to Gnaizda dated November 4, Cesar Chavez asked to be informed of the time and place of any negotiations between the workers and Martin. "The Union wants to be represented at those negotiations and wants to have a voice in any settlement which might be reached," he wrote, but it is unlikely that Gnaizda included the demanding Chavez in the meeting. On December 7 Martin agreed to settle for damages that included reinstatement for all nine men, lifetime employment (subject only to discharge for good cause) with union rights protected, a guaranteed annual minimum wage of $4,500, and punitive damages of $6,750 on the condition that the workers drop their lawsuit against him. The settlement was unprecedented. Although it would take longer (and a trip to the California Court of Appeal) to hold the GFLA, the GSVA, and Houseberg liable for the remaining damages, in 1969 the three were finally convicted of conspiring to violate the right of the nine workers to free association under the California Labor Code. With the help of the CRLA, the Salinas Nine had won a lawsuit that gave not only them, but other agricultural laborers around California the protected right to unionize for the very first time.[17]

The nine farmworkers made labor history once more by serving as plaintiffs in another 1967 CRLA lawsuit, *Ortiz v. Wirtz,* against U.S. Secretary of Labor Willard Wirtz, the Bureau of Employment Security, and the INS to stop the entrance of fifteen hundred braceros into California. In 1967 Mexican nationals working in Monterey County represented more than 20 percent of all contracted foreign agricultural labor in the United States, and the GFLA planned to import fifteen hundred more braceros to the Salinas Valley by the end of September. After filing a restraining order that kept the braceros at bay at the U.S.-Mexico border, CRLA managed to negotiate a settlement with the U.S. Departments of Labor and Justice. The settlement established a more thorough review process for ascertaining growers' eligibility for any foreign labor, bilingual recruitment of domestic workers, and a $1.60 minimum wage for both foreign and domestic workers. Rather than comply with these new terms, California growers gave up on resuscitating the Bracero Program and made plans to live without it. The lawsuit effectively ended bracero importation into California in 1968. "And so these workers did both," Gnaizda concluded of the Salinas Nine. "They won their case for themselves, they established the right to join a union, and they ended the Bracero Program . . . They changed history." Having been the dramatic center of the Chualar tragedy–driven campaign to end the Bracero Program, Salinas was once again the site of change. Historians have overlooked these two important 1967 CRLA lawsuits and the Salinas farmworkers involved, but they were largely responsible for removing the obstacles to future farmworker unionization in California and for making Cesar Chavez's UFWOC organizing vastly easier. The accomplishments of CRLA and the Salinas Nine created such a stir in the state that at a later Senate hearing on migratory labor, Lorenz testified that threatened agribusiness interests and public officials were characterizing them as "a bunch of beatniks" and "a force for social revolution" and calling for their OEO funding to be cut off. Salinas Valley farmworkers continued using CRLA to improve their living and working conditions over the next decade. The 1973 case *Diana v. the State Board of Education* reversed the trend of automatically placing Spanish-speaking schoolchildren in classes for the mentally retarded on the basis of culturally biased and English-only standardized intelligence tests. As a result, twenty-two thousand Chicano children in California were removed from these classes and the California State Board of Education had to revamp its testing methods. *Carmona v. Division of Industrial Safety* emerged out of conversations with Salinas Valley farmworkers who wanted to see *el cortito* banished from the fields for its role in causing permanent back injuries. Because of this case, the tool was finally outlawed in 1975.[18]

Inspired by these legal victories, Mexican Americans across the Southwest spoke out against other forms of inequality and injustice. Regionally, Spanish-surnamed people were completing a median of 9 years of school compared with 12.1 for whites and 10.5 for blacks (in some places, the median educational level was as low as 1.4 years). In California, out of 117,431 state jobs, Mexican Americans only held 4,289 of them (3.65 percent, despite being nearly 15 percent of the state population, at 3.1 million) and their average pay was $1,176 lower than the average pay for whites. In Monterey County, the median income of Spanish-surnamed families was $7,823 compared with $10,285 for all families, and Mexican Americans older than age twenty-five held a median educational level of 8.7 years compared with 12.4 for all county residents. In a letter to the *Salinas Californian*, Salinas resident Ralph R. López asserted it was time for things to change: "The time has passed when Mexican-Americans, American-Indians, Black-Americans, or any other hyphenated Americans will be content with having second-class jobs, second-class pay, second-class rights and benefits, second-class futures and in general, being relegated to the position of second-class Americans." An ex-convict from Salinas used one of his college history papers to write about the discrimination he and other Mexicanos faced, including being called "a dirty Mexican" at the local YMCA and feeling like most Salinas police officers held "a negative view of the Chicano and think of him as being the lowest type of human life on earth." The lack of employment, education, courtroom justice, and upward mobility suffered by Mexican Americans, the author observed, made him continue: "Now that I'm out [of prison] and 'aware' of the problems that are provoked by these prejudiced people only make me that much more adamant in staying out . . . Que Viva La Raza!!!!"[19]

In using the phrase "Long Live the People/the Race," this anonymous author expressed a more radical cultural sensibility that was shared by others as a Chicano Movement began to flourish in Salinas. Though the CSO had dissolved, two MAPA chapters had taken its place shortly after. Led by Salinas residents Maximiano Curiel, Manuel Oliverrez, Crescencio Padilla, Marty Muñoz, and Efrain "Andy" Anzaldua, these two chapters took on activities ranging from picketing the Monterey post office for harassing a Mexican American mailman who had joined the National Association of Letter Carriers union to organizing a local county antipoverty council to registering voters. Voter registrars included former CSO member Sally Gutiérrez and CRLA staff member Amelia Harris. Partly because of MAPA's efforts, voter registration in Monterey County hit record highs in 1966 (78,097) and in 1968 (80,478). While not all Salinas Valley Mexican Americans were eager to join MAPA—some perceived it to be too "radical" a group—the organization helped a wide range of Mexican Americans to become interested or participate in local and national politics. In 1969, Salinas's first Spanish-language newspaper, *El Sol*, was founded, and that same year, a group of Mexican American parents in Alisal fought for hot lunch and summer programs as well as more Spanish-speaking teachers for their children.[20] In 1970, Gutiérrez became the first Mexican American to run for Salinas City Council. Though ultimately unsuccessful, her campaign was a landmark attempt to win political representation for Salinas Mexican Americans.

Meanwhile, the town's Mexican American students began their campaign for an education that included more Spanish-surnamed teachers, a more culturally inclusive curriculum, and less funneling into vocational programs that locked them into low-wage careers and disregarded their other professional ambitions. "La Raza was being organized,"

Alisal high school teacher Peter Crawford remembered of the time. "It was a rallying point and they felt prideful. I think they were starting to speak up and there was a lot of pressure to hire more Spanish-surnamed teachers. It was certainly a time of change." In a particularly heated incident at Gonzalez High School, where Mexican American students made up 70 percent of the student body, school authorities targeted Teacher Corps trainee Paula Alvarez after she helped students form a chapter of the Mexican American Youth Association, took some to visit San Jose State College, and inspired them to begin wearing buttons reading "Boycott Grapes" and "The Grapes of Wrath Revisited." Citing complaints by other teachers regarding "the changing attitudes of the students," school officials dismissed her and her husband, who was working as a school-home liaison. Students and parents protested, CRLA represented the couple in court, and a federal judge ordered school officials to reverse their dismissals. At Hartnell College, instructor Leon Amyx remembered, the first "radical" Chicano student action took place when a group of students constructed a replica of a stereotypical sombrero- and poncho-clad "Mexican" taking a siesta beneath a cactus plant and then buried it on campus. The college's 215 Mexican American students created a MEChA chapter and petitioned the school's board of directors for ten more Mexican American instructors and a full-time minority student recruitment director. In late April 1970 the students confronted Hartnell's board of directors in a "one-hour verbal explosion" iterating their demands. Later that year, the school's first Chicana homecoming queen, MEChA member Sally Peña, was elected.[21] Though no boisterous school walkouts were staged, as they were in Los Angeles, a sea change was occurring in Salinas as evidenced by local Mexican Americans' increased political involvement, protests, and articulations of a "Chicano" identity.

In the fields, Salinas Valley farmworkers had continued to follow the Delano strike closely. Some joined small union committees formed by UFWOC organizers in Salinas, Hollister, Gilroy, and Watsonville and met several times a year to hear union updates and discuss local conditions. When the grape strike finally reached the negotiation stage, this prompted teams of Salinas *lechugueros* (lettuce workers)—mostly single migrants and ex-braceros who traveled between the Imperial and Salinas Valleys—to request a meeting with Chavez to let him know they were ready to be the next group of striking workers. Having experienced the injustices of the bracero era, many of these *lechugueros* were highly class-conscious, and some had even been members of workers' unions in Mexico. Because they often organized themselves into work crews before being hired by employers, *lechugueros* had a special group solidarity that aided in their readiness to strike. Strawberry workers, or *freseros*—who were mostly Tejano migrant men and women in their twenties and thirties—also expressed interest in joining the UFWOC because of its connections to CRLA, the organization that had helped them file lawsuits against the Salinas Strawberries Company a few years before.[22]

Word of mouth proved a powerful way of spreading support for the union. Sabino López, whose father had worked as a bracero in Chicago, Denver, and Salinas during the 1950s, was working with his father and brother in the fields when he met a Mexican American accountant who told him about Chavez's organizing work in Delano. Appalled at how many hours López had worked without overtime pay, the accountant informed him, "Someone's coming to town soon who might put an end to that." López passed the word about the UFWOC to his co-workers. "All we had to do was hear about [the movement] and I think just about everyone in my crew was for it," he recalled. Meanwhile, other farmworkers were learning about the UFWOC from their friends and relatives working in other crops around California. "I had a cousin in grapes and he told us about the strikes over there in Delano . . . 'Why not here?' we thought," recalled one Salinas strawberry worker. Believing a takeover by the UFWOC was imminent, López's employer James Merrill began negotiations with the Teamsters (at this time, the largest union in the country) to sign a preemptory contract. López and his co-workers, however, resisted this decision, which disregarded their needs or consent. One day after picking cauliflower, the crew was ordered by their foreman to sit in a labor bus and listen to a Mexican American Teamsters agent. Twenty-year-old López and his crewmates, however, considered themselves ardent *Chavistas*. "Who sent you? The company sent you here, right?" one worker on the bus shouted at the agent. Others clamored: "Don't you think they should let the farmworkers union come talk to us? Isn't a union something you should choose?" The Teamsters representative, caught off guard, quickly disembarked.

Having seen in Mexico how *sindicatos* (unions) had improved work-ers' lives, Sabino, his brother, and his father joined the UFWOC with others who wanted a union that truly represented their interests.[23]

On July 27, 1970, Chavez and the UFWOC made labor history in Delano. After a five-year grape strike and boycott, grower John Giu-marra—whose family owned the biggest table grape vineyard in the world—finally agreed to a union contract that gave eight thousand grape workers raises from $1.65 to $2.05 an hour, a health and welfare fund, and restrictions on the use of harmful pesticides. These conces-sions were the most comprehensive that any unionized group of U.S. farmworkers had ever won, and by the end of the 1970 harvest sea-son the UFWOC would sign 150 table grape contracts covering thirty thousand workers. As Giumarra and Chavez shook hands in front of the media, applause and shouts of joy erupted from surrounding union members. Yet the celebration would not last for long. A few hours later, Chavez learned that more than 170 Salinas and Santa Maria Val-ley lettuce growers had decided to surreptitiously sign contracts with the Teamsters to prevent their workers from being organized by the UFWOC. "This is a stab in the back. Pack your bags, we're going to Salinas," Chavez told his team.[24]

Fearing a takeover by the UFWOC, growers had gravitated to the more familiar Teamsters union, which had represented the region's transportation, cannery, and warehouse employees since the 1950s. "The grape boycott scared the heck out of the farmers . . . they thought if they could sign a contract with [the Teamsters] it would forestall Ce-sar trying to come in and take over the industry," lettuce grower Daryl Arnold later admitted. Mike Payne, the general manager of the Bruce Church Company at the time, agreed: "The grower community began to get frightened. They needed a contract with somebody to force the UFW[OC] to be at arm's length . . . the union scared us." What these growers had ostracized Bud Antle for doing during the AWOC strike of 1961 was exactly what they did in 1970. Workers were never consulted during the grower-Teamsters negotiations, or given the opportunity to examine and consent to the terms of the contracts. These contracts allowed growers to continue using chemical pesticides despite their damaging effects on farmworkers (the UFWOC included pesticide-restriction clauses in their contracts), and they permitted growers to keep importing braceros if necessary. As Governor Brown's cabinet secretary Frank Mesplé remarked, "the Teamsters supported the bracero program for one very practical reason: they wanted to keep those canneries moving" and keep their other union members in different sectors of the agricultural industry employed. Chavez accused the Teamsters of being corrupt and attacked Salinas growers for being "racist" in their refusal to cooperate with "a group that has strong Mexican-American influence in its leadership." He went on to suggest why the UFWOC struck so much fear into the hearts of growers: "They know that in a few years, farm workers will be sitting on city councils, county boards, and the courts. That's where the Movement is going to lead us. That's why the politicians on the right are so worried. Rural areas will no longer be conservative strongholds." Chavez was right—the Chicano Movement's focus included the agricultural sphere as much as the urban, and Salinas was about to become the next center of *movimiento* activity.[25]

On the evening of July 27, 1970, as Chavez drove to Salinas to speak to farmworkers at a hastily organized rally, he was unsure of how much support he would find. As a former hub of the Bracero Program and a historically antiunion region, the Salinas Valley seemed much tougher to break than Delano. When Chavez entered the doors of a building on Salinas's east side, however, he was shocked by what he saw and heard. Deafening cries of "Viva La Causa!" and "Viva La Raza!" erupted from a waiting crowd of three hundred people that included Mexicano farmworkers and their families, young college students, former CSO members and current MAPA members, and local Mexican American businesspeople. The majority of those cheering had never seen Chavez in person before, hearing of his organizing success only through radio, newspapers, or word of mouth. Sabino López remembered the thrill of seeing Chavez in person for the first time. "There were so many of us waiting, we were ready, ready for him to come," he said. As Chicano Movement leader José Angel Gutiérrez described, farmworkers could relate to the forty-three-year-old Chavez because he "looked mestizo. He was dark skinned, short, with high cheek bones, piercing black eyes . . . He was the embodiment of a Chicano. Chicanos could see themselves in Cesar." After delivering a speech in Spanish, Chavez addressed reporters in English, explaining that the UFWOC demanded immediate negotiations with Salinas growers. "The rage of the workers was just palpable," remembered *Salinas Californian* reporter Eric Brazil, who attended the rally. López agreed: "There was so much anger among people, dating back to the history of the braceros . . . The farmworkers movement gave us a chance to force people to know we existed, that we had decided it was time for better conditions and respect." Jacques Levy, Chavez's biographer, perceived not anger but a quiet determination at the rally. "The workers listened intensely," he noted, adding that AFL-CIO director of organization Bill Kircher remarked, "maybe this quiet attitude is stronger."[26] The diverse Mexican-origin people of the Salinas Valley, who had until this point lived in great tension with each other, finally felt that a more promising and tangible farmworker movement had appeared on the horizon. It was time to walk out of the fields and onto the picket line.

7   A Blossoming of Red Flags

The Salinas UFWOC Strike of 1970

THE DIVERSE CROWD that welcomed the UFWOC to Salinas on the night of July 27, 1970, represented various communities and years of struggle. The farmworker population was mostly of Mexican origin (Mexican American residents, ex-braceros, undocumented migrants, and Tejano migrants) but also included a small number of white, African American, and Filipino farmworkers.[1] Chicano and Chicana college students, MAPA members, Mexican American business owners, newspaper reporters, and curious onlookers also filled the hall. Thanks to the CRLA lawsuits that had established California farmworkers' collective bargaining rights, the idea of attending a union rally seemed much less dangerous and forbidden to these people than it had a mere three years before. Furthermore, the fact that larger and more cohesive "Mexican" neighborhoods had emerged in Salinas likely contributed to the word of mouth that attracted so many people to the rally. Alisal, which was now part of Salinas, had transformed from a Mexicano- "Okie" community to a Mexicano one with Mexican Americans, ex- braceros, and Mexican immigrants living there along with their families. Meanwhile, migrant strawberry workers from the Rio Grande Valley of Texas lived in the La Posada trailer camp in Salinas and a former bracero camp in Soledad. Planting firmer roots in the Salinas Valley, a diverse Mexican-origin population began to invest in the place as home and respond more positively to political collaboration, which the UFWOC promised to facilitate.

The Salinas Valley had to be the UFWOC's next big target, not only because so many growers had evaded the union by signing Teamsters contracts, but because penetrating one of the nation's richest agricultural regions would be a game changer. The valley was producing more than half of all the celery, broccoli, and cauliflower in the United States and a vast portion of the national lettuce crop; its strawberry industry had grossed $150 million. All of this combined to make the Salinas Valley some of the "most lucrative agricultural land in human history." Looking out into the cheering crowd, Cesar Chavez might have thought about how his life had started on a homestead on a piece of land in Yuma, Arizona, that now belonged to Salinas Valley grower Bruce Church. Chavez's family had been pushed off of the land and into the migrant labor stream. Now, Chavez's life and work had brought him to Church's home turf to correct historical injustices against farmworkers and their families. At a post-rally press conference a reporter asked him, "So your big struggle is now here in the Salinas Valley?" Chavez replied, "I would say the big struggle is about to start here, yes."[2]

Unaware of the enthusiasm being displayed at the UFWOC's eastside rally, growers meeting at the GSVA headquarters on the other side of town doubted that the Delano strike could be replicated in Salinas. Previous unionization attempts by the NFLU and AWOC had failed, they told themselves, and the fact that three powerful corporations dominated the area's agriculture lent an additional sense of security. The valley's largest lettuce grower was InterHarvest, a group of agricultural firms under the United Fruit Company. Dubbed "the octopus" in Latin America for its extensive control of plantations, transportation monopolies, and dictatorships, United Fruit placed Portuguese American brothers and Salinas agribusinessmen Tom and Robert Nunes in charge of InterHarvest's twenty thousand acres of lettuce in Arizona and California. The Purex Corporation's farming operation Freshpict covered forty-two thousand acres in California, Arizona, Colorado, and New Mexico. Finally, S. S. Pierce and Company of Boston bought out several strawberry operations in Salinas, Watsonville, and Oxnard and named this conglomerate Pic-N-Pac. Growers believed that these three behemoths would not acquiesce to the demands of Chavez and assumed that a heavily Mexicano UFWOC membership did not have the political unity or capacity to carry out a successful strike.[3]

A few days later on August 2, every preconceived notion grower-employers held about their employees was shattered. Marching from Soledad, Watsonville, King City, Greenfield, and Delano, approximately three thousand farmworkers converged on downtown Salinas for a massive UFWOC rally. After parading through the streets, the crowd gathered on Hartnell College's football field holding wooden crosses and waving flags emblazoned with the UFWOC eagle and the Virgin of Guadalupe. "Chicano Power!" yelled brown beret–clad Hartnell students from the library's rooftop and the back of a flatbed truck, on which Chavez jumped to address the crowd. Alternating between English and Spanish, Chavez accused growers and the Teamsters of ignoring the reality that times had changed. "It's tragic that these men have not yet come to understand that we are in a new age, a new era," he proclaimed amidst boisterous cheers. "No longer can a couple of white men sit down together and write the destinies of all the Chicanos and Filipino workers in this valley." The crowd began chanting, "Huelga! Huelga! Huelga! [Strike! Strike! Strike!]," to which Chavez began pumping his fists in rhythm and shouting the same. According to filmmaker Ray Tellis, this was Chavez's most animated moment ever captured on film. The labor leader eventually had to calm the crowd and explain that a strike would not immediately happen, but that workers should sign UFWOC authorization cards and wait for further instructions.[4]

Despite their employers' threats of termination, blacklisting, and eviction, more than one thousand Salinas Valley farmworkers signed UFWOC cards that afternoon. The next morning more farmworkers inundated MAPA's office in Alisal, which had been transformed into UFWOC headquarters. This level of enthusiasm surprised the union's organizers. "It blew me away because we had really struggled to organize workers in the grape industry," organizer Marshall Ganz said. "[In Delano] the workers were hopeless and terrified . . . In Salinas, all of that was different . . . the people were ready for us." Fellow organizer Jessica Govea agreed: "The Salinas workers were so much more confident than the Delano workers. They were clear about why they were going on strike, and what they wanted to change by going on strike . . .

They were very alive. There was an electricity, a vibrancy that was different from Delano. It wasn't slow or languid. It was like, 'Hey, let's go. Let's do this.'" Salinas Valley farmworkers' readiness to strike was in large part due to greater confidence after the success of Delano, but it was also because they had been preparing locally through political and community organizations to cultivate this movement for themselves. Additionally, the way that *lechuguero* crews were structured as opposed to grape workers played a vital role. *Lechugueros* were almost exclusively male, worked in Salinas over the six-month lettuce season of April to September, and organized themselves into crews even before they approached a supervisor to be hired. Oftentimes, crews were made up of friends or relatives who lived together, traveled through California together, and split their total pay. In 1970 approximately three thousand *lechugueros* worked in the Salinas Valley, and they were some of the most persistent and vocal workers when it came to welcoming Chavez to the region. Ironically, the very monoculture of lettuce that had made Salinas Valley growers rich had also created cohesive crews of farmworkers that were now collectively voting to rebel against them. Along with *lechugueros,* piece-rate crews of *apieros* and *brocoleros* (celery and broccoli workers) began calling themselves *Chavistas* and bringing stacks of signed union cards to UFWOC headquarters.[5]

For some, the desire to join the UFWOC came from their political backgrounds. Some ex-braceros had been members of labor unions back in Mexico before they entered the program. Others were the children of political parents. Ex-bracero Hermilo Mojica's father, for example, was the president of the San Lucas municipality in Michoacán, and another relative was a top leader for Mexican president Lázaro Cárdenas. When he went to the Salinas Valley as a bracero at the end of the 1950s, Mojica exhibited an assertiveness no doubt influenced by his lineage. At his first job picking strawberries in Chualar, he requested that foremen call him by his actual name instead of "Number Sixty-Seven" and even complained about one foreman to the Mexican Consul in San Jose when the man did not properly pay him and his co-workers. Mojica became a "skip" and eventually obtained a green card under sponsorship from a new employer. Pete Maturino, who grew up in the United States, stated that his mother—a Mexican immigrant who became a forewoman for the Harden Packing Company and a member of a rare all-female *lechuguera* crew—was his personal example of leadership. It was while working alongside his mother at Harden that a volunteer for UFWOC approached him and others to join the union. Maturino did and quickly became an organizer. Diverse backgrounds and influences such as these drove masses of farmworkers into UFWOC headquarters. "It was like the experience of [the] movement bursting forth, and it was just incredible," Ganz remembered.[6] The UFWOC had expected "Steinbeck Country" to be the most difficult to organize, given its antiunion history, but the organization had underestimated the thousands of workers who were literally lining up to join the rank-and-file.

A few days after the Hartnell rally fourteen hundred workers at the Freshpict Company and Pic-N-Pac Farms walked off their jobs. Until this point, no more than two hundred farmworkers in one firm had gone on strike simultaneously. The harvesting of lettuce, tomatoes, and strawberries came to a standstill, and celery and broccoli harvests suffered. Faced with a plethora of UFWOC flags and picket lines, the Teamsters realized they held no power over the workers they nominally represented through their grower contracts. The UFWOC organizers believed that if they could persuade the Teamsters to informally turn over all of their farmworker contracts (representing seventy thousand workers) in exchange for UFWOC members returning to work, then growers would feel pressured to meet Chavez at the negotiating table. In meetings mediated by the U.S. Catholic Bishops Committee on Farm Labor, the UFWOC persuaded the Teamsters to do just that. When growers did not respond to this UFWOC tactic, frustrated Salinas *lechugueros* called for the strike to resume, forcing the union's vice president, Dolores Huerta, to leap onto a chair at a union meeting and plead for workers' patience in postponing the strike. Huerta, who had stepped outside of the traditional gender roles of homebound wife and mother to become an essential UFWOC leader and strategist, was impassioned and forceful. The *lechugueros* reluctantly agreed with her plan of action but began creating strike flags anyway, requesting the help of Mexicana *freseras* (strawberry workers) living in the Salinas Strawberries Company camp. The camp, which included 137 trailers and a communal recreation room, pool, and laundry room, was home to workers and their children. In multiple trailers, women set up makeshift *fabricas de banderas* (flag factories) and began sewing, a brazen display of union activity within company housing.[7] When growers finally announced that they planned to keep their Teamsters contracts and refused to negotiate with the UFWOC, what followed was one of the largest agricultural strikes in U.S. history.

THE STRIKE BEGINS

On August 23, four thousand workers assembled at Hartnell College to attend a Catholic mass and express their desire to strike the next day. In addition to carrying UFWOC flags, workers carried banners that identified them by company and crew. The twenty-seven strike committees stepped onstage to declare their vote, and some workers made individual speeches. "Fellow *campesinos,* we are here to show the world our nonconformity—to do our part to uplift the life of our farm worker families," *lechuguero* Raul Castillo said. Farmworker Antonio Sagredo added: "We don't ask the impossible—only that they [the employers] look upon us as human beings. We have the same ambitions as they do. We have families. We have rights. We are people. Why must they continue to treat us like beasts of burden and look for a thousand ways to keep us down[?] . . . But the people know we are right. They will give us their support. We shall triumph." With that simple affirmation, "We are people," Sagredo and other Salinas farmworkers spoke on a literal and figurative platform of protest to those who sought to silence them. Hundreds more people signed UFWOC cards after the rally. "Committees were getting formed then, left and right, by camps, by companies, by crews, just all over the valley. Almost faster than we could keep up with them," Chavez told his biographer Jacques Levy. "It was just a tremendous thing that really swept the valley."[8]

The next day, the strike of nearly six thousand Salinas Valley UFWOC members against thirty-five Salinas growers and shippers began. Red UFWOC flags planted into the earth fluttered next to fields for more than a hundred miles in every direction, spanning multiple counties. Marshall Ganz described the scene:

> . . . it was like an explosion, a blossoming of red flags . . . Now if I were a grower, if I were a member of the Salinas white community I would have been completely, completely freaked out. Because all of a sudden your worst nightmare has happened—the Mexicans are taking over . . . in good ol' Salinas, the Mexicans are taking over. It's a fucking revolution . . . On the other hand the workers were . . . the word "empowered"

just doesn't even begin to go there. They felt a sense of power, and a sense of . . . fullness, fullness of being . . . they'd been completely commodified, and all of a sudden they were agents taking control of their own destiny . . . it was exhilarating.

By August 27 seven thousand farmworkers were striking against forty Salinas Valley ranches. "The growers thought we were kidding," said twenty-one-year-old Brown Beret Tanis Reyna as he stood with others on a picket line. "We're taking pride in our race. We want to be called La Raza or Chicanos. We just don't want to be nothing." Picket leader Ray Huerta demonstrated his historical consciousness by adding: "Those growers still think they're living in the thirties. They think they can just ship us back to Mexico. We've been waiting for Chavez for some time now." In addition to pickets, caravans of UFWOC members drove from field to field blasting car horns, waving red flags, and shouting at those still working in the fields. No longer bent and stooping with *cortitos*, farmworkers were meeting their employers face to face. Mario Bustamante, who served as strike captain for Merrill Farms, remembered an encounter with his bosses Tom and Anne Merrill at the entrance to one of their fields. Bustamante considered the Merrills some of the best employers in Salinas; every year they opened their labor camp early so that workers would have a place to sleep and eat before the first day of harvesting. Yet when Merrill tried to stop Bustamante's caravan from trespassing by calling out, "Mario, don't be a fool," Bustamante led his crew right past the Merrills to talk to a group of Filipino workers before the group was forced off the property by law enforcement officers.[9]

Seeing the effect that Chavez and the UFWOC were having on their workforce, growers responded with various tactics. They argued that the UFWOC had no right to attack them; their farmworkers were indeed unionized (the UFWOC's complaint, however, was that these workers had no choice in the matter and were not asked for their consent to Teamster representation). Some growers hired strikebreakers, schoolchildren and high school athletes, and even their own family members to finish harvesting their dying crops. Others went to the courts to stop the UFWOC from picketing by their fields. On August 25 Judge Anthony Brazil, the father of *Salinas Californian* reporter Eric Brazil, issued a temporary restraining order against the UFWOC that kept the union from picketing at twenty-two farms. Citing the California Jurisdictional Strike Act, Brazil ruled that since growers technically had their workers under a union contract, the battle was between the UFWOC and Teamsters over jurisdiction, not between the UFWOC and the growers. More injunctions were placed on the UFWOC with each passing day. Nevertheless, strikers began to see the real effects of their walkout. The State and Federal Marketing Service estimated that less than half the valley's lettuce was flowing to market. Over the course of the next three weeks, the central coastal berry industry suffered an estimated $2.2 million loss. Meanwhile, state employment officials stopped sending farmworkers to the Salinas Valley because seventy-five workers had picketed the state agricultural labor office in Los Angeles for attempting to send a bus of forty "scabs" to Salinas.[10] The germinal connections that the UFWOC had helped form between California farmworkers were proving themselves to be full-blown networks of communication and support. The union sent volunteers to Los Angeles and San Francisco to strengthen boycott activity at supermarkets. After success in those two cities, the boycott spread rapidly east to cities that included New York and Philadelphia.

More groups of lettuce, tomato, strawberry, and artichoke farmworkers poured into the Salinas UFWOC headquarters (which had since moved to a larger building) asking to be organized. Even those who did not work in the fields counted themselves among the union's supporters. Julianna Martinez, a Filipina produce shed employee, remembered that "every day [we] used to talk about [the strike] in the sheds. Among the women, either their husbands or families were involved in the strike. Most of the workers in the sheds were behind Cesar Chavez." Each evening crowds of up to two thousand people— UFWOC organizers, farmworkers, Hartnell students, local Mexican American residents, members of the clergy, and young members of the SNCC and the Congress of Racial Equality (CORE) who had moved to California to volunteer for the farmworker rights cause—gathered outside of union headquarters to share news of the strike's progress.[11] This collective energy was only amplified by the presence of El Teatro Campesino, founded in 1965 by young Delano native and former SNCC participant Luis Valdez. El Teatro's satirical humor that targeted labor contractors, growers, and foremen in short plays (or *actos*) garnered plenty of fans and made evening meetings all the more lively.

Fig. 7.1. Cesar Chavez stands with women who volunteered to defy picketing injunctions with him in Salinas. (From *El Malcriado*, 15 September 1970, 6; courtesy of Walter P. Reuther Library, Archives of Labor and Urban Affairs, Wayne State University)

In addition to picket lines and plays, the UFWOC strengthened its power by encouraging women's participation in the strike (fig. 7.1). The union already had a strong female leader in Dolores Huerta, who was a main contract negotiator. There were also women like Hope Lopez, who had led grape boycott activities in Philadelphia, and Jessica Govea, the director of boycott operations in Montreal, who showed other women that farmworker activism could cross lines of gender. In Salinas, entire families were becoming involved in the strike through the permission and activism of women. Juanita and Merced Valdez, for instance, left the lettuce and strawberry fields of the Salinas Valley with their seven children and moved to Cincinnati to help with the lettuce campaign. Fifteen women volunteered to picket and risk arrest with Chavez when he decided to picket the Bruce Church Company despite a ban by the Monterey County Superior Court. These women later stood beside Chavez at a press conference where he denounced the court's ban as unconstitutional and affirmed that the union would continue picketing. Huerta noted why Mexicanas were so important for the UFWOC: "Women in the union are great on the picket line. Excluding women, protecting them, keeping women at home, that's the middle-class way. Poor people's movements have always had whole families on the line." As Huerta knew, women in the farmworker movement were the latest in a long line of Mexicana labor activists such as laundresses in El Paso at the turn of the century, cannery workers in California during the 1930s and 1940s, and garment workers in Texas and copper miners' wives in Arizona during the 1950s. In many of these cases, women workers strategically framed their labor struggles around the preservation and well-being of family to gain more public support. Similarly, the UFWOC argued that although farmworkers provided the food for Americans' tables, they were not making a living wage that allowed them to feed themselves and their children.[12]

In addition to women, the UFWOC had amassed a diverse group of allies that included other AFL-CIO unions, students, civil rights organizations, wealthy liberal East Coast donors, antipesticide environmentalists working on the heels of Rachel Carson's 1962 treatise *Silent Spring,* and religious leaders. The Catholic Church, which had been prodded by Mexican Americans to take a stand on social issues including poverty and racism, lent much support to the farmworker cause, while a group of Californian Franciscans gave an interest-free loan of $125,000 to the UFWOC for strike benefits. Some unexpected allies emerged as well. Mexican American inmates at Soledad prison refused to serve as strikebreakers in the fields. The mostly "Okie" lettuce packers and cooler workers of Amalgamated Meat Cutters and Butcher Workmen Local 78A, a union local previously sympathetic to the Teamsters, walked off their jobs in solidarity with the UFWOC. This switch in working-class "Okie" loyalty from an Anglo-dominated union to a Mexicano one was significant, and growers knew it. Having held power in the Salinas Valley for so long, they were experiencing their nightmare of a UFWOC takeover, as Ganz called it. Farmworkers, however, were experiencing their dream. "What is now happening in the Salinas Valley was inevitable," local resident Angel Jesus de los Santos wrote to the *Salinas Californian.* "This humble step towards change and prosperity was long in the making. Thank God it is now here."[13]

On August 31, the UFWOC claimed its first victory when Inter-Harvest signed a contract with the union. This was in part due to United Fruit's CEO Eli Black's desire to reform the company's image, but mostly because Chavez had threatened to initiate a worldwide boycott against all United Fruit–brand products, which included popular Chiquita bananas, Baskin Robbins ice cream, and A&W root beer. The two-year agreement, which covered approximately one thousand field-workers in the Salinas Valley and other parts of California and Arizona, raised hourly wages to $2.10 in 1970 and $2.15 by 1971 and elevated piece rates to 40.5 cents per carton, a huge jump compared with the $1.85 hourly wage and 36-cent piece rate lettuce workers were making under the Teamsters pact. It also contained unprecedented prohibitions against five harmful pesticides, enforced a week of paid vacation, instituted grievance procedures and a hiring hall in the place of contractors, and provided workers and their families with a medical insurance plan. When the contract terms were announced at a nighttime outdoor rally near UFWOC headquarters, "the place went crazy," Ganz remembered. *Lechugueros* jumped for joy and screamed, "Viva la huelga! Viva la unión! Viva Cesar Chavez!"[14]

Stunned by United Fruit's decision, Tom and Robert Nunes left the helm of InterHarvest instead of endorsing the contract. Other anti-UFWOC forces retaliated. A group of local residents, growers' wives, and Teamsters members picketed and closed down the InterHarvest processing plant to prevent company trucks from returning to the fields and UFWOC members from returning to work. This anti-UFWOC group named itself the Citizens Committee for Local Justice, with Anne Merrill and Freshpict president Howard Leach being prominent members. Choosing to use the word "citizens" in its title—a loaded term historically associated with whiteness and white justice—the committee organized anti-UFWOC rallies and blasted Chavez in the media. This encouraged more white Salinas residents to join in the fray, including women and children. "Housewives, some with small children, were lying across the produce companies' driveways and cooling operations so trucks carrying produce could not enter or get into the fields to let farm workers pack the lettuce," local resident and Teamsters office employee Joan Santoro remembered. At a Citizens Committee rally at Hartnell College, a woman who identified herself as a small grower's wife declared to the audience of nearly three thousand people: "I don't want to be anything but what I have been, a housewife trying to take care of her family and her home . . . My husband's family and my family have been here for generations . . . if we are forced into accepting a UFWOC contract, our business cannot survive. In blunt terms, we are fighting for our very lives . . . our area recently has been torn apart by acts of violence, threats, and intimidation. I for one don't want to live this way anymore." On both sides of the strike, the discourse of family, and the actions of women in particular, infused the Teamsters-UFWOC conflict with a sense of higher stakes. The desire to protect the home and family unit, and fight for their survival in the world of agriculture, pervaded grower and farmworker communities alike and created tension that placed every resident of Salinas on edge.[15]

The battle between Chavez supporters and opponents only intensified as hundreds of incidents of violence erupted between the UFWOC and Teamsters during the strike's initial weeks. One of the first involved UFWOC attorney Jerry Cohen, photographer and Chavez biographer Jacques Levy, and union organizer Venustiano Olguin. The three men entered grower Al Hansen's ranch to check on the safety of a group of sit-down strikers and were met by Hansen himself, ten pickup trucks, and fifteen men (thought to be "goons" hired by the Western Conference of Teamsters). When Cohen refused to leave until he received assurance of the strikers' safety, Hansen commanded, "Get 'em, boys." Two men attacked Cohen and beat him severely. Olguin was knocked unconscious, and Levy was beaten and his camera taken when he tried to photograph Cohen's assault. Cohen was hospitalized and slipped into a coma as a result of his injuries. Shortly after, eighteen-year-old UFWOC picketer Lupe Ortiz was punched in the mouth by a man in a moving car who grabbed her UFWOC flag away and shouted, "Your lawyer has died; what's the use of striking?" One of Cohen's attackers was identified as James Charles Plemmons, an alleged organizer for the Western Conference of Teamsters. A Salinas sheriff who witnessed Cohen's beating did not make any arrests, and when Cohen later woke, he refused to sign a complaint created for him by Monterey County law enforcement because it implicated only his two assailants and not Hansen. Evidently, alliances between growers and law enforcement still existed, and in the end no one was prosecuted. Other violent episodes followed. A farm employee intentionally drove a tractor into a group of picketers. Two UFWOC members were separately dragged from their cars and beaten by grower employees. One UFWOC picketer and his friend were beaten at a bar by five men, two of whom were Mexican Americans working under a Mexican American labor contractor. Salinas police laughed at Pauline Carrasco when she complained that a white man had grabbed her UFWOC flag and threatened to "cut [her] up" with a knife. Two UFWOC members were individually struck down by cars, striker Refugio Segura barely missed being sliced with a machete by a passenger in a moving car, and striker Jesus Rodriguez had to leap out of the way when a foreman tried to hit him with his vehicle in front of the Hansen camp. As he drove away the foreman yelled out that he would "like to kill a Mexican greaser like you."[16]

Meanwhile, growers and the Citizens Committee were accusing UFWOC members of wrongdoing such as trespassing on labor camp grounds, damaging vehicles and company property, raping female fieldworkers, and intimidating non-UFWOC workers. The Citizens Committee started collecting incriminating affidavits. Ramon Hernandez complained that more than one hundred UFWOC members had marched into the squash field where he and twenty-five others were working and threatened to "break our arms if we stayed in the field." Gabion Jimenez could not drive a Freshpict bus of employees to their worksite when ten UFWOC members blocked the path and converged on the bus, breaking two windows and "hollering at the workers inside the bus telling them that they shouldn't go to work." Pic-N-Pac supervisor George Otsuki discovered that two fifteen-hundred-gallon diesel booster pumps had been vandalized and drained into nearby strawberry fields, killing approximately twenty-four hundred plants. Anna La Borde reported that a man with a flagpole attacked her in her car, breaking her glasses and leaving scratches, bruises, and lumps around her face and head. In an article in *California Farmer* magazine titled "How to Handle Your UFWOC Troubles," Salinas GSVA vice president E. James Houseberg instructed his fellow agribusiness leaders: "Do not delay. Prepare for battle now." The article went on to suggest that growers set up their own public relations departments and citizens committees, buy American flags for all their road equipment, and begin serving striking farmworkers eviction papers. "Don't underestimate the tremendous organization and experience that the UFWOC has in their operation," the article warned. "They have been in training for years and have learned from agitators like Saul Alinsky and others. Be prepared, for these are far from non-violent people."[17]

Fearful of the strike's violence, Chavez sent a telegram to California attorney general Thomas Lynch in early September. "A vigilante atmosphere hangs heavy over Salinas," he wrote and asked Lynch's office to investigate "the lawless conditions existing in Monterey County . . . before any lives are lost." When Lynch did not immediately respond, the UFWOC contacted the Center for Community Change, an antipoverty organization founded in 1968 that established citizen-based groups in low-income communities of color. Center lawyer Jerry J. Berman visited Salinas from September 11 to 15 and met with UFWOC strikers and officials, news reporters, and representatives from the California Attorney General's Office. "It was obvious that Salinas was a deeply troubled place. Everyone I met with expressed fear of violence," Berman wrote in his report. He also observed that local law enforcement officials in Salinas "appeared to be looking the other way" and had arrested only a few perpetrators of violence despite numerous UFWOC complaints. Berman concluded his report by writing: "A resolution of this conflict is absolutely essential. Violence is intolerable but if the price of the Salinas violence is the loss of an opportunity for the seasonal farm worker to organize and choose a union of his own, this is unconscionable. We are speaking about America's most exploited minority . . . Violence can only perpetuate what is already a nasty, mean, brutish, and short life."[18]

Reminiscent of the chaos of labor strikes in Salinas during the 1930s, the violence and tension of the 1970 strike soon bled onto the pages of local newspapers. In a letter to the *Salinas Californian*, resident Marjorie Cox likened Chavez and UFWOC officials to 1920s "gangsters," while Dollie Schmidt accused the UFWOC's actions of being hypocritical, given Chavez's so-called nonviolent philosophy. Citizens' Committee organizer Richard Ameil proclaimed that Chavez "stands for revolution, destruction, violence, and his main goal is to control the food supply." Committee member Harvey Priddy added: "This boy knows all the commie tactics . . . We want to keep little Cesar from tying up the whole valley and the whole nation. It's time Americans acted like Americans." The *Californian* betrayed its own stance by running headlines such as "Chavez Terror Tactics Hit" and "Reign of Terror," insinuating that Salinas had become as dangerous as Los Angeles, where the widely publicized National Chicano Moratorium march had recently taken place. On August 29, nearly thirty thousand people had gathered in East Los Angeles to protest the high number of Mexican American casualties in Vietnam. Five hundred law enforcement officers charged the crowd, shooting tear gas and beating demonstrators. Four hundred people were arrested, forty were injured, and three were killed, including Rubén Salazar, a popular columnist for the *Los Angeles Times*.[19] In response to the *Californian*'s connection between Los Angeles and Salinas Chicanos, *El Malcriado* ran the headline "Why Vietnam When There Is a Salinas?" alongside a photo of an armed guard overlooking strikebreakers in a Salinas lettuce field (fig. 7.2).

Fig. 7.2. An armed guard patrols a Salinas field during the 1970 strike. (From *El Malcriado*, 15 September 1970, 1; courtesy of Walter P. Reuther Library, Archives of Labor and Urban Affairs, Wayne State University)

It came as no surprise that in a region where access to space, power, and wealth had been historically divided along racial lines, the UFWOC's presence became a racial issue. In a letter to the *Californian,* Citizens Committee leader Bill Hitchcock accused Chavez of creating undue friction in an allegedly well-functioning society. "Until two weeks ago we lived and worked together in relative peace and harmony," he wrote. "Then suddenly our community was split with a deliberate racial wedge." By contrast, UFWOC organizer Marshall Ganz opined that Salinas had long exuded "a racism that was different . . . really organized . . . [and] mechanized . . . it just seemed colder, an established fact." The "ghosts of bracerismo," he observed, still hung over Salinas as evidenced by how labor camps were geographically interspersed with coolers and packing sheds. Farmworkers were housed with other factors of production, resulting in their social segregation and dehumanization. Yet during the strike, growers had to face their employees as equals across the negotiating table. Some growers refused to speak directly to workers or look Chavez and Dolores Huerta in the eye during negotiations. "They hated losing that power," Huerta remembered. "They now had to treat workers decently. They couldn't accept the fact that there could be a farmworker sitting across from you [who] could be just as intelligent as you." Having long believed that Mexicanos were incapable of mobilizing, growers faced the opposite reality.[20]

Racialized debates about the strike continued in the pages of the *Californian* as white and Mexican American residents sparred with each other through the written word. In response to a September 1970 letter by Gloria McCoy that denounced the UFWOC's Hartnell rally and the union's undocumented immigrant membership, Gloria Mercado wrote: "I'm sure she [McCoy] likes some Mexican-Americans as long as they stay quiet and don't complain. We only ask for what we as Americans are entitled to." Raymond Torres agreed, saying of white Salinas Valley residents: "These friends of ours, as they have long told us they were, cannot understand why we, the Mexican-American, feel as we do about Chavez and his 'Huelga.' They cannot understand why we want to do what everyone else has always been doing—fighting for their rights . . . we too are Americans whether you like it or not and never again shall we be the submissive people we were." A particular phenomenon that intertwined race, citizenship, and "Americanness" during the strike was the battle of the flags. In response to the prevalence of UFWOC flags, Teamsters members, growers, and many white residents began flying American flags from their car antennas. By tying Americanness to whiteness, they identified Chavez followers as disloyal, foreign, and undeserving of inclusion in the U.S. body politic. Mexican American UFWOC members then countered by flying the UFWOC and U.S. flags together from their vehicles, reminding their opponents that they possessed bicultural citizenship and loyalty to their American and Mexican roots. Several Mexican American residents defended this action in the *Californian*. "Please, don't forget that we are Americans, too . . . we too have pledged allegiance to the very same flag," Stephanie Frias wrote. Gloria Mercado added: "I would like to reply to all those who just started to display their American flags, as if to let us who carry the red and black banner know that only they are Americans and patriotic . . . This is our flag, our country and many of our men have died to make it so and most of us are fourth and fifth generation Americans."[21]

Though racial tension did characterize the strike, lines of support for and opposition to the UFWOC were not strictly racial. Some white residents expressed support for the UFWOC strikers. "The things that are going on in this Valley make me so ashamed," Pat Swafford wrote. "You can see the racial hatred seeping into people's better judgment when there is absolutely no need for it . . . The American flag belongs to both sides of the farm-labor strike." Jerry Braun agreed: "The American Flag is the symbol of the United States of America, not the growers or any other organization. The Flag protects workers and grower alike." Differing opinions about the UFWOC existed within Salinas's Mexicano community as well. At a September 7 Citizens Committee rally Lena D. García, a Tejana born of Mexican immigrant parents, expressed her opposition to the UFWOC strike and her support for the Teamster-grower alliance. Attacked by other Mexican Americans for her views, García wrote to the *Californian* to defend her position: "[Chavez's supporters] tell me I'm not human, and that I don't respect my race . . . [but Chavez] came into this valley to teach the young generation to hate each other, to make families turn against each other and friends, and fighting in our own Mexican race, too."[22]

Although García was targeted for her minority view, her comments did reveal something important. Not every person in the Salinas Valley's diverse Mexican-origin community supported the UFWOC. Those who did not were influenced by various factors, including class, economics, and identity. Some Mexican Americans who had recently become "middle class" viewed supporting Chavez and the UFWOC as a risk to their further upward mobility, especially because they had struggled so hard to obtain it. Sally Gutíerrez, for instance, did not want to risk losing her job as a court interpreter by publicly taking Chavez's side in the labor conflict, though she privately sympathized with his cause. Others simply did not think the union had the workers' best interests at heart. As Robert Friedrich remembered of his father, Plaza Theater owner Jose Friedrich, "My dad liked the idea of a union, but . . . [he] thought both [the UFWOC and the Teamsters] weren't interested in the workers." He also did not care for the "goon squad tactics" both unions had resorted to during the strike. In the fields, the need for a steady job influenced many individuals' decision to not join the UFWOC. Ex-bracero Ismael Nicolás Osorio, who had acquired a foreman job at the Garin Company after the Bracero Program ended, endured having his truck pelted by rock-throwing UFWOC picketers in order to keep his job. Other ex-braceros who had found work, or migrant farmworkers traveling across California, prioritized putting food on the table over joining the union struggle.[23]

In some multigenerational agricultural families, divisions emerged along lines of age and immigration status. While his father worked as a labor contractor, for example, Ray Villanueva participated in UFWOC rallies as a college student and Brown Beret. José L. Orozco and his older brother went to strike with the UFWOC in Salinas while their father, who had been a bracero from 1946 to 1960 and acquired his residency papers in 1962, continued working in the fields to earn enough money to bring another son from Mexico to the United States. In some cases, these intrafamilial divisions were reconciled. Roberto García, who migrated to Salinas from Texas with his family, stayed in a high-paying foreman position at the Mann Packing Company to financially support his parents when they joined the UFWOC strike. That arrangement changed when García confronted the picket line as he tried to drive a bus of workers into a broccoli field. When García's father approached the bus with a UFWOC flag, a sheriff wordlessly pushed the elder García to the ground. Furious, Roberto hopped off the bus and urged the 150 workers he was transporting to join the strike on the spot. García went on to become one of Cesar Chavez's close friends and a leading Salinas UFWOC organizer.[24]

Like García, some Mexican Americans changed their minds about the UFWOC during the course of the strike, allowing family ties and personal politics to override economic concerns. Others might have silently supported the UFWOC but did nothing, or yelled "Viva Chavez!" at neighborhood rallies but stayed away from picket lines. Recent Mexican migrants who still felt vulnerable as foreign outsiders likely did not feel connected to a U.S.-based "Chicano" identity and farmworker movement. Interestingly, in a conversation with his biographer Jacques Levy, Chavez revealed that he did not consider the Chicano Movement a priority or focus in his organizing. "All that rhetoric about [Chicano] identity . . . comes from the college kids," he said, but he certainly did not prevent those same students from using their rhetoric to draw more attention and followers to the UFWOC.[25] How one identified in terms of culture, politics, and citizenship—Chicano, Mexican American, Mexican, or American—influenced one's actions during the 1970 strike. The Mexican-origin population of the Salinas Valley and the nation writ large was, and always had been, the sum of many parts and an amalgamation of identities. One's loyalty to the UFWOC could not be predicted by class, generation, or nativity alone. Decisions were made on the basis of personal histories, motivation, and self-interest, proving that being Mexicano did not mean thinking in a single way or undertaking a single course of action.

Despite these intraethnic divisions, the UFWOC did help to unify certain groups of people in ways that made 1970 a unique historical moment. For the first time, Mexican Americans, ex-braceros, Tejano migrants, and recent Mexican immigrants in the Salinas Valley were acting in solidarity and benefiting from each other's organizing strengths. U.S.-born and ex-bracero *lechugueros* had initiated conversations with Chavez to bring the UFWOC to the region. Tejano migrants had formed community with each other in shared company housing like La Posada or moved to Salinas already unionized from the 1966 UFWOC strike in the Rio Grande Valley. La Casita Farms, one of the biggest companies affected by that strike, belonged to Harden Farms of Salinas, and some of its workers moved back and forth between the two. Chicano college students articulated a language of racial pride that lent a militant, youthful energy to the movement. And finally—although it had been just ten years before that Salinas's Mexican Americans had fought against the continued presence of braceros and "wetbacks"—Mexican Americans and Mexican nationals were standing side by side on UFWOC picket lines.[26]

Historian David Gutíerrez has argued that it was during the 1950s that Mexican Americans started to realize that cross-national alliances with Mexican immigrants could help their civil rights cause. When it came to communities so heavily dominated by agribusiness like Salinas, however, this change did not and *could not* happen until the Bracero Program had ended and labor competition became a lesser source of intraethnic tension. Ironically, Chavez never intended for or wanted his union to serve Mexican nationals. In fact, at this time he was railing against growers' use of undocumented migrant labor and loudly calling for the INS to increase its patrols along the border. Later, Manuel Chavez would set up a "wet line," or group of tents and patrols, along the Arizona border. Ostensibly, this was an effort to dissuade border-crossers from working in UFW-struck fields, but disturbing stories surfaced about UFW patrols threatening, beating, and robbing migrants.[27] Yet it was green-carders, ex-braceros, and undocumented migrants who made up a significant contingent of the 1970 lettuce strike's participants. Contrary to historical assumptions that the UFWOC struggle was a predominantly Mexican American effort, Mexican nationals proved just as crucial to the success of the union.

By the end of the strike's second week, the UFWOC had signed agreements with some growers, persuaded others to begin negotiations, and sent an estimated two thousand of five thousand picketers back to work. In addition, the California Supreme Court had overturned Salinas judge Stanley Lawson's ban on picketing and work slowdowns under which forty-one UFWOC members had been arrested. But on September 16—Mexican Independence Day—Superior Court judge Anthony Brazil issued a new order banning the UFWOC from picketing approximately thirty Salinas Valley farms still under Teamsters contracts. In response, Chavez ordered picketing and boycotting to be expanded to all non-UFWOC Salinas Valley lettuce growers, including world-leading grower Bud Antle. In a move similar to that which he executed in 1961 against AWOC, Antle moved quickly against the UFWOC by raising company wage rates and piece rates and requesting a preliminary injunction from the Salinas Superior Court to stop the boycott, arguing that his firm had been under Teamsters contract for the past decade.[28]

Undeterred, Chavez continued to make direct attacks on growers and on the city of Salinas for its dark history of farmworker mistreatment. The day after Brazil's ruling, September 17, was the seven-year anniversary of the 1963 Chualar bus-train accident. At a news conference that afternoon, Chavez announced that more than three thousand UFWOC members would march with him from Salinas to a section of railroad tracks near Chualar to memorialize the thirty-two farmworker victims. "We're convinced that those men lost their lives, as so many others have lost their lives, because of the carelessness of the employers, and the fact that employers have not yet come to recognize workers as true human beings," Chavez told reporters. The media followed him to the Catholic memorial service where farmworkers from the home states of the deceased solemnly read the Chualar victims' names over a microphone. In bringing farmworker deaths of the past to bear on the UFWOC's current struggles, Chavez gave an emotionally charged and powerful reminder that the injustices of the past still echoed loudly in the present. On October 8, Monterey County Superior Court judge Gordon Campbell ordered Chavez to halt all boycott activities against Bud Antle. Chávez ignored Campbell's mandate and instructed UFWOC members to keep picketing. The UFWOC proceeded to win a contract with Freshpict after threatening a boycott against its parent company Purex, which produced widely used bleach and other household cleaners. Pic-N-Pac fell soon after, and the D'Arrigo Company agreed to sign a contract with the UFWOC by the end of November. Furious at the disregard for his orders, Campbell called Chavez to appear before him on December 4 to face contempt of court charges.[29]

On the wet, cold, and windy morning of Chavez's hearing, hundreds of UFWOC supporters and farmworkers from around California—including Coachella, Fresno, Delano, and Bakersfield—joined him on a ten-block march to the courthouse. Led by Mexican American and Filipino American UFWOC officials, including Larry Itliong, Dolores Huerta, and Philip Vera Cruz, the procession soon swelled to more than two thousand people. As the crowd approached downtown Salinas, a white man parked his pickup truck near the marchers and fastened an American flag to his radio antenna. "Mexico is that way!"

he shouted, pointing his finger southward. After marching quietly to the courthouse, the crowd filled all three floors of the building and spilled down the stairway out into the courtyard. People stood or knelt for more than three hours and participated in prayers led by Catholic priests from around the San Francisco Bay Area. Declaring Chavez guilty of contempt of court, Campbell ordered a fine of one thousand dollars and imprisonment until he ended the boycott. Chavez, who had strategized and hoped for this sentence, was going to jail for the first time in his organizing career. Before being led away, Chavez communicated a defiant message to his followers and the press: "Boycott Bud Antle! Boycott Dow! And boycott the hell out of them! Viva!" The Dow Chemical Company, which had saved a financially struggling Antle in 1969 by buying seventeen thousand acres of farmland for a fraction of its value and then reselling it to Antle, produced dangerous pesticides as well as napalm used by the United States during the Vietnam War. By verbally connecting the two, Chavez reminded the public of agribusiness's connection to corporations that caused global suffering.[30]

The waiting mass of Chavez supporters erupted in fury upon hearing the verdict. A committee of women attempted to calm the crowd by leading a march to Cristo Rey Church, in part for a union meeting but also to confront Father Humberto Hermosa, who had broken his earlier promise to appear at the courthouse in support of Chavez. As the marchers entered the church, they found Hermosa delivering mass to a group of older Mexicanos. The women, union flags in hand, began singing the Spanish song "De Colores" and proceeded up the aisle on their knees, stopping at Hermosa's feet. "Everything stopped in the church," Ganz remembered. "[Those women found] the courage and the solidarity to confront that jerk . . . they knew exactly what they were doing." Through their defiant actions, the women reminded Hermosa of their role in founding Cristo Rey in the 1950s and the reason why the church had been built in the first place—to respond to the social exclusion of agricultural working-class Mexicanos. As Hermosa moved aside and those in the pews listened, the women began a union meeting in which members decided to hold a twenty-four-hour vigil in the parking lot across from the Salinas jail until Chavez was released. By that evening, farmworkers' wives had created an altar in the back of a pickup truck that consisted of a shrine to the Virgin of Guadalupe, votive candles, flowers, the Mexican and U.S. flags, and pictures of Chavez, Abraham Lincoln, Martin Luther King Jr., John F. Kennedy, and Robert F. Kennedy. As they had done when they sewed strike flags, women created symbols and imagery for the Salinas farmworker movement in this altar. They also made it clear that UFWOC supporters could claim loyalty to both the United States and Mexico, and place their labor struggles on the same level of importance as the African American civil rights movement. Each evening a different priest held mass outside the jail while supporters listened, shared food, and sang songs. In many ways, it was women who helped sustain strikers' morale while Chavez was imprisoned.[31]

Famous women showed their support of the UFWOC as well. Ethel Kennedy and Coretta Scott King paid separate visits to Salinas to visit Chavez and speak to strikers. During her visit on December 6, Kennedy was attacked outside the jail by a crowd of three hundred anti-UFWOC demonstrators that included members of the Citizens' Committee, some Salinas growers, and members of the Monterey County John Birch Society. Waving American flags and shouting "Reds, go home!" and "Ethel, go home!" the demonstrators hurled insults at Kennedy's dead husband (an ardent Chavez supporter) and one grower tried to grab her hair. "I couldn't believe what I was hearing," newspaper reporter Eric Brazil recalled. "I mean, it was dangerous—it felt like someone could be killed." Teamsters employee Joan Santoro agreed: "Growers were on one side of the street, the farm workers on the other . . . The police were nervous and felt there could be bloodshed." During her visit on December 19, King gave a powerful public speech that drew parallels between the African American and Mexican American civil rights movements. "Black people and Brown people are herded at the bottom and told to be quiet and to wait for slow change," King said. "[F]inally together, we have said there is an end to waiting. Cesar Chavez is not an accident; he is a genius of his people." Unlike her late husband, whose personal and financial relationship with Teamsters president James Hoffa precluded him from publicly supporting the UFWOC, Coretta Scott King became an essential bridge between the Mexican American farmworker and African American civil rights activist communities.[32]

Three weeks into Chavez's jail time, the California Supreme Court ordered his release and removed the bans on the UFWOC strike and boycott. On the evening of December 23, five hundred supporters broke into cheers as Chavez stepped out of the jail. Farmworkers, spectators, and photographers waiting with their cameras all clicked their shutters. "For about fifteen or twenty seconds, night became day," photographer Bob Fitch recalled. "So many strobes went off that it was almost like a lightning bolt. It was one big blinding flash of light." In greeting the crowd Chavez did not hesitate to make the jab (splashed all over television), "This jail reminds me of a lot of labor camps," pointing out that it was poorly lit, cold, leaky, and damp. He was not going to ease up on the Salinas Valley anytime soon, and neither was the UFWOC's farm-worker membership. Chavez's imprisonment had not broken strikers' spirit but had strengthened it, and it had brought more publicity to the union's struggle. The lettuce strike and boycott continued until late March 1971, when the UFWOC and Teamsters signed a three-year agreement allowing the former to take over all farmworker contracts in the region.[33]

The UFWOC strike of 1970 certainly elevated the Salinas Valley as a place of importance in the national consciousness, but it was also the culmination of decades of politicization and activism by the region's Mexican American and Mexican immigrant communities. The 1940s had been characterized by antidiscrimination protests in wartime, a zoot suit craze, and bracero skips. In the 1950s, the CSO emerged as an organization that fought for Mexican Americans' rights of citizenship and respectability. Bracero Program backlash, community building, and landmark legal action against agribusiness pervaded the 1960s. By 1970 this confluence of activism, circumstances, and people allowed Cesar Chavez and the UFWOC to thrive. Although the union was the institution, and Chavez the charismatic figurehead, that allowed a diverse Mexican-origin community to mobilize and strike, it was members of this very community—young and old, male and female, U.S.-born and immigrant—who laid the groundwork that made the union's job much easier than it had been in Delano. The 1970 strike was not a sudden outburst of political consciousness and activity led by Chavez. Rather, it was the outcome of years of work by men and women who believed they had grounds for dreaming, the ones who cultivated the fields to be Chavez's stage, who made red flags blossom and the world take notice.

Conclusion

The Farmworker Justice Movement, 1970 to the Present

THE OUTCOME OF the UFWOC strike in 1970 gave its participants every reason to hope that improvements in farmworker conditions were there to stay. It had been a landmark event in the dual struggles for labor justice and Chicano empowerment, and workers had seen what collective action could achieve. Yet it soon became apparent that these battles would continue. After the strike many Salinas Valley agricultural firms simply shut down and reopened under new names to void their UFWOC contracts, turning to labor contractors to hire their employees instead so that they could evade future contracts. Then, when the UFWOC contracts won in 1970 expired in 1973, several growers resisted renegotiating with Chavez and signed contracts with the Teamsters again without elections or their employees' consent. The UFWOC (renamed the United Farm Workers [UFW] in 1972) fought for and benefited from the June 1975 passage of the Agricultural Labor Relations Act that gave California farmworkers the right to choose their union representatives through elections. By the end of that year the UFW won 167 elections in the Salinas Valley representing 24,334 workers, while the Teamsters won 95 representing 11,802 workers. When UFW contracts expired again in 1979, the union organized two marches—one beginning in San Francisco and the other in San Lucas—that converged in Salinas on August 11 with fifteen thousand participants. The major lettuce strike that followed persuaded most Salinas Valley agricultural firms to sign contracts raising starting wages for farmworkers by 40 percent to $5.25 an hour and instituting an improved medical plan, paid vacations, pesticide restrictions, and employer-paid union representatives to monitor workers' conditions locally.[1]

These 1979 victories, however, were the final peak in the UFW's organizing history. The union experienced a rapid decline during the early 1980s, largely because Cesar Chavez's long-held desire to control his union from the top down catastrophically clashed with UFW members' demands for input and power. Beginning in the spring of 1977, Chavez subjected his union's core leadership to a group therapy exercise known as "the Game" from the cultish drug treatment program Synanon, in which participants were required to launch aggressive personal attacks against one another to "cleanse" the organization. The airing of grievances, resentments, and accusations at the union's headquarters in La Paz tore apart various relationships. When UFW lawyer Jerry Cohen and his team suggested moving the union's legal base to Salinas and requested salary raises, Chavez perceived these actions as betrayals of his leadership and the union's principle of voluntary poverty. In 1981 when Salinas worker representatives Sabino López, Cleofas Guzman, and Bertha Batres supported three candidates not approved by Chavez for election to the union's executive board, Chavez fired them all. Although he had conducted union purges as early as 1967 against people who he believed were undermining his leadership, Chavez's systematic purging of his longtime associates, close friends, and valuable union leaders through the Game stymied the union's progress. As Frank Bardacke argued: "Earlier Cesar Chavez had lost control of the first organization he had built, the Community Service Organization. He made sure that would not happen again. But in keeping control of the UFW, he crippled it."[2]

By distancing himself from the fields and actively undermining leadership by farmworkers themselves, Chavez toppled the UFW at the height of its power. At its zenith in the late 1970s the UFW had a membership of fifty thousand, but by 1985 that number had fallen to around six thousand. Additionally, the union's failure to adapt to demographic changes in the 1980s—particularly, new Mexican and Central American migration—meant a lost opportunity for organizing the foreign-born workers who replaced Mexican Americans as the dominant agricultural workforce. By the mid-1980s, less than 10 percent of California farmworkers were U.S.-born.[3] Many have weighed in on Chavez's legacy and focused on his victories and failures, both of which carry equal consequence. During the 1960s and 1970s, Chavez inspired and drew together a diverse following across lines of race, class, geography, and gender. His accomplishments through the union were tremendous, and his status as a civil rights icon today gives Latinos a place in that larger American narrative of struggle. Yet his personal paranoia and desire for control did not let farmworkers evolve into union leaders who could stand beside him. With no paid representatives monitoring conditions at the local level, the union lost its authority and power in the fields.

This organizational tragedy exacted a lasting toll on farmworkers in California and throughout the nation. Many grower-shippers increased their joint ventures with nonunion harvesting companies or discarded their union contracts altogether, and the middleman-labor contracting system reemerged as a way for employers to exempt themselves from labor regulations. Entry-level hourly wages for farmworkers fell from more than seven dollars to five, fringe benefits disappeared, and living conditions worsened. CRLA attorneys had to take up cases such as the infamous "Ranch of the Caves" scandal of 1985, in which a Salinas strawberry grower told his farmworkers to dig their own homes out of a hillside on his property. Almost one hundred workers were found "living in holes in the ground, like rabbits," and the grower was making as much as four hundred dollars in rent per cave each month. A similar discovery was made in San Diego the next year.[4] After Chavez's death in 1993 the union came under the leadership of his son-in-law Arturo Rodriguez. Today, it is active in ten states and in recent years has successfully negotiated contracts for strawberry, rose, and winery workers. Much of its work is digital, including online fund-raising efforts and petitions for legislation concerning employment and pesticide and safety protections for farmworkers. Chavez continues to be revered as a heroic figure in the Latino civil rights and labor movement (in 2011 President Barack Obama proclaimed March 31 Cesar Chavez Day), but the UFW is very different from its former self.

While the UFW's presence and power eventually waned in the Salinas Valley, other important forms of Mexican American protest emerged after 1970. A LULAC chapter was founded and fought on behalf of young Mexican American victims of police harassment and brutality. LULAC's complaints to the U.S. Department of Justice and the FBI, coupled with CRLA lawsuits concerning Monterey County's employment discrimination against minorities, prompted the U.S. Civil Rights Commission to conduct hearings in Salinas in 1976. Community activist Jesse Sánchez developed a Salinas chapter of the Southwest Voter Registration Project, through which Mexican Americans and naturalized Mexican immigrants voted en masse to abolish Salinas's at-large elections system in favor of a district election system. Soon after, in 1989, Simon Salinas, a schoolteacher and ex-bracero's son, won a seat on the Salinas City Council. In 1998 former CRLA attorney Anna Caballero became the first Latina/Latino mayor in Salinas history, and Simon Salinas became the only Latino to be elected to the Monterey County Board of Supervisors in the twentieth century. The Salinas of today looks vastly different from the Salinas of the 1940s. Along with dominating positions in local government, Latinos comprise almost 65 percent of the city's population of 150,000, making it one of the many "minority-majority" cities in California today.[5]

One of the most politically active Latino communities in Salinas and around the United States is the ex-bracero population. After the Bracero Program's end, many men made their homes in the United States by naturalizing, acquiring green cards for permanent residency, or overstaying their contract and becoming undocumented. Several have become involved in the Bracero Justice Movement, which emerged out of the discovery of longtime deductions from braceros' paychecks during the 1940s. Between 1942 and 1949, the United States and Mexico agreed to withhold and deposit 10 percent of each bracero's paycheck in a Mexican governmental account at the Wells Fargo bank of San Francisco. The money would then be sent to either the Banco Agrícola or Banco Nacional de Ahorra in Mexico to create a savings account for each bracero that would encourage him to return home instead of becoming a "skip" or "wetback." Scholars estimate that between $10 million and $100 million was removed from bracero paychecks during the program's first decade, yet many braceros never noticed this provision in their contracts, and government agents and employers did not try to explain the discrepancy. When braceros finally began requesting the money, Mexican banks claimed that the funds had been misdirected or lost.

The Coachella Valley–based organization Braceroproa and other groups, including Braceros del Valle, a self-organized group of ex-braceros in Monterey County, responded by filing the 2001 class action suit *Ramirez, et al. v. United States, et al.* in the U.S. District Court of Northern California. The suit charged the U.S. and Mexican governments and the three banks involved with malfeasance and requested a settlement of $500 million. When Justice Charles Breyer struck down the case in 2002, arguing that the statute of limitations for bracero reparations had passed, braceros turned to their elected representatives for help in bringing greater attention to the "10 percent" issue. In 2005, under pressure from politicians and activists on both sides of the border, the Mexican government agreed to create a bracero compensation fund that would pay each ex-bracero (or his surviving family) a one-time payment of $3,500 if proof of contracting was provided through pay stubs, identification cards, contracts, or other documents. The registration period for these payments ended in March 2006, with 250,000 people signing up for compensation. In a March 2012 visit to Oaxaca City's Instituto del Atención al Migrante (Migrant Rights Office), I witnessed in one afternoon a steady stream of ex-braceros and their families asking for their payments, only to be told to keep waiting. Boxes of folios lined the office's walls, chock-full of braceros' documents proving their service in the program. Some folios even included personal photographs taken of braceros in fields or atop tractors in the United States as pieces of proof. One man I met, a one-hundred-year-old former bracero who had worked in New Jersey, Colorado, Arkansas, Texas, Michigan, Illinois, and California, complained of no longer having the physical strength to keep inquiring at the office for his payment. When Mexican president Enrique Peña Nieto took office in December 2012, the payments stopped. Into 2015, ex-braceros and activists continue to protest and ask that the U.S. and Mexican governments reactivate the fund, but many braceros have died and will die without receiving proper remuneration for their work.[6]

In the Salinas Valley, ex-braceros and Mexican Americans have collaborated in history and memory projects that have created dialogue about the Bracero Program. Local libraries and museums have sponsored documentary film screenings and welcomed the Bracero History Project as it collected oral histories and artifacts for the Smithsonian's National Museum of American History exhibition "Bittersweet

Harvest: The Bracero Program 1942–1964."Meanwhile, the Citizenship Project of Salinas, an organization founded in 1995 by Mexican immigrants, has held a memorial mass for the Chualar crash victims on the anniversary of their deaths every year since 2001. In September 2013, this event was augmented by a dedication ceremony for the Bracero Memorial Highway, the stretch of California's Highway 101 mentioned in this book's beginning (fig. 8.1). After serving as mayor of Salinas, Anna Caballero went on to become a California assemblywoman and in 2010 presented the resolution that made this highway a reality. In the midst of efforts to highlight bracero history, however, there have been reminders that not all embrace this history. In April 2009, Rafael Ramírez, a Mexican artist, painted a mural titled *Los Braceros* on a side wall of the Alisal School District office with the help of local schoolchildren. Ramirez included scenes of braceros being fumigated with DDT upon their arrival and the Chualar accident to ensure

Fig. 8.1. The Bracero Memorial Highway between Chualar and Soledad, California.

Fig. 8.2. A section of *Los Braceros* by Rafael Ramírez, re-creating a famous photograph of braceros being fumigated in Texas in 1956.

that people could see "that that happened" (fig. 8.2). When freelance journalist Todd Brown commended the artwork in the *Salinas Californian,* the backlash was immediate. In the newspaper's online forum, one commenter deemed the mural "another cave painting," while another wrote, "Let us Okies paint a large target on the wall of the Steinbeck building and then line up all the gangbangers . . . POW! POW! POW!," referencing recent gang activity associated with the city's Mexican-origin population. In rejecting the mural's rendition of the bracero experience, these detractors deployed century-old associations between Mexican-ness, primitivity, and violence. This animosity coupled with a willful amnesia about the Salinas Valley's bracero history is chilling and works to thwart the construction of alternative, more inclusive histories that can counter white-, grower-, and Steinbeck-dominated narratives that Salinas currently uses to define itself to residents and visitors.[7]

Like the Smithsonian exhibition, some would call the Bracero Program bittersweet in that the work was grueling and exploitative but the opportunity to earn wages was real. The bitterness in Bracero Program history is too great to ignore, however, when one considers that the U.S. Congress continues to entertain the possibility of reincarnating a similar guestworker program. Agricultural guestworkers in the United States come from various countries such as Peru and Thailand, but the majority of them continue to come from Mexico. In 2010 Mexicans were issued a whopping 90 percent of H-2A temporary agricultural visas, which are very similar to bracero contracts in that they are seasonal and tied to a specific employer, and housing and transportation are provided. If bound to a single employer with little monitoring, workers experiencing abuse are more reluctant to report it for fear of losing their jobs and being deported. According to historian Cindy Hahamovitch, disturbing discoveries of workers going unpaid or being housed in dilapidated or damaged quarters are numerous.[8]

Indeed, the injustices of the past have not left the fields, orchards, and vineyards but continue to permeate the lives of agricultural workers in the United States today. Overwhelmingly immigrant, they are earning wages almost 25 percent lower than what was being paid to their unionized counterparts during the 1970s. Agribusiness continues to evade the institution of a minimum wage, overtime pay, and collective bargaining rights for farmworkers, and the old refrain that "Americans won't do this type of work" keeps agricultural labor marginalized as a "Mexican" or "immigrant" occupation distanced from the eyes and ears of American voters who could demand that new laws be put in place. In addition to abysmally low wages, farmwork continues to be characterized by not enough rest breaks, water, and sanitary facilities. Sexual harassment is prevalent and workers are threatened with firing and deportation if they complain. In some fields, *el cortito* has reappeared. Bureau of Labor Statistics reports reveal that migrant farmworkers are still dying from being transported in overcrowded vehicles, and in March 2011 a farm company supervisor and a labor contractor received no jail time after they ignored the suffering of seventeen-year-old pregnant farmworker Maria Isavel Jimenez while she was working in a Stockton vineyard. She died of heat stroke when her body temperature reached 108 degrees. Migrant and seasonal farmworkers have an average life expectancy of only forty-nine years compared with the seventy-nine-year national average, and 2010 data from the CDC indicate that at least ten to twenty thousand farmworkers suffer from pesticide poisoning each year nationwide. Many more cases go unreported. Pesticides in use today can cause migraines, vomiting, skin rashes, pulmonary and neurological problems, and birth defects. They have also been linked to asthma, elevated rates of Parkinson's disease, and heightened susceptibility to nearly thirty types of cancer.[9]

As agricultural labor's toxic conditions manifest in the bodies of farmworkers and their children, those who are immigrants suffer doubly from toxic discourse and policies regarding their presence in the United States. Since the Reagan administration's effort to legalize undocumented immigrants through the Immigration Reform and Control Act of 1986, the term "amnesty" has been a controversial one in U.S. society. Instead, border militarization has been the chosen course of action. During the early 1990s the Clinton administration, through its strategy of "prevention through deterrence," initiated Operation Hold the Line (1993) and Operation Gatekeeper (1994). High steel fences and floodlights were installed in the El Paso–Juarez and the San Diego–Tijuana areas, and the latter's fourteen-mile fence from the Pacific Ocean to Yuma, Arizona, was soon nicknamed "the Tortilla Curtain." These barriers simply channeled migrants to less visible and more dangerous pathways, such as Arizona's mountainous Sonoran Desert, where thousands have died trying to cross in daytime temperatures of up to 130 degrees and nighttime lows below freezing. The ratification of the North America Free Trade Agreement (NAFTA) in 1994 spurred further migration to *el norte* when an influx of cheaper corn imported from the United States drove half a million Mexican *campesino* families out of business. As a result, the annual number of Mexican migrants to the United States increased by more than 61 percent. Meanwhile, *maquiladoras* (border factories) that boomed in the age of NAFTA continue to exploit the labor of young Mexican women making products for various U.S. companies.[10]

Those immigrants who went to California in 1994 were greeted by the passage of Proposition 187, which barred undocumented immigrants from receiving publicly provided health, education, and welfare services. Though it was eventually ruled unconstitutional some years later, this piece of nativist legislation sent a strong message to Mexican immigrants that they were not welcome. This was only reified by Chris Simcox's establishment in 2004 of the Minutemen Civil Defense Corps in Arizona, which encouraged citizen vigilantes to patrol the U.S.-Mexico border themselves and "do the job the government won't do." The spring of 2006 witnessed large and widespread pro-immigrant demonstrations, work stoppages, and school walkouts involving between 3.5 and 5.1 million people around the country. Arguing that Mexican immigrants powered much of the manual labor and service sectors of the U.S. economy, immigrant rights activists asked U.S. residents to imagine "a day without a Mexican" working in their homes, gardens, restaurants, and construction sites. In 2007 Latinos surpassed African Americans as the largest minority group in the country, and by 2010 the number of people of Latin American and Caribbean origin and heritage in the United States had increased to more than fifty million. Arizona became the center of controversy once more when Senate Bill 1070, which made the failure to carry immigration documents on one's person a crime and gave police broad power to detain anyone suspected of being in the country without authorization, became the toughest state immigration law. Reminiscent of the racial profiling that occurred during Operation Wetback fifty years before, SB 1070 copycat laws that allowed police to investigate people's immigration status during routine stops and forced public schools to determine students' citizenship status passed in the states of Georgia and Alabama. These bills have caused immigrants to flee certain communities, leaving a trail of abandoned homes—and unharvested fields—in their wake. Currently, Congress is debating immigration reform and the implementation of the Development, Relief, and Education for Alien Minors Act (or DREAM Act), which would grant legal residency to minors brought illegally into the country as children but who are willing to complete higher education or serve in the military as a condition of remaining in the United States. This would be one step in preventing the creation of, as sociologist Douglas S. Massey has put it, "a large underclass that is permanently divorced from American society and disenfranchised from its resources, with little hope of upward mobility."[11]

Our twenty-first-century debates around immigrants and immigration policy are nothing new; as this book has shown, they have deep roots in the past. The reality remains that when neighboring countries possess vastly different economies, people will migrate through both legal and illegal channels. For many years, the U.S.-Mexico border has been the most militarized frontier between two countries not at war, but this has failed to address the very real economic, social, and political ties between the two countries that have encouraged migrant flows northward for more than a century. Anxieties related to what anthropologist Leo Chavez has called the "Latino threat narrative"— the idea that Latinos are a threat to America's security, economy, and culture because they have not been "assimilated" to the same extent as European immigrants of the past—have hindered productive immigration reform and better understanding of the reasons why immigrants are both pushed and pulled to the United States. Employers continue to hire authorized and unauthorized immigrants, while generalized "Go back to Mexico" rhetoric rages in the media and the public. These contradictory messages, along with the failure of American societal institutions to incorporate immigrants of Latin American descent as much as those of European descent, have separated Latinos into another category of social citizenship that harms their chances for inclusion and equal rights.[12]

Historically and in the present, California has figured prominently in these immigration debates. Of the 11.4 million undocumented immigrants living in the United States in 2012, approximately 3.2 million resided in California, more than in any other state. Most estimates conclude that approximately 70 percent of California's agricultural workers are undocumented, and the agricultural counties of Monterey and San Benito have the highest percentage of undocumented immigrants. Places like California also show us how diverse the Latino demographic has become over time. New immigrants from South America, Central America, and indigenous communities in Mexico are now working and living beside longtime Mexican American residents and ex-braceros. Just as in the "wetback" era of the 1940s and 1950s, these multiple groups are coexisting and clashing with each other. In 2007, for instance, middle-class Mexican American restaurateurs in Salinas proposed banning taco trucks (mostly operated by recent Latin American immigrants) because of their unfair economic advantage in selling cheap mobile food to fieldworkers. Mexican Americans and ex-braceros also complained that these newcomers overcrowded the Alisal district and created the drug and gang problems that made Salinas a crime capital of California at the turn of the twenty-first century. As Central Americans and indigenous Mexicans began reshaping numerous regions in the United States, including the Deep South and Northeast, California absorbed these new populations as well. Triquis, Mixtecs, and other indigenous groups now comprise 30 percent of the state's farmworkers. In the Salinas Valley town of Greenfield, Mexican American residents took to city council meetings, social media websites, and newspapers to complain that Oaxacan migrants were illegal "invaders" causing community blight and flouting various laws. "It's a shame," Mixtec community leader Eulogio Solano said. "Their fathers or grandfathers came to this country in the same way that our people are coming now."[13]

This book has argued for the importance of agriculture-centered communities in the past, present, and future of Latinos in the United States. Our current histories of Latino labor and political activism can be, and should be, revised by considering how those who lived in the world of agriculture navigated their daily lives as well as significant historical moments and transitions. Likewise, both Latino and agricultural history need to be placed more squarely into larger narratives about immigration, race relations, and politics in the United States. As the 1950s drew to a close, 85 percent of peoples of Mexican descent living in the United States were U.S. citizens, by either birth or naturalization.[14] What if Mexican immigration had stopped there? Through its historic and continued employment of braceros, undocumented laborers, and other immigrants, U.S. agriculture has played a formative role in maintaining this immigrant flow, which in turn has shaped the demographics of our nation and the course of significant federal policies. At the same time, agricultural workers themselves—citizen and immigrant—have profoundly shaped the culture and economy of the United States, as well as that of their countries of origin through remittances and transnational movements.

We are now at a critical juncture, a juncture that has appeared many times before, in which we must decide how to treat the immigrants and farmworkers who labor within our borders. The organic, free-range, and local food movements have permeated our daily lives and discourse as consumers, but they remain disconnected from the labor justice movement and any interrogation of the working conditions of farmworkers who harvest our food. Those performing agricultural work in the United States today are some of the nation's most marginalized, desperate, and vulnerable workers, just like their predecessors. They have grounds for dreaming of something better, and these dreams can be realized in the future only if we pay greater attention to the patterns and mistakes of the past. History is reverberating in our ears and can guide us in seeing the fruit on our kitchen tables, the wine in our restaurants, and the vegetables in our salads as something else—as the toil of humans in need of greater inclusion and rights—as long as we let it.

Notes

INTRODUCTION

1. M. Cristina Medina, "Gathering Remembers Bracero Crash Victims," *Monterey Herald* online, 18 September 2005, www.montereyherald.com/mld/montereyherald/news/12679216.htm; "Full Speed Ahead on Bill for a Bracero Memorial Highway," *Salinas Californian,* 7 August 2010, www.thecalifornian.com/article/20100807/OPINION01/8070301/1014/OPINION/Editorial-Full-speed-ahead-on-bill-for-a-Bracero-Memorial-Highway.

2. McWilliams, *Factories in the Field;* Petrick, "'Like Ribbons of Green and Gold,'" 274; Bardacke, *Trampling,* 341. As of 2000, 91 percent of the agricultural labor force in California were immigrants, one-third were women, and 90 percent were Latino, mostly from Mexico. In contrast, 90 percent of California growers were of European descent. López, "From the Farms," 291.

A note on terminology: In this book "Mexican American" refers to people of Mexican descent born in the United States, or those born in Mexico (Mexicans, or Mexican nationals) who have come to live, acculturate, and feel bicultural in the United States. "Mexicano" or "Mexicana" and "Mexican-origin" are interchangeable as umbrella terms that refer to Mexican Americans and Mexicans together. "Chicana" or "Chicano" refers to those Mexican Americans who adopted this term as an identifier of ethnic pride and a more militant political identity during the 1960s and 1970s. The term "Latino" denotes any person of Latin American or Spanish-speaking descent living in the United States, but this umbrella term appears less frequently in this book because of the specific focus on Mexican-origin people. I use the terms "white," "Anglo," "Anglo American," and "Euro-American" interchangeably but recognize the diversity existing within this population and identify the national origins of white subgroups when necessary and available. At times this book uses the terms "migrant" and "migration" rather than "immigrant" and "immigration," as the latter set can imply a unidirectional path to the United States and elides people's transnational movements back and forth across borders.

3. Scott, "Mexican-American in the Los Angeles Area," 326; Table 6, "Nativity and Parentage of the Foreign White Stock, by Country of Origin, for States with 50,000 or more Foreign-Born White, Urban and Rural: 1940 and 1930," U.S. Bureau of the Census, Sixteenth Census 1940, Population, Nativity and Parentage, 52; Sánchez, *Becoming Mexican American*; Ruiz, *Cannery Women*; Zavella, *Women's Work*; González, *Labor and Community*; Weber, *Dark Sweat, White Gold*; Menchaca, *Mexican Outsiders*; Haas, *Conquests and Historical Identities*; Garcia, *World of Its Own*; Alamillo, *Making Lemonade*; Heidenreich, *"This Land Was Mexican Once"*; Pitti, *Devil in Silicon Valley*.

4. Gutiérrez, *Walls and Mirrors*, 172; Calavita, *Inside the State*; Garcia, *World of Its Own*; Ngai, *Impossible Subjects*; Vargas, *Labor Rights Are Civil Rights*; Camacho, *Migrant Imaginaries*; Jimenez, *Replenished Ethnicity*; Garcia, "Cain Contra Abel"; Hernández, *Migra!*; St. John, *Line in the Sand*; Barajas, *Curious Unions*.

5. The derogatory term "wetback" originally referred to undocumented migrants who entered the United States by swimming across the Rio Grande but was soon applied to any undocumented Mexican migrant during the late 1940s and 1950s. I use the term "wetback" because of its common usage in U.S. media and government documents during this period, but with quotation marks because of its demeaning quality.

6. Mariscal, *Aztlán and Viet Nam*; Chávez, *"¡Mi Raza Primero!"*; Oropeza, *¡Raza Sí!*.

7. Bracero History Archive, www.braceroarchive.org; Galarza, *Merchants of Labor*; Galarza, *Spiders in the House*; Anderson, *Bracero Program in California*; Galarza, *Farm Workers and Agri-business*; Gamboa, *Mexican Labor and World War II*; Calavita, *Inside the State*; Ngai, *Impossible Subjects*; Jacobo, *Los Braceros*; Rosas, "Flexible Families"; González, *Guest Workers or Colonized Labor?*; Camacho, *Migrant Imaginaries*; *Bracero Stories*; *Cosecha Triste*; Cohen, *Braceros*; Mitchell, *They Saved the Crops*; Weise, *Corazon de Dixie*.

8. Apodaca, "They Kept the Home Fires Burning"; Rose, "Gender and Civic Activism"; Pitti, *Devil in Silicon Valley*; Brilliant, *"Color of America Has Changed"*; Bernstein, *Bridges of Reform*.

9. Levy, *Cesar Chavez*; Jenkins, *Politics of Insurgency*; Ross, *Conquering Goliath*; Ferriss and Sandoval, *Fight in the Fields*; Shaw, *Beyond the Fields*; Pawel, *Union of Our Dreams*; Watt, *Farm Workers and the Churches*; Ganz, *Why David Sometimes Wins*; Garcia, *From the Jaws of Victory*; Bardacke, *Trampling*; Barajas, *Curious Unions*; Pawel, *Crusades of Cesar Chavez*; Valdes, *Organized Agriculture*.

CHAPTER 1. THE RACIAL AND LABOR LANDSCAPES
OF THE SALINAS VALLEY

1. Clovis, *Salinas Valley*, 7; Verardo and Verardo, *Salinas Valley*, 16, 21.

2. Takaki, *Different Mirror*, 178; Carey McWilliams, "Minorities in California," paper presented at the annual meeting of the California Library Association, 20 October 1944, 48–49, Carton 4, McWilliams Papers.

3. Barajas, *Curious Unions*, 28; Fisher, *Salinas, Upside Down River*, 29, 40, 43, 124–25.

4. City of Salinas, *Business and Community Profile*, 8; Guinn, *History and Biographical Record*, 305; Breschini, Gudgel, and Haversat, *Early Salinas*, 7–8; Hull Jr., "Effects of Braceros," 49.

5. Johnston, *Salinas, 1875–1950*, 1; Al Parsons, "Black Roots Are Deep in Salinas," *Salinas Californian*, 2 April 1977, n.p., Steinbeck Public Library, Local History Collection; Breschini, Gudgel, and Haversat, *Early Salinas*, 7–8; Jones, "Salinas Valley," 41; Geron, *Latino Political Power*, 164; Guinn, *History and Biographical Record*, 306–7; Hull Jr., "Effects of Braceros," 72; "Monterey City: A Mexican Town Becoming Modernized," *Salinas Weekly Index*, 25 June 1891, 2.

6. Barajas, *Curious Unions*, 27; Kousser, "Racial Injustice," 38; "The Result," *Monterey Weekly Herald*, 23 October 1875, 2; Casas, *Married to a Daughter of the Land*, 14, 51–61; Menchaca, *Mexican Outsiders*, 62.

7. Camarillo, *Chicanos in a Changing Society*; Takaki, *Different Mirror*, 186–87.

8. Verardo and Verardo, *Salinas Valley*, 55–56, 170; López, "From the Farms," 239; Jones, "Salinas Valley," 9, 64, 102; Clovis, *Salinas Valley*, 7; Mueller and Ferrasci interview; "Americanization Class at School to Meet Tonight," *Salinas Daily Index*, 16 October 1923, 5. By contrast, Sicilians were developing a large community in Monterey based on industrialized fishing. Their southern Italian identity served to reinforce Monterey's growing reputation as poorer and less "white" than Salinas. McKibben, *Beyond Cannery Row*.

9. Takaki, *Strangers*, 389; "CHINATOWN: Business Once Flourished Here," *Salinas Californian*, 28 November 2005, 1A. For more on the ethnic succession of Chinese, Japanese, and Filipino laborers in California's fields, see Tsu, *Garden of the World*.

10. Azuma, *Between Two Empires*, 29; Verardo and Verardo, *Salinas Valley*, 89; Ichioka, "Japanese Immigrant Response," 159, 173; López, *Farmworkers' Journey*, 97; Shah, *Stranger Intimacy*, 14, 90, 96; Leonard, *Making Ethnic Choices*, ix, 4.

11. Hernández, *Migra!*, 36; Calleros quoted in Takaki, *Different Mirror*, 312; Monroy, *Rebirth*, 77; Mora-Torres, "Los de casa se van," 23.

12. Mora-Torres, "Los de casa se van," 27; Hernández, *Migra!*, 89; Baldoz, *Third Asiatic Invasion*, 65.

13. Varzally, *Making a Non-White America*, 18–19; Guerin-Gonzales, "International Migration," 158; González, "Mexican Labor Migration," 42; Almirol, *Ethnic Identity*, 23; unidentified author, "Confidential: Spanish-Americans in the Southwest and the War Effort," 18 August 1942, 4, Folder 4, Box 58, Galarza Papers.

14. Monterey County Naturalization Records, Vol. 33; Jones, "Salinas Valley," 99, 103; Wald, "Nature of Citizenship," 278; Varzally, *Making a Non-White America*, 20; Scharlin and Villanueva, *Philip Vera Cruz*, xx; Baldoz, *Third Asiatic Invasion*, 9.

15. Takaki, *Different Mirror*, 321; Almirol, *Ethnic Identity*, 26; Scott, "Mexican-American in the Los Angeles Area," 17; Hull Jr., "Effects of Braceros," 30; Montaño interview.

16. Scharlin and Villanueva, *Philip Vera Cruz*, 12–13; Nelson interview Tape 1; Takaki, *Strangers*, 327–28; Baldoz, *Third Asiatic Invasion*, 141–42; Tsu, *Garden of the World*, 185–86.

17. Other vigilante groups, such as the Gorras Blancas (White Caps) of New Mexico who cut the fences of Anglo ranchers and land developers to protest the exploitative transfer of land after the U.S.-Mexican War, became infamous later in the century. "Murietta in Adventures Near Salinas: Mexican Entered Life of Crime as a Means of Revenge," *Salinas Index-Journal*, 7 March 1936, 1; "Execution of Tiburcio Vasquez," *Hollister Enterprise*, 27 March 1875, 3; "A Reminiscence of Vasquez: The Capturer of the Noted Bandit Reviews the Circumstances of His Capture," *Salinas Daily Journal*, 29 August 1899, 1; "The Trial of Vasquez," *Hollister Enterprise*, 9 January 1875, 22; "The Sentence of Vasquez," *Monterey Democrat*, 30 January 1875, 2; Carrigan and Webb, "Lynching of Persons of Mexican Origin," 413–16, 420, 423; Camarillo, *Chicanos in California*, 18. The *Salinas Valley Standard* was the town's first newspaper, which then turned into the *Salinas Daily Index* in 1871, the *Salinas Index-Journal* in 1928, and the *Salinas Californian* in 1942. Between 1938 and 1968, only one Spanish-surnamed juror served on a Monterey County jury. Don B. Kates Jr., *A Study of Grand Jury Service by Persons of Spanish Surname and By Indians in Selected California Counties*, June 1968, 116, 123, Binder, "News and Other Docs. Crimes Vol. 12," Box 4, Lopez v. Monterey County Collection.

18. Gonzales-Day, *Lynching in the West*, 207–27; Carrigan and Webb, *Forgotten Dead*, 6, Appendices A and B. According to the data collected, Texas claimed 232 victims of mob violence, California 143, New Mexico 87, Arizona 48, Colorado 25, Nevada 3, Louisiana 2, Nebraska 2, Oklahoma 2, Montana 1, Oregon 1, and Wyoming 1, for a total of 547 incidents from 1848 to 1928.

19. Untitled article, *Salinas Weekly Journal*, 15 May 1897, 1; "Our Educational Facilities," *Weekly Herald*, 18 September 1875, 3; "Blood on the San Benito—A Foul Murder," *Salinas Weekly Index*, 13 July 1876, 1; "We were favored with a call this week . . . ," *Weekly Herald*, 26 December 1874, 2; Johnston, *Salinas, 1875–1950*, 2.

20. "Mexican Worker Dies in Fight," *Monterey Peninsula Herald*, 13 October 1938, 2; "Mexican Stabbed," *Monterey Peninsula Herald*, 25 January 1939, 2; "Mexican Arrested on Drunk Driving Charge," *Salinas Index-Journal*, 13 February 1939, 3; "Heavy Sentence for Wife Beater," *Salinas Weekly Index*, 26 August 1909, 4; "Mexican Buried to Neck in Mud, Saved By Police," *Salinas Index-Journal*, 10 October 1938, 10; "Salinas Men Held on Rape Charges Following Assault," *King City Rustler Herald*, 8 December 1941, 1; "Two Guilty," *King City Rustler Herald*, 9 December 1940, 4; "Seek Driver as Man Dies of Injuries," *Salinas*

Index-Journal, 7 July 1936, 4–5; "Mexican Killed When Near Gonzales," *Salinas Index-Journal,* 13 July 1936, 1; "Mexican National Killed in Highway Crash Sunday Night," *King City Rustler Herald,* 15 April 1948, 1; "Farm Worker Seriously Hurt; Believed Victim of Hit and Run Driver Sunday," *Salinas Californian,* 24 June 1952, 2; "Hit-Run Injuries Are Fatal," *Salinas Californian,* 28 June 1952, 1; "Hit-Run Driver Is Located, Arrested," *Monterey Peninsula Herald,* 11 October 1938, 1; "William Rojas Must Do Without Frijoles," *Salinas Daily Post,* 29 December 1933, 1.

21. "Thursday, the 16th . . . ," *Weekly Herald,* 18 September 1875, 3; "Annual Festival at Mission San Antonio Sunday, June 10," *King City Rustler Herald,* 8 June 1939, 1. For more on the concept of the Spanish Fantasy Past, see McWilliams, *North from Mexico;* Pitt, *Decline of the Californios;* Deverell, *Whitewashed Adobe;* Kropp, *California Vieja.*

22. Geron, *Latino Political Power,* 163; Almirol, *Ethnic Identity,* 54, 56.

23. Parsons, "Black Roots Are Deep"; Table 15, In-Migrants, Out-Migrants, and Net Migration, By Age, for States (with Nonwhites for Selected States), 1940, California, U.S. Bureau of the Census, Sixteenth Census 1940, Population, Internal Migration, 162; Bardacke, *Trampling,* 46; Gregory, *American Exodus,* 28–29; Verardo and Verardo, *Salinas Valley,* 89.

24. Gregory, *American Exodus,* 72; Burkett, "The Okies?," 81; Parsons Jr., "Ethnic Cleavage," 370; Bond interview Tape 2; McWilliams, "Minorities in California," 47.

25. Zermeño interview by the author; Sarah Terry-Cobo, "Latino Civil Rights Activist Retiring," *Oakland Tribune,* 24 May 2007, www.insidebayarea.com/ci_5975405; Table 4, Population of Counties by Minor Civil Divisions: 1920 to 1940, U.S. Bureau of the Census, Sixteenth Census 1940, Population, Vol. 1, 124.

26. Grower Profiles; Santoro interview; Santoro, *If You Got the Guts,* 17–18.

27. Barajas, *Curious Unions,* 139; Bardacke, *Trampling,* 50.

28. Jones, "Salinas Valley," 282, 289; Guerin-Gonzales, "International Migration," 169; González, *Mexican Consuls and Labor Organizing,* 122; Takaki, *Different Mirror,* 325.

29. Dewitt, *Violence in the Fields,* 4, 24, 86–87, 91.

30. Baldoz, *Third Asiatic Invasion;* Dewitt, *Violence in the Fields,* 12, 83–87, 91, 93, 102; Tsu, "Grown in the 'Garden of the World,'" 275; Montero interview Tape 1; Dewitt, "Filipino Labor Union," 2.

31. Two main streets in Salinas are currently named after Sanborn and Abbott. Jamieson, *Labor Unionism,* 140; "Blood Flows in Salinas Riot—County's Manpower Mobilized," *Monterey Peninsula Herald,* 16 September 1936, 1; Nelson interview; Verardo and Verardo, *Salinas Valley,* 89, 92–94; Johnston, *Salinas, 1875–1950,* 19; Starr, *California,* 215; "Able-Bodied Men Called to Preserve Law and Order," *Salinas Index-Journal,* 16 September 1936, n.p.; Robbin, *Woody Guthrie and Me,* 22; Street, *Everyone Had Cameras,* 232–47; Kousser, "Racial Injustice," 68–69, 297; Ferriss and Sandoval, *Fight in the Fields,* 25; Galarza, *Merchants of Labor,* 35; Bond interview Tape 1.

32. Bardacke, *Trampling,* 47. Soon after taking office, California governor Earl Warren removed McWilliams from his position, to the delight of farm interests that thought he was a pest. Mitchell, *They Saved the Crops,* 21.

33. Mexican consulates in California attempted to instill patriotism in Mexican immigrants through public celebrations of Mexican national holidays and the building of Spanish schools and libraries. Immigrants felt ambivalent toward the nation they had fled as well as their new home and participated in both Americanization and Mexicanization programs selectively. For more on these programs, see Ruiz, *From Out of the Shadows;* González, *Labor and Community;* Perales, *Smeltertown;* Alamillo, *Making Lemonade;* Sánchez, "'Go After the Women.'"

34. Takaki, *Different Mirror,* 330–31; Vargas, *Labor Rights Are Civil Rights,* 16, 46; Vargas, *Proletarians of the North,* 169–70. Because of protests, the racial classification of "Mexican" was eliminated in the 1940 census, and the category of "Spanish as mother tongue" was incorporated. This revision in classification means that scholars do not have accurate census counts for Mexican Americans living in the United States until 1970.

35. Ruiz, "Citizen Restaurant," 4; Molina, *Fit to Be Citizens?,* 146; Sánchez, *Becoming Mexican American,* 216; Bardacke, *Trampling,* 55; Folder 20, Box 14, Corona Papers. For more on the deportation and repatriation drives, see Hoffman, *Unwanted Mexican Americans;* Guerin-Gonzales, *Mexican Workers;* Balderrama and Rodriguez, *Decade of Betrayal.*

36. Varzally, *Making a Non-White America,* 26; Scharlin and Villanueva, *Philip Vera Cruz,* xx; Tsu, "Grown in the 'Garden of the World,'" 266; Almirol, *Ethnic Identity,* 21; Verardo and Verardo, *Salinas Valley,* 89. The Census Bureau's definition of "white" included people of European and Latin American ancestry. It did not include those of American Indian, Asian, Hawaiian, or Eskimo background.

37. Guglielmo, "Fighting for Caucasian Rights," 1214; Table 6, "Nativity and Parentage of the Foreign White Stock, by Country of Origin, for States with 50,000 or more Foreign-Born White, Urban and Rural: 1940 and 1930," U.S. Bureau of the Census, Sixteenth Census 1940, Population, Nativity and Parentage, 52; Sánchez, *Becoming Mexican American.* El Congreso, spearheaded by Guatemalan-born labor organizer Luisa Moreno, advocated on behalf of the rights of both U.S.-born and immigrant Mexicans. LULAC held that the social advancement of its members would be carried out through assimilation and stated that part of its aims and purposes was "to develop within the members of our race the best, purest and most perfect type of a true and loyal citizen of the United States of America." Orozco, *No Mexicans,* Appendix 3.

38. Bond interview Tape 1; Burkett, "The Okies?," 98.

CHAPTER 2. RACIAL MEETING GROUNDS AND
BATTLEGROUNDS DURING WARTIME

1. Montero interview.

2. Table 14, "Population of Urban Places Having, in 1940, from 5,000 to 25,000 Inhabitants: 1920 to 1940," and Table 2, "Population of Cities of 10,000 or More from Earliest Census to 1940," U.S. Bureau of the Census, Sixteenth Census 1940, Population, Vol. 1, 37, 120.

3. Goldstein-Shirley, "Story and History," 2; Pearson, "Steinbeck's Salinas," 19; National Steinbeck Center, "Valley of the World" exhibit resource guide, 26;

Amyx interview; Cheryl White, "Most Respected Minority Was Once Despised," *Salinas Californian*, 14 July 1979, 15; Salinas Chamber of Commerce, *Survey of Attitudes*.

4. Gamboa, *Mexican Labor and World War II*, 39; Basurto, Delorme Jr., and Kamerschen, "Rent Seeking," 1, 23; Rosas, "Flexible Families," 5; Moore, *Slaves We Rent*. Italian and German prisoners of war were also used as agricultural laborers in the Salinas Valley for a period of time. Anderson, *America's Salad Bowl*, 84.

5. Rosas, "Flexible Families," 2, 37; Hernández, "Crimes and Consequences," 424–25; *Excélsior*, 12 June 1942, n.p.; *Bracero Stories*; Gómez interview, translated by the author.

6. Cohen, "Caught in the Middle," 121–22; Snodgrass, "Bracero Program," 89; Pérez interview, translated by the author; Salazar quoted in Jacobo, *Los Braceros*, 43.

7. Rosas, "Flexible Families," 44, 177–78, 198; *Cosecha Triste*; Office of the California Attorney General, "An Inquiry into the Mexican Migrant Labor Program," 1 December 1959, 25–28, Folder "Bracero Investigation," Box 1, Soto Papers; Ramírez interview; Nicolás Osorio interview with Bocanegra; "A Statement of Conscience and a Review of Evidence by the Emergency Committee to Aid Farm Workers," 29 March 1963, 4-a. Folder 3, Box 1, Farm Worker Organizing Collection, Southern California Library for Social Studies and Research, Los Angeles (hereafter SCLSSR).

8. *Bracero Stories*; Mitchell, *They Saved the Crops*, 330; Cohen, *Braceros*, 107; Henry Anderson, "The Bracero System and the National Honor," June 1961, 13–14, Folder 12, Box 3, Farm Worker Organizing Collection, SCLSSR.

9. By the early 1960s, bracero recruitment stations had been established in Monterey, Nuevo León, Chihuahua, and Empalme in Mexico. The harmful effects of DDT would not be known until the 1970s, when the U.S. government finally banned the chemical. *Bracero Stories*; Ramírez interview; Gómez interview; Rosas, "Flexible Families," 197.

10. "Mexican Labor Group Arrives," *Salinas Californian*, 5 October 1942, 1, 12; "The Pan Sheet," *Honey Dew News*, October 1942, 16; "1,700 Mexican Farm Workers Now Are Employed in Salinas Area," *Salinas Californian*, 13 May 1943, 2; Agricultural Workers Organizing Committee, Statement Before Senate Fact Finding Committee on Labor and Social Welfare, California Legislature, 16 November 1959, 5, Folder 38, Carton 5, McWilliams Papers; "Mexican National and Jamaican Farm Workers Obtained by Contracting Employers Since Inception of the Farm Labor Transportation Program, Number Currently Employed and Orders for 1946 as of January 11, 1946," Folder 8, Box 8, Roth Papers.

11. López Sr. interview; Bureau of Employment Security, "Information Concerning Entry of Mexican Agricultural Workers into the United States," February 1962, iii, 3, 25, Folder 11, Box 3, Quevedo Papers.

12. "530 Mexicans to Arrive Tomorrow," *Salinas Californian*, 14 July 1943, 1; López Sr. interview; Montaño interview; "181 Mexicans for Local Sugar Beet Fields Arrive," *King City Rustler Herald*, 5 October 1942, 1; "Mexicans to Harvest California Crops," *King City Rustler Herald*, 19 October 1942, 1.

13. Bomer interview; "389 Mexicans Assigned to Valley Farms," *Salinas Californian*, 7 March 1945, 14; Montaño interview; Murray, "Abolition of El Cortito," 27–29; "A Statement of Conscience," 17, 20; sample bracero menu, "Report on Bracero Feeding Standards" pamphlet, Folder 7, Box 21, Galarza Papers; De Young interview.

14. Zarazua interview; Guilbault, *Farmworker's Daughter*, 63–64; sample bracero menu; Pérez interview.

15. The Salinas GFLA initially paid braceros' medical expenses, with the bracero expected to repay on a monthly payment plan. This changed in the 1950s when the GFLA forced braceros to buy into a Los Angeles–based insurance program. Calavita, *Inside the State*, 3; Jacobo, *Los Braceros*, 91; Zepeda interview; Ramírez interview; letter to Assistant Secretary of Labor Newell Brown from Juan Gallardo, 24 August 1959, Folder "Employment 1–1, Agricultural Aug 1–Dec 7," Box 3290, RG 16, Records of the Office of the Secretary of Agriculture, National Archives and Records Administration (hereafter NARA) College Park; Bardacke, *Trampling*, 6; Galarza, *Merchants of Labor*, 186; López Sr. interview; Montaño interview; Ames interview; Zermeño interview with the author; Villanueva interview.

16. Kousser, "Racial Injustice," 41; Gamboa, *Mexican Labor and World War II*; Weise, *Corazon de Dixie*; Ramírez interview.

17. López Sr. interview; Zermeño interview with the author; letter to Juan Gonzalez Garcia from Francisca Negrete, October 1943, Folder 2, Box 1, Bracero Letters collection; letter to Jose Estrada from his daughter, 18 November 1943, Folder 4, Box 1, Bracero Letters collection.

18. Chapa interview.

19. "California City Waits Word of 140 Sons in Bataan," *Washington Post*, 10 April 1942, 34; "Trainload of Mexicans to Arrive Here This Weekend," *Salinas Californian*, 1 April 1944, 12; "More Mexican Workers Due," *Salinas Californian*, 6 November 1944, 16; Nicolás Osorio interview with Bocanegra; Zepeda interview; Montaño interview; De Young interview; Alvarez interview; advertisement for Crystal Theatre, *Salinas Californian*, 4 May 1944, 6; "Crystal Theatre," *Salinas Californian*, 7 March 1945, 14; list of area movie theaters, *Salinas Californian*, 27 April 1956, 10A.

20. Alien Registration Figures for 1941 California to Carey McWilliams from the U.S. Department of Justice, INS, Alien Registration Division, Folder 81, Carton 3, McWilliams Papers; "30 Residents of County Are Naturalized," *Salinas Californian*, 10 December 1942, 8; "More New Soldier-Citizens," *Fort Ord Panorama*, 3 March 1944, 4; "Soldiers Get Citizenship," *Monterey Peninsula Herald*, 19 May 1944, 3; "Service Men Naturalized in County," *Monterey Peninsula Herald*, 25 May 1944, 4; "20 Soldiers Win U.S. Citizenship," *Monterey Peninsula Herald*, 3 August 1944, 7; "Thirteen Soldiers Get Citizenship," *Monterey Peninsula Herald*, 25 August 1944, 3; McKibben, *Racial Beachhead*, 42.

21. Table 4, "Population of Counties by Minor Civil Divisions: 1920 to 1940," U.S. Bureau of the Census, Sixteenth Census 1940, Population, Vol. 1, 124; Villanueva interview; "Mexicans Aid Local War Fund," *Salinas Californian*, 12 November 1943, 2; "Mexican Fiesta Planned at Central Park April 2," *Salinas Californian*, 15 March 1944, 8; "Fiesta at Park Sunday," *Salinas Californian*, 1 April 1944, 1; Gutíerrez McQuinn interview; Hollis interview.

22. Gómez interview; Montaño interview; Scruggs, "Texas and the Bracero Program," 258; McCain, "Texas and the Mexican Labor Question," 56; "GNC Report Shows 74 Texas Counties in Mexican Blacklist," *American GI Forum News Bulletin,* 15 November 1952, 1, Folder 1, Box 6, Idar Jr. Papers.

23. Grant deed in joint tenancy for La Rancheria del Carmelo, 26 February 1945, Monterey County Recorder's Office; Varzally, *Making a Non-White America,* 29; Housing and Home Finance Agency, "Housing of the Nonwhite Population 1940 to 1950," July 1952, 1, 3, Folder "Minority Group Housing—Field Letters," Box 3, RG 31, Records of the Federal Housing Administration, NARA College Park.

24. Advertisement by A. V. Rianda, *Salinas Californian,* 2 June 1951, 11; "ATTENTION," *Salinas Californian,* 1 September 1947, 10; "$6,000" and "$5,000," *Salinas Californian,* 1 September 1947, 10.

25. Avila, *Popular Culture,* 31; Montero interview; Al Parsons, "Black Roots Are Deep"; "New Today," *Monterey Peninsula Herald,* 14 and 27 May 1947, 13; "New Select Colored Colony in Seaside," *Daily Peninsula Herald,* 10 October 1946, 14; McKibben, *Racial Beachhead,* 62.

26. Lui, *Chinatown Trunk Mystery;* Shah, *Contagious Divides;* Shah, *Stranger Intimacies;* Yung, *San Francisco's Chinatown;* Zesch, *Chinatown War;* advertisement for the Mexicano City Café, *Salinas Index,* 18–21 July 1940; Montaño interview; petition for including the Republic Café in the National Register of Historic Places, www.parks.ca.gov/pages/1067/files/california_monterey_republic%20cafe _nr%20omination%20draft.pdf; Lee, *Salinas Chinatown Memories,* 6–8; "Nothing Left but Name: Salinas Chinatown Vanished," *Salinas Californian,* 4 September 1968, "Chinese in Monterey County" file, Local History Collection, Steinbeck Public Library.

27. "Pacheco-Morisoli Wedding," *Register,* 16 September 1945, 5; "Hopie Avina Wed," *Register,* 29 July 1946, 3; Almirol, *Ethnic Identity,* 86; Chris Martínez interview; López Sr. interview; Villanueva interview. After World War II, District Attorney Anthony Brazil filed civil injunctions against, and shut down, all the prostitution houses in Chinatown. Young interview.

28. Salinas City Council Minutes, 18 June 1945, Salinas, California.

29. "Mexican Is Stabbed in Fight Here," *Salinas Californian,* 1 November 1943, 8; "Two Soldiers Are Stabbed in Castroville," *Salinas Californian,* 21 July 1952, 2.

30. Garcia, "Intraethnic Conflict," 402; "Lopez Pleads Guilty, Is Sentenced," *Salinas Californian,* 3 December 1943, 3; "Daniels Is Arrested for Murder," *Salinas Californian,* 28 June 1943, 1; "Villapando Sentenced for Murder," *Salinas Californian,* 6 October 1943, 12; Zermeño interview with the author; "Mexican National Murdered," *Salinas Californian,* 3 June 1952, 1; "Two Suspects in Slaying Nabbed by Police Here," *Salinas Californian,* 5 June 1952, 1.

31. Oropeza, *¡Raza Sí!,* 13; Rivas-Rodriguez, *Legacy Greater than Words.* For more on the Sleepy Lagoon trial, see Escobar, *Race, Police, and the Making of a Political Identity;* Pagán, *Murder at the Sleepy Lagoon;* Alvarez, *Power of the Zoot;* Ramirez, *Woman in the Zoot Suit.*

32. Ramirez, *Woman in the Zoot Suit,* xii–xiii; Griffith, *American Me,* 46; Escobedo, "Pachuca Panic," 134.

33. Table 6, "Nativity and Parentage of the Foreign White Stock, by Country of Origin, for States with 50,000 or more Foreign-Born White, Urban and Rural:

1940 and 1930," U.S. Bureau of the Census, Sixteenth Census 1940, Population, Nativity and Parentage, 52; statement of Dr. Carlos E. Castaneda, Special Assistant on Latin-American Problems, to the Chairman of the President's Committee on Fair Employment Practice, Before the Senate Committee on Labor and Education, 8 September 1944, 2, Folder 6, Box 58, Galarza Papers; Gutiérrez, *Walls and Mirrors*, 122.

34. Kelley, *Race Rebels*, 166; Paz, *Labyrinth of Solitude*, 16.

35. Ramirez, *Woman in the Zoot Suit*, 36–37, 152; Lipsitz, *Rainbow at Midnight*, 83. The riots drew international attention that was embarrassing for the United States during a time of war. Latin American countries from Mexico to Argentina questioned the "Good Neighbor Policy" while hundreds of students marched in Mexico City to protest U.S. racism. Other articles on Mexican Americans' mistreatment appeared in papers in Rome, Tokyo, and Berlin. "Outrage to the Race," *Hoy*, 26 June 1943, 1–3; Petition to John Anson Ford from the Citizens' Committee for Latin American Youth, undated, 1, Box 69, Anson Ford Papers; "Axis Broadcasts to Latin America," 6 March 1944, Folder 6, Box 58, Galarza Papers; McWilliams quoted in Varzally, *Making a Non-White America*, 152; Peiss, *Zoot Suit*, 110, 159.

36. "'Pachuco' Held as Murder Suspect," *Salinas Californian*, 19 August 1943, 6; "Housing Blamed," *Salinas Californian*, 8 January 1944, 12; "Seven Youths Are Held for Sailor Fight," *Salinas Californian*, 3 November 1944, 6; "2 Executed at San Quentin," *Salinas Californian*, 5 January 1945, 1; "'Sleepy Lagoon' Defendant Held," *Salinas Californian*, 13 June 1945, 2; "Zootsuiters Sought for Attacking WACs," *Salinas Californian*, 18 September 1945, 12; "'Vell, Vy Not, Ain't Ve Hoodlums, Too," *Salinas Californian*, 17 June 1943, 4; "Noots to Zoot Suits," *Salinas Californian*, 10 November 1942, 4; Barajas, *Curious Unions*, 207; "Judge Colby Puts Ban on Zoot Suiters," *Salinas Californian*, 5 July 1944, 8; "Zoot Suit Girls Fined, Lectured by Police," *Salinas Californian*, 20 February 1945, 12; Escobedo, "Pachuca Panic," 156.

37. "Zoot Suiters Get Warning from Brazil," *Salinas Californian*, 10 July 1943, 12; "Woman Molested by Zoot Suiters," *Salinas Californian*, 12 July 1943, 12; Pagán, "Los Angeles Geopolitics," 238.

38. "Resentment to Zoot-suiters Starts Fight," *Salinas Californian*, 2 July 1943, 14; "Police Halt Zoot-Suiters' Controversy," *Salinas Californian*, 6 July 1943, 1; "Youths Held for Slugging," *Salinas Californian*, 24 May 1944, 16.

39. "Two Injured in Zoot Suit Fight Here," *Salinas Californian*, 26 February 1944, 12; "Zoot Suiters Held for Robbery," *Salinas Californian*, 19 July 1943, 10; "Zootsuiters Take Money from Trio," *Salinas Californian*, 8 June 1945, 2.

40. "'Zoot-Suit' Gang Blamed for Trouble," *Salinas Californian*, 3 April 1944, 1; "Zoot Suiters Cause Riot in Salinas," *Monterey Peninsula Herald*, 4 April 1944, 3; "Zootsuiters' Gang Warfare Is Cut Short," *Salinas Californian*, 12 June 1944, 12; "Two Injured, 40 Held, Following Gilroy Dance," *Monterey Peninsula Herald*, 19 August 1946, 12; "Hollister War Hero Stabbed in Melee with Mexicans," *King City Rustler Herald*, 14 November 1946, n.p.

41. Escobar, "Dialectics of Repression," 1487; "Public Forum," *Salinas Californian*, 15 October 1943, 8; "Public Forum," *Salinas Californian*, 22 October 1943, 10; "Public Forum," *Salinas Californian*, 16 October 1946, 3.

42. López Sr. interview; Galarza, *Merchants of Labor*, 188; Herbert J. Seligmann, "Obreros Mexicanos Son Retenidos En Este Pais Contra Su Voluntad," *El Espectador*, 7 December 1945, 1; "Wahlberg of FSA Predicts—'No Zoot Trouble Here from Mexican Workers,'" *Salinas Californian*, 12 June 1943, 12; McCain, "Texas and the Mexican Labor Question," 64; Table X, "Number and Status of Furloughs Granted Mexican National Farm Workers, by Area and State, Since the Inception of the Farm Labor Transportation Program to March 1, 1946: Southwestern Division," Folder 8, Box 8, Roth Papers.

43. "Farm Workers from Mexico," 2, Folder 6, Box 58, Galarza Papers; *Bracero Stories*; Hull Jr., "Effects of Braceros," 30; López, "From the Farms," 260.

44. Bardacke, *Trampling*, 342.

CHAPTER 3. BOUND IN TENSION

1. Memo to INS Commissioner from San Francisco District Director Bruce G. Barber, 13 May 1953; report of Salinas Patrol Inspector Bruce L. Long, 14 April 1953; statement by Salinas Patrol Inspector James M. Maloney, 14 April 1953; statements by Salinas Patrol Inspector George D. Ward, 14 and 16 April 1953; sworn statement by Leopoldo Rodriguez-Lopez, 16 April 1953; and statements by Thomas Edward Diaz, 14 April and 1 May 1953, all from File 56364/41.11 Pt. 1, Box 83, RG 85, Records of the U.S. Immigration and Naturalization Service, NARA, D.C. Voluntary departure was a preferable option to deportation because if given the former, a migrant would not be barred from legally reentering the United States in the future.

2. During the Bracero Program renegotiation period, the U.S. Department of Labor established a Migration Division in 1948 that imported Puerto Rican agricultural workers to the continental United States. Five thousand men came under contract during the program's first year, increasing to an annual high of nearly twenty-three thousand during the late 1950s before numbers steadily declined over the next two decades. For more, see Valdes, *Organized Agriculture and the Labor Movement*, 101–2.

3. American G.I. Forum and Texas State Federation of Labor, *What Price Wetbacks?*, 1, 5; letter to Herschel T. Manuel from George I. Sanchez and Ed Idar, 21 November 1959, 2, Folder 21, Box 19, Sanchez Papers; Márquez, *LULAC*, 49–50; Henry Anderson, "The Bracero System and the National Honor," June 1961, 5, Folder 12, Box 3, Farm Worker Organizing Collection, SCLSSR.

4. See Gutiérrez, *Walls and Mirrors*; Menchaca, *Mexican Outsiders*; Garcia, *World of Its Own*; Pitti, *Devil in Silicon Valley*; Pitti, "To 'Hear About God in Spanish'"; Ngai, *Impossible Subjects*; Vargas, *Labor Rights Are Civil Rights*.

5. The Taft-Hartley Act of 1947 severely curtailed the power and activities of labor unions. The McCarran-Walter Act of 1952 allowed the government to expel from the country and deny entry to suspected subversives. The specter of a "fifth column" among people of Mexican ancestry dated back to the Spanish Civil War of the 1930s, and in the 1940s and 1950s the FBI investigated LULAC as a possible communist organization. Gutiérrez, "Chicanos and Mexicans under Surveillance," 30, 33, 36.

6. Hernández, *Migra!*, 116; Cohen, "Caught in the Middle," 115; Julian Samora, "Los Mojados" chapter 2 draft, 14, Folder 5, Box 121, Samora Papers; "659 Mexican Nationals Leave Here for 'Home,'" *Salinas Californian*, 5 December 1947, 1; "Roundup of 462 Aliens Completed in Salinas Area; All but Six Mexicans," *Salinas Californian*, 28 May 1948, 20; "450 Mexican Nationals Apprehended in Area," *Salinas Californian*, 28 March 1950, 1; "750 Nationals Returned to Mexico," *Salinas Californian*, 4 April 1950, 1; "2,400 Aliens Are Deported," *Salinas Californian*, 12 May 1950, 2; "1,600 Mexican Nationals Deported from Valley," *Salinas Californian*, 21 April 1950, 2; "2,000 Valley Aliens in Immigration Round-up," *Salinas Californian*, 1 May 1950, 8.

7. Calavita, *Inside the State*, 2; American G.I. Forum and Texas State Federation of Labor, *What Price Wetbacks?*, 7; Kim, "Political Economy," 21; "Braceros: History, Compensation"; Fitzgerald, "Mexican Migration and the Law," 196; Gladwin Hill, "Wetback Users' Serenade," reprinted from the *New York Times* in the *American GI Forum News Bulletin*, September 1954, 4; "Meeting of Users of Mexican Nationals with Immigration Authorities," 9 May 1950, File 56286/203, Box 3161, RG 85, NARA D.C.; letter to Robert Winston, INS Investigator, Los Angeles, from Jack Armstrong, Assistant Manager of the Salinas Growers Farm Labor Association, 10 May 1950, File 56286/203, Box 3161, RG 85, NARA D.C.; letter to James E. Riley, Acting Assistant Commissioner, INS Central Office Enforcement Division, from Bruce G. Barber, District Director, INS San Francisco, 5 May 1950, File 56286/203, Box 3161, RG 85, NARA D.C.; letter to Representative Jack E. Anderson from the Grower-Shipper Vegetable Association, 28 April 1950, 1–2, File 56286/203, Box 3161, RG 85, NARA D.C.; letter to Watson Miller from GSVA, 2–3, File 56286/203, Box 3161, RG 85, NARA D.C.; letter to Bruce Barber from GSVA, 5 May 1950, 2, File 56286/203, Box 3161, RG 85, NARA D.C.; "Seizures of Mexicans in Country Illegally Causes Labor Crisis," *Salinas Californian*, 18 May 1950, 17; "Bias Charges Agriculture Is Used as 'Scapegoat' of Wetback Program," *Salinas Californian*, 22 September 1951, 12.

8. The INS established additional central and northern California offices in Fresno and Sacramento. "Charge Dropped," *Salinas Californian*, 9 January 1952, 2; list of Salinas INS Sub-Office deportation files, NARA San Bruno; California State Advisory Committee to the United States Commission on Civil Rights, "Police-Community Relations in East Los Angeles, California," October 1970, 9, Folder 1, Box 2, RG 453, Records of the Commission on Civil Rights, NARA College Park; Ngai, *Impossible Subjects*.

9. "Federal Agents Report 1,000,000 Mexicans Entered US. Illegally," *Salinas Californian*, 5 September 1952, 5; "Aliens Warned to Register Addresses with Government Sometime in January," *Salinas Californian*, 31 December 1952, 6; Salinas City Council minutes, 2 September 1952; "Expansion of Salinas Is Steady," *Salinas Californian*, 27 February 1967, 86; undated letter to Honorable Bob Wilson, House of Representatives, from INS Commissioner, 1–2, Box 83, RG 85, NARA D.C.; Garcia, *Operation Wetback*, 236.

10. Julian Samora, "Los Mojados" Introduction, n.d., 3, Folder 4, Box 121, Samora Papers; V. H. Mitchell, "Growing Season Returns to Salinas-Pajaro Valleys—and with It Come the 'Wetbacks,'" *Salinas Californian*, 11 April 1952, 4;

Gladwin Hill, "Mexicans Called TB Threat in U.S.," *Los Angeles Times,* 20 May 1951, 39; Report of Criminal Prosecution, Defendant Sixto Rios-Juarez, to INS Commissioner from H. R. Landon, District Director, Los Angeles, 16 May 1951, Box 760, RG 85, NARA D.C.; Report of Criminal Prosecution, Defendants Philip Esparza and Ascencion Garcia-Salazar, to INS Commissioner from H. R. Landon, 17 August 1971, Box 761, RG 85, NARA D.C.; "Three Seized in Smuggling of Wetbacks," *Los Angeles Times,* 10 June 1951, A6; Report of Criminal Prosecution of Amado Trevino-Vidaure to INS Commissioner from H. R. Landon, 28 July 1952, Box 761, RG 85, NARA D.C.; deportation file of Fortino Avalos-Presiado, Folder 1308–5336, Box, RG 85, NARA San Bruno; deportation files of José Solano-Ruíz and José Hernandez-Brambila, Folder 1308–8112, Box 3, and Folder 1308–8373, Box 4, RG 85, NARA San Bruno; "I Crossed the Border Without a Passport: Authentic Story of an Ingenious Mexican Wire Jumper," *El Pueblo,* 4 June 1949, n.p., File 56246/339 (e–f), Box 3056, RG 85, NARA D.C.; letter to President Dwight D. Eisenhower from Ernesto Galarza and Ben Porry, 25 January 1954, Folder 4, Box 21, Galarza Papers.

11. Deportation file of Caroline Venegas-Sinchon, Folder 1308–8020, Box 3, RG 85, NARA San Bruno.

12. Deportation file of Maria Socorro Chávez, Folder 1308–8468, Box 4, RG 85, NARA San Bruno; letter to Officer in Charge, Salinas, from Acting San Francisco District Counsel Milton F. Simmons, 2 August 1954, and letter to Bruce Barber from C. Hobert Lee, 21 July 1954, Folder 1308–8020, Box 3, RG 85, NARA San Bruno.

13. V. H. Mitchell, "Growing Season Returns to Salinas-Pajaro Valleys—and with It Come the 'Wetbacks,'" *Salinas Californian,* 11 April 1952, 4; deportation files of Ernesto Angulo-López, Raul Savedra-Leiva, Enrique Reyes-Padilla, Guadalupe Naranjo-Bravo, and Pedro-Martínez Velasquez, Folders 1308–8051, 1308–8089, 1308–8094, 1308–8155, and 1308–8462, respectively, Boxes 3 and 4, RG 85, NARA San Bruno. For more on the history of photography and immigration policy, see Gordon, *In Sight of America.*

14. Deportation files of Gustavo Ramírez-García, Folder 1308–8544; Gilberto Román-Méndez, Folder 1308–8486; José Gonzáles-Cisneros, Folder 1308–8495; Trinidad Hernandez-Soto, Folder 1308–8496; José Rueda-Medina, Folder 1308–8532; and Maria Estela Jimenez Arce, Folder 1308–8541, all from Boxes 4 and 5, RG 85, NARA San Bruno.

15. Deportation file of Sacramento Ferrel-Rodríguez, Folder 1308–8319, Box 4, RG 85, NARA San Bruno.

16. Letter to Salinas INS office from J. Jesús Farias, 10 January 1952, Folder 1308–5896, Box 1, RG 85, NARA San Bruno; "Table XXIX—Where Apprehended" and "Table XXXXV—Who Reported to Immigration," Folder 5, Box 142, Samora Papers.

17. Statements of INS Commissioner Argyle R. Mackey and Assistant Commissioner Willard Kelly, U.S. Senate Subcommittee on Labor and Labor-Management Relations of the Committee on Labor and Public Welfare, Washington, D.C., 29 February 1952, 748, Folder 3, Box 5, Idar Jr. Papers; Folders 1 and 2, Box 8, RG 174, General Records of the Department of Labor, NARA San Bruno; "Sample

Survey of Mexican Agricultural Labor Skips," 2 November 1953, 3, File 56353/110, Box 3387, RG 174, NARA San Bruno; U.S. Department of Labor, Bureau of Employment Security, "Summary Foreign Farm Labor Program 1953, Region X," 1–2, Folder 4, Box 5, Roth Papers.

18. Parsons Jr., "Ethnic Cleavage," 150, 152–53.

19. Jacobo, *Los Braceros,* 98; Nicolás Osorio interview with the author.

20. Letter to Hon. Robert Murphy from Rocco C. Siciliano, 27 June 1955, Folder "Braceros Jan.–June 1955," Box 879, RG 84, NARA College Park; testimony of Fermín Cepeda, n.d., Folder 7, Box 45, Galarza Papers; statement of Ernesto Galarza, Migratory Labor Hearings before the Subcommittee on Labor and Labor-Management Relations of the Committee on Labor and Public Welfare, U.S. Senate, 82nd Congress, 2nd Sess. on Migratory Labor, Part 1, Feb. and Mar. 1952, 252, Folder 3, Box 5, Idar Jr. Papers; Ernesto Galarza, "Employment Indicators—Aug. 29, 1953," Folder 12, Box 45, Galarza Papers; letter to Louis Braun from Ernesto Galarza, 24 August 1953, Folder 8, Box 49, Galarza Papers; letter to Earl Warren from James E. Murray, 28 August 1953, Folder 8, Box 49, Galarza Papers; letter to Dan Pollitt from James E. Murray, 8 September 1953, 1–2, Folder 8, Box 49, Galarza Papers; Saldívar interview; League for Industrial Democracy and National Sharecroppers Fund, "Down on the Farm: The Plight of Agricultural Labor," n.d., 1, Folder 36, Carton 5, McWilliams Papers; Villanueva interview.

21. Jerry Root, "Jobless List Reflects Change in Salinas: Displaced Lettuce Shed Workers Form 65% of All Claims," *Salinas Californian,* 26 June 1954, n.p.; "CIO Caravan Protests Use of Wetbacks," *Los Angeles Times,* 8 August 1954, 25; "Salinas in Transition," *Carmel Spectator,* 29 June 1955, B4, J2; Hull Jr., "Effects of Braceros," 135; Levy, *Cesar Chavez,* 130; National Farm Labor Union, "The Wetback Strike: A Report on the Strike of Farm Workers in the Imperial Valley of California May 24, June 25, 1951," 7, 10, Folder 3, Box 45, Galarza Papers.

22. "Diocese of Monterey-Fresno, Statistical Data for Period Ending December 31, 1945," *Register,* 19; "Salinas Church Directory," *Salinas Californian,* 27 April 1956, 9A; Parsons Jr., "Ethnic Cleavage," 222; Alvarez interview; "Catholic Priest Realizes Lifelong Ambition in Organization of 'Madonna of Poor Society,'" *Salinas Californian,* 31 August 1956, 4; informational pamphlet, Cristo Rey Church, Salinas, California; list of local churches and services, *Salinas Californian,* 11 December 1954, 7; López Sr. interview.

23. Friedrich interview; *Excélsior* and *Las Ultimas Noticias* reports from American G.I. Forum and Texas State Federation of Labor, *What Price Wetbacks?,* 33.

24. "El Bracero y La Pachuca," *Pachuco Boogie,* by Miguel Salas, recorded by Dueto Taxco and Mariachi Los Caporales del Norte, 1948; Fernandez and Officer, "Lighter Side of Mexican Immigration," 494.

25. Guilbault, *Farmworker's Daughter,* 28; "Baby's Birth by Unattended Woman Here Is Probed," *Salinas Californian,* 6 August 1945, 2; deportation files of Jesus de la Torre-Morales (Folder 1308–8515), Guadalupe González-Chávez (Folder 1308–8513), Roberto Mendoza-Martínez (Folder 1308–7947), and Rafael Ramírez-Trujillo (Folder 1308–8302), Boxes 1, 4, and 5, RG 85, NARA San Bruno.

26. The following story is from Alvarez interview.

27. "Special Farm Labor Committee Recommendations," 5 February 1956, 1–2, Box 154, RG 174, NARA College Park; Calavita, *Inside the State*, 55; Glass, "Conditions," 64; "2000 Braceros Saldrán del Estado de Oaxaca Para el Centro de Preselección de Monterrey," *El Imparcial*, 8 July 1956, 1; "Siguen Haciendo sus Gestiones Ante el Gobierno los Aspirantes a 'Braceros,'" *El Imparcial*, 6 September 1956; Jorge I. Tamayo, untitled article, *El Imparcial*, 14 April 1957, 2; newspaper clipping, "Texas Judge Accused of Serving Dog Food to Mexican Workers," enclosed in letter to V. H. Blocker from Jack D. Neal, 9 October 1951, Folder 361.2, Box 855, RG 84, NARA College Park; translated article from *La Voz de Mexico*, December 1955, Box 87 Part II, RG 85, NARA D.C.; U.S. Department of Labor, Bureau of Employment Security, "Foreign Labor Program, Summary, January 1 Thru December 31, 1959," Folder 3, Box 5, Roth Papers.

28. "Report on Housing Facilities and Inspections, 1959," "Report on Feeding Facilities and Inspections, 1959," "Report of Payroll Inspections, Periodic and Complaints, 1959," "Report of Inspections Made of Transportation Facilities, 1959," and "Transportation and Vehicle Inspections, 1960," all from Folder 3, Box 5, Roth Papers; Ruben Salazar, "Growers Hit 'Meddling' with Bracero Program," *Los Angeles Times*, 23 October 1963, n.p.; Ernesto Galarza, "National Agricultural Workers Union, AFL: Report of Ernesto Galarza," 3 October 1952, 1–2, Folder "Mexican Farm Labor, General Correspondence, 1950–54," Box 2, RG 174, NARA San Bruno; "In the Matter of Growers Farm Labor Association and Atlantic and Pacific Tea Company, 1–2, Folder "Joint Determination, 1960, 1 of 2," Box 4, RG 174, NARA San Bruno; "Analysis of Complaints in Terms of International Agreement and Individual Work Contracts," 1956, 1957, 1958, Folder "Reports and Statistics, 1958–60 (2 of 2)," Box 8, RG 174, NARA San Bruno; Mitchell, *They Saved the Crops*, 216–17; League for Industrial Democracy and National Sharecroppers Fund, "Down on the Farm," 8.

29. "Salinas Man Pleads Guilty," *Salinas Californian*, 26 July 1956, 2; "Laborer Held After Razor Fight Here," *Salinas Californian*, 18 December 1961, 5; Pitti, "To 'Hear About God in Spanish,'" 324; Bishops' Committee on the Spanish Speaking, "A Brief Resume of Public Law 78," 5, Folder 7, Box 21, Vizzard Papers. Indeed, hundreds of thousands of Mexican families were suffering because of the Bracero Program. Bracero wives became single mothers who had to take on extra work or migrate to northern Mexico or the United States to stay financially afloat, while children accepted greater household responsibilities to compensate for the absence of their fathers or older relatives. For more, see Rosas, "Breaking the Silence."

30. A. E. Callin, "Report of Venereal Disease Examination Procedures Followed at the El Centro, California, Reception Center, USDL," 31 October 57, 2, Folder 2, Box 6, Roth Papers; Nate Haseltine, "Meeting the Health Threat of Mexican Migrants," *Washington Post and Times Herald*, 25 February 1959, B7; Denis Richter, "Complacency Due to Penicillin Cure Is Blamed for Alarming VD Increase Among Teen-Agers," *Salinas Californian*, 10 July 1956, 9; letter to Senator Hubert H. Humphrey from Bud Simonson, 18 July 1956, Folder "1956—Mexican Labor Program (July–December)," Box 140, RG 174, NARA College Park.

31. Gilmore and Gilmore, "Bracero in California," 272; Bureau of Employment Security, 1956 and 1957 Annual Reports, Region XII, Agricultural Foreign Labor

Section, Folder "Reports and Statistics, 1958–60 (2 of 2)," Box 8, RG 174, NARA San Bruno; Gutiérrez McQuinn interview; "Citizens Protest: Labor Camp Permits Denied," *Salinas Californian,* 15 March 1956, 1; Salinas City Council minutes, 26 March 1956; "County Planners Delay Action on Permit for Spence Road Labor Camp," *Salinas Californian,* 28 March 1956, 9; "County Planners Deny Labor Camp Permit in Buena Vista Area," *Salinas Californian,* 1 August 1956, 7; "'Tent Labor Camp' Ordinance Hits Snag," *Salinas Californian,* 31 July 1956, 2; Salinas City Council minutes, 27 August 1956; Salinas City Council minutes, 6 June 1955; "Council Delays Action on Industrial Area Labor Camp to Dec. 17 Meeting," *Salinas Californian,* 4 December 1956, 4; Kousser, "Racial Injustice," 54; "Expansion of Salinas Is Steady," *Salinas Californian,* 27 February 1967, 86; Salinas City Council minutes, 19 November 1956; "Pastors 'Concerned' by Labor Camp Locations," *Salinas Californian,* 14 December 1956, 1.

32. "Soledad Residents Fight Labor Camp, Delegation Led by Mayor Alden Anderson," *Salinas Californian,* 14 October 1958, 1; "Council Rejects New Camp," *Salinas Californian,* 18 December 1956, 1; Salinas City Council minutes, 17 December 1956 and 18 February 1957; "County Planners Stand by Approval of Soledad 1,000-Man Labor Camp," *Salinas Californian,* 1 October 1958, 2; "Council OK's Labor Camps by 3–1 Vote," *Salinas Californian,* 19 February 1957, 1–2; "2 Permits for Camps Approved," *Salinas Californian,* 24 January 1957, 1.

33. Verdict, No. 43966, *The People of the State of California v. Eleanor R. Walters,* 25 September 1957, 4, Monterey County Superior Court; "Activity by Individual Employer" and "1958 Report of Selected Activities Participated in by Foreign Labor Service Representatives, District Supervisors and Regional Office Personnel," Folder "Reports and Statistics, 1958–60 (2 of 2)," Box 8, RG 174, NARA San Bruno; letter to Thomas Kuchel from Tony Rios, 16 July 1958, Folder 1, Box 18, Galarza Papers, emphasis mine.

CHAPTER 4. THE COMMUNITY SERVICE ORGANIZATION

1. Zermeño interview with the author; Crawford interview. Many schools remained segregated by custom long after *Mendez v. Westminster* (1948) ruled the racial segregation of Mexican-origin students to be unconstitutional. In California, the desegregation of Mexican students was not officially implemented until 1964. Menchaca, *Mexican Outsiders,* 116.

2. "Text of Grand Jury Report," *Salinas Californian,* 4 September 1953, 1; "3-Way Probe Pushed in Youth Mob Death," *Greenfield News,* 3 September 1953, 1, 4; "Hearing Set Sept. 30 for 46 Youths Involved in 'Gang War' Near King City," *Salinas Californian,* 12 September 1953, 12; "Greenfield Youth Stabbed to Death in Juvenile Gang War," *Salinas Californian,* 28 August 1953, 1; "Hearings Set Sept. 30 for Youths Involved in Mob Battle Near King City," *Greenfield News,* 17 September 1953, 1; "Gang Fight Weapons," *Salinas Californian,* 31 August 1953, 2; "46 Boys Arrested on 'Riot' Charges, 'Gang War' Roundup Announced," *Salinas Californian,* 8 September 1953, 1; "Court Opens Hearing in 'Gang War' Death," *Salinas Californian,* 29 September 1953, 1.

3. "King City Youth Cleared of Murder Charge in 'Gang War,'" *Salinas Californian*, 4 September 1953, 1; "KC Youth Charged in 'Gang War' Slaying," *Salinas Californian*, 29 August 1953, 1; Chávez interview; Folder "CSO News Articles," Box A-16, Gallegos Papers; "46 Boys Arrested on 'Riot' Charges," *Salinas Californian*, 8 September 1952, n.p., and Letter to the Editor, *Soledad Bee*, 1 October 1953, n.p., both from Folder 5, Box 38, Corona Papers; undated reader letters to the *San Francisco Chronicle* and undated editorial, *San Francisco Chronicle*, Folder "CSO News Articles," Box A-16, Gallegos Papers.

4. Zermeño interview with the author; Ledesma interview; "King City Youth Cleared," 1; "Charge Against Ortiz Dismissed in Knife Slaying," *Greenfield News*, 10 September 1953, 1.

5. "Hearing Set Sept. 30," 12; "Court Acts in 'Gang War'—16 Juveniles Cleared of Riot Charges; 9 Placed on Probation," *Salinas Californian*, 8 October 1953, 1; "39 Youths Arraigned on 'Rioting' Charges," *Salinas Californian*, 9 September 1953, 1; "Court Recommends Action to Prevent New 'Gang War,'" *Salinas Californian*, 9 October 1953, 1; "Delinquent Parents Is Topic of Speaker at PTA Meeting Tuesday Night," *Greenfield News*, 17 September 1953, 1.

6. "Mexican Queen Will Be Named Saturday—Votes to Be Tallied at Dance," *Salinas Californian*, 5 September 1952, 4; "Miss Orabuena Is Named Queen for Independence Day Celebration Here," *Salinas Californian*, 10 September 1953, 5; Pitti, "To 'Hear About God in Spanish,'" 169; Joy Ann Zimmerman, "An Organizer's Organizer," *Progressive*, December 1988, 12–13, Folder 8, Box 2, Ross Papers; *CSO Reporter*, n.d., 2, Folder 1, Box 13, Galarza Papers; "The Latin One-Eighth," *Los Angeles Daily News*, 1 July 1949, n.p., Folder 3, Box 58, Galarza Papers; Pawel, *Crusades of Cesar Chavez*, 31; "Mexican Group to Install Officers Here This Evening," *Salinas Californian*, 24 April 1952, 16.

7. Bernstein, *Bridges of Reform*; Brilliant, *"Color of America Has Changed"*; Pitti, *Devil in Silicon Valley*; Apodaca, "They Kept the Home Fires Burning"; Rose, "Gender and Civic Activism"; Underwood, "Process and Politics"; Testimony of Albert Pinon before the Senate Subcommittee on Migratory Labor, 16 March 1955, 2, Folder 5, Box 38, Corona Papers.

8. "The Story of C.S.O.," ca. 1965, 2–3, Folder 1, Box 13, Galarza Papers; Fred Ross, audio recording, 27 April 1985, Folder 330, Box 41, Ross Papers.

9. "What Is CSO" pamphlet, Folder "Community Service Organization—1," Box 8, Roybal Papers; "Move for Attorney General to Enter L.A. Police Probe," *Daily News*, 21 March 1952, 2, 53; "Cop Showup in Brutality Case Sought," *Los Angeles Mirror*, 21 March 1952, n.p., and "Sergeants Admit Seeing Jail Prisoners Slugged," *Los Angeles Examiner*, 14 March 1952, n.p., both from Folder "Bloody Christmas Case 1952," Box 1, Civil Rights Congress Collection, SCLSSR; Fred Ross, unpublished manuscript on CSO, 80, Folder 6, Box 20, Ross Papers; Bernstein, "Interracial Activism," 237; American Council of Spanish Speaking People Civil Liberties Newsletter, 5 February 1952, 4, and 17 March 1952, 4, Folder 1, Box 13, Galarza Papers; G. W. Sherman, "Around the U.S.A.: A People Comes of Age," *Nation*, 28 March 1953, 256; "Final Census in Salinas Is Upped 268 to Make It 18,319," *Salinas Californian*, 8 September 1952, 1; "Special Salinas Census to Start This Week—3000 Boost in Population Is Forecast," *Salinas Californian*,

11 August 1952, 1; "Final Census in Salinas Is Upped 268 to Make It 18,319," *Salinas Californian,* 8 September 1952, 1; "Population," *Salinas Californian,* 22 February 1952, 28a.

10. Chávez interview.

11. Zermeño interview with the author; Sánchez interview; Sarah Terry-Cobo, "Latino Civil Rights Activist Retiring," *Oakland Tribune,* 24 May 2007, www .insidebayarea.com/ci_5975405.

12. Soledad CSO meeting minutes, 10 June 1957, Folder 15, Box 6, Ross Papers; Friedrich interview; naturalization record of Sophie Cásarez, Monterey County Naturalization Records, Vol. 30.

13. López Sr. interview; "Fallece Benigno López, Pionero Hispano del Valle de Salinas," obituary, *El Sol,* 1992, n.p., given to the author by Ben López Jr.; Gutíerrez McQuinn interview; Hortensia Lopez, "Latino Community Leader Continues Fight," *Monterey County Herald,* 8 September 1992, 7A; "Sally Gutierrez: Salinas's First Court Interpreter," *El Observador,* 2 May 1960, 6E; Gutíerrez interview.

14. Edward Roybal speech at 1954 CSO Convention, Folder "Speeches," Box 40, Roybal Papers; Lopez, "Latino Community Leader Continues Fight"; "'Americanism' Project Planned for Valley," *Salinas Californian,* 19 December 1953, 2; "Citizenship Program of the Community Service Organization of Fresno County," Folder 22, Box 4, Ross Papers. By 1950 the CSO was conducting 108 citizenship classes throughout California. "The Story of C.S.O.," 7.

15. Naturalization records of Mario Luis Marquez and Raul Francisco Fernandez, Monterey County Naturalization Records, Vols. 30 and 33. Some Mexican nationals who served in the U.S. Armed Forces during World War II were allowed the same privilege of naturalization after completing their service.

16. Various naturalization records, Monterey County Naturalization Records, Vols. 30, 32, and 33.

17. Naturalization records of Bruno Espino, Sophie Cásarez, Marguerite Villegas, Josefa Gonzales Enriquez, Jesus Enriquez, Teresa López Gilpas, and Jose Enrique Friedrich, Monterey County Naturalization Records, Vols. 30, 32, and 33; Friedrich interview.

18. Naturalization records of Mario Luis Marquez, Celia Terrazas Arroyo, Manuel Cota Bautista, Frances Chavez Morales, Refugia Burrela de Carranza, Vincent Tana Sanchez, Jose Mendoza Barragan, and Rosa Maria Gallegos, Monterey County Naturalization Records, Vols. 30 and 33.

19. Report to CSO National Convention from the Monterey County CSO, 1954, Folder "CSO Second National Convention," Box A-14, Gallegos Papers; "You Can't Vote Unless You Are Registered—," *Salinas Californian,* 27 April 1956, 32A; Fred Ross, notebook entry, 22 August 1956, Folder 2, Box 30, Ross Papers; Monterey Peninsula Council for Civic Unity, "Spanish Speaking Voters Double," *Civic Unity Reporter,* March 1954, Folder 15, Box 6, Ross Papers; letter to Hon. Chet Holified from unknown, Brawley, California, 2, Folder 10, Box 11, Ross Papers.

20. Monterey County CSO chapter report, 1955, 1, Folder 4, Box 5, Ross Papers; Monterey County CSO chapter report, 1956, 2, Folder 24, Box 4, Ross Papers; Zermeño interview with the author.

21. Monterey County CSO chapter report, 1955, 1, Folder 4, Box 5, Ross Papers; Monterey County CSO chapter report, 1956, 1, Folder 24, Box 4, Ross Papers; "Officers of CSO to Be Nominated," *Salinas Californian,* 6 January 1955, 15; "CSO Praised for Aid in TB Survey," *Salinas Californian,* 24 May 1955, 13; Senate Resolution No. 204, offered by California Senator Fred Farr, 11 June 1957, Folder 7, Box 13, Galarza Papers.

22. CSO Executive Board meeting minutes, 16 March 1956, Folder 2, Box 9, Roybal Papers; list of CSO chapters, n.d., 1–4, Folder 8, Box 13, Galarza Papers; "CSO—Third National Convention, 1956," Folder 6, Box 6, Ross Papers; CSO Mailing Directory, December 1962, Folder 15, Box 6, Ross Papers.

23. "Gender in the CSO" panel, comments by Danny Robles; Chapter Reports, Fourth Annual CSO Convention, Fresno, 23–24 March 1957, 2, Folder 2, Box 9, Roybal Papers.

24. Zermeño interview with the author; Chávez and Sánchez interviews; "Gender in the CSO" panel, comments by Danny Robles and Ana Chávez; Rose, "Gender and Civic Activism," 181; "The Story of C.S.O.," 11; CSO meeting minutes, 14 July 1956, 9, 15, Folder 25, Box 4, Ross Papers; CSO Mailing Directory, 17 November 1960, Folder "Community Service Organization—1," Box 8, Roybal Papers.

25. "To Fred W. Ross, West Coast Director of the Industrial Areas Foundation," scroll, ca. 1958, Folder 9, Box 2, Ross Papers; Zermeño interview with the author; Chávez interview.

26. Monterey County CSO Report to CSO National Convention, 1954, Box A-14, Gallegos Papers; Minutes of the Founding Convention, CSO, 20 March 1954, 15, Box A-16, Gallegos Papers; Zermeño interview with the author; Chávez interview.

27. Fred Ross, Work Diary, 1957, Folder 19, Box 1, Ross Papers; "Total number of labor camps by county as of December 31, 1960," Folder 7, Box 49, Galarza Papers; Monterey County CSO Chapter Report, 1957, 1, Folder 2, Box 9, Roybal Papers.

28. Zermeño interview with CSO Oral History Project; Fred Ross, notebook entry, 27 August 1956, Folder 2, Box 30, Ross Papers.

29. Bernstein, "From California to the Nation," 88; Vern Partlow, "Bypassed 'Islands' of L.A. Experience Awakening," *Daily News,* 27 December 1950, n.p., and Los Angeles CSO Quarterly Report, 1 March 1956 to 30 June 1956, 3, both from Folder 24, Box 4, Ross Papers; "Two San Joseans Face Race Relations Suits," *San Jose Evening News,* 29 August 1958, 2; letters to Fred Ross from Abe Chávez, "C.S.O. Adult Education," 6 and 13 May 1957, Folder 4, Box 6, Ross Papers.

30. "Population," *Salinas Californian,* 27 April 1956, 34A; Fred Ross, notebook entry, 3 March 1958, Folder 18, Box 5, Ross Papers; Zermeño interview with the author; Fred Ross, notebook entry, 8 February 1957, Folder 6, Box 30, Ross Papers; Fred Ross, notebook entry, 27 July 1959, Folder 1, Box 31, Ross Papers.

31. Fred Ross, notebook entry, 27 July 1959, Folder 1, Box 31, Ross Papers; Fred Ross, work diary entry, 3 March 1958, Folder 18, Box 5, Ross Papers; "CSO Voter Registration Drive Report, April 16, 1960," 5, Folder "Community Service

Organization—1," Box 8, Roybal Papers; "Cesar Chavez Talks About Organizing and the History of the NFWA," 3, Folder 8, Box 3, Steiner Papers, Series 3; "CSO Mailing List," CSO Newsletter, 1 November 1964, 2, Folder 5, Box 38, Corona Papers; CSO Directory 1963, Folder 12, Box 6, Ross Papers.

32. Biography of Alex Zermeño; Zermeño interview with the author; Ledesma interview; Chávez interview.

33. Gutiérrez, *Walls and Mirrors,* 170; Fred Ross, unaddressed letter draft, Folder 12, Box 6, Ross Papers; "Demographic, Economic, and Social Characteristics of the Spanish-Surname Population of Five Southwestern States," U.S. Commission on Civil Rights Staff Report, 1–3, Box 25, RG 453, NARA College Park; Garcia, *Rise of the Mexican American Middle Class,* 313.

34. "The Story of C.S.O.," 3; testimony of Albert Pinon, 2; Fred Ross and César Chávez, audiorecording, n.d., Tape 369b, Box 41, Ross Papers; Levy, *Cesar Chavez,* 129.

35. Pawel, *Crusades of Cesar Chavez,* 12; Andrew Gindes, "A Man on the Moon: The NFWA Political Farm Unionism in California," 31, Folder 13, Box 1, Beard Papers; Ferriss and Sandoval, *Fight in the Fields,* 12, 21; Jerry Roberts, "Fred Ross—Helped Unionize Farm Workers," *San Francisco Chronicle,* 1 October 1992, D8; news release to all CSO Chapter Presidents from CSO President Anthony P. Rios, 16 July 1958, Folder 1, Box 18, Galarza Papers.

36. "A Statement of Conscience and a Review of Evidence by the Emergency Committee to Aid Farm Workers," 29 March 1963, 61–62, Folder 3, Box 1, Farm Worker Organizing Collection, SCLSSR; Office of the Attorney General, State of California, "An Inquiry into the Mexican Migrant Labor Program," 1 December 1959, 16, Folder "Bracero Investigation," Box 1, Soto Papers; State of California Department of Employment, Table, "Foreign Contract Labor as a Percentage of All Seasonal Labor Used on Farms in Selected Counties: California, 1950–1959 (Through Oct. 31)," 10 November 1959, Folder 7, Box 20, Galarza Papers; Ernesto Galarza, "Salinas Vegetable Growers Association," Folder 12, Box 45, Galarza Papers. By 1960 close to 14,000 Puerto Ricans, 8,900 British West Indians, and 8,600 Canadians had been recruited to work on U.S. farms in addition to 1,730 Japanese workers in California who were obliged to pay for their own transportation to and from Japan but could work for six-month terms up to three years in the state. Fay Bennett, "The Condition of Farm Workers in 1961," 3–4, Folder 1, Box 1, Farm Worker Organizing Collection, SCLSSR; "The Bracero Program and Its Aftermath: An Historical Summary," 9, 10, Folder 10, Box 7, Roth Papers.

37. Agricultural Workers Organizing Committee, "The Future Disposition of Public Law 78," 30 July 1959, 10–11, Folder 37, Carton 5, McWilliams Papers; Ganz, *Why David Sometimes Wins,* 61; National Advisory Committee on Farm Labor, "The Plight of American Farm Workers—Related to the Mexican Farm Labor Program (Public Law 78)," Folder 10, Box 5, R. P. Sanchez Papers; "Report on Farm Labor," February 1959, 36, Folder 36, Carton 5, McWilliams Papers; Fay Bennett, "Still the Harvest of Shame," *Commonweal,* 10 April 1964, 84, Folder 8, Carton 12, McWilliams Papers; Camarillo, *Chicanos in California,* 78; analysis and report to AWOC Director Norman Smith from Louis Krainock, 9 October 1959, 1, Folder 8, Box 23, Vizzard Papers.

38. Howard Kennedy, "Goldberg Aide to Enter Imperial Lettuce Strike," *Los Angeles Times,* 5 February 1961, 10; "13 Lettuce Growers Lose Right to Employ Mexican Field Hands," *Los Angeles Times,* 26 February 1961, 9; Ganz, *Why David Sometimes Wins,* 73.

39. Ganz, *Why David Sometimes Wins,* 74; "Los Engañan a Los Trabajadores de Salinas," *El Malcriado,* 12 August 1966, 22, Box 2, *El Malcriado* Collection; Santoro, *If You Got the Guts,* 20; Glass, "Organization in Salinas," 26; "3 Salinas Valley Strikes Settled," *San Jose Mercury,* 9 July 1960, n.p.; "Vegetable Crop Strikes Settled," *Los Angeles Times,* 9 July 1960, 6; "Strawberry Workers Strike Salinas Company: Union Protests Bracero Use in Fields; Telegram Sent to Mexican Government," *Los Angeles Times,* 27 April 1961, B6; "Strawberry Strike Rated Bona Fide," *Los Angeles Times,* 2 May 1961, 22. "Strawberry Strike in Salinas Area Spreads," *Monterey Peninsula Herald,* 28 April 1961; "Salinas Valley Strike Extends to Five Ranches," *Monterey Peninsula Herald,* 29 April 1961; Roy Hurlbert, "Picketing Spread Berry Walkout Momentum," *San Jose Mercury,* 29 April 1961; "Strawberry Strike Enters Second Week," *Monterey Peninsula Herald,* 3 May 1961; and "U.S. Says Braceros Stay on Struck Berry Farms," *San Jose Mercury,* 4 May 1961, all n.p., Newspaper Clipping Collection, Monterey Public Library.

40. San Francisco FEPC Commission, "Californians of Spanish Surname," May 1964, 24, 41, Folder 12, Box 4, Ross Papers; Fred W. Ross, "Mexican-Americans on the March," 2, Folder 1, Box 13, Galarza Papers. In 1961 the California legislature did extend disability insurance coverage to farmworkers for the first time, and the State Industrial Welfare Commission made the state minimum wage one dollar an hour for men, women, and children working in agriculture. Fay Bennett, "The Condition of Farm Workers in 1961," 5, Folder 1, Box 1, Farm Worker Organizing Collection, SCLSSR.

41. Fred Ross and Cesar Chavez, audiorecording, n.d., Tape 369b, Box 41, Ross Papers; Zermeño interview with the author; Garcia, *From the Jaws of Victory,* 26; Seventh CSO Annual Convention Minutes, March 19–20, 1960, 6, Folder "CSO Second National Convention," Box A-14, Gallegos Papers; Ferriss and Sandoval, *Fight in the Fields,* 58–60, 62; Pawel, *Crusades of Cesar Chavez,* 131.

42. Ruben Salazar, "U.S. Charges Falsifying of Bracero Pay Books," *Los Angeles Times,* 7 December 1962, 31; "Extension of Bracero Use Proposed," *Los Angeles Times,* 19 February 1963, 8; "Bracero Defeat Shocks State, County Growers," *Salinas Californian,* 30 May 1963, 5.

CHAPTER 5. A TOWN FULL OF DEAD MEXICANS

Epigraphs. Henry Anderson, "Blood on the Lettuce," KPFA radio broadcast transcript, Berkeley, California, 18 September 1963, 2, Folder 3, Box 11, Galarza Papers; Ric Masten, song, "Hindends and Elbows," 1966, used by permission.

1. "Crash Kills 27: Train Smashes Makeshift Bus," *Los Angeles Times,* 18 September 1963, 1; "27 Mexican Celery Workers Die as Train Hits Bus in California," *New York Times,* 18 September 1963, 43.

2. Claudia Meléndez Salinas, "Second Survivor of 1963 Chualar Bus Crash Emerges," *Monterey Herald,* 1 March 2014, www.montereyherald.com/news/

ci_25256461/second-survivor-1963-chualar-bus-crash-emerges?source=rss; "Crash Kills 27," 1; Gutiérrez McQuinn interview; Hollis interview.

3. Galarza, *Tragedy at Chualar,* 11; Salinas, "Second Survivor."

4. See, for example, Galarza, *Tragedy at Chualar,* and Pitti, "To 'Hear About God in Spanish.'"

5. "Perecen 27 Braceros en un Grave Choque en California" and "Zapatos, Sombreros y Cuchillos Estaban Esparcidos Por Todas Partes," *Novedades,* 18 September 1963, 7; *Cosecha Triste;* M. Cristina Medina, "Gathering Remembers Bracero Crash Victims," *Monterey Herald* online, 18 September 2005, www .montereyherald.com/mld/montereyherald/news/12679216.htm.

6. Galarza, *Tragedy at Chualar,* 1; Loza, "Braceros on the Boundaries," 27, 52.

7. Ernesto Galarza, Report on the Farm Labor Transportation Accident at Chualar, 5, Folder 7, Box 16, Galarza Papers; Folder "Reports and Statistics, 1961, 1963–64," Box 9, RG 174, NARA San Bruno; Dale Polissar, "Labor Director Blasts Bracero Program," *Lodi News-Sentinel,* 27 August 1963, 2–3. In addition to braceros, 22,353 other foreign workers were employed around the United States in 1963. British West Indians (11,856) and Bahamians (1,074) worked primarily in Florida sugar cane and citrus, Connecticut tobacco, and Virginia vegetable fields; Canadians (8,500) worked Maine's potato harvest; and Japanese (923) worked in California. "Administratively Confidential: Use of Labor in Agriculture and Effects of Ending the Bracero Program," 2–3, 6, and Table, "Number of Foreign and Domestic Seasonal Workers and Time of Seasonal Peak Employments for State Employing 1,000 or more Foreign Workers at that Time, 1963," Folder "Agricultural [2 of 2]," Box 4115, RG 16, NARA College Park.

8. "Inquiry Vowed in Salinas Crash," *Los Angeles Times,* 19 September 1963, 3; "Bracero Bus Called Safe by Growers," *Los Angeles Times,* 9 October 1963, A3; "Playing Politics with Tragedy," *Salinas Californian,* 19 September 1963, 6; "Two Kinds of Blame in Birmingham and Salinas," *East Bay Labor Journal,* 27 September 1963, 1; letter to James Vizzard from William Garin, 20 September 1963, 2, Folder 8, Box 23, Vizzard Papers.

9. Creagan, "Public Law 78," 553; "Bracero Defeat Shocks State, County Growers," *Salinas Californian,* 30 May 1963, 5.

10. "6 Mexican Nationals Killed, 12 Hurt as SP Passenger Hits Truck," *Salinas Californian,* 19 February 1953, 19; Jeff Boehm, "There Is Blood on Your Salad!," *Santa Clara County AFL-CIO Union Gazette,* 27 September 1963, 1; "8 Killed, 6 Hurt at Rail Crossing: Freight Hits Labor Truck Near Chualar," *Salinas Californian,* 27 October 1955, 1; "12 Die in Bus Fire, 19 Are Taken to Hospital; Probes Start," *Salinas Californian,* 17 June 1958, 1; U.S. Department of Labor statement, 29 May 1958, and National Agricultural Workers Union press release, 11 June 1958, both from Folder 10, Box 16, Galarza Papers; "Inquiry Vowed in Salinas Crash," 3; "U.S.-State Probes of Bracero Bus Crash Pressed as Vote Nears on PL 78 Extension," AFL-CIO California Labor Federation Weekly Newsletter, 27 September 1963, 4, and Paul Jacobs, "The Forgotten People," *Reporter,* 22 January 1959, both from Folder 1, Box 4, Farm Worker Organizing Collection, SCLSSR; Fay Bennett, "Still the Harvest of Shame," *Commonweal,* 10 April 1964, 84, Folder 8, Carton 12, McWilliams Papers; Mitchell, *They Saved the Crops,* 313.

11. Pasquale Marranzino, "A Shameful and Black Practice," *American G.I. Forum News Bulletin,* May–June 1955, 2, Folder 1, Box 6, Idar Jr. Papers; Moore, *The Slaves We Rent,* 18; "Galarza Raps Labor System," *Salinas Californian,* 20 April 1964, 1; Galarza, Report on the Farm Labor Transportation Accident, 55, 57; "Treating Humans Like Cattle," *Corpus Christi Caller,* 2 November 1954, B-2.

12. Cited in Calavita, *Inside the State,* 143.

13. Letter to David Lowe from Louis Krainock, December 1960, Folder 11, Box 2, AWOC Records; Anderson, "Blood on the Lettuce" and "Beyond the Bracero System," KPFA radio broadcast transcripts, 31 July and 1 August 1963, 2–3, Folder 3, Box 11, Galarza Papers.

14. MAPA Resolution Against Public Law 78, Folder 7, Box 3, Galarza Papers; Burt, *Search for a Civic Voice,* 193–94.

15. MAPA Resolution Against Public Law 78; "Two Kinds of Blame," 1.

16. "Two Kinds of Blame," 1; Boehm, "There Is Blood on Your Salad!," 8; Vizzard quoted in Pitti, "To 'Hear About God in Spanish,'" 364, 383.

17. Galarza, *Tragedy at Chualar,* 10–11; Eric Brazil, "Manuel Silva Missed Labor Bus—and Missed Death," *Salinas Californian,* 19 September 1963, 1, 4; "750,000 Due Families in Bus Crash," *Los Angeles Times,* 20 September 1963, 13; Galarza, Report on the Farm Labor Transportation Accident, 4.

18. Galarza, Report on the Farm Labor Transportation Accident, 4–5, 54; Galarza, *Tragedy at Chualar,* 12.

19. "Macabre Funeral Hassle Develops over Braceros," *Salinas Californian,* 20 September 1963, 1; advertisement for Sanchez-Hall Mortuary, *El Malcriado,* 1 August 1968, 7; "Workers' Rites Planned Here," *Salinas Californian,* 21 September 1963, 1; letter to Ernesto Galarza from José Rafael Ramos, 7 November 1963, Folder 4, Box 16, Galarza Papers.

20. M. Cristina Medina, "Gathering Remembers Bracero Crash Victims," *Monterey Herald* online, 18 September 2005, www.montereyherald.com/mld/montereyherald/news/12679216.htm; "3,000 Mourn Victims of Bus Crash," *San Jose Mercury News,* 26 September 1963, 1; "Mass for 32 Mexicans Slated at Palma High," *Salinas Californian,* 24 September 1963, 1; "9,000 Attend Mass for 32 Bracero Dead," *Salinas Californian,* 26 September 1963, 1; "Macabre Funeral Hassle," 1; "Workers' Rites Planned Here," 1.

21. Galarza, *Tragedy at Chualar,* 11; "Bracero Bus Damage Suit Filed Today," *Salinas Californian,* 28 January 1964, 1; "750,000 Due Families in Bus Crash," 13; "Families of 31 Dead in Crash to Get $750,000," *Chicago Tribune,* 21 September 1963, N: A24; Hector Moreno, "Chualar Tragedy Still Under Probe," *San Jose Mercury-News,* 26 July 1964, 2; letter to Mercedes Ramirez from Margarita Vasquez, 12 January 1964, and letter to Margarita Vasquez from Ernesto Galarza, 19 March 1964, both from Folder 1, Box 16, Galarza Papers, translated by the author; Gutíerrez McQuinn interview. In January 1964, 180 relatives of the dead and injured braceros filed a $4,475,000 indemnity suit against Espinosa, the Earl Myers Company, the David E. Meyers Company, Harden Farms, Horme and Siefert, and David E. Myers. The Mexican and U.S. governments determined that the accused had violated Public Law 78 by failing to have the bus inspected at specified intervals, but it is unclear whether the victims received any financial compensation.

"Braceros' Relatives File Indemnity Suit," *The News* (Mexico City), 29 January 1964, Folder 5, Box 16, Galarza Papers; Final Joint Determination, in the Matter of Growers Farm Labor Association, Demco Farms, and Mr. David E. Myers, 18 February 1964, 1, Folder 7, Box 16, Galarza Papers.

22. "9,000 Attend Mass," 1, 4; "28 BRACEROS KILLED," *Salinas Californian,* 18 September 1963, 1.

23. "Inquiry Vowed in Salinas Crash," 14; Galarza, *Tragedy at Chualar,* 2.

24. "Farm Group Deplores Selection of Galarza," *San Jose Mercury News,* 25 October 1963, n.p.; Congressional Record, Proceedings and Debates of the 88th Congress, First Session, Vol. 190, No. 166, 16 October 1963, 18638–9; Galarza, *Spiders in the House,* 164; Galarza, *Tragedy at Chualar,* 2, 36; Galarza, Report on the Farm Labor Transportation Accident, 10, 33; "Bracero Train-Truck Crash Toll Reaches 31," *Monterey Peninsula Herald,* 20 September 1963, 1; copies of bracero contracts, Folder 2, Box 16, Galarza Papers.

25. State of California Department of Employment, Farm Placement Technical Section, "Estimates of Mexican Citizens with Green Card Permanent Visas Working in California Agriculture During 1962," 20 February 1963, 1, Folder 8, Box 8, Roth Papers.

26. Galarza, Report on the Farm Labor Transportation Accident, 26–27; Galarza, *Tragedy at Chualar,* 46–48; Ames interview; Ernesto Galarza, "Interview—Robert Ames," and "Selected Notes on Interviews," 2, both from Folder 6, Box 16, Galarza Papers.

27. "Prosecution Rests Case in Bus Tragedy Trial," *Salinas Californian,* 11 December 1963, 3; Ames interview; Eric Brazil, "Constriction of Vision Claimed," *Salinas Californian,* 11 December 1963, 1–2; Galarza, Report on the Farm Labor Transportation Accident, 1, 25–26, 29; Gutíerrez McQuinn interview; Galarza, *Tragedy at Chualar,* 45, 48; "Espinosa Sobs Heavily After Acquittal Verdict," *Salinas Californian,* 13 December 1963, 1; "Bus Driver Cleared in Crash That Killed 32," *Los Angeles Times,* 14 December 1963, 16; Eric Brazil, "Fate of Pancho Espinosa: Is Driver Dead or Alive?," *Salinas Californian,* 15 September 1964, 2; "Bracero Death Bus Driver Executed?," *Los Angeles Times,* 16 September 1964, 1; "Slaying of Bus Driver in Mexico Discounted," *Los Angeles Times,* 16 September 1964, 1–2.

28. Galarza, *Tragedy at Chualar,* 48–49; unknown Galarza associate, "Trip to Salinas, Nov. 1–2, 1963," 3, Folder 7, Box 16, Galarza Papers.

29. "Trip to Salinas, Nov. 1–2, 1963," 2, Folder 7, Box 16, Galarza Papers; Galarza, Report on the Farm Labor Transportation Accident, 24–25, 28; Galarza, *Tragedy at Chualar,* 8, 43–44, 49; Ernesto Galarza, "Survivors," "Interview—8 Braceros—Camp Colorado—Oct 10, 1963," and "S. Brunet—Mx Dept. Labor," all from Folder 6, Box 16, Galarza Papers.

30. Galarza, "Selected Notes on Interviews," 4, and "General Impressions," both from Folder 6, Box 16, Galarza Papers.

31. Basurto, Delorme Jr., and Kamerschen, "Rent Seeking," 26; Pitti, "To 'Hear God in Spanish,'" 303; surveys from California, 1962, Folder 3, Box 140, Samora Papers; Henry Rodriguez, "Report of Bracero Committee," 12 January 1964, 2, Folder 16, Box 7, Ruiz Papers.

32. Telegram to California Governor Edmund G. Brown from unknown author, n.d., Folder 8, Box 3, Quevedo Papers; Brilliant, *"Color of America Has Changed,"* 211; biographical document about Manuel Ruiz, 31 May 1966, 1, Box 1, Ruiz Papers; "Governor's Meeting with Mexican-American Community Roster," 28 December 1965, Folder 8, Box 3, Quevedo Papers; letter to Anthony Barieri from James Delgadillo, 6 July 1965, Folder 10, Box 3, Quevedo Papers; MAPA State Executive Board, "Resolution on Statewide Unity of Mexican-American Organization," 25 April 1965, Folder 11, Box 3, Quevedo Papers; Bert Corona, Welcome Speech to MAPA 8th Convention, 14–16 July 1967, Folder 5, Box 7, Ruiz Papers. In 1965 Chavez and Huerta briefly clashed with MAPA when they learned the latter had volunteered to work with farm labor offices in northern and central California to recruit domestics. Huerta called MAPA leaders "middle-class sellouts" and asserted, "If you are helping the growers, you are not helping the farmworkers." Yet when the UFWOC initiated the Delano grape strike later that year, Chavez asked for MAPA's support in meetings with state officials. Burt, *Search for a Civic Voice,* 220, 222.

33. Anderson, "Blood on the Lettuce," 2.

34. Brazil interview; letter to Kennedy M. Crockett, Esq., from William T. Pryce, 9 December 1963, Folder "Labor and Manpower, Migrant Labor, July–December," Box 14, RG 59, NARA College Park; Garcia, *From the Jaws of Victory,* 16; Bardacke, *Trampling,* 468; "Farmers Hiring Indians to Replace Braceros," *San Jose News,* 19 January 1965, n.p., Folder 25, Carton 5, McWilliams Papers; Mitchell, *They Saved the Crops,* 387.

35. Neuburger, *Lettuce Wars,* 25–26; letter to Lyndon B. Johnson from Walter P. Reuther, 27 October 1964, 1–2, Folder 1, Box 21, Vizzard Papers; "A Statement on Farm Labor," *GI Forum News Bulletin,* February 1965, 1, 4, Folder 5, Box 85, Garcia Papers; Roger W. Benedict, "Bracero Battle: Farmers Dispute Labor, Government on Impact of Foreign Worker Ban," *Wall Street Journal,* 26 April 1965, 1, 8; "Loophole in Bracero Law," *San Francisco Examiner,* 9 August 1964, 12; U.S. Department of Labor, "Summary Table on Prevalence of Foreign Ag. Labor in the U.S.A. for June 1964," Folder 8, Box 1, Farm Worker Organizing Collection, SCLSSR.

36. "Wirtz Helps Growers—A Little," *Business Week,* 17 April 1965, 46.

37. Mitchell, *They Saved the Crops,* 382; "Where Braceros Once Worked," *Business Week,* 16 January 1965, 32; "Grapes of Wrath—New Style," *Economist,* 3 April 1965, 52.

38. Frank C. Porter, "Growers Attack Wirtz Bitterly for Barring Use of Braceros," *Washington Post,* 11 May 1965, A9; Harry Bernstein, "First Mexicans Cross Border for Farm Jobs," *Los Angeles Times,* 19 May 1965, 28; Salinas City Council minutes, 10 May 1965; "Gate Is Opened by U.S. for 1,000 More Braceros," *Washington Post,* 21 May 1965, A25; Harry Bernstein, "Another 1,000 Mexican Farm Workers OKd," *Los Angeles Times,* 20 May 1965, 3, 32; Harry Bernstein, "Panel Rejects All Pleas for Foreign Farm Labor," *Los Angeles Times,* 30 May 1965, B, 26; "Wirtz to OK Ban on Foreign Farm Workers," *Los Angeles Times,* 1 June 1965, 26; resolution of King City and Southern Monterey County Chamber of Commerce and Agriculture, 4 May 1965, Folder "Agri. May 13–24," Box 4282, RG 16, NARA College Park; letter to Thomas McNamara from Assistant Secretary of Agriculture

George L. Mehren, 14 May 1965, Folder "Agri. May 13–24," Box 4282, RG 16, NARA College Park; telegram to unknown recipient from H. Stephen Chase, 24 August 1965, Folder "Agri. Aug 5–Sept 8," Box 4282, RG 16, NARA College Park; "Growers Warn of Sharp Crop Cuts: Farm Chief Says Labor to Be Adequate Despite Departure of Braceros," *Los Angeles Times,* n.d., 1, Folder 25, Carton 5, McWilliams Papers; "Mexican-American Intensive Recruitment Program—1965," 3–6, Folder 5, Box 9, Roth Papers; Dick Flood, "Angry Mexican-Americans Rap Tieburg's Farm Report," *San Jose Mercury,* 17 June 1965, 45.

39. Mitchell, *They Saved the Crops,* 388; Frank C. Porter, "Growers Call Wirtz A-Team Farce," *Washington Post,* 2 August 1965, A4; "Many Athletes Leave Salinas Farming Jobs," *Los Angeles Times,* 26 June 1965, 13; "Laborers Coming Shortly," *Salinas Californian,* 21 August 1965, 1; Verardo and Verardo, *Salinas Valley,* 112.

CHAPTER 6. THE FARMWORKER MOVEMENT IN THE POST-BRACERO ERA

1. In February 1969 the federal minimum wage for farmworkers was raised to $1.30 an hour, but that law applied only to workers on farms that sold their produce in interstate commerce. California had no minimum wage for men, and growers resisted paying the $1.65 state minimum wage for women and $1.35 for minors. "Farm Workers Begin to Collect Minimum Wages," *El Malcriado,* 2 December 1968, 6; "New Farm Minimum Wage," *El Malcriado,* 15 February 1969, 14; J. B. Lieber, "Chavez and the Farm Workers: 'We Have Our Patience,'" *Nation,* 3 September 1973, 175; Verardo and Verardo, *Salinas Valley,* 112; "Farm Workers Average $1,247/Yr," *El Malcriado,* 2 December 1968, 7; "A Statement of Conscience," 25; Lee G. Burchinal, ed., "Rural Youth in Crisis: Facts, Myths, and Social Change," n.d., Folder 1, Box 123, Samora Papers.

2. This number of 5.5 million did not take into account those Mexican-origin people not counted by the census or those who did not claim Spanish as their "mother tongue." José Antonio Villarreal, "Mexican Americans in Upheaval," *Los Angeles Times,* 18 September 1966, W20–21; State of California Division of Fair Employment Practices, Information Memo No. 25, Re: 1965 Population Estimates for Ethnic Groups in California, Folder 1, Box 2, Quevedo Papers; U.S. Bureau of the Census, Eighteenth Census 1960: Median School Years; Galarza, Gallegos, and Samora, *Mexican-Americans in the Southwest,* 38; "Migrant and Seasonal Farmworker Powerlessness" hearings, statement of Dr. Hector P. Garcia, 1521; "Tío Taco Is Dead," *Newsweek,* 29 June 1970, 22, 28.

3. Ganz, *Why David Sometimes Wins,* 4; Pawel, *Union of Our Dreams,* 20; *El Malcriado,* 30 June 1966, 8; "Migrant and Seasonal Farmworker Powerlessness" hearings, Garcia statement, 1531–32; "Tío Taco Is Dead," 23.

4. Bardacke, *Trampling,* 326; "Remembering Cesar Chavez and the Farm Workers Movement" panel, remarks by Matt Garcia; "Farm Union Reaps First California Victory," *Business Week,* 16 April 1966, 159; chronology of UFW strikes, unnamed author, 1, Folder 7, Box 17, Cruz Papers.

5. Ganz interview; Shaw, *Beyond the Fields,* 25; Garcia, *From the Jaws of Victory,* 52.

6. Salinas Chamber of Commerce, "Things to Know About Salinas and Monterey County, California," Binder, Socio Eco. Vol. 45, Box 12, Lopez v. Monterey County Collection; Pawel, *Crusades of Cesar Chavez,* 100; Bardacke, *Trampling,* 126–27; Stan Cloud, "Program to Organize Salinas Farm Labor," *Monterey Peninsula Herald,* 17 June 1966, 1, 6; "A Look into Our Strike in Salinas," *El Malcriado,* 15 September 1970, 7.

7. Ganz interview.

8. "Esclavos de Mexico Trabajando Otra Vez," *El Malcriado,* 19 May 1966, 6; "Brown Buys Braceros," *El Malcriado,* 19 May 1966, 6; *El Malcriado,* 16 June 1966, 15.

9. Sally Gutíerrez, letter to *El Malcriado,* 29 March 1967, 5; "Fight in the Fields" panel, remarks by Teresa Serrano; Jose Andere, "Crooked Contractors," letter to *El Malcriado,* 10 May 1967, 4.

10. Appellants' opening brief, in the Court of Appeal of the State of California, *Fred Wetherton et al. v. Growers Farm Labor Association et al.,* 23 January 1968, 4.

11. Gnaizda interview; "Public Forum: Discourtesy, Rudeness Is Charged," *Salinas Californian,* n.d., n.p., Folder 3, Box 62, records of the UFW Office of the President: Cesar Chavez (hereafter UFWOP-CC Records).

12. "Hector de la Rosa, Sr.—The Man Who Changed His World."

13. Letter to Fay Bennett from David S. North, 18 March 1966, 1, Folder 7, Box 24, Vizzard Papers; "Second Complaint Filed Against Strawberry Firm," *Salinas Californian,* 2 June 1967, 2; Marty Glick, e-mail correspondence with the author, 19 November 2012.

14. "Filth in the Fields," *Advocate,* February–March 1968, Folder 1, Box 61, UFWOP-CC Records; "Do Growers Flout the Law?," *California AFL-CIO News,* 23 February 1968, 1 and n.p., Folder 17, Box 60, UFWOP-CC Records; "Farm Sanitation Charges Test State Labor Referral," *Salinas Californian,* 7 June 1968, 26, and "Farm Worker Wins Jobless Insurance," *Monterey Herald,* 11 June 1968, 6, both from Folder 1, Box 61, Part 1, UFWOP-CC Records; Marty Glick, "Cases from the Offices," *Noticiero,* 1 November 1968, 6, Folder 10, Box 62, Part 1, UFWOP-CC Records; "Judge Rules Agricultural Labor Not Suitable Employment," *El Malcriado,* 15–31 July 1969, 11.

15. In the Court of Appeal of the State of California, *Wetherton et al. . . . .* 4, 9–11, 17–18, 24; *Fred Wetherton et al. v. GFLA et al.,* 28 July 1969; Gnaizda interview.

16. Marty Glick, e-mail correspondence with the author, 24 September 2009; letter to Alan Marer from Jim Lorenz, n.d., Folder 15, Box 60, Part 1, UFWOP-CC Records; letter to Cesar Chavez from Jim Lorenz, 13 February 1967, 1, Folder 12, Box 60, Part 1, UFWOP-CC Records; letter to Jim Lorenz from Cesar Chavez, 16 February 1967, Folder 12, Box 60, Part 1, UFWOP-CC Records; Gnaizda interview.

17. Gnaizda interview; letter to Robert Gnaizda from Cesar Chavez, 4 November 1967, Folder 15, Box 60, Part 1, UFWOP-CC Records; Brief, *Wetherton, et al. v. Martin Produce, Inc., et al.;* in the Court of Appeal of the State of California, *Wetherton et al. . . . .* 6; Harry Bernstein, "Farm Worker Can't Be Fired for Union Activity, Court Rules," *Los Angeles Times,* 31 July 1969, OC: A1.

18. "Nine File Lawsuit to Block Braceros: Hearing Slated in U.S. Court for Injunction," *Salinas Californian*, 9 September 1967, 1, 3; Glick interview; Kousser, "Racial Injustice," 42; Eric C. Brazil, "New Safeguards Won by Domestic Workers," *Salinas Californian*, 13 September 1967, 1; Marty Glick, e-mail correspondence with the author, 19 November 2012; Gnaizda interview; "Migrant and Seasonal Farmworker Powerlessness" hearings, statement of James D. Lorenz, 1587–88; "Use of Short-Handled Hoe Banned by State," *Los Angeles Times*, 8 April 1975, 20; Murray, "Abolition of El Cortito." The high-profile cases won by CRLA in the 1970s provoked the ire of Cesar Chavez, who believed that CRLA staff should perform union work and be directed by UFWOC attorneys. His demands, which were illegal and unethical under terms of CRLA's founding, maintained the tension between the two organizations. Pawel, *Crusades of Cesar Chavez*, 202.

19. Table P-2: Social Characteristics of the Population, Monterey County; Table P-3: Labor Force Characteristics of the Population, 1970; Table P-4: Income Characteristics of the Population: 1970—Salinas—Income in 1969 of Families and Unrelated Individuals; and Table P-8: As Applies to the Spanish-Language Population, Summary of Characteristics of Population and Housing, all from U.S. Bureau of the Census, Nineteenth Census 1970, Population; Salinas Chamber of Commerce, "Things to Know About Salinas and Monterey County, California," and unnamed author, "Chicano—The Social Conflicts in Salinas," 11 May 1972, 1, 3–4, 6, both from Binder "Socio Eco. Vol. 45," Box 12, Lopez v. Monterey County Collection; Patricia McNally, "Census Reveals County Ethnic Data," *Salinas Californian*, 20 June 1971, 2; Kousser, "Racial Injustice," 43–44; Congressional Record, Senate, 21 April 1971, S-5282, Folder 55, Carton 7, McWilliams Papers; Ralph R. López, "Farm Workers Deserve Every Cent They Get," *Salinas Californian*, 4 September 1970, 4.

20. "Mexican-U.S. Political Unit Formed in Area," *Salinas Californian*, 4 June 1964, 17; "Castroville Man to Head MAPA Group," *Salinas Californian*, 21 August 1964, 13; "Candidates Air Views at MAPA," *Salinas Californian*, 9 September 1964, 17; "MAPA Chapter Hears Six Speakers on School Crisis," *Salinas Californian*, 17 September 1964, 15; "Spanish-Speaking Voter Registrars Announced," *Salinas Californian*, 8 April 1970, 22; "Registration Hits 80,478," *Salinas Californian*, 30 September 1968, 1; Parsons Jr., "Ethnic Cleavage," 219; "Mexican Group Makes Requests to Alisal Unit," *Salinas Californian*, 10 April 1969, 29.

21. Crawford interview; Michael Harris, "A Fired Teacher's Victory in Court— Job Restored," *San Francisco Chronicle*, 5 April 1969, 2; Helen Manning, "200 Confront Hartnell Board on Mexican-American Plea," *Salinas Californian*, 22 April 1970, 23; Andre, *Hartnell*, 126.

22. Bardacke, *Trampling*, 360; Ferriss and Sandoval, *Fight in the Fields*, 165; Ganz, "1979 Lettuce Strike," 1; Ganz interview; Wells, *Strawberry Fields*, 82.

23. Sabino López interview with the author; Sabino López interview with Rachel Goodman, 6; Ferriss and Sandoval, *Fight in the Fields*, 159, 165; Wells, *Strawberry Fields*, 81.

24. "Teamster Raids Repelled," *El Malcriado*, 15 August 1970, 5; Verardo and Verardo, *Salinas Valley*, 108; Bill Boyarsky, "Handshakes Seal Pact Ending Grape Boycott," *Los Angeles Times*, 30 July 1970, 3; Kousser, "Racial Injustice," 69–70;

Lieber, "Chavez and the Farm Workers," 172; "Chavez and the Teamsters," *Nation,* 2 November 1970, 428; Gordon, "Poisons in the Fields," 51.

25. Ferriss and Sandoval, *Fight in the Fields,* 161; "Fight in the Fields" panel, remarks by Mike Payne; "From Clovis to the Capitol: Building a Career as a Legislative Liaison," Mesplé interview, 42; "Chavez Calls for Boycott of Chain in Lettuce Dispute," *Salinas Californian,* 21 September 1970, 3, 20; Harry Bernstein, "Growers Plan United Action on Bargaining," *Los Angeles Times,* 1 April 1971, A30; Kousser, "Racial Injustice," 75. While the Teamsters colluded with growers in California, it formed different alliances in different states. In Crystal City, Texas, for example, the Political Association of Spanish-Speaking Organizations allied with the cannery workers' division of the Teamsters to topple the entrenched Anglo leadership of the local schools and city council in 1963. Geron, *Latino Political Power,* 1.

26. López interview with the author; Jensen and Hammerback, *Words of Cesar Chavez,* xvi; Ferriss and Sandoval, *Fight in the Fields,* 165; Pawel, *Crusades of Cesar Chavez,* 215.

CHAPTER 7. A BLOSSOMING OF RED FLAGS

1. Though Filipinos are a vital part of farmworker history and the history of the UFWOC, their numbers were much larger in the San Joaquin Valley and southern California than they were in the Salinas Valley by 1970. This was due to immigration restrictions and patterns in addition to Filipinos being pushed out by Mexican American and bracero labor over time.

2. Bardacke, *Trampling,* 346–47; press conference with Cesar Chavez, undated transcript, 890, Folder 149, Box 2, Jacques E. Levy Research Collection on Cesar Chavez (hereafter Levy Collection).

3. Bardacke, *Trampling,* 350.

4. Ferriss and Sandoval, *Fight in the Fields,* 164; Bardacke, *Trampling,* 361.

5. Ganz interview; Wells, *Strawberry Fields,* 81; Bardacke, *Trampling,* 342–43, 351.

6. Bardacke, *Trampling,* 343–46; Maturino interview; Ganz interview.

7. "Teamster Raids Repelled," *El Malcriado,* 15 August 1970, 1–2, 5–6; Jensen and Hammerback, *Words of Cesar Chavez,* 47; Ferriss and Sandoval, *Fight in the Fields,* 164, 169; Harry Bernstein, "1,000 Berry Workers Join Chavez Strike," *Los Angeles Times,* 12 August 1970, 3; Harry Bernstein, "Teamsters Give Chavez Clear Field to Organize Farm Hands," *Los Angeles Times,* 13 August 1970, 1, 30; "Chavez Movement Gains," *Los Angeles Times,* 16 August 1970, F5; Ganz interview; Monterey County Agricultural Housing Photo Binders, worker camp descriptions, Vol. 1, 41.

8. "4,000 Attend Salinas Strike Meeting," *El Malcriado,* 1 September 1970, 3–5; "Farm Workers Vote to Strike in California," *Washington Post,* 24 August 1970, A2; conversation between Cesar Chavez and Jacques Levy, tape transcript, 1015, Folder 153, Box 3, Levy Collection.

9. Ganz interview; "Chavez and the Teamsters," *Nation,* 2 November 1970, 429; Bardacke, *Trampling,* 372.

10. Doug Willis, "Calif. Lettuce Rots as Farm Unions Clash," *Washington Post,* 28 August 1970, A6; Wells, "Legal Conflict and Class Structure," 55; Harry Bernstein, "Growers Losing $500,000 a Day," *Los Angeles Times,* 27 August 1970, 1; Harry Bernstein, "Chavez-Grower Contract Talks Stalled by Suit," *Los Angeles Times,* 29 August 1970, A1.

11. Julianna Martínez interview; Bernstein, "Growers Losing $500,000 a Day," 1; Levy, *Cesar Chavez,* 196.

12. Barbara L. Baer and Glenna Matthews, "The Women of the Boycott," *Nation,* 23 February 1974, 234; Rose, "From the Fields to the Picket Line," 273, 276; Rose, "Women in the United Farm Workers"; "A Look into Our Strike in Salinas," *El Malcriado,* 15 September 1970, 6; "Chavez Defies Court Order on Picketing but Escapes Arrest," *Los Angeles Times,* 10 September 1970, 3; Levy, *Cesar Chavez,* 416.

13. Bardacke, *Trampling,* 372; Ganz, *Why David Sometimes Wins,* 229; Ganz interview; Harry Bernstein, "Two Salinas Valley Growers Prepared to Sign with Chavez," *Los Angeles Times,* 30 August 1970, 26; Angel Jesus de los Santos, letter to the *Salinas Californian,* 3 September 1970, 4.

14. Bardacke, *Trampling,* 361; "Chavez Union Signs Pact with Major Vegetable Grower," *Los Angeles Times,* 31 August 1970, 3; "UFWOC Signs with Valley's Largest Lettuce Grower," *El Malcriado,* 1 September 1970, 7; Ganz interview.

15. "A Look into Our Strike in Salinas," 5; "Salad Luncheon to Aid Citizens Committee," *Salinas Californian,* 15 October 1970, 3; audiotape of anti-UFWOC rally, 1970, Tape 6, Folder 213, Box 86, Series 11, Levy Collection.

16. Ganz interview; "Chavez and the Teamsters," 429; Jerry J. Berman, "A Report on Violence in Salinas, California and Its Effects on Farm Worker Organizing," 22 September 1970, 3–4; letter to George E. Coelho from Thomas C. Lynch, 24 December 1970, 4; declaration by Lupe Ortiz, 31 August 1970; timeline of violence, 2; declaration by Francisca Aguilera, n.d.; declaration by Tomas Cadena, 9 September 1970, 1–2; declaration by Pauline Carrasco, 31 August 1970; declaration by Refugio Segura Jr., 1 September 1970; declaration by Jesus Rodriguez, 9 September 1970; and declaration by Luis Herrera and Roberto Cortez, n.d., all from Folder 48, Box 36, Part 2, UFWOP-CC Records.

17. "From Salinas—How to Handle Your UFWOC Troubles," *California Farmer,* 7 November 1970, n.p., Folder 172, Box 1, Agricultural Workers History Collection; declaration of Ramon Hernandez, 26 August 1970; declaration of Gabion Jimenez, 27 August 1970; declaration of George Otsuki, 2 September 1970; and declaration of Anna La Borde, 29 August 1970, all from Folder 15, Box 49, National Farm Worker Ministry Records.

18. Telegram to Attorney General Thomas Lynch from Cesar Chavez, Folder 48, Box 36, Part 2, UFWOP-CC Records; Berman, "A Report on Violence in Salinas," 1, 2, 12.

19. Dollie Schmidt, "Chavez Owed Vote of 'No Thanks,'" letter to the *Salinas Californian,* 5 September 1970, 4; Marjorie Cox, "Country Much Too Good to Be Abused Union Members Docked," letter to the *Salinas Californian,* 10 September 1970, 4; Bill Akers, "Anti-UFWOC Movement Launched," *Watsonville Register Pajaronian,* 14 September 1970, n.p.; "A Look into Our Strike in Salinas," 6; *Salinas*

Californian, 2 September 1970, 33; California State Advisory Committee on the United States Commission on Civil Rights, Report, "Police-Community Relations in East Los Angeles, California," October 1970, 14–18, Folder 1, Box 2, RG 453, NARA College Park; Escobar, "Dialectics of Repression," 1483–84.

20. "Chavez Terror Tactics Hit," "Reign of Terror," and "Citizens Group Holds Rally to Explain Growers' Side," *Salinas Californian,* 7 July 1970, 1; "Huge Rally Backs Growers," *Salinas Californian,* 8 September 1970, 1; Ganz interview; Ganz, "1979 Lettuce Strike," 1; "Fight in the Fields" panel, remarks by Dolores Huerta.

21. Gloria Mercado, "Only Asking for What Is Due," letter to the *Salinas Californian,* 5 September 1970, 4; Raymond Torres, "Parsons Report Proven Correct," letter to the *Salinas Californian,* 25 September 1970, 4; Stephanie Frias, "Letter to Concerned Citizens," letter to the *Salinas Californian,* 12 September 1970, 4; Jose Granados, "Keep Flags on Proper Pedestals," letter to the Editor, *Salinas Californian,* 12 September 1970, 8.

22. Pat Swafford, "Must Work Out Differences," letter to the Editor, *Salinas Californian,* 12 September 1970, 4; Jerry Braun, "Answer Lies at Conference Table," *Salinas Californian,* 12 September 1970, 4; Lena D. García, "My Valley and My Children's Valley," letter to the *Salinas Californian,* 10 October 1970, 4.

23. Gutíerrez interview; Friedrich interview; Nicolás Jr. interview.

24. Villanueva interview; Orozco interview; "Fight in the Fields" panel, remarks by Roberto Garcia.

25. Principal Cesar Chavez Tape Collection Transcript, 759cc, Folder 131, Box 1, Series 1, Levy Collection.

26. "Harden Farms," *El Malcriado,* 30 June 1966, 19.

27. Gutíerrez, *Walls and Mirrors;* Pawel, *Crusades of Cesar Chavez,* 81, 288–89.

28. Harry Bernstein, "10 Salinas Growers OK Chavez Meeting," *Los Angeles Times,* 12 September 1970, C12; Harry Bernstein, "Salinas Valley Farm Workers Dispute Easing: Some Pickets Leave as 10 Strawberry Growers Agree to Chavez Talks," *Los Angeles Times,* 12 September 1970, B1; Harry Bernstein, "Ban on Striking by Chavez Union Lifted," *Los Angeles Times,* 16 September 1970, D7; "2 Firms Ask Chavez Talks," *Los Angeles Times,* 17 September 1970, A4; Harry Bernstein, "Chavez Calls for Boycott of Lettuce Lacking Union Label," *Los Angeles Times,* 18 September 1970, 3, 24; Harry Bernstein, "Lettuce Strike Gaining Support of Other Unions," *Los Angeles Times,* 28 August 1970, 3; Bardacke, *Trampling,* 388.

29. Transcript of press conference with Cesar Chavez, 17 September 1970, 1038, Folder 153, Box 3, Levy Collection; "Boycott Scab Lettuce," *El Malcriado,* 1 October 1970, 4–5; Ganz interview; Jean Hewitt, "Here to Spur Boycott of Lettuce, Farm Workers Urge: Remember the Grape," *New York Times,* 9 October 1970, 60; "Chavez May Face Jail or Fine in Court Contempt Action," *Los Angeles Times,* 25 November 1970, A3; Levy, *Cesar Chavez,* 417; Harry Bernstein, "Another Grower Signs Contract with Chavez Union," *Los Angeles Times,* 9 October 1970, 3; Jim Stingley, "Chavez Signs 3rd Big Salinas Grower," *Los Angeles Times,* 10 October 1970, A1; "Chavez, Salinas Lettuce Grower Agree to Pact," *Los Angeles Times,* 21 November 1970, C5.

30. "Cesar Jailed, Boycott Goes On," *El Malcriado*, 15 December 1970, 3; "Chavez Jailed for Contempt," *Watsonville Register-Pajaronian*, 4 December 1970, n.p.; Bardacke, *Trampling*, 389; Paul Booth, "Farm Workers Call for Lettuce Boycott," New University Conference Newsletter, Vol. 4, No. 7, 20 December 1970, 6–7, Folder 46, Box 1, Agricultural Workers History Collection.

31. Ganz interview; "Farm Workers Hold 500-Hour Vigil for Cesar," *El Malcriado*, 1 January 1971, 5.

32. "Anti-Chavez Pickets Boo Mrs. Robert Kennedy," *New York Times*, 7 December 1970, 57; "Joins March to Jail: Ethel Kennedy Visits Chavez," *Los Angeles Times*, 7 December 1970, A3; Brazil interview; Harry Bernstein, "Jailing of Chavez May Rally Support for Lettuce Boycott," *Los Angeles Times*, 6 December 1970, B, 20; Santoro, *If You Got the Guts*, 35; Coretta King, speech transcript, 19 December 1970, 2–3, Folder 458, Box 21, Levy Collection; Araiza, *To March for Others*, 108.

33. "Jailed Three Weeks: Chavez Set Free," *Los Angeles Times*, 24 December 1970, 1; Eric Brazil, "State Court Lets Chavez Out of Jail," *Salinas Californian*, 24 December 1970, 1; Street, *Everyone Had Cameras*, 471. In 1972 the California Supreme Court ruled that employers who grant exclusive bargaining status to labor organizations that they know do not actually represent a substantial number of their workers may not obtain injunctive relief against a competing union.

CONCLUSION: THE FARMWORKER JUSTICE MOVEMENT

1. Cesar Chavez, "Why the Farm Labor Act Isn't Working," *Los Angeles Times*, 17 November 1975, B7; "Growers Fight Back," *El Malcriadito*, n.d., 1, Folder 10, Box 2, Farm Worker Organizing Collection; Richard Steven Street, "UFW's March for Justice: The Lettuce Strike Story," *Nation*, 19 January 1980, 47; Shaw, *Beyond the Fields*, 260–61.

2. Pawel, *Crusades of Cesar Chavez*, 150; Bardacke, *Trampling*, 721.

3. Bardacke, *Trampling*, 2, 490.

4. Frank Bardacke, "Decline and Fall of the UFW: Cesar's Ghost," *Nation*, 26 July/2 August 1993, 130; Kousser, "Racial Injustice," 56; Susan Krohn, "Workers Housed in Caves," *Modesto Bee*, 22 June 1987, B-4; Marcus B. Brown, California Rural Legal Assistance open letter, 31 March 1986, Folder 37, Box 4, Huerta Papers.

5. "Latin League Asking Probe of City Police," unnamed author and newspaper, 20 September 1974, Binder "News and Other Docs. Crimes Vol. 12," Box 4, Lopez v. Monterey County Collection; Geron, *Latino Political Power*, 167–69, 175, 177, 184; County of Monterey web page, Simón Salinas biography, www.co.monterey.ca.us/d3_supervisor.htm; Geron, *Latino Political Power*, 163; Camarillo, "Cities of Color."

6. Pitti, "Bracero Justice"; "Braceros: History, Compensation"; Camille T. Taiara, "Pay Dirt: Mexican Farmworkers Look for Money Owed After 60 Years," *San Francisco Bay Guardian*, 17 July 2002, www.sfbg.com/36/42/news_dirt.html; *Bracero Stories*; Uribe, "Guest Worker Programs"; Lorena Figueroa, "Mexican Braceros to U.S.: Open Bracero Program's Files," *El Paso Times*, 20 February 2014, www.elpasotimes.com/news/ci_25186147/mexican-braceros-want-their-money.

7. M. Cristina Medina, "Gathering Remembers Bracero Crash Victims," *Monterey Herald* online, 18 September 2005, www.montereyherald.com/mld/montereyherald/news/12679216.htm; "Full Speed Ahead on Bill for a Bracero Memorial Highway," *Salinas Californian*, 7 August 2010, www.thecalifornian.com/article/20100807/OPINION01/8070301/1014/OPINION/Editorial-Full-speed-ahead-on-bill-for-a-Bracero-Memorial-Highway; Todd R. Brown, "What Many Hands Do" and "Racist Reactions to Bracero Talk," blog entries, 24 February 2009, http://tantrapantry.blogspot.com/20090201archive.html; Todd R. Brown, "Salinas Mural Celebrates Bracero Labor: Alisal District Office Project Teaches 'What Many Hands Do,'" *Salinas Californian*, 24 February 2009, www.thecalifornian.com/article/20090224/NEWS01/90224001/1002.

8. Fitzgerald, "Mexican Migration and the Law," 188; Global Workers Justice Alliance, "Visa Pages," www.globalworkers.org/visa-pages; Cindy Hahamovitch, "Protecting Immigrant Farm Workers," *Miami Herald*, 13 March 2013, www.miamiherald.com/2013/03/13/v-fullstory/3284165/protecting-immigrant-farm-workers.html.

9. Ganz, *Why David Sometimes Wins*, 239; López, "From the Farms," 250, 345; Hansen and Donohoe, "Health Issues," 156; López, *Farmworkers' Journey*, 130, 133–34; Austin, "Struggle for Health," 203; Centers for Disease Control and Prevention, "Pesticide Exposure Tracking," http://ephtracking.cdc.gov/showPesticideTracking.action. Studies of contemporary farmworker conditions include Estabrook, *Tomatoland*; Holmes, *Fresh Fruit, Broken Bodies*; and Gray, *Labor and the Locavore*.

10. Overmyer-Velázquez, "Histories and Historiographies," xxxix; Marrow, "Race and the New Southern Migration," 30; Massey, Durand, and Malone, *Beyond Smoke and Mirrors*, 93; Zavella, *"I'm Neither Here nor There,"* 32–33.

11. Marrow, "Race and the New Southern Migration," 131; Massey, "Epilogue," 259, 263; Zavella, *"I'm Neither Here nor There,"* x; Overmyer-Velázquez, "Histories and Historiographies," xxi, xliv.

12. Chavez, *Latino Threat*.

13. Zong and Batalova, "Frequently Released Statistics on Immigrants and Immigration"; C. Kelly Nix, "Monterey County No. 1 in Illegal Immigrants," *Carmel Pine Cone*, 29 July 2011, www.pineconearchive.com/110729-3.htm; Claudia Meléndez Salinas, "Monterey, San Benito Counties Have Highest Percentage of Undocumented Immigrants in State," *Santa Cruz Sentinel*, 2 August 2011, www.santacruzsentinel.com/localnews/ci_18602889; Carolyn Marshall, "Proposed Ban on Taco Trucks Stirs Animosity in a California Town," *New York Times*, 15 June 2007, www.nytimes.com/2007/06/15/us/15taco.html; Gosia Wozniacka, "Latino-Indigenous Divide Stirs California Town," Associated Press, 15 August 2011, www.thonline.com/news/national_world/article_8a411feb-76fc-5bfe-b914-72c7e27fd169.html?mode=story.

14. Garcia, *Rise of the Mexican American Middle Class*, 313.

Bibliography

INTERVIEWS

Unless otherwise noted, interviews were conducted by the author.

Alvarez, Catalina. 28 July 2008, Salinas, California.

Ames, Robert. 30 September 2008, Salinas, California.

Amyx, Leon K. Conducted by Pauline Pearson. 30 March 1981, Salinas, California. Oral History Collection, Steinbeck Public Library.

Bomer, Betty. Conducted by Pauline Pearson. 20 November 1980, Salinas, California. Oral History Collection, Steinbeck Public Library.

Bond, Frank. Conducted by Pauline Pearson. 19 July 1980, Salinas, California. Oral History Collection, Steinbeck Public Library.

Brazil, Eric. 13 September 2009, Sacramento, California.

Chapa, Sonia. 2 June 2013, Monterey, California.

Chávez, Anna. Conducted by the CSO Oral History Project, University of California, San Diego, undated.

Crawford, Peter. 28 October 2012, telephone interview. Name changed.

De Young, Fred. Conducted by Kristine Navarro. 28 July 2005, Salinas, California. Bracero History Archive.

Friedrich, Robert. 11 June 2012, telephone interview.

Ganz, Marshall. 5 September 2009, Los Altos, California.

Glick, Martin. 24 September 2009, San Francisco, California.

Gnaizda, Robert. 19 July 2009, San Francisco, California.

Gómez, Ignacio. Conducted by Mireya Loza. 28 July 2005, Salinas, California. Bracero History Archive.

Gutíerrez, Sally. 1 July 2009, Salinas, California.

Gutíerrez McQuinn, Sally. Conducted by Steve Velásquez. 28 July 2005, Salinas, California.

Hollis, Gary. 28 June 2009, telephone interview. Name changed.

Ledesma, Frank. Conducted by Alex Zermeño, CSO Oral History Project, University of California, San Diego, undated.

López Jr., Ben. 29 September 2008, Salinas, California.

López Sr., Ben. Conducted by George Robinson. 1 December 1976, Salinas, California. Oral History Collection, Steinbeck Public Library.

López, Sabino. 1 September 2009, Salinas, California.

López, Sabino. Conducted by Rachel Goodman, Salinas, California. "The Boomtown Chronicles: Reflections on a Changing California." Undated transcript. http://coastridge.org/boomtown/transcripts/Sabino-Lopez.pdf.

Martínez, Chris. 14 September 2008, telephone interview.

Martínez, Julianna. 28 June 2012, Salinas, California.

Maturino, Pete. 28 June 2012, Salinas, California.

Mesplé, Frank. Conducted by James H. Rowland. 29 September 1978. Regional Oral History Office, Bancroft Library, University of California at Berkeley.

Montaño, Luis. 29 July 2008, telephone interview.

Montero, George. Conducted by Pauline Pearson. 30 March 1981, Salinas, California. Oral History Collection, Steinbeck Public Library.

Mueller, Annette, and Jack Ferrasci. 11 November 2009, Salinas, California.

Nelson, Walter O. Conducted by Pauline Pearson. 18 April 1981, Salinas, California. Oral History Collection, Steinbeck Public Library.

Nicolás Jr., Ismael. 9 April 2014, telephone interview.

Nicolás Osorio, Ismael Z. Conducted by Leti Bocanegra. 28 July 2005, Salinas, California. Bracero History Archive.

Nicolás Osorio, Ismael Z. 2 October 2008, Salinas, California.

Orozco, José L. Conducted by Mireya Loza. 28 July 2005, Salinas, California. Bracero History Archive.

Pérez, Pedro de Real. Conducted by Mireya Loza. 28 July 2005, Salinas, California. Bracero History Archive.

Ramírez, Isidoro. Conducted by Steve Velásquez. 13 July 2005, San Jose, California. Bracero History Archive.

Saldívar, Annie. 30 July 2008, telephone interview.

Sánchez, Cecilia. Conducted by the CSO Oral History Project, University of California, San Diego, undated.

Santoro, Joan. 29 June 2009, Salinas, California.

Villanueva, Ray. 7 September 2008, Salinas, California.

Young, Bertram N. Conducted by Pauline Pearson. 2 February 1981, Salinas California. Oral History Collection. Steinbeck Public Library.

Zarazua, Aquilino. 28 July 2008, Salinas, California.

Zepeda, Audómaro G. Conducted by Mireya Loza. 28 July 2005, Salinas, California. Bracero History Archive.

Zermeño, Alex. 28 July 2009, Woodland, California.

Zermeño, Alex. CSO Oral History Project, University of California, San Diego, undated.

NEWSPAPERS AND PERIODICALS

American GI Forum News Bulletin
Business Week
Carmel Pine Cone
Commonweal
Corpus Christi Caller-Times
Daily News
East Bay Labor Journal
Economist
El Espectador
El Imparcial
El Malcriado
El Observador
El Paso Times
Fort Ord Panorama
Greenfield News
Hollister Enterprise
Honey Dew News
Hoy
King City Rustler Herald
Lodi News-Sentinel
Los Angeles Mirror
Los Angeles Times
Miami Herald
Modesto Bee
Monterey County Herald
Monterey Democrat
Monterey Peninsula Herald
The Nation
Newsweek
New York Times
Novedades

Oakland Tribune
The Register
Salinas Californian
Salinas Daily Index
Salinas Daily Journal
Salinas Daily Post
Salinas Index-Journal
Salinas Weekly Index
Salinas Weekly Journal
San Francisco Chronicle
San Francisco Examiner
San Jose Evening News
San Jose Mercury News
Santa Clara County AFL-CIO Union Gazette
Santa Cruz Sentinel
Wall Street Journal
Washington Post
Washington Post and Times Herald
Watsonville Register Pajaronian
Weekly Herald

ARCHIVAL SOURCES

Agricultural Workers History Collection. Walter P. Reuther Library, Wayne State University.

Agricultural Workers Organizing Committee (AWOC) Records. Walter P. Reuther Library, Wayne State University.

Beard (Samuel N.) Papers, 1929–1968. Special Collections and Archives, University of California at Santa Cruz.

Bracero History Archive. www.braceroarchive.org.

Bracero Letters Collection, 1943. Department of Special Collections, Stanford University.

Civil Rights Congress Collection, Los Angeles, late 1940s–1950s. Southern California Library for Social Studies and Research, Los Angeles, California.

Corona (Bert N.) Papers, Department of Special Collections, Stanford University.

Cruz (Ricardo). Católicos por la Raza Papers. Special Collections, University of California at Santa Barbara.

El Malcriado Collection. Department of Special Collections, Stanford University.

Farm Worker Organizing Collection, Southern California Library for Social Studies and Research, Los Angeles, California.

Ford (John Anson) Papers, 1928–1971. Manuscripts Department, Huntington Library.

Galarza (Ernesto) Papers, 1936–1984. Department of Special Collections, Stanford University.

Gallegos (Herman) Papers. Department of Special Collections, Stanford University.

Garcia (Clotilde) Papers. Benson Latin American Collection, The University of Texas at Austin.

Huerta (Dolores) Papers. Walter P. Reuther Library, Wayne State University.

Idar Jr. (Eduardo) Papers. Benson Latin American Collection, The University of Texas at Austin.

Farmworker Movement Documentation Project. Presented by the UC San Diego Library. https://libraries.ucsd.edu/farmworkermovement.

Jacques E. Levy Research Collection on Cesar Chavez. Beinecke Rare Book and Manuscript Library, Yale University.

Local History Collection. Steinbeck Public Library, Salinas, California.

Lopez v. Monterey County Collection, 1855–1991. Department of Special Collections, Stanford University.

McWilliams (Carey) Papers, 1921–1980. Bancroft Library, University of California at Berkeley.

Monterey County Agricultural Housing Photo Binders. Monterey County Agricultural and Rural Life Museum, King City, California.

Monterey County Naturalization Records. Salinas Courthouse, Salinas, California.

Monterey County Recorder's Office, Salinas, California.

National Archives and Records Administration, College Park, Maryland.
   Records of the Commission on Civil Rights (RG 453)
   Records of the Department of Labor (RG 174)
   Records of the Federal Housing Administration (RG 31)
   Records of Foreign Service Posts of the Department of State (RG 84)
   Records of the Office of the Secretary of Agriculture (RG 16)

National Archives and Records Administration, San Bruno, California.
   Records of the Department of Labor (RG 174)
   Records of the Immigration and Naturalization Service (RG 85), San Francisco District Office, Salinas Sub-Office

National Archives and Records Administration, Washington, D.C.
   Records of the Immigration and Naturalization Service (RG 85).

National Farm Worker Ministry Records. Walter P. Reuther Library, Wayne State University.

Newspaper Clipping Collection, California Room, Monterey Public Library, Monterey, California.

Oral History Collection. Steinbeck Public Library, Salinas, California.

Quevedo (Eduardo) Papers. Department of Special Collections, Stanford University.

Ross (Fred) Papers. Department of Special Collections, Stanford University.

Roth (Raymond) Papers. Department of Special Collections, University of California at Davis.

Roybal (Edward) Papers, 1947–1962. Department of Special Collections, Charles E. Young Research Library, University of California at Los Angeles.

Ruiz (Manuel) Papers. Department of Special Collections, Stanford University.

Salinas City Council Minutes, 1940–1970. Salinas City Hall, Salinas, California.

Samora (Julian) Papers. Benson Latin American Collection, The University of Texas at Austin.

Sanchez (George I.) Papers, Benson Latin American Collection, The University of Texas at Austin.

Sanchez (R. P.) Papers, Benson Latin American Collection, The University of Texas at Austin.

Soto (Anthony) Papers. Department of Special Collections, Stanford University.

Steinbeck Public Library, Salinas, California.

Steiner (Stan) Papers. Department of Special Collections, Stanford University.

Superior Court of California Records, Monterey County, Monterey County Superior Courthouse, Monterey, California.

UFW Office of the President: Cesar Chavez Records, Walter P. Reuther Library, Wayne State University.

Vizzard (James) Papers. Department of Special Collections, Stanford University.

PUBLISHED AND UNPUBLISHED SOURCES

Alamillo, José. *Making Lemonade Out of Lemons: Mexican American Labor and Leisure in a California Town, 1880–1960*. Urbana: University of Illinois Press, 2006.

Almirol, Edwin B. *Ethnic Identity and Social Negotiation: A Study of a Filipino Community in California*. New York: AMS Press, 1985.

Alvarez, Luis. *The Power of the Zoot: Youth Culture and Resistance During World War II*. Berkeley: University of California Press, 2009.

American G.I. Forum and Texas State Federation of Labor, *What Price Wetbacks?* Austin: The Forum, 1953.

Anderson, Burton. *America's Salad Bowl: An Agricultural History of the Salinas Valley.* Salinas: Monterey County Historical Society, 2000.

Anderson, Henry P. *The Bracero Program in California.* Manchester: Ayer, 1976.

Andre, Dick, ed. *Hartnell: The First 70 Years, 1920–1990.* Salinas: Hartnell College, 1990.

Apodaca, Maria Linda. "They Kept the Home Fires Burning: Mexican-American Women and Social Change." Ph.D. diss., University of California, Irvine, 1994.

Araiza, Lauren. *To March for Others: The Black Freedom Struggle and the United Farm Workers.* Philadelphia: University of Pennsylvania Press, 2014.

Austin, Colin. "The Struggle for Health in Times of Plenty," in Charles D. Thompson Jr. and Melinda F. Wiggins, eds., *Human Cost of Food: Farmworkers' Lives, Labor, and Advocacy.* Austin: University of Texas Press, 2002, 198–218.

Avila, Eric. *Popular Culture in the Age of White Flight: Fear and Fantasy in Suburban Los Angeles.* Berkeley: University of California Press, 2006.

Azuma, Eiichiro. *Between Two Empires: Race, History, and Transnationalism in Japanese America.* Oxford: Oxford University Press, 2005.

Balderrama, Francisco, and Raymond Rodriguez. *Decade of Betrayal: Mexican Repatriation in the 1930s.* Albuquerque: University of New Mexico Press, 1995.

Baldoz, Rick. *The Third Asiatic Invasion: Empire and Migration in Filipino America, 1898–1946.* New York: New York University Press, 2011.

Barajas, Frank. *Curious Unions: Mexican American Workers and Resistance in Oxnard, California, 1898–1961.* Lincoln: University of Nebraska Press, 2012.

Bardacke, Frank. *Trampling Out the Vintage: Cesar Chavez and the Two Souls of the United Farm Workers.* London: Verso, 2011.

Basurto, L., C. D. Delorme Jr., and D. R. Kamerschen. "Rent Seeking, the Bracero Program, and Current Mexican Farm Labor Policy." *International Economic Journal* 15, No. 1 (Spring 2001): 21–40.

Bernstein, Shana. *Bridges of Reform: Interracial Civil Rights Activism in Twentieth Century Los Angeles.* Oxford: Oxford University Press, 2010.

———. "From California to the Nation: Rethinking the History of 20th Century U.S. Civil Rights Struggles Through a Mexican American and Multiracial Lens." *La Raza Law Journal* 18 (2007): 87–95.

———. "Interracial Activism in the Los Angeles Community Service Organization: Linking the World War II and Civil Rights Eras." *Pacific Historical Review* 80, No. 2 (May 2011): 231–67.

Biography of Alex Zermeño. Community Service Organization, Organizers. www.csoproject.org/Organizers.html#AZ.

Biography of Simon Salinas. County of Monterey. www.co.monterey.ca.us/d3_supervisor.htm.

"Braceros: History, Compensation." *Rural Migration News,* Vol. 12, No. 2 (April 2006). http://migration.ucdavis.edu/rmn/more.php?id=1112_0_4_0.

Bracero Stories. Directed by Patrick Mullins. Cherry Lane Productions, El Paso, 2008.

Breschini, Gary S., Mona Gudgel, and Trudy Haversat. *Early Salinas.* Images of America series. Charleston: Arcadia, 2005.

Brief, *Wetherton, et al. v. Martin Produce, Inc., et al.,* No. 63696, Superior Court, Monterey County, filed 25 August 1967.

Brilliant, Mark. *"The Color of America Has Changed": How Racial Diversity Shaped Civil Rights Reform in California.* Oxford: Oxford University Press, 2010.

Burkett, Lynn. "The Okies? Why They're Some of Salinas' Best Citizens." Master's thesis, University of California at Santa Cruz, 1978.

Burt, Kenneth C. *The Search for a Civic Voice: California Latino Politics.* Claremont: Regina Books, 2007.

Calavita, Kitty. *Inside the State: The Bracero Program, Immigration, and the I.N.S.* New York: Routledge, 1992.

Camacho, Alicia Schmidt. *Migrant Imaginaries: Latino Cultural Politics in the U.S. Mexico Borderlands.* New York: New York University Press, 2008.

Camarillo, Albert. *Chicanos in a Changing Society: From Mexican Pueblos to American Barrios in Santa Barbara and Southern California, 1848–1930.* Cambridge: Harvard University Press, 1979.

———. *Chicanos in California: A History of Mexican Americans in California.* San Francisco: Boyd & Fraser, 1984.

———. "Cities of Color: The New Racial Frontier in California's Minority-Majority Cities." *Pacific Historical Review* 76, No. 1 (February 2007): 1–28.

Carrigan, William D., and Clive Webb. *Forgotten Dead: Mob Violence Against Mexicans in the United States, 1848–1928.* Oxford: Oxford University Press, 2013.

———. "The Lynching of Persons of Mexican Origin or Descent in the United States, 1848 to 1928." *Journal of Social History* 37, No. 2 (2003): 411–38.

Casas, María Raquél. *Married to a Daughter of the Land: Spanish-Mexican Women and Interethnic Marriage in California, 1820–1880.* Reno: University of Nevada Press, 2007.

Centers for Disease Control and Prevention, "Pesticide Exposure Tracking," 25 July 2014, http://ephtracking.cdc.gov/showPesticideTracking.action.

Chávez, Ernesto. *"¡Mi Raza Primero!" (My People First!): Nationalism, Identity, and Insurgency in the Chicano Movement in Los Angeles, 1966–1978.* Berkeley: University of California Press, 2002.

Chavez, Leo. *The Latino Threat: Constructing Immigrants, Citizens, and the Nation.* Stanford: Stanford University Press, 2008.

City of Salinas. *2007–2009 Salinas Valley Business and Community Profile.* Steinbeck Public Library, Salinas, California.

Clovis, Margaret E., and the Monterey County Agricultural and Rural Life Museum. *Salinas Valley.* Images of America series. Charleston: Arcadia, 2005.

Cohen, Deborah. *Braceros: Migrant Citizens and Transnational Subjects in the Postwar United States and Mexico.* Chapel Hill: University of North Carolina Press, 2011.

———. "Caught in the Middle: The Mexican State's Relationship with the United States and Its Own Citizen Workers, 1942–1954." *Journal of American Ethnic History* 20, No. 3 (2001): 110–32.

Community Service Organization (CSO) History Project. www.csoproject.org/.

Congressional Record, Proceedings and Debates of the 88th Congress, First Sess., 16 October 1963. Vol. 190, No. 166, Washington, D.C.

Cosecha Triste (Harvest of Loneliness). Directed by Gilbert G. González and Vivian Price. Films Media Group, 2010.

Creagan, James F. "Public Law 78: A Tangle of Domestic and International Relations." *Journal of Inter-American Studies* 7, No. 4 (October 1965): 541–56.

Deverell, William. *Whitewashed Adobe: The Rise of Los Angeles and the Remaking of Its Mexican Past.* Berkeley: University of California Press, 2005.

Dewitt, Howard A. "The Filipino Labor Union: The Salinas Lettuce Strike of 1934." *Amerasian* 5, No. 2 (1978): 1–21.

———. *Violence in the Fields: California Filipino Farm Labor Unionization During the Great Depression.* Saratoga: Century Twenty One, 1980.

Escobar, Edward J. "The Dialectics of Repression: The Los Angeles Police Department and the Chicano Movement, 1968–1971." *Journal of American History* 79, No. 4 (March 1993): 1483–514.

———. *Race, Police, and the Making of a Political Identity: Mexican Americans and the Los Angeles Police Department, 1900–1945.* Berkeley: University of California Press, 1999.

Escobedo, Elizabeth Rachel. "The Pachuca Panic: Sexual and Cultural Battlegrounds in World War II Los Angeles." *Western Historical Quarterly* 38, No. 2 (2007): 133–56.

Estabrook, Barry. *Tomatoland: How Modern Industrial Agriculture Destroyed Our Most Alluring Fruit.* Kansas City: Andrews McMeel, 2011.

Fernandez, Celestino, and James E. Officer. "The Lighter Side of Mexican Immigration: Humor and Satire in the Mexican Corrido." *Journal of the Southwest* 31, No. 4 (Winter 1989): 471–96.

Ferriss, Susan, and Ricardo Sandoval, eds. *The Fight in the Fields: Cesar Chavez and the Farmworkers Movement.* New York: Harcourt Brace, 1997.

"The Fight in the Fields" panel. 31 May 2009. Steinbeck Public Library, Salinas, California.

Fisher, Anne B. *The Salinas, Upside Down River.* New York: Farrar and Rinehart, 1945.

Fitzgerald, David. "Mexican Migration and the Law," in Mark Overmyer-Velázquez, ed., *Beyond La Frontera: The History of Mexico-U.S. Migration.* Oxford: Oxford University Press, 2011, 179–203.

Galarza, Ernesto. *Farm Workers and Agri-business in California, 1947–60.* Notre Dame: University of Notre Dame Press, 1977.

———. *Merchants of Labor: The Mexican Bracero Story: An Account of the Managed Migration of Mexican Farm Workers in California 1942–1960.* San Jose: Rosicrucian Press, 1964.

———. *Spiders in the House and Workers in the Field.* Notre Dame: University of Notre Dame Press, 1970.

———. *Tragedy at Chualar: El Crucero de las Treinta y Dos Cruces.* Santa Barbara: McNally & Loftin, West, 1977.

Galarza, Ernesto, Herman Gallegos, and Julian Samora. *Mexican-Americans in the Southwest.* Santa Barbara: McNally & Loftin, 1969.

Gamboa, Ernesto. *Mexican Labor and World War II: Braceros in the Pacific Northwest, 1942–1947.* Seattle: University of Washington Press, 2000; 1st ed. Austin: University of Texas Press, 1990.

Ganz, Marshall. "The 1979 Lettuce Strike." Summary of Marshall Ganz's Report to the National Farm Worker Ministry Board in Salinas, California, 5/15/79. NFWM, July 1979. https://libraries.ucsd.edu/farmworkermovement/essays/essays/MillerArchive/062%20The%201979%20Lettuce%20Strike.pdf.

———. *Why David Sometimes Wins: Leadership, Organization, and Strategy in the California Farm Worker Movement.* Oxford: Oxford University Press, 2010.

Garcia, Juan Ramon. *Operation Wetback: The Mass Deportation of Mexican Undocumented Workers in 1954.* Westport: Greenwood, 1980.

Garcia, Matt. "Cain Contra Abel: Courtship, Masculinities, and Citizenship in Southern California, 1942–1964," in James Campbell, Matthew Guterl, and Robert Lee, eds., *Race, Nation and Empire in American History*. Chapel Hill: University of North Carolina Press, 2007.

———. *From the Jaws of Victory: The Triumph and Tragedy of Cesar Chavez and the Farm Worker Movement*. Berkeley: University of California Press, 2012.

———. "Intraethnic Conflict and the Bracero Program During World War II," in Donna R. Gabaccia and Vicki L. Ruiz, eds., *American Dreaming, Global Realities: Rethinking U.S. Immigration History*. Urbana: University of Illinois Press, 2006.

———. *A World of Its Own: Race, Labor, and Citrus in the Making of Greater Los Angeles, 1900–1970*. Chapel Hill: University of North Carolina Press, 2001.

Garcia, Richard A. *Rise of the Mexican American Middle Class: San Antonio, 1929–1941*. College Station: Texas A&M University Press, 1991.

García y Griego, Manuel. "The Importation of Mexican Contract Laborers into the United States, 1942–1965," in David G. Gutiérrez, ed., *Between Two Worlds: Mexican Immigrants in the United States*. Wilmington: Scholarly Resources, 1996, 45–85.

"Gender in the CSO" panel. CSO Reunion Conference, 17 November 2008, Asilomar, California.

Geron, Kim. *Latino Political Power*. Boulder: Lynne Rienner, 2005.

Gilmore, N. Ray, and Gladys W. Gilmore. "The Bracero in California." *Pacific Historical Review* 32, No. 3 (August 1963): 265–82.

Glass, Judith Chanin. "Conditions Which Facilitate Unionization of Agricultural Workers: A Case Study of the Salinas Valley Lettuce Industry." Ph.D. diss., University of California at Los Angeles, 1966.

———. "Organization in Salinas: Technological Changes Providing a More Structured Market Facilitate Unionization Among Fieldworkers in the Lettuce Industry of California." *Monthly Labor Review*, June 1968, 24–27.

Global Workers Justice Alliance. "Visa Pages: U.S. Temporary Foreign Worker Visas," 2010, www.globalworkers.org/visa-pages.

Goldstein-Shirley, David. "Story and History: Rural Asian California Around 1940." *Australasian Journal of American Studies* 14, No. 1 (July 1995): 1–14.

Gonzales-Day, Ken. *Lynching in the West: 1850–1935*. Durham: Duke University Press, 2006.

González, Gilbert. *Guest Workers or Colonized Labor? Mexican Labor Migration to the United States*. Boulder: Paradigm, 2006.

———. *Labor and Community: Mexican Citrus Worker Villages in a Southern California County, 1900–1950*. Urbana: University of Illinois Press, 1994.

———. *Mexican Consuls and Labor Organizing: Imperial Politics in the American Southwest*. Austin: University of Texas Press, 1999.

———. "Mexican Labor Migration, 1876–1924," in Mark Overmyer-Velázquez, ed., *Beyond La Frontera: The History of Mexico-U.S. Migration*. Oxford: Oxford University Press, 2011, 28–50.

Gordon, Anna Pegler. *In Sight of America: Photography and the Development of U.S. Immigration Policy*. Berkeley: University of California Press, 2009.

Gordon, Robert. "Poisons in the Fields: The United Farm Workers, Pesticides, and Environmental Politics." *Pacific Historical Review* 68, No. 1 (February 1999): 51–77.

Gray, Margaret. *Labor and the Locavore: The Making of a Comprehensive Food Ethic*. Berkeley: University of California Press, 2014.

Gregory, James. *American Exodus: The Dust Bowl Migration and Okie Culture in California*. Oxford: Oxford University Press, 1989.

Griffith, Beatrice. *American Me*. Boston: Houghton-Mifflin, 1948.

Grower Profiles of Bruce Church, Russ Merrill, Gene Harden, and Bud Antle. Program of the 2005 Valley of the World Awards, National Steinbeck Center, Salinas, California, 9 June 2005.

Guerin-Gonzales, Camille. "The International Migration of Workers and Segmented Labor: Mexican Immigrant Workers in California Industrial Agriculture, 1900–1940," in Camille Guerin Gonzales and Carl Strikwerda, eds., *The Politics of Immigrant Workers: Labor Activism and Migration in the World Economy Since 1830*. New York: Holmes & Meier, 1993.

———. *Mexican Workers and American Dreams: Immigration, Repatriation, and California Farm Labor, 1900–1939*. New Brunswick: Rutgers University Press, 1994.

Guglielmo, Thomas. "Fighting for Caucasian Rights: Mexicans, Mexican Americans, and the Transnational Struggle for Civil Rights in World War II Texas." *Journal of American History* 92 No. 4 (March 2006): 1212–37.

Guilbault, Rose Castillo. *Farmworker's Daughter: Growing Up Mexican in America*. Berkeley: Heyday, 2005.

Guinn, J. M. *History and Biographical Record of Monterey and San Benito Counties and History of the State of California Containing Biographies of Well-Known Citizens of the Past and Present*. Los Angeles: Historic Record, 1910. Monterey Public Library, California Room, Monterey, California.

Gutiérrez, David. *Walls and Mirrors: Mexican Americans, Mexican Immigrants, and the Politics of Ethnicity in the Southwest 1910–1986*. Berkeley: University of California Press, 1995.

Gutiérrez, José Angel. "Chicanos and Mexicans Under Surveillance: 1940 to 1980." Renato Rosaldo Lecture Series Monograph 2, Spring 1986, 28–57.

Haas, Lisbeth. *Conquests and Historical Identities in California, 1769–1936.* Berkeley: University of California Press, 1996.

Hansen, Eric, and Martin Donohoe. "Health Issues of Migrant and Seasonal Farmworkers." *Journal of Health Care for the Poor and Underserved* 14, No. 2 (May 2003): 153–64.

"Hector de la Rosa, Sr.—The Man Who Changed His World." Biographical packet given to the author by Hector de la Rosa.

Heidenreich, Linda. *"This Land Was Mexican Once": Histories of Resistance from Northern California.* Austin: University of Texas Press, 2007.

Hernández, Kelly Lytle. "The Crimes and Consequences of Illegal Immigration: A Cross-Border Examination of Operation Wetback, 1943 to 1954." *Western Historical Quarterly* 37, No. 4 (2006): 421–44.

———. *Migra! A History of the U.S. Border Patrol.* Berkeley: University of California Press, 2010.

Hoffman, Abraham. *Unwanted Mexican Americans in the Great Depression: Repatriation Pressures, 1929–1939.* Tucson: University of Arizona Press, 1973.

Holmes, Seth. *Fresh Fruit, Broken Bodies: Migrant Farmworkers in the United States.* Berkeley: University of California Press, 2013.

Hull Jr., Frank Leroy. "The Effects of Braceros on the Agricultural Labor Market in California 1950–1970: Public Law 78 and Its Aftermath." Ph.D. diss., University of Illinois at Urbana-Champaign, 1973.

Ichioka, Yuji. "Japanese Immigrant Response to the 1920 California Alien Land Law." *Agricultural History* 58, No. 2 (April 1984): 157–78.

In the Court of Appeal of the State of California, First Appellate District, Division Four. Fred Wetherton, John Watson, Jesus Robles, Jose Perez, Manuel Ortiz, Domingo Longoria, Anthony Cervantes, Antonio Castaneda, Ignacio Burgos, Plaintiffs and Appellants, vs. Growers Farm Labor Association, Grower Shipper Vegetable Association, E. James Houseberg, Defendants and Respondents. No. 1/Civil 25822. 23 January 1968 and 28 July 1969.

Jacobo, Jose-Rodolfo. *Los Braceros: Memories of Bracero Workers 1942–1964.* San Diego: Southern Border Press, 2004.

Jamieson, Stuart Marshall. *Labor Unionism in American Agriculture: American Farmers and the Rise of Agribusiness.* New York: Arno, 1975.

Jenkins, J. Craig. *The Politics of Insurgency: The Farm Worker Movement in the 1960s.* New York: Columbia University Press, 1985.

Jensen, Richard J., and John C. Hammerback. *The Words of Cesar Chavez.* College Station: Texas A&M University Press, 2002.

Jimenez, Tomás. *Replenished Ethnicity: Mexican Americans, Immigration, and Identity.* Berkeley: University of California Press, 2009.

Johnston, Robert B. *Salinas, 1875–1950: From Village to City.* Fidelity Savings and Loan Association in Cooperation with the Monterey County Historical Society, 1980.

Jones, William Orville. "The Salinas Valley: Its Agricultural Development, 1920–40." Ph.D. diss., Stanford University, 1947.

Kelley, Robin. *Race Rebels: Culture, Politics, and the Black Working Class.* New York: Free Press, 1996.

Kim, Joon K. "The Political Economy of the Mexican Farm Labor Program, 1942–64." *Aztlán* 29, No. 2 (Fall 2004): 13–53.

Kousser, J. Morgan. "Racial Injustice and the Abolition of Justice Courts in Monterey County," 9 September 2000. www.hss.caltech.edu/~kousser/redistricting/Racial%20Injustice.pdf.

Kropp, Phoebe. *California Vieja: Culture and Memory in a Modern American Place.* Berkeley: University of California Press, 2008.

Lee, Wellington. *Salinas Chinatown Memories.* Self-published for Steinbeck Public Library.

Leonard, Karen B. *Making Ethnic Choices: California's Punjabi Mexican Americans.* Philadelphia: Temple University Press, 1992.

Levy, Jacques E. *Cesar Chavez: Autobiography of La Causa.* New York: W. W. Norton, 1975.

Lipsitz, George. *Rainbow at Midnight: Labor and Culture in the 1940s.* Urbana: University of Illinois Press, 1994.

López, Ann Aurelia. *The Farmworkers' Journey.* Berkeley: University of California Press, 2007.

———. "From the Farms of West Central Mexico to California's Corporate Agribusiness: The Social Transformation of Two Binational Farming Regions." Ph.D. diss., University of California Santa Cruz, 2002.

Loza, Mireya. "Braceros on the Boundaries: Activism, Race, Masculinity, and the Legacies of the Bracero Program." Ph.D. diss., Brown University, 2011.

Lui, Mary Ting Yi. *The Chinatown Trunk Mystery: Murder, Miscegenation, and Other Dangerous Encounters in Turn-of-the-Century New York City.* Princeton: Princeton University Press, 2007.

Mariscal, Jorge. *Aztlán and Viet Nam: Chicano and Chicana Experiences of the War.* Berkeley: University of California Press, 1999.

Márquez, Benjamin. *LULAC: The Evolution of a Mexican-American Political Organization.* Austin: University of Texas Press, 1993.

Marrow, Helen B. "Race and the New Southern Migration, 1986 to the Present," in Mark Overmyer-Velázquez, ed., *Beyond La Frontera: The History of Mexico-U.S. Migration.* Oxford: Oxford University Press, 2011, 125–60.

Massey, Douglas. "Epilogue: The Past and Future of Mexico-U.S. Migration," in Mark Overmyer-Velázquez, ed., *Beyond La Frontera: The History of Mexico-U.S. Migration.* Oxford: Oxford University Press, 2011, 251–65.

Massey, Douglas S., Jorge Durand, and Nolan J. Malone. *Beyond Smoke and Mirrors: Mexican Immigration in an Era of Economic Integration.* New York: Russell Sage Foundation, 2002.

McCain, Johnny M. "Texas and the Mexican Labor Question, 1942–1947." *Southwestern Historical Quarterly* 85, No. 1 (July 1981): 45–64.

McKibben, Carol. *Beyond Cannery Row: Sicilian Women, Immigration, and Community in Monterey, California, 1915–99.* Urbana: University of Illinois Press, 2006.

———. *Racial Beachhead: Diversity and Democracy in a Military Town.* Stanford: Stanford University Press, 2012.

McWilliams, Carey. *Factories in the Field: The Story of Migratory Farm Labor in California.* Boston: Little, Brown, 1939.

———. *North from Mexico: The Spanish Speaking People of the United States.* Philadelphia: J. B. Lippincott, 1948.

Menchaca, Martha. *The Mexican Outsiders: A Community History of Marginalization and Discrimination in California.* Austin: University of Texas Press, 1995.

"Migrant and Seasonal Farmworker Powerlessness." Hearings before the Subcommittee on Migratory Labor of the Committee on Labor and Public Welfare, U.S. Senate, Ninety-First Congress, First and Second Sessions on Farmworker Legal Problems, 8 August 1969, Part 4-B. Washington, D.C.: U.S. Government Printing Office, 1970.

Mitchell, Don. *They Saved the Crops: Labor, Landscape, and the Struggle over Industrial Farming in Bracero-Era California.* Athens: University of Georgia Press, 2012.

Molina, Natalia. *Fit to Be Citizens? Public Health and Race in Los Angeles, 1879–1939.* Berkeley: University of California Press, 2006.

Monroy, Douglas. *Rebirth: Mexican Los Angeles from the Great Migration to the Great Depression.* Berkeley: University of California Press, 1999.

Moore, Truman. *The Slaves We Rent.* New York: Random House, 1965.

Mora-Torres, Juan. "Los de casa se van, los de fuera no vienen": The First Mexican Immigrants, 1848–1900," in Mark Overmyer-Velázquez, ed.,

Beyond La Frontera: The History of Mexico-U.S. Migration. Oxford: Oxford University Press, 2011, 3–27.

Murray, Douglas L. "The Abolition of El Cortito, the Short-Handled Hoe: A Case Study in Social Conflict and State Policy in California Agriculture." *Social Problems* 30, No. 1 (October 1982): 26–39.

National Steinbeck Center, "Valley of the World" exhibit resource guide. Salinas, California, undated.

Neuburger, Bruce. *Lettuce Wars.* New York: Monthly Review Press, 2013.

Ngai, Mae. *Impossible Subjects: Illegal Aliens and the Making of Modern America.* Princeton: Princeton University Press, 2004.

Oropeza, Lorena. *¡Raza Sí! ¡Guerra No! Chicano Protest and Patriotism During the Viet Nam War Era.* Berkeley: University of California Press, 2005.

Orozco, Cynthia. *No Mexicans, Women, or Dogs Allowed: The Rise of the Mexican American Civil Rights Movement.* Austin: University of Texas Press, 2009.

Overmyer-Velázquez, Mark. "Histories and Historiographies of Greater Mexico," in Mark Overmyer-Velázquez, ed., *Beyond La Frontera: The History of Mexico-U.S. Migration.* Oxford: Oxford University Press, 2011, xix–xlv.

Pagán, Eduardo Obregón. "Los Angeles Geopolitics and the Zoot Suit Riot, 1943." *Social Science History* 24, No. 1 (Spring 2000): 223–56.

———. *Murder at the Sleepy Lagoon: Zoot Suits, Race, and Riot in Wartime L.A.* Chapel Hill: University of North Carolina Press, 2003.

Parsons Jr., Theodore William. "Ethnic Cleavage in a California School." Ph.D. diss., Stanford University, 1965.

Pawel, Miriam. *The Crusades of Cesar Chavez: A Biography.* New York: Bloomsbury, 2014.

———. *The Union of Our Dreams: Power, Hope, and Struggle in Cesar Chavez's Farm Worker Movement.* New York: Bloomsbury, 2009.

Paz, Octavio. *The Labyrinth of Solitude.* New York: Grove, 1961.

Pearson, Pauline L. "Steinbeck's Salinas: A Bus Tour." Rev. ed. Salinas: National Steinbeck Center Archives, 1992.

Peiss, Kathy. *Zoot Suit: The Enigmatic Career of an Extreme Style.* Philadelphia: University of Pennsylvania Press, 2011.

Perales, Monica. *Smeltertown: Making and Remembering a Southwest Border Community.* Chapel Hill: University of North Carolina Press, 2010.

Petrick, Gabriella M. "'Like Ribbons of Green and Gold': Industrializing Lettuce and the Quest for Quality in the Salinas Valley, 1920–1965." *Agricultural History* 80, No. 3 (Summer 2006): 269–95.

Pitt, Leonard. *The Decline of the Californios: A Social History of the Spanish Speaking Californians, 1846–1890.* Berkeley: University of California Press, 1966.

Pitti, Gina Marie. "To 'Hear About God in Spanish': Ethnicity, Church, and Community Activism in the San Francisco Archdiocese's Mexican American Colonias, 1942–1965." Ph.D. diss., Stanford University, 2003.

Pitti, Stephen J., "Bracero Justice: The Legacies of Mexican Contract Labor." Proceedings of "Repairing the Past: Confronting the Legacies of Slavery, Genocide, and Caste," Seventh Annual Gilder Lehrman Center International Conference at Yale University, 27–29 October 2005, New Haven, CT. www.yale.edu/glc/justice/pitti.pdf.

———. *The Devil in Silicon Valley: Race, Northern California, and Mexican Americans.* Princeton: Princeton University Press, 2003.

Ramirez, Catherine. *The Woman in the Zoot Suit: Gender, Nationalism, and the Cultural Politics of Memory.* Durham: Duke University Press, 2008.

"Remembering Cesar Chavez and the Farm Workers Movement." Panel discussion, Organization of American Historians Conference, 13 April 2013, San Francisco, California.

Rivas-Rodriguez, Maggie. *A Legacy Greater than Words: Stories of U.S. Latinos and Latinas of the WWII Generation.* Austin: U.S. Latino & Latina WWII Oral History Project, 2006.

Robbin, Edward. *Woody Guthrie and Me: An Intimate Reminiscence.* Berkeley: Lancaster Miller, 1979.

Rosas, Ana Elizabeth. "Breaking the Silence: Mexican Children and Women's Confrontation of Bracero Family Separation, 1942–64." *Gender and History* 23 No. 2 (August 2011): 382–400.

———. "Flexible Families: Braceros' Families Lives Across Cultures, Communities, and Countries, 1942–1964." Ph.D. diss., University of Southern California, 2006.

Rose, Margaret. "From the Fields to the Picket Line: Huelga Women and the Boycott, 1965–1975." *Labor History* 31, No. 3 (1990): 271–93.

———. "Gender and Civic Activism in Mexican American Barrios in California: The Community Service Organization, 1947 to 1962," in Joanne Meyerowitz, ed., *Not June Cleaver: Women and Gender in Postwar America, 1945–1960.* Philadelphia: Temple University Press, 1994, 177–200.

———. "Women in the United Farm Workers: A Study of Chicana and Mexicana Participation in a Labor Union, 1950 to 1980." Ph.D. diss., University of California, Los Angeles, 1988.

Ross, Fred. *Conquering Goliath: Cesar Chavez at the Beginning.* Keene: El Taller Grafico, 1989.

Ruiz, Vicki L. *Cannery Women, Cannery Lives: Mexican Women, Unionization, and the California Food Processing Industry, 1930–1950*. Albuquerque: University of New Mexico Press, 1987.

———. "Citizen Restaurant: American Imaginaries, American Communities." *American Quarterly* 60, No. 1 (March 2008): 1–21.

———. *From Out of the Shadows: Mexican Women in Twentieth Century America*. New York: Oxford University Press, 1998.

Salinas Chamber of Commerce. *Survey of Attitudes of Salinas Citizens Toward Japanese Americans During World War II*. Salinas: ca. 1942–1945.

Sánchez, George J. *Becoming Mexican American: Ethnicity, Culture, and Identity in Chicano Los Angeles, 1900–1945*. Oxford: Oxford University Press, 1993.

———. "'Go After the Women': Americanization and the Mexican Immigrant Woman, 1915–1929," in Vicki Ruiz and Ellen Carol Du Bois, eds., *Unequal Sisters: A Multicultural Reader in U.S. Women's History*. New York: Routledge, 1994, 284–97.

Santoro, Joan. *If You Got the Guts, Run Baby Run*. Bloomington: Xlibris, 2008.

Scharlin, Craig, and Lilia V. Villanueva. *Philip Vera Cruz: A Personal History of Filipino Immigrants and the Farmworkers Movement*. Seattle: University of Washington Press, 2000.

Scott, Robin Fitzgerald. "The Mexican-American in the Los Angeles Area, 1920–1950: From Acquiescence to Activity." Ph.D. diss., University of Southern California, 1971.

Scruggs, Otey M. "Texas and the Bracero Program, 1942–1947." *Pacific Historical Review* 32, No. 3 (August 1963): 251–64.

Shah, Nayan. *Contagious Divides: Epidemics and Race in San Francisco's Chinatown*. Berkeley: University of California Press, 2001.

———. *Stranger Intimacy: Contesting Race, Sexuality, and the Law in the North American West*. Berkeley: University of California Press, 2011.

Shaw, Randy. *Beyond the Fields: Cesar Chavez, the UFW, and the Struggle for Justice in the 21st Century*. Berkeley: University of California Press, 2008.

Snodgrass, Michael. "The Bracero Program, 1942–1964," in Mark Overmyer-Velázquez, ed., *Beyond La Frontera: The History of Mexico-U.S. Migration*. Oxford: Oxford University Press, 2011, 79–102.

Starr, Kevin. *California: A History*. New York: Modern Library, 2007.

St. John, Rachel. *Line in the Sand: The History of the Western U.S.-Mexico Border*. Princeton: Princeton University Press, 2012.

Street, Richard Steven. *Everyone Had Cameras: Photography and Farmworkers in California, 1850–2000*. Minneapolis: University of Minnesota Press, 2008.

Takaki, Ronald. *A Different Mirror: A History of Multicultural America.* Boston: Little Brown, 1994.

———. *Strangers from a Different Shore: A History of Asian Americans.* New York: Penguin, 1990.

Tsu, Cecilia. *Garden of the World: Asian Immigrants and the Making of Agriculture in California's Santa Clara Valley.* Oxford: Oxford University Press, 2013.

———. "Grown in the 'Garden of the World': Race, Gender, and Agriculture in California's Santa Clara Valley, 1880–1940." Ph.D. diss., Stanford University, 2006.

Underwood, Katherine. "Process and Politics: Multicultural Coalition Building and Representation in Los Angeles' Ninth District, 1949–1962." Ph.D. diss., University of California, San Diego, 1992.

Uribe, Mónica Ortiz. "Guest Worker Programs Have a Long History in U.S." *Fronteras,* 17 April 2013. www.fronterasdesk.org/content/guest-worker-programs-have-long-history-us.

U.S. Bureau of the Census. Sixteenth Census of the United States Taken in the Year 1940, Population, Internal Migration 1935 to 1940. Washington, D.C.: U.S. Government Printing Office, 1943.

———. Sixteenth Census of the United States Taken in the Year 1940, Population, Nativity and Parentage of the White Population, Country of Origin of the Foreign Stock, by Nativity, Citizenship, Age, and Value or Rent of Home, for States and Large Cities. Washington, D.C.: U.S. Government Printing Office, 1943.

———. Sixteenth Census of the United States Taken in the Year 1940, Population, Vol. 1. Number of Inhabitants. Washington, D.C.: U.S. Government Printing Office, 1942.

———. Eighteenth Census of the United States Taken in the Year 1960, Median School Years Completed by Spanish Surname, Total White and Nonwhite Populations, 1950 and 1960. Washington, D.C.: U.S. Government Printing Office.

———. Nineteenth Census of the United States Taken in the Year 1970, Population, 1970. Washington, D.C.: U.S. Government Printing Office.

Valdes, Dionicio N. *Organized Agriculture and the Labor Movement Before the UFW: Puerto Rico, Hawai'i, and California.* Austin: University of Texas Press, 2011.

Vargas, Zaragosa. *Labor Rights Are Civil Rights: Mexican American Workers in Twentieth Century America.* Princeton: Princeton University Press, 2005.

———. *Proletarians of the North: A History of Mexican Industrial Workers in Detroit and the Midwest, 1917–1933.* Berkeley: University of California Press, 1993.

Varzally, Allison. *Making a Non-White America: Californians Coloring Outside Ethnic Lines, 1925–1955.* Berkeley: University of California Press, 2008.

Verardo, Jennie Dennis, and Denzil Verardo. *The Salinas Valley: An Illustrated History.* Chatsworth: Windsor, 1989.

Wald, Sarah. "The Nature of Citizenship: Race, Citizenship, and Nature in Representations of Californian Agricultural Labor." Ph.D. diss., Brown University, 2009.

Watt, Alan. *Farm Workers and the Churches: The Movement in California and Texas.* College Station: Texas A&M University Press, 2010.

Weber, Devra. *Dark Sweat, White Gold: California Farm Workers, Cotton, and the New Deal.* Berkeley: University of California Press, 1994.

Weise, Julie M. *Corazon de Dixie: Mexico and Mexicans in the U.S. South Since 1910.* Chapel Hill: University of North Carolina Press, forthcoming.

Wells, Miriam J. "Legal Conflict and Class Structure: The Independent Contractor-Employee Controversy in California Agriculture." *Law & Society Review* 21 No. 1 (1987): 49–82.

———. *Strawberry Fields: Politics, Class, and Work in California Agriculture.* Ithaca: Cornell University Press, 1996.

Yung, Judy, and the Chinese Historical Society of America. *San Francisco's Chinatown.* Charleston: Arcadia, 2006.

Zavella, Patricia. *"I'm Neither Here nor There": Mexicans' Quotidian Struggles with Migration and Poverty.* Durham: Duke University Press, 2011.

———. *Women's Work and Chicano Families: Cannery Workers of the Santa Clara Valley.* Ithaca: Cornell University Press, 1987.

Zesch, Scott. *The Chinatown War: Chinese Los Angeles and the Massacre of 1871.* Oxford: Oxford University Press, 2012.

Zong, Jie, and Jeanne Batalova. "Frequently Released Statistics on Immigrants and Immigration in the United States," Online Journal of the Migration Policy Institute, 26 February 2015, www.migrationpolicy.org/article/frequently-requested-statistics-immigrants-and-immigration-united-states#Unauthorized%20Immigration.

Index